CHRISTIAN WORSHIP
IN REFORMED CHURCHES
PAST AND PRESENT

The CALVIN INSTITUTE OF CHRISTIAN WORSHIP LITURGICAL STUDIES SERIES, edited by John D. Witvliet, is designed to promote reflection on the history, theology, and practice of Christian worship and to stimulate worship renewal in Christian congregations. Contributions include writings by pastoral worship leaders from a wide range of communities and scholars from a wide range of disciplines. The ultimate goal of these contributions is to nurture worship practices that are spiritually vital and theologically rooted.

Available

Gather into One
Praying and Singing Globally
C. Michael Hawn

My Only Comfort: Death, Deliverance, and Discipleship in the Music of Bach
Calvin R. Stapert

Christian Worship in Reformed Churches Past and Present
Lukas Vischer, Editor

Christian Worship in Reformed Churches Past and Present

Edited by

LUKAS VISCHER

WILLIAM B. EERDMANS PUBLISHING COMPANY

GRAND RAPIDS, MICHIGAN / CAMBRIDGE, U.K.

Wm. B. Eerdmans Publishing Co.
255 Jefferson Ave. S.E., Grand Rapids, Michigan 49503 /
P.O. Box 163, Cambridge CB3 9PU U.K.
www.eerdmans.com

Printed in the United States of America

08 07 06 05 04 03   7 6 5 4 3 2 1

Library of Congress Cataloging-in-Publication Data

Christian worship in Reformed Churches past and present / edited by Lukas Vischer.
    p.   cm.
    Includes bibliographical references and index.
    ISBN 0-8028-0520-5 (pbk.: alk. paper)
      1. Public worship — Reformed Church.   2. Reformed Church — Liturgy.
  I. Vischer, Lukas.

    BX6825.C47   2003
    264'.042 — dc21

                    2002029490

Bruce Prewer's poems "If you have breath" (© Bruce Prewer, from *Kakadu Reflections*) and "God of space shuttles" (© Bruce Prewer, from *Jesus Our Future: Prayers for the Twenty-First Century*) are used by permission of Bruce Prewer.

Contents

Series Preface

"One holy, catholic, and apostolic church." This book is about the all-encompassing biblical vision of the church captured in these six creedal words. It is a book that helps us sense the underlying *unity* of the body of Christ, as it describes worship practices across great divides of both time and space. It is a book about *holiness,* as it bears witness to efforts at liturgical purity, truth, and integrity, and names work yet to do. It is a book about *catholicity:* even though it is a book about only one tradition within the Christian faith, it describes a tradition that bears witness to the catholicity of the church and attempts to enhance it through tangible decisions about how to worship, preach, and celebrate the sacraments. It is a book about *apostolicity:* its global scope is itself a witness to the missionary work of the church in declaring the good news of Christ's gospel worldwide. Reading the essays in this book is an exercise in making these creedal statements a part of our working theological imagination. Taken together, these essays can help us experience Christ's church in a new and more profound way.

These essays also have much to teach us about worship. Nearly all of today's challenges and controversies about the practice of Christian worship relate to the church's posture toward culture. All Christian congregations must somehow decide how their worship can at once transcend, reflect, and critique culture in their local environment. Most churches are better at one of these postures than the others. Some congregations have an identity that is defined over against culture; others almost entirely reflect culture. The only way to gain perspective on how to achieve balance in being "in, but not of" the world is somehow to step outside of our own world, to find a perspective from which to perceive the water in which we swim. This book promises to be a significant resource for Reformed Christians in particular to do just that — to learn how fellow Christians, with a common theological and ecclesiastical heritage, have practiced their faith in very different times and places. The goal here is to invite a deeper level of reflection about how a given theological vision can become enfleshed in a local cultural context.

For its part, the Roman Catholic Church has the wonderful advantage of having centuries of practice at thinking globally. Some of its most mature efforts at addressing questions of worship and culture after Vatican II bear witness to this legacy. Perhaps this book can play a small role in challenging Protestants to gain a deeper level of understanding about the interplay of ecclesiastical tradition and cultural context in shaping patterns of worship in a global context. In this task, this book will complement a fine volume of essays on worldwide Methodism: *The Sunday Service of the Methodists: Twentieth Century Worship in Worldwide Methodism,* ed. Karen B. Westerfield Tucker (Kingswood Books, 1996).

In addition, this book can help many of us Reformed Christians to sense the global scope of the Reformed branch of the Christian church. It has often been tempting to equate Reformed Christianity with particular ethnic identity (whether that be Hungarian, Korean, Scottish, or Dutch), and then, when that ethnic identity erodes, to assume that Reformed Christianity has little more to offer. This book helps us understand how the Reformed tradition need not be dependent on a particular ethnic or cultural context.

Perhaps this book can also serve as an invitation to further work in the field. This book can't begin to encompass even all the many voices within the Reformed tradition — either culturally or theologically — to say nothing of the potential comparative studies of various Christian traditions in many particular cultural contexts.

All of us who benefit from this book are indebted to Lukas Vischer and the John Knox Center for hosting the consultation that produced this volume and for editing these essays for publication.

JOHN D. WITVLIET
Calvin Institute of Christian Worship
Calvin College and Calvin Theological Seminary
Grand Rapids, Michigan

Introduction

The renewal of worship is today on the agenda of many Reformed churches, and the need for adaptation and new approaches is acutely felt in many circles. How can the church faithfully worship God in the midst of rapidly changing situations? How can it constructively relate to widely differing cultural contexts — in the countries of both the North and the South? What is its place in the wider ecumenical scene?

The purpose of the present volume is to provide some help to those engaged in responding to these questions. For some years the International Reformed Center John Knox has conducted studies on worship. In 1994 it organized a first international consultation on the "Place and Renewal of Worship in Reformed Churches," issuing a report that was published and widely shared throughout the family of Reformed churches. It surveyed the issues at stake and addressed in particular the topics of the "sacraments" and of "text, context, and culture." It also suggested that an effort should be made to write a "history of worship in the Reformed tradition." The present volume is an attempt to build upon the beginnings made in 1994. It is the result of a second international consultation held at the John Knox Center from January 5-12, 2001, which was attended by theologians and liturgical scholars from a wide range of churches and countries.

The volume offers first (Part I) a history of worship in Reformed churches. Behind this effort is the conviction that, as the 1994 report put it, an awareness of history is required to be freed for a creative future. In order to know where we are to go, we need to know where we have come from. The pages that follow do not give a complete and detailed history of all ramifications and aspects of Reformed worship through the centuries. Instead, they

provide a general survey of the most important developments and seek to identify the major "ingredients" of the Reformed worship tradition.

The history of Reformed worship displays a wide variety of forms and
has been multivocal from the very beginning. As history progressed, it was
further diversified. In the encounter with new situations new emphases developed and insights were gained that went beyond the original impulse of the sixteenth-century reformers. As the Reformed family developed stage by stage
into a worldwide communion, the Reformed heritage was appropriated in a
wider range of contexts. Growing variety is therefore a characteristic of the
Reformed tradition.

What does this simultaneously rich and confusing picture mean for us
today? How do we deal with the legacy of history? A tentative answer to this
question is given in the chapter following the historical section: "A Common
Reflection on Christian Worship in Reformed Churches Today" (Part II). The
participants in the second consultation made an attempt to identify the main
issues that arise as we engage in the renewal of worship in today's Reformed
churches. Their report, included here, offers a summary of the discussions.

The last part of the volume (Part III) offers contributions on aspects of
worship that are today particularly relevant for a constructive discussion in
Reformed churches.

It is our hope that this volume will contribute to a new interest in the renewal of worship. It will have achieved its purpose if it helps to promote discussion, exchange, and also action.

As editor I would like to thank all who have participated in this effort and
given time and energy to it. To build together a volume like this was an extraordinary experience. Special thanks are due to Professor Marsha M. Wilfong,
who helped produce the report and patiently and skillfully accommodated the
remarks of all participants. Good drafters are like people with the gift of arranging flowers. The flowers are not theirs — but the bouquet is their achieve-
ment!

LUKAS VISCHER

Part I

A Historical Survey

Reformed Worship in the Sixteenth Century

Elsie Anne McKee

The sixteenth-century Reformation is most often remembered as a reform of theology or church politics, but it was also and especially a reform of worship. Central to the theological arguments was the conviction that God was not being worshiped as God willed, and therefore human salvation was in danger. The major changes Protestants effected in theology and church organization were expressed with equal clarity in their worship. There were a number of common convictions shared by all those who broke with Rome, but there was also considerable variety in the way particular groups shaped the new or reformed patterns of worship and Christian life, and sometimes even within groups there continued to be slight or even significant differences.

To appreciate the way the Reformed tradition understood and practiced worship, it is important to examine it in the context of the larger picture. The first part of that historical context is an outline of the heritage Protestants received. This begins with certain significant reforming movements of the later Middle Ages and early modern period: the Waldensians, the Modern Devotion, the Hussites, and the new intellectual currents of humanism. I will then examine the most prominent features of the medieval church's worship tradition and practice as the reformers understood those, and sketch the common Protestant response. The central section of the chapter is a three-part picture of the specific ways the different members of what is now called the Reformed tradition developed their ideas and practices. After more brief attention to Huldrych Zwingli and the Zürich reform of worship, and mention of other influential centers such as Strasbourg, our primary focus will be on Calvin and Geneva, because that pattern is usually regarded as the most significant for later Reformed theology and worship. The third brief part of this examination of the Reformed tradition identifies the family of churches that developed out of the Zürich-Strasbourg-Geneva matrix. The conclusion then summarizes some of the distinctive characteristics of the Reformed tradition and its possible contributions to the wider church today.

The Protestant Heritage

The Protestant reform of theology, worship, and religious practice presented a distinctively new movement in the Western church, but it did not appear out of nowhere. Rather, it built on a number of earlier reforms.

Earlier Reforming Movements

Among the antecedents of Protestantism were notable institutional reforming efforts, some of which the church at Rome condemned as heretical but which Protestants recognized as forerunners displaying some of their own convictions. The earliest movement of particular significance for the Reformed tradition was the lay reform of the Waldensians. This group traces its origin to the late twelfth century, when a wealthy merchant of Lyons, France, named Waldes, felt called to lead an apostolic life of poverty and preach to all who would listen. For this purpose he procured some vernacular copies of parts of the Bible and began his mission. Soon he had a number of followers.

The Roman church, however, did not allow lay people to preach, and thus the Waldensians were first silenced, and then, when they refused to stop preaching, excommunicated and labeled heretics. Persecution did not end the movement; instead, some parts of it gradually became less willing to accept other traditional teachings of the Roman church. Waldensians considered the Bible the sole authority for doctrine and practice; they also rejected Masses and prayers for the dead and allowed preaching by women. Some permitted lay administration of the sacraments where a priest was not available; others went further and chose their own clergy. Eventually this movement went underground, but the coming of the new Protestant teaching in the sixteenth century attracted Waldensians; in 1532 their representatives met with William Farel at Chanforan and the two streams merged.

Two other important late medieval reforming movements, the Modern Devotion and the Hussite church, are better known. The Modern Devotion, centered in the Dutch-speaking Low Countries, encouraged lay as well as monastic piety, which was particularly noted for its simplicity and the inward focus of its spirituality. While quite orthodox in doctrine, the Modern Devotion gave less weight to ecclesiastical structure and external ceremony than was usual in the medieval church, and more attention to personal religious attitudes. It also made less distinction between lay and clerical lifestyles: all were to aim at the same devotion and practice of their faith. This movement remained within the church even as it quietly and indirectly challenged aspects of hierarchy and worship practice.

The Hussite churches, in contrast, were considered heretical. Here one of the key issues was the nature of the church and what religious authority it has, especially in relation to the Bible. Jan Hus's own writings emphasized the role of election: the church is made up of the elect, not determined by the clerical hierarchy. Common Hussite teaching focused on the primacy of Scripture and the preaching of God's pure word, and the offering of the cup (as well as the bread) to the laity in the Lord's Supper. Like the other two reform movements, the Hussites also espoused apostolic poverty and moral reform of Christian life. At the time of the Reformation, Martin Luther was accused of being a Hussite, a heretic. The Hussite churches themselves welcomed many of the new ideas being taught by Protestants, and contacts between the various reformers were established, although the churches did not merge at this time.

In the early modern period a different kind of intellectual reform, usually called humanism, also made important contributions to the thinking of Protestants as they began to re-envision the character of Christian theology, practice, and (not least) worship. Humanism can be defined in various ways, but perhaps the most useful definition identifies humanism less with specific ideas than with a methodology, a way of learning ("back to the sources"), and a pedagogical approach that sought more to persuade than to prove.

Northern European humanists in particular were interested in getting back to the pure sources of faith: the Bible in the original languages and the earliest church fathers as the best interpreters of Scripture. In addition, the purpose of teaching these original sources was more to awaken faith and conviction in the hearers than to offer them syllogistic proofs of truth, which might not actually make any difference in their lives. Younger humanists began to delve into the New Testament in Greek and the Old Testament in Hebrew and to read the early church commentators, and as they did so they began to conclude that what they had been taught in church dogma was not in fact the same as what they were now reading. Protestants believed that they were persuaded of the Bible's truth by the work of the Holy Spirit, not by human wisdom. They also believed that the Spirit who inspired the Bible would not contradict or go beyond it; the Spirit would not continue to add further revelations (whether through church traditions or charismatic inspiration of individuals). So it was necessary to teach only the Bible, as faithfully and intelligently and carefully as possible, because that was seen as the instrument of the Spirit's power, which God has given to believers to draw them into the truth.

Protestant Views of Medieval Worship

So the new Protestant reformers, encouraged by the earlier reforming movements, and building on the wonderful resources of the new scriptural insights, became increasingly dissatisfied with the doctrine and practice of the church — including its understanding and practice of worship. Protestant reforms were prompted to a large degree by the dissonance between what the reformers inherited and what they were now learning from the renewed study of the Bible in its original languages and in its historical context. In order to understand why and how Protestants reformed worship it is helpful to sketch briefly the medieval worship practices they received and to which they reacted. (It is also important to bear in mind that every reaction was precisely that: a reaction, an effort to set right what was wrong. In the process of correcting, the reformers usually went too far in the opposite direction, emphasizing what had been neglected and downplaying what had been overemphasized, rather than creating a perfectly balanced situation.)

Although they shared many concerns with earlier reformers, Protestant reactions to the medieval church were also distinctive because their understanding of these common ideas was re-shaped by new theological insights. The most important new insight concerned the character of the relationship between God and human beings: that all are justified by faith alone and not by the church's sacraments or by their own good deeds (such as Masses and pilgrimages). In light of this insight, Protestants clearly affirmed that all Christians are equal; the distinction between laity and clergy is one only of function, not of rank. There is a priesthood of believers, all of whom equally belong to God and owe God their worship and praise. This new understanding of how God wills to be known and to save human beings came to Protestants through the Bible, and thus they insisted that Scripture is the sole source of right religious knowledge and that it must be preached without human additions (although this does not mean without human ministry or interpretation). The shape of Protestant worship reforms was therefore part of a larger reforming movement that focused on Scripture, preaching, and full participation for laity, and included a movement away from elaborate external ceremony and toward a more inward spirit and ecclesiastical simplicity. Also important was the central role given to the new theology, which denied that worship was a good work or something humans could design to please themselves.

Those who broke with Rome criticized in particular the sacramental teaching that was the basis of Catholic worship. This theology seemed to make the church with its sacraments, saints, and good works the source of salvation, rather than God. The sacramental system was *the* means of salvation; the objective practice of the sacraments was sufficient to compel God to give grace. The Mass, for example, was regarded as a sacrifice offered to God by the priest on the people's behalf. Neither the people nor even the priest had to understand the precise meaning of the words; if the sacramental words were recited in Latin and the right acts done, then grace was automatic. On the other hand, if a baby died without baptism, it went to limbo, and those people who died without the sacrament of penance were not sure of their ultimate salvation. Persons who prayed to the saints, however, and gave alms or endowed Masses could hope that when they died the Virgin Mary and the saints would intercede and perhaps reduce the time their souls would spend in purgatory.

The Roman church's theology and practice was additionally problematic for the Protestants because it cultivated ignorance of what they considered essentials. The liturgical year gave so much space to the feasts of the saints and especially to the Virgin Mary that the reformers worried people might lose sight of the distinctiveness of Sunday. The life of the day's saint became more important than the gospel reading, and this seemed to make Christ one among many intercessors. Since salvation was essentially through the sacraments, saints, and good works, it was not necessary to study the Bible. Knowledge of the Bible, which to Protestants was essential, was rather limited in the Middle Ages. This was partly because relatively few people could read, and fewer yet possessed even a part of the Bible (since inexpensive printed copies were not yet available). It was also partly because in most parishes preaching was only occasional and the content of sermons was more likely to be moral stories or saints' lives than an explanation of the biblical text from the lectionary. In fact, most biblical sermons were themselves thematic, focused on a single word or idea, not expository treatments of a whole passage.

In addition, the experience of corporate worship was clearly divided between the celibate clergy and the rest of the people, who might have some complementary roles but essentially observed rather than participating actively.[1] In the Mass, for example, the laity normally did not commune; usually

---

1. Some scholars have pointed out that medieval lay people had their own parallel patterns of worship, which were complementary to those of the priest. Cf. Virginia Reinburg, "Liturgy and the Laity in Late Medieval and Reformation France," *The Sixteenth Century Journal* 23 (1992): 526-46. Others describe how many people carried on their private devotions — reciting their private prayers, reading their books of hours, etc. — while the Mass was been said in Latin (with parts of it spoken too softly for anyone to hear). These lay devotions might indeed have

only the priest did, while the people watched reverently. Most people came to communion only once a year (as was required) or somewhat more often if they were very devout, and then they received only the bread, not the wine. The people usually had no voice in the liturgies, and commonly they did not understand the words or participate in singing, even if there were choral responses. Occasionally a few vernacular responses were sung, but most often the music was polyphonic and could be performed only by trained (clerical) choirs. There the Latin language was not the only barrier to understanding: often different melodic voices would also have different texts, sung at various tempos, so that even if one knew Latin it was not possible to hear all the words, much less to join in the song. In fact, however, intellectual understanding was not the critical thing in worship. For most medieval Christians, individual sight and touch were more important than corporate hearing; the beauty of the liturgy, churches, statues, and paintings, and the concreteness of relics and holy things, all these were understood as means to teach, to draw people to God.

Common Protestant Values and Changes

Based on their renewed understanding of Scripture and of the way human beings receive God's justifying grace through faith alone, Protestants thought the kind of worship they had inherited dishonored God in a number of ways. In the first place, they regarded the object and conception of worship in the Roman Catholic Church as wrong. God alone is to be worshiped, they proclaimed, and for this reason no trust may be put in saints or human sacramental acts and other good deeds. People must understand that they cannot give God anything (such as the sacrifice of the Mass) but only receive from God, because grace is purely a free gift, not something one can earn. Humans also do not choose for themselves how to worship God; they learn from God's word what is pleasing to the Lord. All the reformers agreed that nothing in worship may contradict Scripture, and some went further and made Scripture the paradigm for right worship. Thus, although the inner heart was seen as the most important thing in worship, training the mind in biblical teaching was also necessary because understanding is a foundation for obedience. (Protestants, especially the Reformed tradition, put much more weight on ear than

---

been very sincere, but they were often only tangentially related to what the priest was doing. When the ideal of both Protestant and Catholic reformers became having the whole assembly involved in the same service, this older pattern of parallel but different activities on the part of priest and people was sharply rejected as a contradiction of the meaning of public worship.

eye, on the corporate preaching and hearing of God's word rather than on the visual depiction of the holy as a means of educating. The voice rather than statues or paintings therefore became the primary means of praise.) Furthermore, worship was not something that could be left to specially qualified persons, because there are no human beings who are intrinsically more holy than others, and especially because worship is the joy and responsibility of all Christians equally. No fixed forms of liturgy were sacrosanct, no words magical, but all was to be fitted to the purpose of God's glory and the people's edification.

The primary changes that almost all Protestants introduced were intended to correct these problems. First, because salvation is not by works but by trusting that God in Christ is the sole savior, the meaning of worship was shifted from something done to please God and earn divine favor, to worship as a response to God's gift and obedience to God's word. Second, because the promise of grace in Christ is known by the preaching of the gospel, which the Holy Spirit will impress on human hearts but which God has chosen to proclaim through human means (the church), therefore responding to God includes learning both what Christ's grace is and how to respond in gratitude. Generally, worship became less mechanical and individualistic for Protestants and more demanding; it required understanding, active attention, and some specific acts of participation in a common service. Visual arts with their many layers of meaning for individual appropriation give way to verbal art, the corporate focus of a gathered people.

Reacting against the earlier ignorance of the people, the reformers intended to make their church services more edifying; as a result, Protestants have (with some reason) been accused of making worship overly intellectual. In fact, they were as much concerned with heart as head, but they put new emphasis on worshiping God with the understanding and sometimes the proper balance was lost. Ministers were still necessary in Protestant worship, but now as preachers and pastors rather than as priests (privileged intercessors). Liturgies — that is, planned acts of corporate worship — were still vitally important, but these were now in the language of the people ("inculturated") and adapted to the historical community and culture of the worshipers.

With this as the foundation, other changes followed naturally. Prayer was to be offered only to the triune God and not to the saints. Public worship was to be based on biblical preaching and the exposition of Scripture, while nonbiblical matter was to be excluded. Usually liturgies of some kind were printed and followed. (The balance between form and freedom was fluid in the sixteenth century; no one specific form was essential or salvific, but Protestants generally agreed on the usefulness of having a prepared text for most parts of the service. This form could be altered to meet the needs of different communities, but it was never to be changed merely on individual whim, because worship belongs to the whole people, who need to know what is being said and done.) All worship was to be conducted in a language the people could understand, and it should also be corporate; the priest could no longer commune alone in the Lord's Supper, but the congregation was to share in both bread and wine. The people should also have a voice in the praise of God and public prayer, usually through singing, and this meant greatly simplifying the music. Normally everyone would sing in unison, one syllable per note, so that the text could be understood and the whole people might pray with mind and voice. The seven sacraments were reduced to the two that Christ had instituted — baptism and the Lord's Supper — and these acts were not considered saving in themselves, without faith. The same standards were to apply to the lives of all Christians, since all are equally saved by faith and not by their own acts of holiness. Protestant clergy were therefore strongly urged to marry: there was no holy status for celibate people, no orders of monks or nuns. Families and communities were all to practice the same kind of biblical piety.

These values were common to virtually all Protestants, but when they put them into concrete practice, differences began to develop. Groups, including those that later came to be called "Lutheran," "Zwinglian," "Calvinist," and "Anglican," argued over theology and church order and rejected each other's ways. (For the present purposes, Anabaptists are not included under the heading of Protestant, but the Church of England is.) Usually the criterion that finally determined whether two groups actually separated was the doctrine of the sacraments. There was a common acceptance of infant baptism among Protestants, though they interpreted the rite differently and this could at times cause conflict. The key concern, however, was the Lord's Supper. Those who could share the Supper together became a kind of family of churches; those who could not do so developed more and more separate lives and sometimes enmity.

Even a willingness to share the Supper did not, however, mean perfect agreement, but rather that the members chose to hold unity above (some) differences of theology. In the first thirty years of the Reformation two groups — the followers of Zwingli led by Heinrich Bullinger, and ones now called Calvinist — agreed in 1549 to share communion. This "Zürich Consensus," as the document ratifying the agreement is called, expressed some concessions on Calvin's part and probably somewhat greater ones from Bullinger in modifying Zwingli's teaching, but it serves as evidence of how the defense of pure doctrine and devotion to church unity could be combined in the sixteenth century. In practice, the joining of the Zwinglian and Calvinist streams of reform created what is now identified as the "Reformed tradition." The combined "river" also continued to include some theological variety, particularly on the doctrine of the church and, specifically, matters of worship. Thus, to understand Reformed worship in the sixteenth century, it is necessary to study the several streams that flowed into the Reformed tradition, and then to identify some of the common features, along with the continuing ecumenical diversity.

The Zwinglian Reformed Tradition

Zwingli and Zürich

In the early years of the Reformation, leaders appeared in a number of different places, especially in Germany and German-speaking Switzerland. Huldrych Zwingli (1484-1531) was a Swiss priest with strong humanist training, who was called to be the chief preacher in the primary church of Zürich, the Grossmünster, beginning in 1519. Zürich was one of the largest and most influential Swiss cantons, and Zwingli was a learned, courageous, and forceful voice for reform. Like other humanists, Zwingli went back to the sources: the Bible and the early church fathers. Like the Modern Devotion, and like Erasmus and other humanists, the Swiss preacher reacted sharply against the great weight put on external matters in worship. One of Zwingli's favorite verses was John 6:63 ("The spirit gives life, the flesh profits nothing"), and he moved toward a very strong emphasis on the spiritual, where *spiritual* could sometimes mean the opposite of material. Thus, for Zwingli, reform signified purifying religion of everything that was not plainly biblical and emphasizing the spiritual over the material, the invisible over the visible.[2]

The Word and Liturgical Time

The most important thing for Zwingli was the preaching of the Bible, in the language of the people, on a regular basis. Almost everything else was stripped away. Saints' days were essentially abolished and Sunday became the central day of worship. The daily Mass was replaced by frequent sermons, not only on Sundays but also on many weekdays. The old lectionary system, which selected

2. See Carlos Eire, *War Against the Idols: The Reformation of Worship from Erasmus to Calvin* (Cambridge: Cambridge University Press, 1986). Eire's interpretation of Zwingli is very helpful, though his presentation of Calvin is less good; he tends to see Calvin as more Zwinglian than he was.

individual pericopes from different New Testament books and verses from the Psalms (but did not include other Old Testament books), was replaced with *lectio continua,* a system of continuous reading in which the minister preached straight through a given biblical book. This was exegetical preaching, not the thematic sermons on a single word or phrase customary in the Middle Ages. In this way, none of the Bible was omitted, and, if they lived long enough, parishioners might eventually hear all of every book expounded from the pulpit. Of course, this was the ideal, and not every minister could preach on all the Bible, but the amount of biblical exposition was greatly expanded to include the Old Testament and many neglected parts of the New. It was common to all Protestants to put special emphasis on the Pauline Epistles, but the Reformed tradition made preaching on the Old Testament a regular part of the worship sequence as well. Usually this was done on weekdays, but in some places (such as Scotland) there were sermons on the Old Testament even on Sundays.

Prayer, Music, and Art in Worship

Like other Protestants, Zwingli strongly believed in giving the people a voice in public prayer, but his way of doing this was unique. Although he was himself the most gifted musician among the reformers, Zwingli rejected the use of music in public worship. Instead, during the Lord's Supper service he wanted antiphonal recitation of psalms, hymns, and the Creed by the two sides of the congregation, men on one side and women on the other. Unhappily, the Zürich authorities would not allow this, and so the spoken praise was put back in the mouths of the clergy. Some areas influenced by Zürich did not follow this pattern, however, and so some Zwinglian churches, such as that in Constance, Switzerland, published and used song books.[3]

Music was not the only one of the arts changed; visual artistic expression was among the aspects of worship most visibly affected by the reformers, although not everyone went as far as Zwingli did. In accordance with his under-

---

3. For an English translation of Zwingli's Sunday service and Lord's Supper service (where the antiphonal recitation is found), see Bard Thompson, *Liturgies of the Western Church* (Cleveland: Meridian Books, 1961), pp. 147-56. The fullest examination of Zwingli's liturgical practices is found in the writings of Fritz Schmidt-Clausing, especially *Zwingli as Liturgiker* (Göttingen, 1952); and *Zwinglis liturgische Formulare* (Frankfurt a.M., 1970). For an edition of the original German liturgies of Zwingli and the Zwinglian-influenced Basel and Bern services, see Bruno Bürki, chap. 9 (Das Abendmahl nach den Zürcher Ordnungen), chap. 10 (Das Abendmahl nach den Basler Ordnungen), and chap. 11 (Das Abendmahl nach der Berner Ordnung 1529), in *Coena Domini* vol. 1, ed. I. Pahl (Freiburg i.S., 1983), pp. 181-236.

standing of the Ten Commandments, Zwingli emphasized the importance of eliminating all visual arts from the church building. The Roman church, since the time of the church father Augustine, had divided the Decalogue into two tables of three and seven commandments. The break came between the law about the Sabbath and the one about honoring parents; the words about making "no graven image" were thus interpreted by the Catholic church as part of the first commandment to have "no other gods" before God, and the commandment not to covet was divided in half to produce two laws. Following, perhaps, the early Christian scholar Origen, Zwingli and other Reformed Protestants (though not some other non-Reformed Protestants, such as the Lutherans) divided "no other gods" and "no graven image" into two commandments, and combined the words about coveting, thus making two tables of four and six commandments respectively. The "new" division of the first commandment into two led the Reformed to take very seriously the prohibition on visual representations of God and any other beings considered sacred. Pictures of holy beings lead to idolatry, to transferring trust from the one or ones represented to the images. In the case of images of saints, to allow religious pictures could also appear to give the saints a status as intercessors, which Protestants denied they could have.[4]

Zwingli's church building and liturgy were thus severely, beautifully simple, stripped of everything except the preaching of the word and the prayers, and the reformed sacraments.

The Sacraments

The two sacraments of baptism and the Lord's Supper, which all Protestants agreed were clearly instituted by Christ, were practiced by the Zürich church, but in an austerely simple fashion. Both sacraments were to be public events; there were to be no private baptisms, no private Masses. After some wavering, Zwingli decided to keep the practice of infant baptism as an expression of the covenant of adoption, like the Old Testament practice of circumcision. He clarified his ideas in arguments with the Anabaptists, who required confession of faith first, and therefore only baptized adults. For Zwingli, baptism was a sign of the Christian community, to be given to all children born into the covenant. (To do otherwise was, in his view, to claim to establish a church of the

4. For these aspects of Zwingli's work, see Charles Garside, *Zwingli and the Arts* (New Haven: Yale University Press, 1966), and Lee Palmer Wandel, "Envisioning God: Image and Liturgy in Reformation," *The Sixteenth Century Journal* 24 (1993): 21-40.

elect only, something he did not believe human beings could determine.) Since here on earth it is not possible to separate the wheat from the chaff, baptism should be given to all the children of church members. Baptism was not, however, a magical act, and the church was responsible for seeing that all of those baptized were taught the meaning of the faith in order to be able to affirm it personally. In Zürich as elsewhere, especially among the Reformed, this catechetical instruction was required before a child could be admitted to the Lord's Supper.[5]

Zwingli understood the Supper as a thanksgiving to God, a pledge of faith, a memorial of Christ's death. It was to be celebrated four times a year, in the context of a service of the word, with the whole (adult) congregation participating. The Supper was for Zwingli symbolic — a rich, moving symbol, but not one that conveys grace. Grace, he believed, is given by the Holy Spirit to the human spirit of the believer, but there is no connection with the bread and wine. Preaching, rather, is the means of grace, the Supper the symbolic illustration; consequently, preaching was supposed to be frequent, while it was sufficient to have the Supper at regular intervals. (It should be noted, however, that Zwingli's plan of four times per year was three times more often than medieval Christians had been required to commune.)

In reacting to the earlier overemphasis on the sacramental system and its function as *the* means of grace, Zwinglian Protestants have been accused with some justice of overemphasizing preaching, almost to the denigration of the Supper, but that was certainly not Zwingli's intent.[6]

Beyond Zürich

The new interpretation of theology and worship developed by Zwingli spread quickly, especially in German-speaking Switzerland and also into Alsace, along the Rhine, where it encountered the Lutheran theological influence coming from the north. A number of Swiss cantons, particularly Bern and Basel, became Protestant in Zwinglian form, and other areas such as Con-

---

5. Cf. Zwingli, "Of Baptism," in *Zwingli and Bullinger,* ed. G. W. Bromiley (Philadelphia: Westminster Press, 1953), pp. 119-75. The rite itself is translated in J. D. C. Fisher, *Christian Initiation: The Reformation Period* (London: SPCK, 1970), pp. 126-31. For an overview of Reformed baptismal liturgies, see Hughes Oliphant Old, *The Shaping of the Reformed Baptismal Rite in the Sixteenth Century* (Grand Rapids: Eerdmans, 1992), which also includes considerable attention to catechesis.

6. See Zwingli, "On the Lord's Supper," in *Zwingli and Bullinger,* ed. Bromiley, pp. 176-244.

stance followed. South German cities like Strasbourg shared the Zwinglian sacramental theology in the 1520s, when arguments over the Lord's Supper began to divide Luther and Zwingli and their followers into two camps. By the 1530s, however, parts of South Germany, especially in Alsace and led by Strasbourg, were developing a mediating position between the Lutherans and the Zwinglians. The major figure in this process was Martin Bucer of Strasbourg, and this Rhineland tradition of Reformed theology and worship was one of the most influential factors in the emergence of the other major branch of the Reformed tradition, called "Calvinist."[7]

The Calvinist Reformed Tradition

What is now called the "Reformed tradition" has most often been called "Calvinist," after its single most important sixteenth-century theologian, and Calvin's city of Geneva has often been seen as the headquarters of the Reformed tradition. Both the leading man and the most important city need, however, to be understood in context if one is to appreciate rightly their unique contributions and the contributions of others who have sometimes been overshadowed by Calvin and Geneva.

Calvin and Geneva

The patterns of teaching and church practice that are often called "Calvinist" were strongly influenced by the nearly twenty years of Protestant Reformed developments in the city of Strasbourg before John Calvin arrived there in 1539. The young Frenchman learned a great deal from Bucer and other senior colleagues like William Farel. Calvin himself, though, brought to his work as a reformer particular gifts and life experiences that were outstanding even

---

7. For Bucer's most Zwinglian stage, see his book *Grund und Ursach,* in English as *Basic Principles: Translation and Commentary on Martin Bucer's Grund und Ursach, 1524,* by O. F. Cypris (Ph.D. Dissertation, Union Seminary, N.Y., 1971). Bucer's Lord's Supper liturgy is also translated in Thompson, *Liturgies of the Western Church,* pp. 167-81. The fullest picture of Strasbourg's liturgical reform is René Bornert, *La réforme protestante du culte à Strasbourg au XVIe siècle (1525-1598)* (Leiden, 1981). For a discussion of the cooperative way in which Reformed liturgical scholars (especially those in South Germany and Switzerland) worked and of their effort to develop a liturgy in accord with the early church without slavishly copying it, see Hughes Oliphant Old, *The Patristic Roots of Reformed Worship* (Zürich: Theologischer Verlag, 1975).

among the remarkable group of Protestant leaders. Not a warmly outgoing personality or a creative initiator like Martin Luther, Calvin was one of the most gifted and coherent thinkers, and perhaps the most creative organizer of thought and practice, among the reformers. He was a brilliant writer and, despite his natural shyness, also a highly self-disciplined leader. Calvin's work, however, was shaped not only by his personal gifts but also by the time and place in which he lived.

This is most obvious with regard to time. Calvin came into the Protestant movement as a member of its second generation, and almost the only major figure who had never been a priest or a monk. He was a first-generation Protestant who had grown up in the same Catholic world as the first-generation reformers and shared their reactions to medieval theology and worship. His theological work drew on various earlier Protestant thinkers: Luther and Bucer were the key influences, with Zwingli mostly mediated through Bucer. Because Calvin entered the movement later, however, there were already many divisions among Protestants and conflicting interpretations of theology and worship to consider, and so his gifts of synthesis and organization were particularly important. Similarly, Calvin inherited a liturgy that had already been markedly changed from the Mass. Geneva was using a Zwinglian service when the young Frenchman arrived, and he also learned a great deal from the fuller liturgy that Bucer and other colleagues had developed in Strasbourg. In this context, it was the shaping of the various common Protestant elements, and their development, that was more important than creativity. And yet, the way Calvin shaped what he inherited made it something new and powerful.

The question of how Calvin's place affected his work is less often appreciated. Calvin lived out his vocation as an exile, and thus he brought to the role of reformer personal experiences different from those of most of the first generation. He was the most important of the reformers to work outside his homeland, and one of the few who spent his entire ministry as a resident alien in a foreign land. So the reformer of Geneva shaped his church order, his worship and piety, in the context of an international perspective that had existential roots unlike those of Luther, Zwingli, Bucer, Cranmer, or even Knox, a Lasco, and others, all of whom completed their work wholly or at least partially in the regions in which they were born.

Geneva itself was a small, precariously independent city-state (not a part of Switzerland until 1815), with no pretensions to university-educated leadership. Calvin worked, therefore, in an unimportant city of sturdy small-town burghers, which had been first converted to Protestantism in a Zwinglian form by Farel. Over the years, Calvin reshaped Geneva into a church pattern identifiable as "Calvinist," which became the most important model for the international spread of the Reformed tradition beyond the German-speaking world.

The following overview of Calvin's teaching and practice of worship gives primary attention to the liturgy, i.e., corporate worship and its components, without entirely neglecting the personal piety that shaped daily life.[8] Geneva in Calvin's day had a full series of services of the word: there were four on Sundays (dawn, mid-morning, catechism at noon, and afternoon), and one or sometimes two on other days of the week. In addition to this regular schedule of public worship, there were also other institutions — schools, the consistory, and the family — to support the up-building of the people of God in the service of God, because worship was supposed to run through the Christian's whole life. Thus, my sketch concludes by pointing to some aspects of the daily piety that came to mark Calvinists so distinctively.

The Word and Liturgical Time

Calvin shared the common Protestant conviction that preaching the word was one of the most critical factors that needed to be re-introduced and maintained as a vital part of public worship. Like other Reformed theologians, Calvin set aside the "selected lectionary" and followed the *lectio continua* system, working straight through one biblical book after another. On Sundays he preached on the New Testament, on weekdays on the Old, though psalms were also expounded on Sundays.

Also like other Reformed leaders, Calvin greatly simplified the liturgical calendar, putting central emphasis on Sundays, and eliminating not only all of the saints' days but also most of the other holy times such as Advent and Lent. Commonly Zwinglian churches kept Christmas (December 25), Circumcision (January 1), Annunciation (March 25), Easter, Ascension, and Pentecost. Calvin dropped Circumcision and Annunciation as well (the latter was popularly remembered as a Marian feast, the Conception), and celebrated the other four holy days on Sundays. Usually on these days Calvin interrupted the regular *lectio continua* pattern to preach on a text suited to the day, unless the New Testament book he was then expounding lent itself to that particular feast. In ad-

8. For a brief summary, see Elsie Anne McKee, "Context, Contours, Contents: Towards a Description of Calvin's Understanding of Worship," in *Calvin Studies Society Papers, 1995, 1997*, ed. D. Foxgrover (Grand Rapids, 1998), pp. 66-92. Full liturgies for Sundays with and without the Lord's Supper and for weekdays, including the baptismal liturgy, and for the Day of Prayer, are found in part 3 of Elsie Anne McKee, *John Calvin: Writings on Pastoral Piety* (New York: Paulist Press, 2001), a volume in the Classics of Western Spirituality series.

dition, during the week before Easter, there was also a break in the *lectio continua* pattern for a series of sermons on the Passion; Calvin sometimes chose the Gospel of John but especially liked Matthew, which was the favorite Synoptic Gospel in the sixteenth century because it was believed to be the oldest.[9]

Many people have criticized this Reformed revision of the calendar, which is related to the change from a selected lectionary to the *lectio continua* method of choosing Scripture, without fully understanding the reasons it was done. One purpose was to see that all the Bible was preached, including the Old Testament. A second reason was the re-orientation of religious time as part of the Protestant re-envisioning of the holy. No longer was one time considered more holy than any other, just as no places or persons were intrinsically holy. Sunday was kept as *the* holy day and the only full holiday (free of work). For Calvin, however, the observance of Sunday, although it was critically important, was not a law that had to be kept in order to be saved, but rather an obedient recognition of God's accommodation to humanity. All of time is holy, all seven days are owed to God, but God requires only one to be set aside for worship and rest, while the other six may be used for work. (Calvin never thought of changing the day of worship, but he did object to the superstitious idea that Sunday was essentially different from the other days. He would probably have been as disappointed that the later Reformed tradition developed a strong Sabbatarianism as he would have been shocked by how lightly many modern people treat Sunday.)

At least in the sixteenth century, this extreme revision of the liturgical year did not mean there was less concern for salvation history. One has only to look at Calvin's prayers to see that the death and resurrection of Jesus Christ were themes throughout the year.[10] If no time is sacred but all time belongs to God and has been redeemed by the Passion and resurrection of Christ, then every moment is holy, every moment is a time for worship. The Reformed idea of liturgical time reflects a very strong sense of God's providence and presence acting in history, a worship conscious of the here and now as lived in God's sight and offered to God.

This present-focus of liturgical time is most clearly seen in the establish-

9. The material in this section, including questions of liturgical time and the Day of Prayer, will be further developed in my book in process, *The Pastoral Ministry in Calvin's Geneva,* chaps. 2-3. It should be noted that not all "Calvinist" churches followed Genevan practice; the Netherlands, for example, continued to celebrate Christmas more fully, while some communities, such as Scotland and the English Puritans, carried further the elimination of traditional holy days.

10. See McKee, *John Calvin: Writings on Pastoral Piety,* part four and prayers in part three.

ment of the weekly Day of Prayer, which in Geneva was held on Wednesdays. This was a time of repentance for sins, thanksgiving for mercies, and intercession for the afflicted, prompted especially by careful observation of God's working in the world. The "current events" of Christian lives — the dangers that served as God's chastisement and education, acts of deliverance that manifested God's gracious mercy, and regular awareness of all sisters and brothers who suffered or were in need — these were the focus of the Day of Prayer. Together with the restructuring of the liturgical year to give key prominence to Sunday, this special "holy day" (a partial holiday in Geneva: no work was allowed until after the services) helped to shape Calvinist Reformed liturgical time in a way that orients worship toward taking very seriously the here and now in which Christians serve God. In addition, it also helped to give Calvinist worship a strongly ethical and activist bent; remembering and interceding for all brothers and sisters, both those immediately at hand and those far away, meant that one could never forget the obligation to love one's neighbors.

Prayer, Music, and Art in Worship

Prayer was a central concern for Calvin; in fact, his liturgy is called "The Form of Prayers." Putting the words of prayer and praise in the mouths of the whole congregation was vital, and a fitting way to express this public prayer was through singing. Although he shared Zwingli's sense that music could be seductive, Calvin was prepared to risk that danger for the sake of the greater gift of moving cold hearts. But that very fact — the power of music — made it all the more important that the words the people sang should be fitting; not just any texts were appropriate to sing for the glory of God and the edification of God's people.

For Calvin, only biblical words were appropriate, so he sponsored the translation and publication in French of metrical psalms and a few canticles such as the Decalogue and Song of Simeon. The first psalm booklet appeared in 1539, the complete Psalter in 1562. Although the words were the first concern, Calvin gave particular attention also to the music; it needed to be worthy of the texts and the worship of God, and therefore the French Psalter tunes were almost always written specifically for the psalms they were to accompany. (In a few instances several psalms used the same melody.) The complete Psalter with 150 psalms and 2 canticles was provided with 125 tunes in many different meters. Psalms were the people's prayers and praise in public worship, and they became the language of their private devotions as well. In public worship singing was always a cappella and in unison, led by a cantor and schoolboys (who were trained in music) to keep the congregation on the melody. In private, psalms could be sung in harmony.[11]

Like Zwingli and other Reformed Christians, Calvin generally rejected the use of visual arts for religious purposes, on the basis of the second commandment forbidding graven images. He did not, however, share Zwingli's identification of the spiritual with the nonmaterial; in fact, Calvin could speak of the sacraments, with the bread and wine and water, and the right liturgical ceremonies such as preaching, as the "living image of God."[12] Of all the visual arts, Calvin probably gave most thought to architecture; he was concerned that the place where Christians gathered to worship should be suitable for the purpose. Reformed congregations might meet in various kinds of buildings (Catholic critics spoke of Calvinist places of worship as being like schools, if not like more secular buildings), but the point was that everyone present should be able to hear the word of God and see the table where the Supper was celebrated, and that the surroundings should not distract the worshipers. In general, Reformed worship chiefly called on the ears and voice, not the eyes: the word was spoken and heard, the Psalms and prayers said and sung. The sacraments were to be clearly visible as well, but seeing was not a primary sense in Reformed worship.[13]

11. Calvin's foreword to the Psalter, which expresses something of his liturgical ideal as well as his understanding of singing in public and private worship, is found in two places: McKee, *John Calvin: Writings on Pastoral Piety,* pp. 91-97, and Charles Garside, *The Origins of Calvin's Theology of Music: 1536-1543* (Philadelphia: American Philosophical Society, 1979), pp. 31-33, which is the fullest discussion of Calvin's understanding of music. For the development of the Psalter see Pierre Pidoux, "Au XVIe siècle: La Genève de Calvin et le chant des psaumes," *Revue musicale de Suisse romande* 44, no. 3 (1991): 139-59 (a brief summary by the scholar who has mastered the sources). For a wide-ranging overview aiming to set the Psalter in a larger sociocultural context than is usually done, see John Witvliet, "The Spirituality of the Psalter: Metrical Psalms in Liturgy and Life in Calvin's Geneva," in *Calvin Studies Society Papers,* 1995, 1997, ed. Foxgrover, pp. 93-117.

12. *Institutes* 1.11.13; 4.1.5; and the Easter sermon on Matt. 28:1-10 on 14 April 1560 (*Supplementa Calviniana* 7, p. 96, translated in McKee, *John Calvin: Writings on Pastoral Piety,* p. 122) are just three examples.

13. Two Catholic critics are Antoine Cathalan and Florimond de Raemond. (See citations in McKee, *The Pastoral Ministry in Calvin's Geneva.*) Calvin's own ideas on art and architecture must be gathered from a variety of places, *Institutes* 1.11-12 being the most obvious. For an unpublished summary overview on Calvin and architecture by Edward A. Dowey, see citations in McKee, *The Pastoral Ministry in Calvin's Geneva.*

The Sacraments

The sacraments were, however, a very important part of Reformed worship, especially for Calvin. They are the aspect of worship on which Zwinglian and Calvinist Reformed differed the most significantly. Generally, the two branches understood the practice of infant baptism in similar fashion, but there were some differences in their teaching. Both agreed that baptism is the pledge of the covenant, given to the children of all members of the church, which must be completed by training that enables the child to affirm the faith for himself or herself. In accordance with his strong conviction that the sacraments are seals of God's promises, however, Calvin understood baptism primarily as a means of grace, with the human pledge in second place, and he insisted that it must always be celebrated in the context of a public service of the word.[14]

On the doctrine of the Lord's Supper, the two reformers were further apart, although again the basic reason was the same: whether or not the material sacrament could function as the seal of a spiritual promise.[15] Calvin's teaching includes some similarities to the thinking of Zwingli, especially on the place of the resurrected body of Christ. With Zwingli and against Luther, Calvin affirmed that Christ's human body is in heaven, and it is not made ubiquitous in every celebration (as the developed Lutheran position taught); Christ's presence in the bread and wine is spiritual, not local. In other significant ways, however, Calvin's teaching on the Supper was closer to Luther's than to Zwingli's. This is evident in two issues: the question of presence of Christ and that of means of grace. Calvin did not share Zwingli's idea of the Supper as a memorial only. Instead, like Luther, Calvin affirmed that there is a

14. See *Institutes* 4.15.1 (anonymous gentle criticism of Zwingli); *Institutes* 4.15-16 deals with various aspects of baptism. For several recent studies of Calvin and Reformed baptism, see J. W. Riggs, *The Development of Calvin's Baptismal Theology, 1536-1560* (Ph.D. Dissertation, Univ. of Notre Dame, 1986), and Old, *Shaping of the Reformed Baptismal Rite*.

15. Calvin's single fullest presentation of the Lord's Supper (not in a polemical treatise) is in *Institutes* 4.17. The "Short Treatise on the Lord's Supper" (published in 1541) is perhaps the most helpful and attractive way to approach Calvin's teaching; see Calvin, *Theological Treatises*, ed. J. K. S. Reid (Philadelphia: Westminster Press, 1954), pp. 142-66. Here the concluding comments on Luther and Zwingli are rather gentle, though they illustrate how Calvin understood himself to present a position that avoided the errors of both of his honored predecessors. Calvin does not use the categories outlined here, but they are implicit in his discussion of the Supper and seem the best way to give modern readers a grasp of what was at stake in the debates. For a helpful modern theological discussion of the Supper in its larger context, see B. A. Gerrish, *Grace and Gratitude: The Eucharistic Theology of John Calvin* (Minneapolis: Fortress Press, 1993).

real presence of Christ's body and blood (though he insisted that this is spiritual and not physical), and he considered the sacrament a means of grace. The bread and wine are not transubstantiated into body and blood (as the Catholic church taught), but the body and blood of Christ are truly offered with the bread and wine; they are received by faith. Someone without faith receives only the bread and the wine, but for the person with faith, the body and blood are conveyed with the elements, which are thus an instrument of grace. (The operative word is *with,* in contrast to the Lutheran *in, with,* and *under*).

This understanding of the meaning and purpose of the Supper influenced Calvin's view of how frequently it should be celebrated and what constitutes worthiness to partake.[16] The Supper is a means of sealing the grace of the promises that are preached, to make the doubting human heart more sure of the truth of God's acceptance in Christ. (Word and Supper offer the same grace, but in different ways; the sacrament or "visible word" serves to confirm the promises tangibly because of human weakness.) The Supper should therefore be held frequently, as often as the people are able to receive it — that is, as often as all the communicant members of the congregation can be prepared. The reason to limit frequency is thus that people must be fit to partake. There is much confusion about was meant by worthiness, but Calvin insisted that what makes one fit to receive is not perfection but trust in Christ alone, along with repentance, and reconciliation with God and one's neighbors. This ideal is common to most other reformers, but the Reformed added a distinctive corporate factor: the Supper is the meal of the whole body, not just those who happen to feel worthy on a given day, and therefore worthiness has a corporate dimension.

Thus, although Calvin said that the ideal would be to hold the Supper every Sunday (according to Acts 2:42), he took very seriously the importance of preparation for the sacrament, and this meant corporate as well as individual work. If everyone who is permitted is also expected to partake, then the community has to be prepared both by teaching and by examination. While the necessary preparation of faith and trust in Christ is inward, repentance and reconciliation must be outwardly manifested, and these are as much corporate as individual. The leadership of the church, the consistory, was to keep watch for any flagrant ignorance or open scandal, to teach and correct the transgressors for the honor of God and the health of both the church and the erring member. The leaders also had to attempt to reconcile those who were at odds with each other; no one should come to the Supper with a heart full of bitterness against another. Someone who was judged by the corporate church lead-

---

16. For a fuller discussion of this, see McKee, *The Pastoral Ministry in Calvin's Geneva,* chap. 3.

ership to be not sufficiently prepared should not, said Calvin, be allowed to share the Supper. Such exclusion by the judgment of the church was normally temporary, however; the object was to restore each and every person to fellowship so they would be ready to partake at the next celebration of the Supper.

And so, unless and until adequate preparation could be insured for the biblical ideal of a weekly celebration, Calvin was content with a monthly Supper. The right celebration — all the body gathered together in faith and peace with God and each other, to receive the tangible seal of the preached word of forgiveness in Christ — was more important than frequent celebrations at which only some members participated. On the other hand, to be content with infrequent celebration was to dishonor God and deprive oneself of one of the greatest gifts God gives. Calvin's careful balance must be remembered.

Nonetheless, the Genevan authorities refused to allow the Supper more than four times per year (which was still more often than the people had been accustomed to commune), and so the frequency of celebrating the Lord's Supper was the same in Geneva as in Zürich. This similarity of practice did not imply the same theology, but the effect was that eventually Calvin's different interpretation of the Supper was rather obscured by the assimilation of its practical frequency to the Zwinglian tradition.

Fellowship: Linking Liturgy with Love

It might appear that all the components of liturgy had been covered: word, prayer, sacraments. The Calvinist Reformed paradigm for worship, however, included one more element, based on the teaching of Acts 2:42: "They continued steadfastly in the teaching of the apostles and the fellowship and the breaking of the bread and the prayers."[17] That fourth element was fellowship, and those four aspects of worship together — preaching the word, fellowship, the Supper, and prayers — were regarded as necessary components of the right worship gathering, not a specific order of service.

Fellowship was most often concretely expressed as almsgiving, though Calvin also mentions the kiss of peace. Another aspect of this fellowship would be an awareness of mutual needs, physical as well as spiritual, which might include also announcements about the sick and needy in the congregation. (In Calvin's Geneva, however, these were a constant part of daily prayers and in particular a major theme on the Day of Prayer, so they received less at-

17. For a full study of this paradigm in context, see Elsie Anne McKee, *John Calvin on the Diaconate and Liturgical Almsgiving* (Geneva: Libr. Droz, 1984), chaps. 3 and 10.

Calvin's Genevan Service of the Word and Sacrament

(Order of 1562, with three psalms)

Liturgy of the Word

Psalm

Invocation

Confession of Sin

Psalm

Minister's Extempore Prayer for Illumination-Sealing

Biblical Text and Sermon-Exposition

Liturgy of the Table

Confession of Faith (Apostles' Creed)

Decalogue (sung)

Scripture (1 Cor. 11:23-29) and Exhortation

Distribution (men and then women file up in order, a lector reads aloud
   from the Gospel of John chap. 13 and following)

Thanksgiving

Song of Simeon

Benediction

tention on Sunday.) This fourth element of Acts 2:42, fellowship, is the most elusive and often neglected component of the Calvinist Reformed liturgical definition. In part this is because it seems "extrinsic" to the liturgy, being directed to human need and not focused on God. It points, however, to a very significant factor in Calvin's understanding of worship: the way service of God is linked with service of the neighbor.

Daily Worship: Piety and Ethos

Calvinist worship was strongly corporate and was intended to encompass the whole of Christians' lives. In the list of the components of a full Sunday liturgy, two aspects — the word and especially prayer — spill over into the daily life of the Christian, and a third, fellowship, has its primary place there. First, hearing the word of God was not just a Sunday activity for Genevans; there were daily sermons in several churches, and on Fridays also a regular Bible study for clergy and lay people together. (Although he expected Christians to read their Bibles, Calvin put less emphasis on private Bible study than some later Reformed theologians, probably because so much daily preaching was provided in Geneva.) Second, besides the injunction "to pray without ceasing," Calvinists were instructed to stop at intervals throughout the day to pray, and texts were provided. Chief among these were the metrical psalms that were sung in the liturgy but also intended for private use. In addition, other daily prayers were provided in the catechism and liturgy for use at home and at school; these included prayers for morning and evening, before and after meals, and before school or daily work. Some of these were to be said by individuals, others were for families; parents and householders were expected to train the little churches in their homes as well as they were able.

In the worship service the fourth point of Acts 2:42, almsgiving, was not a major component, but this liturgical expression of concern for others linked Calvinist liturgy with daily life. There fellowship, mutual concern of the members of the body for each other, actually had an important role as a witness to faith. Although Calvin clearly stated that the love and worship of God take precedence over all else, he also insisted that one of the most sincere expressions of the service of God is love for the neighbor. Liturgy can be hypocritical; love and service of those in need can hardly be counterfeited. And so Calvin expected the daily life of Christians to evidence their worship of God; they were to serve the good of all people and honor the image of God in all. The daily vocation of each Christian must also reflect the worship of God; as Calvin said so succinctly, "We are not our own. . . . We are God's!"[18] That affirmation should transform our lives.

The Reformed Family of Churches

To say that all belong not to themselves but to God does not mean that all must or can be uniform, but that they all share the same allegiance and try to live as

---

18. The full passage, from the *Institutes* 3.7.1 on *The Sum of the Christian Life,* is well worth quoting: "We are not our own: let not our reason nor our will, therefore, sway our plans and deeds. We are not our own: let us therefore not set it as our goal to seek what is expedient for us according to the flesh. We are not our own: in so far as we can, let us therefore forget ourselves and all that is ours. Conversely, we are God's: let us therefore live for Him and die for Him. We are God's: let His wisdom and will therefore rule all our actions. We are God's: let all the parts of our life accordingly strive toward Him as our only lawful goal (Rom. 14:8)."

one faithful body of many members. Diversity in unity was part of the Reformed tradition from the beginning. The several originating figures themselves had somewhat varied theological viewpoints "inculturated" in different vernaculars. They worked to bring these viewpoints into fellowship, but they never spoke with only one voice: it was more like a choir, singing to one God a song of praise in multiple parts.

The fruit of this early chorus or fellowship of Reformed voices was a family of churches: brothers and sisters and cousins, all with a clear family resemblance but also individual differences. The Reformed family developed a variety of national or linguistically distinct confessions and church organizations, but each of these church bodies affirmed and practiced communion with the others, and each of the confessions revealed common traits. The influence of the Zürich stream was most significant in German-speaking lands, but it was also apparent in other places — for example, Heinrich Bullinger's stature in the sixteenth-century Church of England was in some ways greater than that of Calvin. The center of influence for much of the international Reformed movement, especially that in Hungary and Poland, France and the Netherlands, Scotland and Puritan parts of England, as well as for scattered groups of Italian- and Spanish-speaking believers, was the stream flowing from Bucer and Calvin. In part the reason for this was the international character of Bucer's and especially Calvin's vision; in part it was the influence of the refugees from all across Europe who flocked to Geneva. The liturgical work of the Strasbourg circle, mediated through and shaped by Calvin, and given particular weight by his increasing importance as the most representative voice of international Reformed thought, spread widely.

Worship and church order in the Reformed tradition were thus particularly marked by Calvin's masterful synthesis, though the broad family of churches that came to be called Reformed maintained an internal variety within their fellowship of mutual recognition, mutual aid, and mutual exchanges across geographic and linguistic lines. (No one interpretation of doctrine or particular liturgy became *the* accepted doctrine or liturgy throughout the entire Reformed communion.) The family also developed a presence in many lands of Europe and beyond, in new continents where Reformed peoples moved.

The remainder of the chapters in this volume trace not only the geographic spread but also significant features of the continuing development of the Reformed family, taking into account new perspectives on church order (congregationalism) and worship (issues of form and freedom); on cultural and historical adaptation to new lands and centuries; on political, social, and aesthetic questions; and more. Before turning to that broadening river, it is useful to note some of the characteristic features of the classical Reformed teaching on worship, and how those distinctive traits may contribute to the wider church — both Reformed and ecumenical — in the modern world.

Some Concluding Comments on the Distinctive Features of Calvinist Reformed Worship

While recognizing that the Reformed tradition was not the work of any one person, and that it had roots in more places than Geneva, it can still be said that in many ways the work of John Calvin in the small city beside Lake Leman was critical for the formation of this religious heritage. This is particularly true for the teaching and practice of worship. Thus, while endeavoring to set the Reformed tradition itself in the wider context of the Protestant re-envisioning of Western Christian worship, and while acknowledging the contributions of other leaders such as Zwingli and especially Bucer, it is appropriate to recognize that Calvin and Geneva provide the most important key to the classical Reformed tradition in worship. In conclusion, therefore, while bearing in mind the diversity within the tradition and celebrating that capacity for a kind of "ecumenical" conversation, it is worthwhile to highlight some of the distinctively Reformed features of sixteenth-century Reformed worship, particularly as they were defined by John Calvin.

Preaching and Liturgical Time

Since all Protestant (and also Catholic) reformers shared in the renewal of preaching in the sixteenth century, it is important to see what the particular contribution of the Reformed tradition was. Reformed people may have been more insistent than other Protestants on the necessity of carefully prepared expository preaching, but the two most significant contributions were perhaps the choice to set the canon of Scripture above the liturgical calendar, thus making a very clear revision of religious time, and the emphasis given to the Old Testament. Both of these decisions about the word of God and time were notable characteristics of Reformed Protestants. Both choices included potential future dangers but also very obvious gifts in the sixteenth-century context.

A clear decision was made to give the canon of Scripture precedence over the traditional religious cycle. This did not mean a complete leveling of time; Sundays were red-letter days, and Sundays when the Lord's Supper was celebrated were (at least among Calvinists) times of very great importance:

high holy days. It did mean a new, more linear sense of time. While this could in the long term spell dull routine, in fact it set a high standard; it required its members to see all of time as lived in God's sight, and the present as the place to look for God's acting, to recognize God's rebuke, to rejoice in God's deliverances, to intercede for God's people. The interweaving of the doctrine of providence with worship is plain. While this pattern did not locate salvation history so clearly in special seasons of the calendar, the great events of Christ's passion and resurrection were never forgotten, but carried through each day and week.

The Reformed reaction against the medieval dominance of calendar over canon was extreme and could lead to various problems. In a time when people no longer attended worship several times a week or more, the *lectio continua* pattern would necessarily limit their hearing the full scope of Scripture, eventually leading to a pedestrian neglect of certain themes that the liturgical year would have made prominent. It could also allow preachers to choose their favorite books and no others. Nonetheless, the new vision of religious time was an important corrective in the sixteenth century, and its orientation to the here and now still has something to teach the church about the relevance of worship to life in the world where God's people are working and suffering.

The Reformed choice to require regular exegetical preaching on the whole of the Bible, including the entire Old Testament, also was important because of the implicit prophetic element built into this pattern. The determination to have exegetical sermons on the whole range of Scripture clearly expanded the amount of the Bible that ordinary people would hear and know. (It also was one of the main reasons for the Reformed insistence on a learned ministry.) In particular, this new vision, with its strong emphasis on the Old Testament, gave to Reformed preaching a prophetic orientation that was not equalled anywhere else until the African-American and other free-church voices of the modern period. While its promise was not always fulfilled, this principle, which made the Exodus and the prophets almost as familiar as Jesus and his disciples, was no small contribution to the ecumenical church.

Psalms and Music

A second area of worship and piety distinct to the Calvinist Reformed is the role of the psalms as the words of prayer and praise. Unlike other Protestants, Calvinists (and most other Reformed) did not sing human compositions, but they made of the Psalter a treasury of public and private worship. The memorization of a body of biblical songs formed an important basis for Reformed piety, a language of prayer that gave a particular coherence to public and private worship. No longer could Sunday worship be separated from that of the rest of the week; all of time was offered to God in the same biblical prayers. In addition, the fact that the kind of music sung was considered important also distinguished Calvinists, and the sober-yet-singing quality of the tunes written for the psalms gave a specific character to the artistic sense of Reformed Christians (though not all Reformed Psalters were as successful as the Genevan French). The scope might be narrow, but the appreciation for beauty was channeled rather than cut off.

The Sacraments

With regard to the sacraments, one of the important marks of the Reformed tradition, especially of Calvinists, was the consistent requirement that these be corporate. Public baptisms in the presence of the whole worshiping community were essential: there were no emergencies that necessitated private baptisms. Also, the common participation of the whole communicant membership in the Lord's Supper, and proper preparation for it, mark the Reformed practice as different from most Protestants. Here Calvin shaped the tradition more strongly than Zwingli by giving oversight of preparation to the corporate leadership of the church rather than to the Christian state. Zwinglians and Calvinists differed in their understanding of the Lord's Supper, and other views were also possible (Bullinger's position being somewhere between that of Zwingli and Calvin).[19] In no case, however, was there any denigration of the sacraments, but instead a very strong effort to make them rightly valued. For Zwingli, this meant as pledges of the community's faith and thanksgiving to God, something Calvin recognized also. For Calvin, however, the sacraments were first of all seals of the promises of God, means of grace, conveying what they offered to those who had faith.

A particular concern of Calvin's was that right participation in the Lord's Supper necessitated prior repentance, trust in God, and reconciliation with one's neighbors. The value placed on preparation and discipline is usually regarded as distinctively Reformed, but in addition its corporate character must also be noted. Calvin's discipline had as one purpose seeing that the whole body of Christ in any place ate his Supper together. Frequency of celebration has become an issue again in modern times, and Calvin certainly had a

---

19. For an overview of the continuing diversity on the Supper, see B. A. Gerrish, "The Lord's Supper in the Reformed Confessions," in *Theology Today* 23 (1966-67): 224-43.

more urgent sense than Zwingli of the need to share the Supper often. It is helpful, however, to remember the conditions in which Calvinists believed the Supper should be held: frequent celebration did not honor God or serve the people if preparation was neglected; celebration by only a self-selected few who felt ready, while the rest of the people observed, was also a travesty of the common feast.

Love/Ethos/Piety

The discussion of the sacraments leads naturally into the issue of piety, the lived worship of the Christian life. Sharing the Supper, the Reformed taught, should strengthen the members of Christ's body for active service and love of others. In addition, they made a very clear connection between the worship of God in a strict sense — prayer, liturgy, preaching — and the worship of God in daily life, in the mundane situation of each person's vocation. Partly thanks to the importance of the Old Testament, the Decalogue, and the prophets, and partly owing to the way the transcendence of God — the totality of God's claim on human life — was understood, for the Reformed tradition the worship of God included the love of the neighbor. Both prayer and love are daily, continuous activities. While this vision was certainly not confined to the Reformed tradition, a sense that serving the glory of God means transforming the world has always been particularly strong among Reformed Christians.

For Further Reading

Eire, Carlos. *War Against the Idols: The Reformation of Worship from Erasmus to Calvin.* Cambridge: Cambridge University Press, 1986.

Garside, Charles. *The Origins of Calvin's Theology of Music: 1536-1543.* Philadelphia: American Philosophical Society, 1979.

———. *Zwingli and the Arts.* New Haven: Yale University Press, 1966.

Gerrish, B. A. "Calvin's Eucharistic Piety." In *Calvin Studies Society Papers, 1995, 1997,* ed. D. Foxgrover. Grand Rapids, 1998. Pages 52-65.

———. "The Lord's Supper in the Reformed Confessions," *Theology Today* 23 (1966-67): 224-43.

McKee, Elsie Anne. "Context, Contours, Contents: Towards a Description of Calvin's Understanding of Worship," in *Calvin Studies Society Papers, 1995, 1997,* ed. D. Foxgrover. Grand Rapids, 1998. Pages 66-92.

———. *John Calvin: Writings on Pastoral Piety.* Classics of Western Spirituality.

New York: Paulist Press, 2001. (Texts of Calvin's liturgies with sermons, foreword to Psalter, dedication to commentary on Psalms, prayers of many kinds, exposition of Lord's Prayer, etc.)

Old, Hughes Oliphant. *The Patristic Roots of Reformed Worship.* Zürich: Theologischer Verlag, 1975.

———. *The Shaping of the Reformed Baptismal Rite in the Sixteenth Century.* Grand Rapids: Eerdmans, 1992.

Parker, T. H. L. *Calvin's Preaching.* Louisville: Westminster/John Knox, 1992.

Thompson, Bard. *Liturgies of the Western Church.* Cleveland: Meridian Books, 1961. (An older text with Sunday and especially Lord's Supper liturgies for many Reformed and other theologians, e.g, Zwingli, Bucer, Calvin, Knox, Church of England, English Puritans.)

Witvliet, John. "The Spirituality of the Psalter: Metrical Psalms in Liturgy and Life in Calvin's Geneva," *Calvin Studies Society Papers,* 1995, 1997, ed. D. Foxgrover. Grand Rapids, 1998. Pages 93-117.

Zwingli, Ulrich. "Of Baptism" and "On the Lord's Supper." In *Zwingli and Bullinger,* ed. G. W. Bromiley. Philadelphia: Westminster Press, 1953. Pages 119-244.

Reformed Worship in Continental Europe since the Seventeenth Century

Bruno Bürki

Introduction

The historical and geographic limits of this chapter call for some explanation, or possibly even justification. Today, churches and congregations of the Reformed confessional family are found everywhere in the world. Even in the sixteenth century they were beginning to fan out from Europe. At first this was due to difficult historical circumstances that caused many Reformed Christians to emigrate or become refugees, rather than to an impetus for world mission. Regardless of the reason they went, they carried their congregational structures and customary forms of worship into every country in the world. There, new encounters and conditions brought about changes in the accustomed ways of doing things.

All Reformed Christians look to Geneva as the definitive birthplace of Reformed worship, and to Calvin for the roots of their style of church leadership and guidance for pastoral ministry. In the previous chapter on Reformed worship in the sixteenth century we spoke of this, and justifiably concentrated first on Zwingli and then especially on John Calvin. This common heritage later took on different liturgical and synodal forms and structures of church discipline. In France Reformed churches were scattered, and were separate from and often persecuted by the state. In the Swiss sovereign territories, the followers of Zwingli and Calvin developed mixed church-state governments along Calvin's lines. Other forms appeared in Heidelberg, for the Electoral Palatinate, or in the Netherlands. Protestants in eastern European countries, too, received inspiration and support from Geneva, but then grew in accordance

The author is indebted to Marcel Barnard for his contribution to the survey on the Netherlands.

with their own history. In England and Scotland, and thence into the widening English-speaking world, the Presbyterian form of the church made its home. In 1618, Reformed church representatives from a number of countries met in Dordrecht, Holland, to establish orthodox principles for church doctrine and church life, as a defense against the Arminian weakening of the belief in predestination.

The origins of Reformed worship in the Netherlands are both typical and special enough to merit a particular place in our account. An order of worship was developed in the Dutch refugee communities in England and on German soil (in Wesel, Emden, Frankfurt, and finally in the Electoral Palatinate). This order of worship, parts of which are still in use today, was ratified at synods in Dordrecht in 1574 and 1578. The former Polish priest Johannes a Lasco, Maarten Micron, and especially Petrus Dathenus (1531-1590) had much to do with its development. Their church polities show Calvinistic influences, as do the polities of Strasbourg, Württemburg (Germany), and especially the Palatinate.[1]

Two examples are the Dutch celebration of the Lord's Supper in London, under Maarten Micron, and the order of worship adopted in Dordrecht under Petrus Dathenus, with an important order for baptism. These are both typical of Reformed worship theology and clearly influenced by the situation of Dutch congregations. In the exile community in London there was, in addition to Sunday worship, a service on Thursdays in which "prophets" put questions to the preacher. The Bible was read through in continuous installments. The Lord's Supper was celebrated every second month, with the members of the congregation sitting at table together and serving one another, and the liturgical actions were performed by the preacher and congregation together. The mystery of the Supper is the *communio* with Christ, portrayed in the communicative actions of the congregation. In opposition to Luther, the emphasis was on the breaking of the bread, and on the eating and drinking of bread and wine, rather than on Christ's presence in the elements. In the words of Maarten den Dulk, it was a Protestant breakthrough from the ontological to the functional.[2]

The form of the Lord's Supper adopted by the Dordrecht Synod in 1578 gives an important place to the self-examination of the faithful between the words of institution and the table fellowship. This self-examination consisted

---

1. For information on the influence of the Dutch model of worship on South Africa and Indonesia, see the chapters by Coenraad Burger and Ester Pudjo Widiasih in this volume.

2. Maarten den Dulk, *Een huis naast de synagoge. Herlezing van de brief aan Timoteüs met het oog op de gemeente* (Zoetermeer, 2000), p. 151.

of three steps: accepting one's misery, redemption, and thanksgiving, followed by the assurance of mercy and the turning away of the unrepentant. In the order for baptism adopted by the same synod, baptism is not itself the means of grace. Rather, the Father makes known and affirms the covenant of grace through baptism, the Son confirms the purification through his blood, and the Spirit assures the baptized persons of its presence. It is a cognitive process focused on the life of the believer. The decisive element in the understanding of baptism is the forgiveness of sins, but also an ethical obligation on the part of the baptized.

We will confine ourselves here essentially to worship in the churches of the German- and French-speaking parts of the European continent, but will also return to the Dutch churches and briefly touch on the worship tradition of the Reformed Church in Hungary. Beginning with the worship practice of the Reformed churches in the century following the Reformation, we will see how worship developed during the Enlightenment and during the subsequent periods in the history of ideas, of the church, and of the society.

It is important to discuss the Enlightenment because it brought about more of a break than we are accustomed to acknowledging in the life of the churches. From the eighteenth century onward, the Reformed churches, though preserving much of their heritage, belonged to a modern world that differed in important ways from the era of the Reformation. Moreover, our present-day churches by and large, particularly in Europe, are still under the influence of cultural and intellectual attitudes grounded in the Enlightenment. This is a good reason to offer a summary of the history of worship in continental Europe from the seventeenth to the twentieth century.

We will then examine the encounter of this worship practice with the development and challenges of worship communities from other cultures and eras, and the creation of a worshiping community first within the Reformed family of churches, and then reaching out beyond them ecumenically. But attention must also be paid and honor be done to our communion's liturgical heritage from the church of the first millennium.

Preserving the Reformation Heritage in the Period of Orthodoxy

In the period of the Reformed orthodoxy, worship was a part of public life in town and countryside in the Reformed areas of Switzerland, Germany, and other countries. It took place on Sundays and certain days during the week. Attendance was a citizen's duty, and the authorities had efficient means of assuring that this duty was fulfilled. In France, however, membership in the Reformed Church and attendance at worship were purely the church's affair, and followed the rules laid down in the synodal *Discipline.*

In accordance with the order established by the Reformation, Reformed worship was mainly a matter of listening. Through the preaching of the word the congregation was taught and admonished. Reformers such as Calvin introduced the practice of preaching series of sermons on books of the Bible, a practice that lasted until the emergence of more freedom in preaching customs. The heart of worship was thus the proclamation of the word by the minister. Biblical content in preaching presupposed the hearer's familiarity with the Scriptures of both Old and New Testaments, which could be increased by reading the Bible alone or with one's family. Regular catechism sessions for young and old ensured knowledge of the articles of faith.

The prayers that were offered aloud in worship were of considerable length and theological weight and emphasized the teaching character of worship. In many respects, they extended the lessons and admonitions of the sermon. The word had acquired great weight following the impetus from the Reformation and from contemporary humanist culture. The widespread effect of such word-dominated religion should be neither over- nor underestimated.

In Geneva and elsewhere (in France, for instance), the sermon began and ended with the singing of a psalm in unison, according to well-known melodic and verse settings. In Zürich such singing in worship was not allowed until 1598. Accompaniment on the organ was forbidden everywhere until the nineteenth century. A leader sang each line for the congregation to follow, and in the course of time there were also trumpeters. In France the language of the psalms was modernized in the latter half of the seventeenth century by Valentin Conrart and Marc-Antoine de la Bastide, French literary figures well known to the public. (Conrart was the father of the Académie Française.) The goal was to adapt the psalms of the Huguenots to new linguistic sensibilities. This new version of the psalms for singing also came to Switzerland, by way of Geneva. In their revisions Conrart and de la Bastide also included the prayers of the Calvinist liturgy, which were often published together with the psalms in one volume.

German-speaking regions preserved the sixteenth-century "Lobwasser Psalter" for many years. Ambrosius Lobwasser (d. 1585), a Prussian Lutheran, translated the Huguenot Psalter to create the German Reformed *Psalmenbuch,* which remained in exclusive use until the end of the eighteenth century.

On high feast days the sermon was followed by the celebration of the Lord's Supper. It was considered important for members of the congregation to be dressed in a dignified manner if they wished to participate. The central act in the celebration of the sacrament was "the breaking of the bread." The use of ordinary bread for the Lord's Supper was considered proof of Calvinist orthodoxy. The wording for the Lord's Supper prescribed by Calvin, and by the church rules of the Electoral Palatinate, was preserved practically unchanged in the churches of their respective areas. In Zürich the same was true of Zwingli's liturgical order, on into the nineteenth century. For all members of the congregation who were admitted, the Lord's Supper represented a solemn and impressive moment. The word made visible did not add anything new to the message proclaimed in the sermon, but allowed the divine character of the word to be clearly felt. With the detailed admonishments to the congregation with regard to receiving communion, and the long prayers continuing the catechismal intonation, worship was under the spell of verbal communication even during the sacrament. Other than the procession to the table, there was not much "to do" or "to see," except the "breaking of the bread" (carried out with dignity by the pastor) and the actual individual act of receiving communion. Going to the Lord's Supper was nonetheless an obligation that each person felt strongly and that established a person's place in the congregation. The feeling of being united as a social group by the same confession enhanced, especially in Switzerland, the sense of membership. Worship had an integrative and sometimes even exclusive character.

In Hungary and France the Reformed churches preserved their worship life even during periods of oppression. Lutheran influence had begun to make itself felt in Hungary around 1520, and around the middle of the sixteenth century the Reformed movement increasingly gained ground in the country. Soon after its publication, Debrecen adopted the Second Helvetic Confession (1566). In church life the distinction between Lutherans and Reformed was not as clearly recognizable as in theological teaching. The Hungarian churches adopted the forms of worship of Zürich and Geneva, and, oppressed by the Roman Catholic majority, Protestants organized themselves in districts in order to survive. The Diet of Sopron of 1681 guaranteed freedom of worship in certain places, whereas "orphan congregations" elsewhere were only allowed family worship in private homes. For baptisms and weddings, members of such congregations had to go to the recognized congregations, after paying the fees to their local Catholic priest. Reformed members of "orphan congregations" also had to observe the Catholic feast days. Burials took place in great secrecy, usually at night, with an elder reading the Bible and praying, the congregation quietly singing its psalms, and no pastor allowed. Even so, the Reformed faith was passed on and celebrated from generation to generation in these orphaned congregations. The situation did not change until Emperor Joseph II's Decree of Tolerance in 1781.[3]

As in Hungary, life was hard for the Reformed churches of France. This was especially in the south during the "Desert Period" from the Revocation of the Edict of Nantes in 1685 to the Edict of Tolerance in 1787.[4] Church members who had not been imprisoned or gone into exile were encouraged at first by itinerant preachers, and met in homes or in remote places in the countryside at the risk of their lives and possessions. Charismatic figures, both women and men, played a role. Prophets from the Cévennes Mountains strengthened the spirit of resistance among the faithful. In the secret gatherings a particular Huguenot spirituality developed. The excesses of such inspired groups were held in check by pastors trained abroad, especially in Lausanne, and the synods they reestablished. One of the first "Desert" synods decided in 1716 that "the same forms of congregational worship should be followed that we knew when we were free, and that are customary in Geneva and in Switzerland." Scripture reading and psalm singing, the appointed prayers as well as free prayer, the sermon (by those appointed to preach), and other familiar elements of worship were preserved. During the eighteenth century, however, Enlightenment views of the faith and new forms of worship such as prayers for feast days also spread through French Protestantism and neighboring churches, especially by means of books for use in home worship, since public worship was forbidden. One can then see why Napoleon was later joyfully hailed as the new "Cyrus" who freed the church and its worship.

Ostervald's Adoption of Anglican Forms in the Early Enlightenment

Pastor Jean-Frédéric Ostervald (1663-1747) of Neuchâtel represents a reasoned orthodoxy touched by the early Enlightenment.[5] In the first decade of the eighteenth century, in the Reformed Church of Neuchâtel, he started an extensive pastoral reform, of which the renewal of worship was an essential element. The

3. At the meeting in the John Knox Center, Erzsébet Horvath presented a paper on the history of Protestant worship in Hungary; it has been used in this survey.

4. Otto Erich Strasser-Bertrand, "Die evangelische Kirche in Frankreich," in *Die Kirche in ihrer Geschichte*, ed. Bernd Moeller (Göttingen, 1965), vol. 3, pp. 136-91.

5. Bruno Bürki, "Beispielhaft reformierte Form der Liturgie in Neuchâtel," in *Liturgiereformen*, ed. Martin Klöckener and Benedikt Kranemann (Münster, 2001), vol. 1, pp. 417-35. Pierre Barthel, *Jean-Frédéric Ostervald l'Européen 1663-1747, Novateur neuchâtelois* (Geneva, 2001).

Principality of Neuchâtel was a special case in the area of what is now Switzerland, in that the clergy exercised leadership of the church without interference from the secular authorities. As a young man Ostervald was already an influential spokesman for the "classe des ministres" and was able to implement his ideas for reform of the worship service and religious feeling ("du culte et des sentiments"). His aim was to go beyond the fossilized system of orthodox doctrine and practice in worship and to breathe new life into the church. Ostervald and Neuchâtel were in fact almost a hundred years ahead of other Protestant churches that were trying to renew their worship in the spirit of the Enlightenment. Thus Neuchâtel met with resistance, especially from its influential neighbor Bern, which was still very strictly oriented to Calvinist orthodoxy.

Ostervald had studied at the modern Academy of Saumur in France, which was no longer governed by orthodoxy, and had acquired his theological and philosophical orientation from England and the Netherlands, where Enlightenment thinking was in full swing. Thus it did not seem incongruous to him to take prayers and rites from the Anglican liturgy as models for his renewal. Large sections of Ostervald's liturgy for Neuchâtel, especially for celebrating baptism and the Lord's Supper, came from the *Book of Common Prayer.* Ostervald had strongly condemned the Calvinist Reformation's break with liturgical tradition, and in this way the Reformed churches regained contact with that common Christian liturgical tradition.

By reconnecting with the Anglican liturgy, Ostervald took a step full of consequences for the whole Reformed French-speaking world of Calvinist tradition. Reformed sister churches did not directly follow the example of Neuchâtel and its liturgy, but it was the signal for the beginning of liturgical openness toward the catholic or common Christian tradition. This orientation is still detectable today, distinguishing the French-speaking Reformed churches from the German-speaking ones in Germany and Switzerland. It set the stage for an affinity of French-speaking Reformed churches with the English-speaking Presbyterians.

Certainly the best and most far-reaching element of Ostervald's worship reforms was the development of daily prayer services on the model of the Anglican Morning and Evening Prayers. These "offices" complemented the weekday sermons that had been usual in Neuchâtel as in other cities of the Calvinist tradition. In connection with these prayer services Ostervald also developed not only hymns to be recited in the congregation but also a biblical lectionary to take the place of the Reformation-style sermon series or the free choice of a sermon text by the worship leader.

In the area of sacraments of initiation, Ostervald borrowed from the Anglican baptismal service to create his liturgies. He especially wanted to bring back the celebration of confirmation, conceiving of it as a promise made to God by the Christian person entering adulthood, with a typically Enlightenment-style moral impetus.

The celebration of the Eucharist in the Neuchâtel liturgy acquired, through Ostervald's reform, a prayer of consecration, following the example of the Anglican Eucharistic prayer and largely taken from it word for word. In Reformed worship the accompanying gestures are exclusively oriented toward the communion.

It must be noted, however, that Ostervald's entire liturgical project suffered from a deficient view and practice of sacramental theology. For him, a sacrament was not really a gift of God and means of grace, but rather a moral duty for Christians. In this regard, Ostervald's practice of baptism and the Lord's Supper was markedly inferior to the Reformation's understanding of the sacraments, particularly that of Calvin. What was perhaps gained in the area of liturgical forms was lost with regard to the content in terms of faith. Human beings were left to themselves instead of participating, as Calvin said, in the body and blood of the risen Christ through the Holy Spirit.

According to Ostervald, worship was not merely to serve the moral education of individual Christians and the local congregation to which they belonged. It was also to promote community among Christians of different nations. Through contact with like-minded people in England and church leaders in Berlin, with whom Neuchâtel had ties as a principality of the Prussian king, relationships among the churches of the Reformation in Europe were promoted. This meant that people talked about plans for union, although this remained a utopian dream, a pre-ecumenical project. In view of the French policy on religion under Louis XIV, these discussions were in a polemical and defensive vein.

The Influence of Pietism and the Enlightenment on the Reformed Liturgy of German-Speaking Switzerland and the Netherlands

These two spiritual currents in Europe — Pietism and the Enlightenment — essentially gave a new shape to worship life in German-speaking Switzerland.[6] In general, the effects of the Enlightenment on church liturgy became noticeable only little by little in the course of the eighteenth century. With regard to

6. Emanuel Kellerhals, *Geschichte des Gottesdienstes in der reformierten deutschen Schweizer Kirche* (Manuskriptdruck, 1973).

Pietism, at least in the area of worship, the Awakening of the nineteenth century must be seen in relation to the older Pietism with roots in the seventeenth century. It is not easy to decide whether the Enlightenment and Pietism should be viewed as spiritually related twin sisters or as warring brothers. The moral impetus, and the shift of emphasis from the congregation as a whole to the individual person standing alone before God and the world, is common to both. Worship in the received tradition seemed insufficient to both. For both the Enlightenment and Pietism the main purpose of religion was to strengthen individual religiosity on the basis of spiritual experience. The call to assume responsibility in personal freedom, the legalism of either the "born again" Christian or the idealistic activist, can be perceived in the forms of worship and in the liturgical texts.

The Enlightenment brought about the softening of the strict Calvinistic confession of sins into a more general opening prayer in worship services, despite the *Assoziationseid,* the oath imposed by the orthodox leaders of Bern in 1699 (directed against the Pietists as much as against Arminians and Socinians). It was Pietism that created, as an opening prayer, the one prayer for Sunday that has been preserved and widely used from the middle of the eighteenth century to the present: "High and eternal God, Thou who dwellest in heaven and whose Name is holy . . ." The creed and the reading of the Ten Commandments, no longer seen as being sufficiently related to particular situations, disappeared from the regular liturgy. Around the middle of the eighteenth century, Pastor Johannes Konrad Wildermett, a friend of Ostervald's in Biel, created a prayer book containing many texts with an Enlightenment bias.

The Pietist movement introduced new prayers for feast days in which its theological concerns were included with urgent emphasis. This can be heard in a Christmas prayer from strongly pietistic St. Gallen: "Lord Jesus . . . Thou, the creator of the whole world, wast born in Bethlehem so that we might be reborn as new creatures. Thou tookest a stable for thy lodging, that we might dwell in houses and secure dwelling places in peace. Thou wast content with a hard manger, that we might be lifted up into the soft bosom of Abraham. Thou wast wrapped in swaddling clothes, that we might put on the garments of righteousness and be adorned with the pure silk of holiness. . . ." In Zürich, on the other hand, there were prayers in Enlightenment style to "Lord Jesus, Thou most precious Friend of humankind." At the end of the eighteenth century, the word "worship" in the church book was replaced by the favorite Enlightenment expression "doing reverence to God," in order to get rid of the last orthodox bones of contention. In the course of the seventeenth and eighteenth centuries the custom of kneeling for prayer, which was in use during the Reformation, was given up and even forbidden in some congregations.

The intensive debate that went on in Germany during the Enlightenment about the freedom of the clergy to use new liturgies did not take place in the same way in Switzerland. Within the Swiss Confederation, "church books" remained in general use, and were revised when deemed necessary and adapted to the spirit of the times. No one developed a private worship book as was being done in Germany.

The decline, or rather the disappearance, of worship services held during the week became a clear sign of "modern" worship practices during the Enlightenment. The idea in Zürich of getting rid of the "big gloomy cathedral" shows a fundamental distancing from inherited piety. As for Pietism itself, it shifted its emphasis from public congregational worship to household prayers and gatherings in homes, in the home of the pastor if he himself was an adherent of Pietism. This was the case of the "father" of church Pietism in Basel, Hieronymous Annoni (d. 1770). He also wrote verse for hymns, and people came from other parishes to hear him preach in Muttenz, a phenomenon that the church governing bodies tried to stop through warnings and restrictive decrees. In Bern as well, private religious gatherings and preaching in the local dialect were forbidden. Even before 1750 there were trials and persecution of Pietists in Bern. The Pietists soon emphasized spontaneity and free prayer in their gatherings, and importance was given to allowing the laity to speak during worship. This phenomenon of house and small group gatherings for worship in early Pietism was used even more during the later Awakening movement as an instrument of missionary efforts, when the relationship to Anglo-Saxon Methodism was a relevant influence in piety and worship.

For the Reformed churches in Switzerland, a basic freedom to question inherited orders of worship and to try new forms became an important stimulus that pointed the way toward the future, from the Enlightenment and Pietism all the way to "modern" worship practice.

Pietism made a lasting and sustaining contribution to religious devotion and worship life through its widely distributed instructive literature and a wealth of new hymns. This new burst of creativity came in response to a felt need for much more sentiment and mystical depth in religious language. It also brought a blending of elements across confessional and national boundaries. Martin Luther became a greatly honored figure for the Swiss Reformed. The Synod of Bern (1532) was now also being respected far beyond the borders of Bern as a source for Protestant thought. "True Christianity" as expounded by the German Lutheran Johann Arndt became a source of mystical and uplifting inspiration in Switzerland and the rest of Europe. The hymns of Zinzendorf (1700-1760), a founder of the Moravian Church (previously the Bohemian Brotherhood), and of Tersteegen (1697-1769), a converted and enlightened reformer from the lower Rhine with an element of deep mysticism, became familiar through home worship and later widely used in hymnbooks for congregational worship. Pietism bypassed the distinction between private spiritual songs and hymns for the church in both Switzerland and Germany. The hymns of the orthodox Lutheran Paul Gerhardt were also beginning to be sung in Switzerland at this time.

In the Dutch *Hervormde Kerk,* the liturgical forms established since the end of the sixteenth century remained essentially unchanged into the twentieth century. This does not mean, however, that pastors were not free in their use of them, especially in the nineteenth century. At the end of the eighteenth century, atmosphere became an important element in worship. The Lord's Supper was celebrated in the evening by candlelight. On Good Friday there was an emphasis on sharing in Jesus' suffering. Reformation Sunday and the last day of the year became popular occasions for worship.

Dutch churchgoers of the eighteenth century, as children of the Enlightenment, began to find the traditional translation of the Psalms by Petrus Dathenus unbearable, particularly its anthropomorphic portrayal of God and its coarse poetic imagery. On government initiative, a new version of the Psalms was introduced in 1773 and continued to be used until 1968 and even beyond. This 1773 version is considered an "exponent of the Reformed Enlightenment in the Netherlands."[7] There was also a call for new evangelical hymns such as those in use elsewhere. A collection of such hymns was distributed in 1807 and also enjoyed a long life in active use. Remorse for one's sins, remembrance of Christ's sufferings, and the Reformed schema of misery, redemption, and thanksgiving for being able to live with Christ as one's example were the marks of these hymns for the church.

Theological Trends and Liturgy in German-Speaking Reformed Churches in Switzerland in the Nineteenth Century

One influential figure on the German-speaking Reformed churches was Friedrich Schleiermacher (1768-1834), the son of a Reformed army chaplain who received his schooling from the Moravian Brotherhood at Herrnhut, Germany. He later considered himself a "Herrnhuter [Pietist] of a higher order."[8] In

7. Cf. Roel A. Bosch, *En nooit meer oude Psalem zingen. Zing'end geloven in een nieuwe tijd, 1760-1810* (Zoetermeer, 1996), p. 104.
8. Ralf Stroh, *Schleiermachers Gottesdiensttheorie* (Berlin, 1998).

two theological statements in 1804 he advocated Lutheran-Reformed union, and in putting together worship services from the elements of liturgy, singing, prayer, and religious discourse, he kept to a middle course between the Lutheran and Reformed worship traditions. Most notably, however, he developed the new concept of worship as the celebration of the Christian community, a representation and communication of the Christian experience and of the awareness of God. For him, worship took place in dialogue, in the alternation of receiving and spontaneous response. Worship was "the life of the community coming out into open view."[9]

Schleiermacher opposed Prussian King Frederick William III's claim that as sovereign he had the right to prescribe church liturgy by law, as well as the worship book established by the king for the churches of the Union in Prussia. In the long run, his theological development of the concept of worship became influential for Reformed theologians and churches The impressive figure of Schleiermacher, with his theory of worship as a cultic event, thus stands symbolically at the gateway to all of modern Protestantism.

In German-speaking Reformed Switzerland during the nineteenth century, traditional "church book" liturgies and customary worship practices continued to be translated and modified, although the main text of previous editions was preserved. New prayers for feast days were added to the general prayers of the church, which had previously been quite general and few in number.

The order for Sunday worship was as simple as possible everywhere. The opening hymn was followed by the pastoral prayer and the sermon. Then followed another prayer, followed by intercessions, a hymn, and the benediction. The "Our Father" came sometimes at the end of the first prayer, sometimes at the end of the second. In Bern certainly, and perhaps elsewhere as well, a Bible reading was held while the bells were ringing and people were arriving for worship; this was given by sextons on the pastor's instructions, with the intention of preventing gossiping in the church. On high feast days the Lord's Supper was celebrated following the preaching service, using the order that had scarcely been changed in the different churches since the Reformation, even during the Enlightenment. The offering was collected in the belled offering bag as the worshipers left the church. The use of the official liturgy particular to each canton was expected in all the churches of the canton — an "obligatory" liturgy.

Up until this time, it had been expected that pastors would wear the official attire of the magistrates, a habit with a ruff around the neck, plus a pulpit

9. Peter Cornehl, "Article Gottesdienst VIII," in *Theologische Realenzyklopaedie* 14 (1985): 64f.

mantle, but this practice was gradually replaced. Instead, the Lutheran-style robe, which appealed to the Romantic spirit of the times, was adopted from Germany and became widespread.

Disputes arose over theology and church policy between those who held on to the traditional faith (those in the politically and socially conservative "positive" wing) and those in the liberal wing, including those feeding on the political and scientific spirit of the times following the French Revolution. These disputes had effects on worship life as well, and the rash of societies that blossomed after the French Revolution only added to the debate. Many of these societies were founded for spiritual purposes, and they were especially popular among the Pietists, beginning with the "German Christendom Society" in Basel. The theological left was also organized as the "Church Reform Association." In the latter half of the nineteenth century the prayers in all the "church books" followed one track or the other, under the influence of the liberal and conservative parties. Worship services too were under either "liberal" or "positive" influence, led by preachers who represented one or the other school of thought. There were actually two churches living amicably under one institutional roof, though sometimes in heated and even public conflict with one another.

Representatives of the liberal or "freethinking" wing — certain of support from the state authorities — took it upon themselves to remove the Apostles' Creed from the liturgies for baptism, confirmation, and ordination, or sometimes from Sunday worship. Until then it had been obligatory for all adolescent and adult church members to recite and regularly invoke the official creed. The requirement to use the official liturgy of one's canton was also revoked, and the prayers formulated by the liberals used Enlightenment-oriented or deistic forms of addressing God.

The "positive" wing endeavored to keep orthodox Trinitarian and Christological expressions in their prayers, which resounded with the theme of redemption through the sacrifice of Jesus Christ. In the definitions of Christian faith and obedience, Pietistic affirmations had their place; this was true particularly in Basel. The time when the congregation only sang psalms was over for good. Confirmation as an "edifying" act of worship was welcomed as modern by both Pietists and Enlightenment followers.

Express reference to liturgical development in Reformed Switzerland was made in Germany by the theologian and churchman August Ebrard (1818-1888), in the development of his liturgical thought and his gift of a "worship book" *(Kirchenbuch)* to the German Reformed Church, to guide them in their worship.[10] Ebrard took part in founding the Reformed Federation in Ger-

10. August Ebrard, *Versuch einer Liturgik vom Standpunkte der reformirten Kirche* (Frank-

many. He can be considered the Reformed exponent of the Erlangen school of theology, which is mainly Lutheran, and which made use of the stimuli from the Awakening movement and its theology of experience.

Ebrard began by creating a "liturgy from the Reformed church viewpoint," establishing Reformed worship principles over against the Lutheran understanding with its "Romanizing" (Catholicizing) tendencies. Worship belongs, he argued, to the internal ministry of the church, as opposed to its external ministry that aims to make faith in Christ accessible. The outward historical event of salvation through Christ is to be communicated to the faithful, while the power of the Holy Spirit brings them into an inner relationship of faith in Christ. The sermon, prayers, and Lord's Supper belong together in the worship of the community of those who confess Christ. From the inherited wealth of prayers of the Reformed church, including the hymns of Ostervald and a lectionary, Ebrard's worship book developed a genuinely Reformed order of worship. It was the first of the German Reformed "worship" or "church books" and was subtitled "A collection of prayers and forms of church worship introduced into the Reformed churches."

During the same period, European liturgy was carried to the daughter churches being founded on other continents by missionary societies. The Basel Mission Committee decided in the period from 1852 to 1860 to approve for its worship the Lutheran liturgical tradition of Württemberg.[11] But Moravian and even Anglican orders of worship were also used as models — always without explicit confessional designations. Obviously the richer forms were more in demand for occasions such as baptisms and the Lord's Supper than the simpler Swiss orders of service. In Ghana, China, or India, inculturation remained limited to songs in the local language, which accompanied and were used in parallel with the worship service. The practice was similar in Francophone areas where the Paris mission worked, in which evangelical (in today's sense of the term) worship customs tended to be widespread.

---

furt a.M., 1843). Cf. August Ebrard, *Reformirtes Kirchenbuch. Sammlung von in der reformirten Kirche eingeführten Kirchengebeten und Formularen;* newly revised second edition by Gerhard Goebel (Halle 1889).

11. Wilhelm Schlatter, *Geschichte der Basler Mission 1815-1915,* vol. 2 (Basel, 1916), pp. 62-67; and Wilhelm Schlatter and Hermann Witschi, vol. 4 (Basel, 1965), pp. 228-45. Württemberg, though Lutheran, belongs to the base of the Basel Mission.

The Influence of Eugène Bersier
in French-Speaking Protestantism

Pastor Eugène Bersier (1831-1889) was unique in continental European Protestantism as a representative of Pietism, more precisely of the Awakening movement, who played a weighty role in the historical development of liturgy.[12] Bersier was molded by the spirit of Romanticism. He was pastor of the Paroisse de l'Etoile in Paris, which grew out of the free-church movement. Theologically he belonged to the Calvinist wing of the Reformed church and to the spirituality of the Awakening movement. He took his evangelical congregation into the French Reformed Church because he believed it to be the true representative of the Reformed tradition. This was even more important to him than separation of church and state, though the latter was also a concern of his. (The Reformed churches at that time had a concordat with the state.) Bersier saw in the Reformed churches the possibility of adhering to the common Christian tradition, a purpose for which he found the evangelical free churches too narrow.

At first Bersier created for his own congregation a liturgy intended to renew traditional Reformed worship and to connect it to the common or catholic tradition. This led him to submit a highly motivated worship book proposal with a detailed commentary to all the Reformed synods of France. His intent was to bring about a fundamental liturgical renewal. At that time, of course, the synods did not have the foresight to join this project. They contented themselves instead with a halfhearted renewal of the traditional Reformed liturgy. Nevertheless, Bersier's liturgical reform met with a wide response in manifold unofficial ways in the Reformed churches in France, and also in French-speaking Switzerland, in the late nineteenth and early twentieth centuries. It gave a new and distinctive face to Reformed worship in general through its emphasis on liturgical components that were unusual in the traditional Reformed world. The most striking characteristic of this liturgical style was the widespread use of sung responses by the congregation in the course of a worship service.

The source of Eugène Bersier's liturgical inspiration is worth noting. During his own scholarly liturgical research he had consulted as many liturgi-

---

12. Bruno Bürki, *Cène du Seigneur: eucharistie de l'Eglise. Le cheminement des Eglises réformées romandes et françaises depuis le 18ᵉ s., d'après leurs textes liturgiques,* 2 vols. (Fribourg, Switzerland, 1985), vol. B, pp. 36-46. See the doctoral thesis of Stuart Ludbrook (at the Université de Paris Sorbonne [Paris IV] and Institut catholique de Paris), *La liturgie de Bersier et le culte réformé en France: "ritualisme" et renouveau liturgique* (1999).

cal sources as possible. A decisive influence on him was Catholic liturgical tradition as taken over by the English Irvingite church. The missal and rituals of the Holy Catholic Apostolic Church of the so-called Irvingites (after its Scottish Presbyterian founder, Edward Irving) were distributed by an Englishman, J. B. Cardale, and came into Bersier's hands in French translation. In the nineteenth century the Catholic Apostolic Church, which was expecting the second coming of Christ and was strongly institutionalized according to the pattern of early Christianity, was well known in Europe. Later the New Apostolic movement grew out of it.

In his prayers for feast days and church rites, Bersier developed a liturgical style that remained influential in French-speaking areas for several generations. In contrast to the rational or "liberal" development within Protestantism, he aimed to uphold the heritage of Reformed theology. The Trinitarian faith, confessing the divinity of Jesus Christ, was fundamental for him. His emphasis on redemption through the sacrificed blood of the Crucified One came from his Awakening-style piety. Rather than individual conversion, however, he stressed praise for God as holy and transcendent. The social-ethical commitment of this representative of nineteenth-century Protestantism is noteworthy.

Bersier developed his liturgical principles clearly, both in the liturgy he personally created for the Paroisse de l'Etoile and in the project he presented to the synods. He indicated these principles in the headings he gave to sets of rules or liturgical formulas. Orders for worship and the development of the church year were of concern to him. His principles are still worth attention even in the light of modern liturgical movements or renewal, and have remained remarkably relevant. For him, worship was not merely for instructing the faithful, as had too often been the case in Reformed history, but should offer a space for adoration of God. Prayers and liturgical actions, he believed, are expressions of the Christian tradition and of the common Christian faith. Through the sung responses, the congregation should actively help to carry the worship service. It became important for worship to have the character of a dialogue. A more extensive reading aloud of passages from the Bible, which did more than merely provide the sermon text, became part of worship. This form of worship has a churchly character, rather than being the affair of an individual preacher from a particular epoch or trend. Bersier's format was Reformed worship with the traditional elements and those common to all Christians, which express the catholic character of the celebration. An essential and primary element was Holy Communion, in which — true to the faith of Calvin — Bersier argued that Christ is present and shares himself with those who receive him in faith.

Taking care to worship rightly was, above all, an ecclesiological concern for Bersier, and he is not to be classified merely as a nineteenth-century catholicizing ritualist. His emphasis on the sacraments is to be understood first and foremost as community-building rather than institutional. He was an evangelical pastor, and his motivation was pastoral, the care of souls. Through congregational worship and the various rites of the church — baptism and confirmation, marriage, burial of the faithful, and also ordination (consecration) of the church's servants — the congregation is built up as the body of Christ. Strengthened by worship, it can then fulfill its Christian responsibility in the public, political sphere and in its social surroundings. Those redeemed by Jesus Christ, as they assemble for worship, form the spiritual unity of God's people according to God's will. The eucharistic community is an essential expression of this. Bersier wanted to distance himself both from the general Protestant rationalism of his time and from a common catholic conception of merit. In his theory of worship, Bersier cites Schleiermacher's feeling of religious dependence.

The redeemed, those converted and baptized, form the communion of saints. With baptism, reception of confirmands, and admission to membership in the Reformed Church, Bersier developed a cycle of initiation rites. The act of ordination too was seen in this vein. Bersier's concept of the Lord's Supper as the feast of the redeemed is in the vein of "salvation history" theology and is eschatological. This is also expressed in the celebration of marriage and in the burial liturgy. Thus his was a solid theology and a full liturgy. The church building Bersier erected for his Paroisse de l'Etoile has in many ways become a model for the furnishing of Reformed places of worship in France and beyond. He also had an interest in leadership of informal prayer groups and educational gatherings.

The Twentieth-Century Liturgical Movement in French-Speaking Switzerland

After what has been said about Ostervald and Bersier, it will not be especially surprising that the twentieth-century liturgical movement in French-speaking Protestantism, particularly in the French-speaking, Reformed area of Switzerland, developed an independent and creative branch. The influence of this liturgical movement on neighboring Reformed churches, and ecumenically, is worthy of note (though it had little impact on the churches in the German-speaking parts of Switzerland).[13]

13. André Bardet, *Un combat pour l'Eglise. Un siècle de mouvement liturgique en Pays de Vaud* (Lausanne, 1988).

"Church and Liturgy" was a group of pastors and motivated laypersons that formed in the early twentieth century. Its goal was an ecumenically-oriented renewal of the concept of the church and the reform of worship in line with evangelical catholicity. The starting-point for the reform was the challenge of the First World Conference on Faith and Order, which was held in Lausanne in 1927.[14] The reformers already had in Lausanne a local forerunner in the area of liturgy, in the person of Pastor Jules Amiguet (1867-1946), who on his own initiative had already made extensive studies of the history of liturgy and implemented what he had learned in his own congregation of Saint-Jean on the Avenue de Cour.

"Church and Liturgy" essentially developed out of a vision of the church and its celebrations that could be called evangelical-catholic, and this vision was embodied by its founder, Pastor Richard Paquier (1905-1985). Paquier was an enthusiastic devotee of the Anglican world and also had an extensive knowledge of the liturgical traditions of both the Western and the Eastern churches. Besides his leadership of the "Church and Liturgy" group, Paquier was lifelong pastor in two congregations in the canton of Vaud (of which Lausanne is the capital), in Bercher and later in Saint-Saphorin/Lavaux. His theological competence was recognized by the University of Neuchâtel by an honorary doctorate.

The "Church and Liturgy" group never spread outside the canton of Vaud and did not survive into a second generation after its original members were gone. This was the result of its projects being limited to local churches and of the rather traditionalist thinking of its principal leaders. Unlike, for example, the Catholic representatives of the liturgical renewal in France around the Centre National de Pastorale Liturgique, "Church and Liturgy" was unable to really connect with modernity in the late 1960s. Incompatibilities appeared, opportunities were missed, and the movement's leaders lacked the openness that would have particularly benefited the liturgical renewal.

This does not, however, take away from the pioneering achievements of "Church and Liturgy." These consisted first of all in recognizing that renewal of worship is inseparable from ecclesiologically responsible reform of congregational life, on behalf of the whole church, and that such renewal must also have an ecumenical dimension. At the level of liturgical form and content, Paquier and his group managed to create and distribute a complete, ecumenically recognizable eucharistic prayer. From the beginning of the 1930s, this prayer appeared in several versions, and a final formulation appeared in 1952 —

---

14. For a more detailed discussion of the impact of the ecumenical movement, see Coenraad Burger's chapter in this volume.

two decades before the new Catholic eucharistic prayers were composed. Also to the credit of "Church and Liturgy" is its important work on the liturgical development of the church year, in which its central concern to have the high point be the Easter Eve celebration was soon recognized. Daily prayers at the canonical hours, for which orders of worship were created for at least two daily offices, became a new reference point for the Christian life of groups, individuals, and in many places even of congregations. Liturgical and pastoral renewal in the practice of various rites of the church, as well as the rediscovery of individual confession, had beneficial pastoral and community-building effects.

The liturgical life of the Taizé Community in France, as well as that of the Grandchamp Community in Switzerland, was inspired by "Church and Liturgy." The liturgy created for the French Reformed Church after World War II was also stimulated by the group in Vaud, as was the "Liturgy for the Use of the Reformed Churches of French-speaking Switzerland" later in the twentieth century. The work of Jean-Jacques von Allmen in the theology of liturgy also owes a debt to Richard Paquier.

The twentieth-century liturgical movement was only a partial phenomenon in the history of the church in the twentieth century. It caused, however, an unmistakable shift in the worship life of the Reformed world and set standards that have endured.

The Influences of the Liturgical Movement in the German-Speaking Swiss Reformed Churches

Impulses from liturgical movements are neither sought after nor appreciated in Switzerland, and Swiss congregations do not crave innovations in worship. Simplicity, even meagerness, of liturgical forms seems to suit the religious character of the people. The more austere, the closer worship seems to them to the inexpressible divine Truth, and to the piety that people who have few words or gestures for whatever moves them deeply hesitate to show. This is true for human love and friendship as well as religion. Outside observers are amazed at the sobriety and awkwardness of the Swiss.

There are, however, notable exceptions worthy of attention. In Zürich from 1916 to 1917, through the efforts of Pastor Theodor Goldschmid of Winterthur, a newly revised church book was published in three volumes, based on the principles of two teachers in Strasbourg, Friedrich Spitta (1852-1924) and Julius Smend (1857-1930).[15] This worship book attracted attention

15. Konrad Klek, *Erlebnis Gottesdienst, Die liturgischen Reformbestrebungen um die*

and was used far beyond the Zürich area, which is clear proof that it met expectations. The liberal "older liturgical movement" of Spitta and Smend, with its lack of emphasis on doctrine, could be called the continuation of Schleiermacher's understanding of worship. Worship is important as an integrative factor in church life and is related to society. It is the community's festive celebration, the experience of being Christians. It borrows from the common liturgical tradition and recomposes what it takes freely, according to need and inclination.

After World War II a branch of the German Protestant Michael Brotherhood *(Michaelsbruderschaft),* which grew out of the Berneuchener Conference, became active in Switzerland.[16] The Reformed members of the brotherhood were not very numerous but were confident and enterprising in their work as pastors or committed lay members in congregations, where they started a noteworthy renewal of worship. Its most important dimension was its use of symbols with Trinitarian significance — the Word made flesh taking shape in worship. The sacramental life of the church took on an unaccustomed meaning for Reformed Christians. Development of eucharistic prayer and the eucharistic liturgy as a whole were promoted, and more frequent celebration of the Eucharist was an early goal. Daily prayers at the canonical hours as a regular spiritual exercise for individuals or small groups was a new discovery for the Protestant Reformed. Although it often met with smiles or reprimands as being extravagant or "not Reformed," this liturgical movement called attention to notorious gaps in church practices. During the national-socialist period and in the period following, there was a felt need to avoid according an improperly sacred status to nature. In this group, this led to an emphasis on Christian tradition, with restoration tendencies, in opposition to the approaches taken originally in the youth movement. Nevertheless, the future renewal of worship throughout the church, later in the century, was being prepared.

The two-volume worship book published by the Reformed church of the canton of Aargau in 1950 is a sign of such church-wide renewal.[17] It appeared primarily as a result of the commitment of a president of the church commission, Willy Meyer (1903-1987), and his prudence and qualities as a mediator. It

---

Jahrhundertwende unter Führung von Friedrich Spitta und Julius Smend (Göttingen, 1996). Rüdiger Siemoneit, *Julius Smend. Der evangelische Gottesdienst als lockende Macht* (Frankfurt a.M., 1999).

16. G. Hage, ed., *Die Evangelische Michaelsbruderschaft* (Kassel, 1981). See also *Das heilige Amt. Eine Handreichung für den Gottesdienst der Kirche,* revised and commented upon by Paul Kramer (Bern, 1960).

17. *Liturgie für die Evangelisch-reformierte Landeskirche des Kantons Aargau,* 2 vol. (Aarau, 1950; 2nd ed., 1959).

brought substantial content from the liturgical tradition into the Reformed service of the word and prayers of the congregation. The orders of worship, or "formulas," for Sunday worship and the celebration of the sacraments, as well as various rites of the church, were given liturgical form. The rules for worship inherited from the Reformation were also treated with increasing scholarly competence, and Calvin's prayers received due respect within the Reformed liturgical world.

Several personalities came to the study or practice of liturgy from the world of music, bringing with them considerable professional musical knowledge for the benefit of liturgy. This was true of Adolf Brunner (1901-1992), Gerhard Aeschbacher (b. 1917), and Markus Jenny (1924-2001).[18] Jenny in particular researched the basic intentions of Reformation liturgy, insofar as they can be historically documented, which still offer guidance for every Protestant trend in worship. On the French-speaking side, Pierre Puidoux (b. 1905) and André Bardet (b. 1913) stand out in a similar way as professional musicians and liturgists.

This church-wide liturgical renewal in Reformed Protestantism would later be consecrated and further developed in the cooperation, which included liturgy, between the Protestant Reformed and Roman Catholic churches following the Second Vatican Council. The liturgical reform begun by Vatican II was not only observed attentively and with good will by the Reformed churches, but in important ways also emulated. That in so doing none of the churches needed to, or could, give up its own historical identity is one of the important conditions that the contemporary ecumenical movement has learned to observe. This condition is also valid in the area of liturgy.

Dialectical Theology and Liturgy in the Thought of Karl Barth (1886-1968)

The starting point and the center of Karl Barth's work in theology and church was truly a question of worship: how can the word of God be proclaimed? The embarrassment and desperation of the pastor of a congregation as worship leader and preacher made Barth a theologian. Radical concentration on the issue of proclaiming the word certainly produced among Barth's students, and even in himself, an attitude toward issues of worship that could easily be considered hostile to liturgy.

18. The latter produced a significant liturgical study: Markus Jenny, *Die Einheit des Abendmahlsgottesdienstes bei den elsässischen und schweizerischen Reformatoren* (Zürich, 1968).

What was important to Barth, however, was the realization that the word of God is communicated by God's own activity alone. The message centered on Christ should be understood first of all as exclusive, in the sense that the miracle of divine revelation does not need any help from secondary sources. Neither the Catholic sacraments nor the natural meaning and dynamic experienced in symbolic liturgical acts should be considered as mediating instruments. God the Three in One alone will accomplish it, and has already done so in Christ. Worship is seen as the real presence of Jesus Christ. This actually renders all forms irrelevant, whether rhetorical (the liberal art of oratory), moral (pietistic devotion), or even liturgical.

Just as revelation has an exclusively divine beginning, the worship to which it gives birth in the church is fully human — the wholly human response to the divine act that has been accomplished. Hence worship is the Christian life, especially in its involvement in real life, political life. As Bonhoeffer said, "Only those who have publicly cried out against the persecution of the Jews may sing Gregorian chant."

Karl Barth never provided sufficiently precise theological information on *how* baptism with water should be administered in correlation with baptism by the Holy Spirit, or how the church should celebrate the Lord's Supper or even proclaim the word. But he maintained that congregational worship should take the form of an ellipse with two foci — the proclaimed word and the breaking of the bread.[19] So worship in the church responds to God's initiative through complete obedience. While some time later the Constitution on the Sacred Liturgy of Vatican II named the elements of a comprehensive liturgical reform for the Catholic church, Barth's contribution consisted in pointing to the foundation of worship as response to God's revelation in Christ.

Not much could be expected of Barth in terms of inventing liturgical forms, which is not surprising given his cultural and confessional background. Nevertheless, he became the theological mentor of a fundamental renewal of worship. The church receives the answer to its worship as a gift from the Holy Spirit. We must realize that one of the most solid though simple Reformed liturgies for worship was developed under Barth's influence, and that one of the most exciting ecumenical liturgical theologians of Reformed origin comes from the school of Karl Barth. We are referring to the *Baselbieter Kirchenbuch (Liturgy of Basel-Campagne)* of 1949 and to the ecumenical theologian Jean-Jacques von Allmen (1917-1994).

---

19. Karl Barth, *Final Testimonies,* ed. Eberhard Busch, trans. Geoffrey W. Bromiley (Grand Rapids: Eerdmans, 1977), p. 46; cf. also *Gotteserkenntnis und Gottesdienst* (Zollikon, 1938), p. 198.

The *Baselbieter Kirchenbuch* captivates with its theologically well-considered orders of worship and the strong formulations of its prayers, which are both expressive and to the point.[20] There is an emphasis on returning to our heritage of prayers from the Reformation fathers. It is also not by accident that among the orders provided for celebration of the Lord's Supper is one which, gracefully and without making a point of it, brings the elements of eucharistic celebration from the common church tradition into the Reformed liturgy. All this takes place in the simplicity of authentic Reformed worship and in strict theological coherence.

Through his theological teaching, based on Barth's theology of revelation that was inspired by the confessional writings of the Reformation, Jean-Jacques von Allmen developed an ecumenical vision that is recognized worldwide. It has become important to the World Council of Churches' Commission on Faith and Order in the dialogues with the Orthodox churches and with the Roman Catholic Church, particularly because of its sacramental dimension. In addition, von Allmen had a definite ecumenical influence on the liturgical life of the local church in Neuchâtel where he was pastor.

Faithfulness to Tradition in the Reformed Alliance of Germany

Between 1941, during the war, and the 1980s, the Moderamen (governing body) of the Reformed Alliance published a *Worship Book* with a definite Reformed emphasis of its own stamp for the churches and congregations of the Alliance.[21] There were three editions and revisions, and we will have occasion in a later section to speak of the most recent of them. The members of the Reformed Alliance are the Reformed churches of Bavaria and Northwest Germany, the Church of Lippe, and the Synod of the Evangelical Old Reformed Church, formed from congregations in various parts of Germany. The *Worship Book* contains "Prayers and Orders of Worship for the Community Gathered under the Word."

There were two historically important reference points for the liturgical order in this Reformed *Worship Book*. One was the order of worship in the

---

20. *Liturgie für die reformierten Kirchgemeinden des Kantons Basel-Landschaft* (Liestal CH, 1949).

21. *Kirchenbuch. Gebete und Ordnungen für die unter dem Wort versammelte Gemeinde*, edited by the Moderamen of the Reformed Alliance (Neukirchen Kreis Moers, 1951; 2nd ed. 1956; 3rd ed. 1983).

book of rules for the church of the Electoral Palatinate of 1563, with its Calvinistic prayers. The other was the close relationship with the struggle of the churches under national socialism and with the Confessing Church. During this trial the Reformed community had learned to pray and to confess its faith anew. Worship became an existential act of faith. Karl Halaski had an important role in editing the Reformed liturgy; for a long time he kept watch over the preservation of the Reformed confession through the prayers used in Reformed churches in Germany. The sermon prayers of John Calvin were regarded as an important model. The *Worship Book* preserved and transmitted them in German language versions.

Prayers that were close to being proclamations, such as those Karl Barth used in his own formulations and earnestly recommended for preachers of God's word, were the special marks of this consciously Reformed liturgy. These sermon prayers are often quite extensive, and their content is as much intended to teach as it is to build community. They are filled with biblical imagery.

Behind this specifically Reformed worship practice can be discerned the late medieval tradition of the "preaching" worship service, which was always clearly set apart from the Mass, and out of which Reformed worship first developed. In certain cases — certainly more often in recent generations than at any time since the Reformation — a preaching service also includes the distribution of the Lord's Supper, with the appropriate admonitions and the prayer for the Lord's Supper, as well as the words of institution and the breaking of the bread. In addition to the pastor who proclaims the word and administers the sacraments, the elders are important reference persons for the congregation "gathered under the word." They have remained visible even though the role originally entrusted to the elders in the presbytery, that of maintaining discipline in the life of the congregation, has been discontinued. The proclamation of the word and the rules for the congregation, for the sanctification of individuals and of the whole community, belong together. This remained an immediate concern for congregations even during their struggle with the state under national socialism.

At the level of liturgy in particular, the Reformed order of worship, with its simple and relatively unstructured sequence, and its concentration on the proclamation of the word with the observance of the sacraments playing a lesser role, has been a model followed in many congregations, including Lutheran and United churches at least in southern Germany. Thus it has developed as a second basic form of worship in addition to the liturgy of the German Mass, one that is characterized by its focus on the sermon. It has become the common heritage of all German-speaking Protestant churches, and in the *New Liturgy* or *Protestant Worship Book* of the Lutheran and United churches of Germany, that which has been borrowed from the Reformed worship tradition is explicitly identified. In addition, prayer texts from the Reformed *Worship Book* have been included in this all-Protestant worship book in which the German Reformed churches were not directly involved.

It seems to fit the structure of Reformed churches that, in a traditional Reformed church, liturgical forms are provided not only for Sunday worship but also for the rites of the church and, of course, the sacrament of baptism. The German *Worship Book* takes this fully into account. In the Reformed world, not only the Sunday assembly of the congregation with the word and sacraments is part of the liturgy but also the Christian life in the community. The Heidelberg Catechism (which was an organic part of the Palatinate church constitution of 1563) juxtaposes two perspectives: the section on the redemption of humankind is followed by the section on gratitude for God's gifts. In this classical framework the contemporary concerns of community and of personal spirituality now find liturgical expression.

Contemporary Theological and Ecclesiastical Developments in Worship

It is a pleasure to speak first of all of two movements for renewal in worship that originated in the "grassroots" church and then became subjects for reflection by theologians as they developed. These are the reform of worship in Zürich beginning in the 1960s and '70s and the Swiss Protestant Synods of 1983 to 1987. Church members, both laypersons and office-holders, made decisions and confidently seized the opportunity to do something new in and about worship in the Reformed church.

In Zürich since the mid-1960s there had been a desire to emphasize the nature of worship as a journey,[22] as well as the thematic structuring of the parts of a worship service, so as to overcome the so-called Reformed sobriety in liturgical matters and the sterile opposition between the sermon and the liturgical "framework." Advocates of reform emphasized that the members of the congregation come from their various walks of life and gather together before God. In adoration and praise of God, the congregation in that place takes on the experience of the church in every age with the same God. The sermon is

22. Alfred Ehrensperger, "Die Gottesdienstreform der evangelisch-reformierten Zürcher Kirche von 1960-1970 und ihre Wirkungsgeschichte," in *Liturgie in Bewegung/Liturgie en mouvement,* ed. Bruno Bürki and Martin Klöckener (Freiburg [Schweiz])/Geneva, 2000), pp. 192-205.

the experience of God's presence in word and spirit, and the intercessions are an encounter with the world and the reality of life. In the blessing and sending, the congregation is sent out to take the next stage in its journey.

Communication in familiar everyday language and participation by the members of the congregation have been important concerns in the reform of worship in Zürich, which was supported by a new *Worship Book* with variable patterns for worship instead of traditional formulas. The adoration of God is a central concept; a sermon, talk, should not be all there is to worship. However, the sacramental dimension and the salvation-history or Christological core of worship are still underdeveloped, beyond the following of formal models. The free choice of liturgical materials and the many and diverse possibilities for putting them together are likely to be too great a challenge for those assigned to lead worship.

The "Swiss Protestant Synod," in its assemblies between 1983 and 1987 of around two hundred delegates from the most varied church circles, not only debated present-day problems with their challenges for the individual and the community, but also emphasized its concerns for church and world and brought its hopes for them into the worship celebrations.[23] "Worship renewal" was a central theme of the Synod. Here, in an informal fellowship of Christians from all over Switzerland, it was self-evident that lay participation and especially that of women was a central concern, particularly in worship. The Swiss Protestant Synod made the celebration of the Lord's Supper a central point of its meetings, in awareness of the possibilities for liturgical renewal appearing on the ecumenical horizon. New hymns were practiced in many languages. Here indeed a theology of worship that laypersons can understand, and that is eucharistic and compatible with the ecumenical scene, is being developed and given liturgical, celebratory form. Especially for many German-speaking Reformed Christians in Switzerland, these were completely new perspectives. They were further developed in preparing the *Hymnbook of the Evangelical Reformed Churches of German-speaking Switzerland,* published in 1998.

In recent years theological reflection and research in both German-speaking and French-speaking areas have been conducted particularly by representatives or followers of a liberal theological orientation. Two very individual books come to mind, which consciously distance themselves from liturgical traditions and movements: *Worship With an Open Choir* by Laurent Gagnebin (Paris) and *Protestant Worship, Liturgical diversity in the religious and*

---

23. Marianne Périllard, "Le Synode protestant suisse (1983-1987) et le renouveau du culte," in *Liturgie in Bewegung*, pp. 324-37.

social milieu by Theophil Müller (Bern).[24] Both authors are professors of practical theology at Protestant theological schools. Müller's concern is for worship to be grounded in personal experience — this has remained important to him personally from his Protestant Methodist heritage — and to be expressed in everyday language, which is closest to the obvious truth. Gagnebin also pleads for openness, beginning with his metaphor of knocking down the choir screen, through which the connection of the Reformed essence with modern and postmodern art and society is envisioned.

The continuation of a Reformed theology of liturgy along the lines of Faith and Order should also be noted. Such liturgical study stands in succession to scholars such as that old master of the liturgical movement and ecumenical ecclesiology, Jean-Jacques von Allmen of Neuchâtel, or of the Methodist Geoffrey Wainwright, born in England but now active in the United States. Apart from noteworthy theological approaches and traces in the "worship books" to be described in the next section, I would like with all due modesty to mention my own work within the ecumenical community: I contributed a chapter on "Worship in the Reformed Context" to the *Handbook of Liturgy,* the new standard work on the subject for German Protestantism. Certain professional colleagues in Switzerland, fellow members of the international and ecumenical Societas Liturgica, have made their own contributions to the ecumenical study of liturgy. Alfred Ehrensperger, who works in the area of Zürich and St. Gallen, has done research in the liturgy of the Enlightenment and has recently published a study entitled *Worship — Visions.* Daniel Neeser, liturgical scholar in Geneva, edits the French-language journal for spirituality and liturgical practice *Vie et liturgie (Life and Liturgy),* which in its short life has already achieved wide recognition. The roots of Christian worship in the Old Testament tradition are important to him. In Germany the Moderator of the Reformed Federation, Peter Bukowski, does creative work in liturgy in addition to being a church leader.[25]

A Variety of New Worship Books

In Europe in recent decades many new worship books have been planned and adopted for use, which are not periodic revisions of existing orders for wor-

24. Laurent Gagnebin, *Le culte à chœur ouvert, Introduction à la liturgie du culte réformé* (Paris/Geneva, 1992); Theophil Müller, *Evangelischer Gottesdienst. Liturgische Vielfalt im religiösen und gesellschaftlichen Umfeld* (Stuttgart, 1993).

25. Alfred Ehrensperger, *Gottesdienst. Visionen, Erfahrungen, Schmerzstellen* (Zürich, 1988).

ship but rather, in many ways, new books. I regard this as not only a sign of vitality — fostered, of course, by a situation of material security — in the churches concerned, but also as proof of their readiness to keep moving forward in worship. Their synods, or at least the church leadership, are thus fulfilling their responsibility for the organization of worship in the church, in the authentic Reformed tradition.

The new liturgy books reflect first of all the rich and varied worship traditions in the European Reformed churches. In French-speaking Switzerland the form of worship created in Geneva by Calvin has been further developed, but has always remained recognizable as such. In German-speaking Switzerland the tradition of the service of the word, with a sermon, has been preserved across the centuries in different local variations, all of which hark back to Zwingli. The Reformed churches in Germany have remained true to the Palatinate church polity of the sixteenth century, with its admonitions and biblical seriousness, until the present day. The Reformed churches of France, scattered around the country but gathered in one national synod, at first simply adopted (without an explicit decision by the synod) the Genevan order for worship, and preserved it even under persecution. Only after the French Revolution did they develop their own French liturgy, still strongly influenced by that of Geneva. The bringing together of the separated Evangelical and Reformed churches of France in the French Reformed Church, since 1938 and especially after World War II, offered an opportunity for a new joint liturgy. The "Liturgy of the French Reformed Church," known as the "Green Liturgy," rightly gained respect even outside France as a path-finding example of liturgical renewal.[26] This liturgy did much to help the United Church in France discover its identity. On the Dutch Reformed churches, see the special section below. These brief indications make it impossible to overlook the observation we made at the beginning: the Reformation heritage has nowhere come down to us without the decisive influence of the Enlightenment and of Pietism.

The exciting variety of contemporary worship books demonstrates, on the one hand, the diversity of worship customs that have rightly been preserved and further developed. It is neither necessary nor desirable to have one standard liturgy for the Reformed churches — even though Calvin's "Form for prayers and songs of the church" (with its translations into other languages) guaranteed, in its time, something like a standard Reformed liturgy (not unlike, if I may dare to make such a comparison, the Tridentine *Missale Romanum* in the Catholic church). On the other hand, the lack of balance among contrasting worship books today indicates that people no longer know

26. Eglise réformée de France, *Liturgie* (Paris, 1963).

what to do liturgically, in the Reformed confessional family as in others. At a more fundamental level, in my opinion, our liturgical heritage and the situation of the church in the world call upon us to overcome this confusion and to practice a "Form for prayers of the church," as John Calvin called it, that can be acknowledged at the ecumenical level and that responds to the Trinitarian revelation of God.

The churches in French-speaking Switzerland published between 1979 and 1986 a two-volume liturgical work for worship on Sunday and feast days entitled *Liturgy for the Use of the Reformed Churches in French-speaking Switzerland.*[27] This publication was the fruit of a relatively independent working group, including competent professionals, which has carried on its work for decades. It is a sound reappraisal of the entire Western tradition along the lines of contemporary liturgical renewal and has received recognition from the ecumenical community and liturgical scholars. There is even admiration, and rightly so, for its beautiful "White Liturgy." It must be admitted, however, that overall it has a quite conventional air, culturally and theologically, which has not succeeded in reconciling the post-1968 generation with the liturgy and institutions of the church. This in no way denigrates the merit of the liturgical work of Jean-Louis Bonjour (1920-2001).

Neighboring German-speaking Switzerland lies on the other side of a considerable cultural and social divide from the "Suisse romande." Here work has been going on since 1964 on the first book of liturgies for the entire Swiss German-speaking region, in many volumes that have not yet all been published.[28] Originally planned as a compilation, it still offers the most varied formulas and texts, but no single clear liturgical choice. Contemporary experiments in diverse liturgical rites appear side by side with adaptations of prayers and orders of worship from the Reformation and other centuries. Strikingly new for the Swiss region are also Roman Catholic *ordines,* which have been taken in with very little editing. The individual volumes give the impression of always being behind current developments, for instance in language. Less confusing than the work as a whole are small books for congregational use and pocket liturgies, which were part of the concept early on. And theological awareness of liturgy is growing as the work continues.

Most worthy of mention at present is the German-language *Evangelical Reformed Hymnal* of 1998 (in parallel with the Roman Catholic and the Old Catholic hymnals) as a promising liturgical work from the Reformed churches

---

27. *Liturgie à l'usage des Eglises réformées de la Suisse romande,* 2 vol. (Lausanne).

28. *Liturgie,* edited by the Liturgiekonferenz der evangelisch-reformierten Kirchen in der deutschsprachigen Schweiz, vol. 1-5 (Bern, 1972-2000).

in the ecumenical community.[29] Besides having a wealth of old and new hymns to choose from, it is noteworthy for its teaching about liturgy and its spiritual guidance for church members, and the relatively clear options for contemporary liturgies.

The Moderamen of the Reformed Federation of Germany commissioned a revision of the *Reformed Liturgy,* which appeared in 1999.[30] This successor to the *Worship Book* of the postwar period is a complete liturgy in a handy format for Reformed congregations throughout Germany, which brings together old and new concerns in a wise and moderate way. The old concern is to preserve the scriptural and traditional Reformed "Prayers and Ordinances for the Congregation Assembled under the Word." New is the desire to be in concord with the Lutheran and United churches in Germany, which use the New Liturgy of the *Protestant Worship Book.* Important decisions have been made on principles for celebration of the Lord's Supper. Here too, the Lord's Supper has been integrated into Sunday worship and is to be celebrated more often. The eucharistic prayer is a Protestant adaptation from that of the Mass, and the traditional Reformed admonitions on receiving Communion are not given as alternatives, but rather are brought into relationship with one another.

For the first time in the Swiss churches, inclusive language with its prerequisites and far-reaching implications is a topic of discussion and is used throughout the liturgy. Never before, to my knowledge, has such care been taken with a major problem of contemporary society. Previously some concessions had been made and a few corrections granted. But now the concept has been followed through with all its social and theological consequences.

The French Reformed Church adopted in 1996 a new liturgy for congregational worship and the rites of the church.[31] The church has always been conscious of its liturgical heritage going back to Calvin, and in the mid-twentieth century it had created a liturgy that was important for liturgical renewal at the time. By the late twentieth century this needed to be revised for an age in which French Reformed congregations are becoming more and more scattered and their minority situation is an important fact — hence the need for the new liturgy. The Protestant witness to God's grace above all was to be the decisive characteristic in the proposed orders of worship for the various

29. *Gesangbuch der Evangelisch-reformierten Kirchen der deutschsprachigen Schweiz* (Basel-Zürich, 1998).

30. *Reformierte Liturgie. Gebete und Ordnungen für die unter dem Wort versammelte Gemeinde,* commissioned by the Moderamen of the Reformed League, ed. Peter Bukowski et al. (Wuppertal, Neukirchen, and Vluyn, 1999).

31. *Liturgie de l'Eglise réformée de France* (Paris, 1996).

celebrations, printed as removable individual brochures. Respect is shown for the various theological viewpoints within the church. Ecumenical responsibility and awareness of Reformed uniqueness stand side by side and are clearly noticeable in the individual liturgical options. This liturgy was composed by a commission of persons involved in the church at the local level and then approved by the synods. There is much about this book in which one senses the fleeting character of the contemporary liturgical scene. The Communion supper shared by the congregation and its common life and witness, as well as the responsibility of each church member in daily life, stand at the center.

Liturgical Renewal in the Netherlands

The Dutch churches came into the twentieth century with a variety of traditionally confessional, liberal, and evangelical free-church traditions. The liturgical movement here was represented by the internationally known scholar of the phenomenology of religion, Gerardus van der Leeuw (1890-1950), who was later Minister of Education and Cultural Affairs of the Netherlands, and by Reverend J. H. Gerretsen of The Hague. The *Dienstboek in Ontwerp* (Draft Worship Book) produced in 1955 by the Dutch Reformed Church was strongly influenced by this movement.

In the last decades of the twentieth century, the Dutch Reformed Church, the Reformed Churches in the Netherlands, and the Evangelical Lutheran Church decided to move closer together with the goal of eventual union. In liturgics the Lutheran influence is worthy of notice. In 1956, long before the Leuenberg Agreement, the Reformed and Lutheran churches of Holland came to an agreement on the Lord's Supper. A common *Liedboek voor de Kerken* (Hymnal for the Churches) appeared in 1973, with a revised psalmody and nearly five hundred hymns, both traditional hymns and those produced by a workshop of contemporary poets and composers, from Ambrosius to Huub Osterhuis. Another important stage in the process was marked by the *Ecumenical Ordinarium* of 1978, published by the Van der Leeuw Foundation, which did so much for development of liturgy in Holland. The *Ordinarium* was characterized by sung responses for the congregation and especially the promotion of regular celebration of the Lord's Supper.

Twenty years later, in 1998, the *Dienstboek een proeve* was published jointly by the two Reformed churches together with the Evangelical Lutheran Church in the Netherlands.[32] The liturgy they propose "for testing," for the

---

32. *Dienstboek een proeve, Schrift, Maaltijd, Gebed* (Zoetermeer, 1998).

celebration of the word and of Communion with liturgical prayer, points toward the future in several ways and is especially significant ecumenically. Several issues in worship that need to be resolved in the Reformed churches and beyond become strikingly apparent in this work.

This current liturgy is characterized by its ecumenical inspiration and openness in various directions. Sunday worship, in this Dutch worship book, is intended in principle to be a service of the word with celebration of Communion. It provides forty-two different eucharistic prayers, showing a willingness for variety that is desirable for liturgical reasons, but also raising the question whether there is a limit to diversity and whether some uniformity might also be desirable in church liturgy. New eucharistic prayers are found side by side with a Calvinistic order for the Lord's Supper and the classic Dutch Reformed order established in Dordrecht in 1578. Similar questions come to mind with regard to the various lectionaries for Sunday worship that appear side by side: a Lutheran lectionary, then one based on the three-year Roman Catholic *Ordo lectionum Missae,* a further one that extends over nine years in connection with Nature Year and other commemorations and themes (such as synagogue and church), and finally a Torah lectionary with psalms, which leaves one wondering about the place of the New Testament in Christian worship. The Old Testament was very important in twentieth-century Dutch theology. The recollection of the 110,000 Jewish fellow citizens who never returned to Amsterdam, out of 140,000 transported to Auschwitz and other camps, continues to play a role in this respect.

Perhaps this worship book leaves too many theological and church decisions up to individual congregations and their worship leaders. The concept of "unity in diversity" remains a difficult one.

What is progressive for the Reformed community, helpful in a pastoral sense, and edifying for congregations in this book is the guidance provided for regular, and not merely occasional, daily prayers at the traditional hours of the Western church. There is also a wealth of liturgical music for congregational worship, which makes use of the best prayer book and hymnal traditions and provides a link to the *Ordinarium* of the Latin church, which has become ecumenically familiar. The music is drawn from international sources, including the melodies of the Orthodox churches that are now also becoming familiar to Reformed and Lutheran Christians.

Finally, the worship book is educational with regard to liturgical language and theological thinking, offering a great many new formulations, especially for the daily prayers. These are largely based on the three-year cycle of Bible readings, but they also bring in concrete and contemporary human experience and religious expectations. Particular attention has been given to ways of addressing God, in the sense of a richer image of God not pre-empted by dogma and often limited simply to a divine "Thou" as in the Hasidic tradition.[33] New ways of speaking about Christ and attentiveness to human beings as they are today go hand in hand. It is also important to note, in judging this worship book, that new formulations are placed side by side with traditional forms of prayer.

The challenge to, and limitation of, this most recent Dutch Reformed worship book is its reception in Reformed and Lutheran congregations. A common worship book for both Lutheran and Reformed churches is not to be taken for granted even today. Tradition-conscious and liberal Protestant groups each have their own reasons for distancing themselves from it. And so-called liturgically aware congregations will continue to enjoy putting together their own worship services from various sources, and will use the worship book at best as a treasure trove in which to hunt for alternative texts or tunes. The growing influence of evangelical and charismatic currents has hardly yet been taken into account in the official liturgies of the churches. This newest Dutch worship book reveals the precarious position of Reformed liturgy, and of Protestant liturgy in general.

Conclusion

It is not my view that Reformed worship in European countries is headed unavoidably toward ever greater differentiation and diversity among the congregations that celebrate it, even though the churches live under quite varied circumstances and differences in theological and human history. Splinter movements, and doing as one pleases, in no way need become the marks of Reformed liturgy. Instead, as we move on, we can sense a convergence of situations and a community of ways in which this convergence is being met, liturgically and otherwise. Christians do not have an unlimited number of answers to the decisive questions they encounter, but rather one Savior only, Jesus Christ. This is expressed today, as it has always been, in liturgical celebration, in the form that we will ultimately share ecumenically. Grace is received and God is praised in every time and every place, with one heart and one mind. It is up to us to celebrate coherently together the *one* ground of our being, liturgically as in every other way.

---

33. Frieder Schulz, "Entchristologisierung der gottesdienstlichen Gebete?" [Are prayers in worship being de-Christologised?], in *Liturgisches Jahrbuch* 50 (2000): 195-205.

For Further Reading

Bonjour, Jean-Louis. "Le culte des Eglises réformées de Suisse romande." In *Saint-Pierre de Genève au fil des siècles,* ed. Clefs de Saint-Pierre. Geneva, 1991.

Bürki, Bruno. "Gottesdienst im reformierten Kontext." In *Handbuch der Liturgik,* ed. Hans-Christoph Schmidt-Lauber, Karl-Heinrich Bieritz, and Michael Meyer-Blanck. Göttingen, 2003.

Gagnebin, Laurent. *Le culte à chœur ouvert. Introduction à la liturgie du culte réformée.* Paris/Geneva, 1992.

Oskamp, Paul, and Niek Schuman, eds. *De Weg van de Liturgie Traditties, Achtergronden, Praktijk.* 3rd ed. Zoetermee, 2001.

Spinks, Bryan D., and Iain R. Torrance. *To Glorify God: Essays on Modern Reformed Liturgy.* Edinburgh, 1999.

The Origins of the Antipathy to Set Liturgical Forms in the English-Speaking Reformed Tradition

Bryan D. Spinks

In 1763 the Dutch church in New York decided the time had finally arrived when English must replace Dutch as the language of their worship and preaching, and the New York consistory began the process to call an English-speaking pastor. An approach to the Church of England was ruled out because it was a church "where the doctrines of pure grace are scarcely to be found." The obvious solution was to call either an English or a Scottish Presbyterian minister. There were, however, problems with this solution as well. Most English Presbyterians had either become Unitarian or were crypto-Unitarians, and the idea of a Scottish Presbyterian minister was also less than perfect. Already in 1751 the Synod of North Holland had warned the New Yorkers, "But now it becomes known that the Scotch Presbytery is not only entirely independent, but without Forms of doctrine and Liturgies, so that neither now, nor ever, can one be sure of its opinions."[1]

In the end a Scottish minister, one Archibald Laidlie, a member of the Dutch classis in Zeeland, accepted the call. He, together with John Henry Livingstone, would ensure that the liturgy of the Netherlands, translated into English, would continue to be used by the New York Dutch Reformed Church. Use of the Psalm Book was important to Dutch Reformed spirituality, containing, as it did, the morning prayers of public worship that the minister was expected to recite. It was precisely because English and Scottish Presbyterian ministers were known to be without a liturgy (and because of suspicions that they leaned toward Unitarianism) that they were not regarded as suitable pastors for the congregation.

---

1. Daniel James Meeter, "Bless the Lord, O My Soul," in *The New-York Liturgy of the Dutch Reformed Church, 1767,* Drew University Studies in Liturgy 6 (Lanham, Md.: Scarecrow Press, 1998), p. 42.

It remains a quirk of history that from Zürich, through Bern, Neuchâtel, Geneva, Strasbourg, Ulm, the Palatinate, and the Netherlands, the Reformed churches published agendas or forms for public worship which the minister was expected, for the most part, to follow, while the English-speaking Reformed tradition became one which, to parody Karl Barth's words, was without liturgical forms and even hostile to such forms.[2] This chapter attempts to trace an outline of the origins of this hostility, which developed in the time up to the making of the Westminster Directory and culminated in that work being itself largely abandoned.

There is, as far as I can discover, no clear and single cause for this phenomenon. I want to suggest that it came about through a number of interrelated factors and developments. First, it can be traced to the sixteenth-century English disputes over ceremonies and phraseology of the *Book of Common Prayer,* which, for some of tender conscience and continental taste, seemed too close to Rome for comfort. Second, and related to it, was the dispute over the authority of Scripture vis-à-vis the magistrate and ceremonies. Third, it was a negative reaction to the attempts of the magistrate, in the person of the bishops and archdeacons, to enforce compliance, and to the punishment of those who refused, both in England and, after 1618, in Scotland. A final contributing factor was the development of an evangelical piety and radicalism in Scotland beginning in the 1620s.

Sixteenth-Century Disputes over the *Book of Common Prayer*

In 1559 a new Act of Uniformity required for the Elizabethan church the use of the *Book of Common Prayer* for all forms of public worship. Cranmer's second *Book of Common Prayer* had been finished in 1552, and, with the exceptions of three minor changes and alterations to the royal prayers, its liturgy was essentially that supported by the 1559 Act. The precise history of the 1549 and 1552 Prayer Books need not detain us, though we should observe that although the book of 1552 certainly contained more Protestant and Reformed liturgy than that of 1549, it was nevertheless, in ethos and format, very different from the liturgies of the continental Reformed Churches.[3] It is no accident that the

2. See Karl Barth, *The Knowledge of God and the Service of God,* trans. J. L. M. Haire and Ian Anderson (London: Hodder and Stoughton, 1938), p. 131. Barth's original reference was to sacraments.

3. G. J. Cuming, *The Godly Order* (London: Alcuin Club/SPCK, 1983); Bryan D. Spinks, "Treasures Old and New: A Look at Some of Thomas Cranmer's Methods of Liturgical Com-

Marian exiles who moved to Frankfurt attempted to adapt the 1552 book to conform more to a Reformed ethos. Indeed, the rumor that Cranmer was preparing a book a hundred times better than that of 1552 may have been deliberately invented by the exiles to justify their ad hoc liturgical reforms.[4] The *Liturgy of Compromise* of 1555 reduced and adapted the Prayer Book material for a more Reformed environment — for example, removing versicles and responses.[5] Neither is it accidental that those exiles who journeyed to Geneva produced a liturgy that drew on Prayer Book material but that was much nearer the shape, format, and ethos of Calvin's Genevan rite.[6]

Whether Cranmer's work of 1552 would have been his final form or was merely one in a series, we will never know. Dairmaid MacCulloch observes that Elizabeth's solution to the dilemmas she faced in 1559 was to establish a version of the Edwardian church that proved to be a snapshot, frozen in time, of the church as it had been in September of 1552, ignoring the progress made in further changing the Church of England after that date.[7] In fact, Elizabeth turned the clock back slightly. For those who had tasted Reformed worship when in exile, what they returned to was just too unreformed for comfort. Thus immediately there was opposition to the wearing of the surplice, tippet, and hood. But the anti-vestarianism began to develop into a larger agenda over ceremonial, which included kneeling for Communion. Contrasting what they envisioned as the usage of the apostolic church with the Elizabethan worship, Field and Wilcox complained in *An Admonition to the Parliament* of 1572 that

> They ministred the sacrament plainely. We pompously, with singing, pypyng, surplesse and cope waeryng. They simply as they receeved it from the Lorde. We, sinfullye, mixed with mannes inventions and devises. And as for baptisme, it was enough with them, if they had water, and the partie to be baptised faith, and the minister to preach the word and minister the sacraments.

---

pilation," in *Thomas Cranmer: Churchman and Scholar,* ed. Paul Ayris and David Selwyn (New York: Boydell Press, 1993), pp. 175-88.

4. *A Brieff Discours off the Troubles begonne at Frankford in Germany Anno Domini 1554,* ed. E. Arber (1908).

5. Robin Leaver, ed., *The Liturgy of the Frankfurt Exiles 1555,* Grove Liturgical Study 38 (Bramcote: Grove Books, 1984).

6. Dan G. Danner, *Pilgrimage to Puritanism: History and Theology of the Marian Exiles at Geneva, 1555-1560* (New York: Peter Lang, 1999); W. D. Maxwell, *The Liturgical Portions of the Genevan Service Book,* 2nd ed. (London: Faith Press, 1965); Bryan D. Spinks, *From the Lord and "the Best Reformed Churches": A Study of the Eucharistic Liturgy in the English and Puritan Separatist Traditions, 1550-1663* (Rome: CLV, 1984).

7. D. MacCulloch, *Thomas Cranmer* (New Haven: Yale University Press, 1996), p. 620.

Nowe, we must have surplesses devised by Pope Adrian, interrogatories ministred to the infant, godfathers and godmothers, brought in by Higinus, holy fonts invented by Pope Pius, crossing and suche like peces of poperie, which the church of God in the Apostles times never knew (and therfore not to be used) nay (which we are sure of) were and are mannes devises, broght in long after the puritie of the primitive church.[8]

Similar complaints were made some thirty years later in the Millenary Petition presented to James I. The petitioners requested the removal or emendation of the following:

1. In the church service: that the cross in baptism, interrogatories ministered to infants, confirmations, as superfluous, may be taken away: baptism not to be ministered by women, and so explained: the cap and surplice not urged: that examination may go before the communion: that it be ministered with a sermon: that divers terms of priests and absolution and some other used, with the ring in marriage, and other such like in the book, may be corrected: the longsomeness of service abridged: church-songs and music moderated to better edification: that the Lord's day be not profaned: the rest upon holydays not so strictly urged: that there may be an uniformity of doctrine prescribed: no ministers charged to teach their people to bow at the name of Jesus: that the canonical scriptures only be read in the church.[9]

Despite petitions and attacks in books and pamphlets, few concessions were made. Some ministers, such as Richard Greenham, Vicar of Dry Drayton, were given private dispensation from the surplice and use of the cross in baptism by their bishop, and indeed, those who kept quiet and were popular with their congregation seemed to be left alone.[10] On the other hand, others who were vocal — such as Field and Wilcox, or in the case of the Millenary petition, Arthur Hildersham — were disciplined and, if conformity was not forthcoming, suspended. This was on the grounds that these things were not contrary to Scripture and were therefore matters indifferent, and the magistrate had the right to require use of things indifferent. It was the duty of

8. In W. H. Frere and C. E. Douglas, *Puritan Manifestoes: A Study of the Origin of the Puritan Revolt* (London: SPCK, 1907), p. 14.

9. In E. Cardwell, *A History of Conferences and other Proceedings Connected with the Revision of the Book of Common Prayer* (Oxford: University Press, 1841), pp. 131-32.

10. John H. Primus, *Richard Greenham: Portrait of an Elizabethan Pastor* (Macon, Ga.: Mercer University Press, 1998); Kenneth L. Parker and Eric J. Carlson, *"Practical Divinity": The Works and Life of Revd. Richard Greenham* (Aldershot, England: Ashgate, 1998).

Christian people to obey and (in the words of the prayer book) to be "godly and quietly governed."

It will be noted that thus far this chapter has avoided use of the term "Puritan." Older historiography operated with a distinction of Anglican and Puritan, with the understanding that Puritans opposed the Elizabethan Settlement and Anglicanism. It now seems difficult to speak of Anglicanism before 1662. The period of 1559 to 1662 is perhaps better understood as a struggle of different groups within an English national church to establish one overriding theology and ethos, with many contenders. It has become commonplace to speak of the theology of this period as being a "Calvinist consensus" in terms of theology being in the main shared with continental Reformed churches. Tom Webster has preferred to call those of tender conscience "godly" rather than Puritan, since most Puritans were also members of the Church of England, and thus Anglican.[11] But amongst the godly we should distinguish between conformists, such as William Perkins and Richard Sibbes, and nonconformists such as Arthur Hildersham, who were suspended for periods of time for their failure to observe the ceremonies they complained of, but were Church of England clergy, and remained members of that church. These in turn must be distinguished from the Separatists, who left voluntarily, and who regarded Geneva as being as unreformed as the Church of England.

The Authority of Scripture versus the Authority of the Magistrate

In the debate over ceremonies, the "godly" appealed to the word of God as the final arbiter in such matters. William Fulke could thus write, "The church of God is the house of God, and therefore ought to be directed in all things according to the order prescribed by the Householder himself, which order is not to be learned elsewhere but in his holy word."[12] William Bradshaw wrote the following:

> IMPRIMUS. They hould and maintaine that the word of God contained in the writings of the Prophets and Apostles, is of absolute perfection, given by Christ the head of the Churche, to bee unto the same, the sole Canon and rule of all matters of Religion, and the worship and service of

11. Tom Webster, *Godly Clergy in Early Stuart England* (Cambridge: Cambridge University Press, 1997).

12. W. Fulke, "A Brief and Plain Declaration," in *Elizabethan Puritanism*, ed. Leonard J. Trinterud (New York: Oxford University Press, 1971), p. 243.

God whatsoever. And that whatsoever done in the same service and worship cannot bee iustified by the said word, is unlawfull.[13]

The Admonitioners had requested that those in authority allow Christ to "rule and raygne in his church by the scepter of his worde onely."[14] In the apostolic church nothing was taught but God's word, but now "Princes pleasures, mennes devices, popish ceremonies, and Antichristian rites in publique pulpits defended."[15] And Thomas Cartwright was to urge in the Second Admonition, "We must be in daunger of a premunire if we folowe not the lawes of the land, thoughe they be against the Scriptures, and in daunger of a twelve monthes imprisonment, if we speake against the booke of common prayer, though it be againste the word of God."[16]

What was at stake was obedience to Scripture rather than the magistrate. The result was a heightened view of scriptural authority which would, with John Owen in the seventeenth century, result in the view that every jot and tittle was inspired by God. Whereas the authorities of the Church of England urged that things indifferent could be used with a good conscience, for many of the "godly," things without explicit warrant in Scripture were not indifferent at all, but stumbling blocks to true obedience to the word of God. In other words, those of tender conscience were forced back to a position where everything must have some warrant in Scripture. Thus all matters of worship came under scrutiny.

Resentment of Injustice, Resentment of Liturgical Forms

Many of the "godly" wanted the *Book of Common Prayer* either further reformed or replaced by a Reformed liturgy. Various editions of the 1556 *Genevan Service Book* circulated, and there is evidence that in some groups it was used. In 1584 and again in 1586 attempts were made through Parliament to authorize use of editions of the *Genevan Service Book* in place of the *Book of Common Prayer,* but both attempts were thwarted by royal intervention.[17] There is evidence that some godly groups borrowed the liturgies of the English

13. William Bradshaw, *English Puritanisme, Containening the maine opinions of the rigidest sort of those that are called Puritanes in the Realme of England* (1605), pp. 1-2.

14. Frere and Douglas, *Puritan Manifestoes,* p. 9.

15. Frere and Douglas, *Puritan Manifestoes,* p. 12.

16. Frere and Douglas, *Puritan Manifestoes,* pp. 93-94.

17. These were known after their printer and place of printing — the Waldegrave Liturgy 1584 and the Middleburg Liturgy 1586. See Spinks, *From the Lord,* pp. 113-21.

"stranger" churches — those foreign groups of Dutch and French Reformed who settled in England and were allowed their own ministers and own liturgical forms. The most important of these were the *Forma ac Ratio* of John a Lasco, the "Superintendent of the London foreigners," for the use at Austin Friars Church, London. French and Italian translations were made, and there was a Dutch adaptation by Maarten Micron.[18] Valerand Poullain, who was pastor of a French congregation in Glastonbury, produced a version of Calvin's Strasbourg liturgy, *Liturgia Sacra,* in 1551.[19]

Thus, the "godly" were not opposed to liturgical forms *per se,* but simply the unreformed nature of the *Book of Common Prayer.* Amongst Separatists, however, in the late 1580s, we find an unequivocal repudiation of any set form of worship, be it from Canterbury, Geneva, Zürich, or Amsterdam. The Separatist leaders found no warrant in Scripture for set forms, but found instead the ministerial gift for public prayer through the Spirit. In the apostolic church, so Henry Barrow claimed,

> They alwaies used spiritual praiers according to their present wantes and occasions, and so taught all churches to pray, alwaies, with all maner of praier and supplication in the spirit, and therby to make knowen their wantes, and to shew their requestes in al thinges unto God their heavenly Father.[20]

If prayer was essentially the gift of the Spirit, then written or "stinted" prayer represented a blasphemous attack on the Spirit; those who use written prayers

> take the office of the Holie Ghost awaie, quench the spirit of the ministrie, and of the whole church, stop and keepe out the graces of God, thrust their idle devices upon the whole church, yea, upon God himselfe, whether he wil or no.[21]

Most of the "godly" saw Separatism as an intolerable danger, yet the Separatist view of set forms of prayer began to be absorbed by the some of the nonconformist godly. Already in William Fulke we find an appeal to Scripture

---

18. Spinks, *From the Lord,* pp. 96-113. See also Andrew Pettegree, *Foreign Protestant Communities in Sixteenth-Century London* (Oxford: Oxford University Press, 1986); Dirk W. Rodgers, *John a Lasco in England* (New York: Peter Lang, 1994).

19. A. C. Honders, ed., *Valerandus Pollanus, Liturgia Sacra (1551-1555)* (Leiden: Brill, 1970).

20. "A Brief Discoverie of the False Church 1590," in *The Writings of Henry Barrow 1587-1590,* ed. Leland H. Carlson (London: Allen and Unwin, 1970), p. 366.

21. A Plaine Refutation, in *Writings of Henry Barrow 1590-1591,* ed. Leland H. Carlson (London: Allen and Unwin, 1966), p. 100.

which, while not ruling out set forms, nevertheless did not endorse them. Fulke viewed worship as something inseparable from the church and its ministry, both of which were dependent on the word. Worship in terms of public prayer was dealt with as belonging to the office of the pastor. Thus the pastor was to teach and exhort (2 Tim. 3:16–4:2); it was also his duty to pray, as in Acts 16:16. The congregation might join in the singing of psalms (cf. 1 Cor. 14:15, 26), "for this custom hath continued in the Church from the beginning, that the congregation have praised God with psalms singing together." But it belonged essentially to the office of pastor to make prayer, and "the rest to pray with him in silence and to answer 'Amen'" (cf. 1 Cor. 4:16).[22] And in *The Admonition to the Parliament* Field and Wilcox noted,

> Then ministers were not tyed to any forme of prayers invented by man, but as the spirit moved them, so they powred forth hartie supplications to the Lorde. Now they are bound of necessitie to a prescript order of service, and booke of common prayer in which a great number of things contrary to Gods word are contained. . . .[23]

In April of 1593 the Act to Retain the Queen's Subjects had been passed, making nonconformity punishable by exile. Some went to prison, some were exiled, and some chose exile before they could be arrested. Thus William Ames fled from Cambridge for Holland in 1611 rather than face a bishops' court. He would later become Professor of Divinity at Franaker. His teacher and mentor, William Perkins, was a conformist Calvinist, and had defended the use of set forms of worship. Ames, however, in his *The Marrow of Theology,* wrote of "Instituted Forms" of worship that "No instituted worship is lawfull unless God is its author and ordainer. Deut. 4.1-2; 12.32, *Keep all things which I shall command you. . . . Add not to the word which I command you, neither take from it. . . . Everything which I command you observe to do: Add not to it, or take from it. . . . Our Lord broke in on us, because we did not seek him rightly.*"[24]

Of course, this left open the possibility that a set form of worship might have God as its author, and being in the orbit of the Dutch Reformed Church, Ames must have known that that church used a set form. His condemnation of "will worship" and his discussion of ceremonies and idolatry had in mind the *Book of Common Prayer* as well as the Roman liturgical forms. Elsewhere Ames argued that the Lord's Prayer was an example of set prayer and that to

---

22. Trinterud, *Elizabethan Puritanism,* pp. 268-70.

23. In Frere and Douglas, *Puritan Manifestoes,* p. 11.

24. William Ames, *The Marrow of Theology,* ed. and trans. John D. Eusden (Grand Rapids: Baker Books, 1997), p. 279.

keep to its text would mean no proficiency in the spirit and gift of prayer.[25] William Bradshaw, writing in 1605, had explained that the most rigid of those called Puritan in England held it as gross superstition "for any mortall man to institute and ordaine as parts of divine worship, any mysticall rite and Ceremonie of Religion whatsover, and to mingle the same with the divine."[26] In this same work Bradshaw was clear that the magistrate might have authority over church members, and must be a member of the church and subject to Scripture. He further explained,

> They hould that in the assemblie of the Church, the Pastor onely is to be the mouth of the Congregation to God in prayer, and that the people are onely to testifie their assent by the word Amen. And that it is a Babilonian confusion, for the Pastor to say one peece of a prayer & the people with mingled voices to say another, except in singing, which by the very ordinance and instinct of nature, is more delightfull, and effectuall, the more voyces there are ioyned & mingled together in harmonie and concent.
>
> They hould that the Church hath no authoritie to impose upon her Pastors or any other of her offices, any other minisyteriall duties, Offices, Functions, Actions, or ceremonies, eyther in Divine worship or out of the same then what Christ himselfe in the scriptures hath imposed upon them, or what they might lawfully impose upon Christ himself, if hee were in person upon the Earth, and did exercise a ministeriall office in some Church.[27]

Though this did not rule out set forms *a priori,* there is here a tendency to place public prayer solely in the hands of the minister, as a gift of the Spirit for ministry, and reserve congregational participation to "Amen" and psalm singing. If public prayer is a gift of the Spirit, then no set liturgy is required. Such views seemed to harden amongst many of the "godly" during the so-called Laudian rule, when most bishops were encouraged to impose strict compliance with rubrics, with increasingly severe penalties for those who stubbornly resisted. John Watson made the point:

> If a man declines to use a liturgy and you crop his ears and split his nose to encourage him, human nature is so constituted that he is apt to grow more obstinate, and to conceive a quite unreasonable prejudice against the book.[28]

25. William Ames, *Conscience with the Power and Cases thereof* (London, 1643), bk. 4, p. 41.

26. Bradshaw, *English Puritanisme*, p. 3.

27. Bradshaw, *English Puristanisme*, p. 10.

28. John Watson, *The Cure of Souls* (New York: Dodd, Mead, 1896), p. 254.

The trajectory of Ames and Bradshaw can be seen in the views set forth by John Cotton. Cotton was a graduate from Emmanuel College, Cambridge, where Perkins's teacher, the aging Laurence Chaderton, was Master. He had been converted by the preaching of the conformist Calvinist Richard Sibbes and was an ordained minister of the Church of England. In 1612 he was appointed to St. Botolph's in the town of Boston in Lincolnshire, which was a well known "godly" congregation. He eventually espoused a congregational polity and claimed to have been influenced by the writings of Robert Parker, Paul Baynes, and William Ames. But all his views could be seen as a trajectory of Bradshaw's book. In 1633 he was to leave for New England, but would later be nominated to the Westminster Assembly.

In his *A Modest and Cleare Answer to Mr. Ball's Discourse of Set Formes of Prayer,* 1642, Cotton argued that the imposition of a set liturgy was unwarranted by God's word, which was the only book necessary for worship.

> A man may give unto another holy directions, and rules for Prayer, and may also set downe some forms of Prayer as examples of such rules, but not to prescribe them as set forms to them, to be used by them for their Prayers. . . . We hold it in like manner unlawfull for one Church to receive such set forms of Prayer from another, and to use them for their own Prayers.[29]

Reading a prayer by others is, according to Cotton, like reading the sermons of others — which was a common practice with the less theologically articulate clergy; it is as dishonorable to Christ and as superfluous for the governors of the church to prescribe to ministers set forms of prayer as it would be to prescribe a printed sermon to be read.[30] For Cotton, "in conceived prayer, the Spirit of God within us teacheth us what to pray."[31] How, he asked, could men have power to prescribe to the church methods and forms of speech in prayer when God had prescribed nothing? What God had commanded was the reading of Scriptures and singing psalms. He conceded that it was lawful to recite the Lord's Prayer, but that was because Christ is the author. The minister was given gifts of preaching and praying. In *The Way of the Churches of Christ in New England,* Cotton wrote of their worship:

> First then when we come together in the Church, according to the Apostles direction, 1 Tim. 2.1., wee make prayers and intercessions and

---

29. John Cotton, *A Modest and Cleare Answer to Mr. Ball's Discourse of Set Formes of Prayer* (1642), pp. 4-5.

30. Cotton, *A Modest and Cleare Answer,* p. 28.

31. Cotton, *A Modest and Cleare Answer,* p. 13.

Thanksgivings for our selves and for all men, not in any prescribed forme of prayer, or stinted Liturgie, but in such a manner, as the Spirit of grace and of prayer (who teacheth all the people of God, what and how to pray, Rom. 8.26, 27) helpeth our infirmities, wee having respect therein to the necessities of the people, the estate of the times, and the worke of Christ in our hands.[32]

But psalmody was a different matter, for this indeed was pure Scripture, and so accuracy was demanded, and a new translation was needed.[33] The singing of psalmody is defended by Cotton, and in his work of 1647, *Singing of Psalmes a Gospel Ordinance,* contended that "carnell men and Pagans" are obligated to sing the psalms as much as are "Church-members and Christians."[34] Thus, what had been a hallmark of the Separatist position on set forms was adopted by some of the seventeenth-century "godly" divines, disenchanted by the fact that their earlier pleas for further Reformation had been ignored.

The Rise of Hostility to Liturgy in Scotland

The fortunes of the English and Scottish churches were brought together with the accession of James VI to the English throne in 1603. The Church of Scotland had adopted Reformation principles in 1561, and had adopted for liturgical use the form drawn up by Knox and his colleagues at Geneva in 1556. This brought together phraseology and material from the Book of Common Prayer of 1552, from Calvin's Genevan liturgy, and from a liturgy Knox had composed for use at Berwick on Tweed in 1550.[35] It provided a Sunday Morning service, and rites for baptism, the Lord's Supper, marriage, visitation of the sick, and burial, as well as a catechism and private prayers. It did allow for free prayer, but seems to have been used by many ministers as a set liturgy, with daily services in some parishes during which the prayers were read by a "Reader."[36]

The Church of Scotland had, however, dispensed with many of the cere-

32. John Cotton, *The Way of the Churches of Christ in New England* (London: Printed by M. Simmons, 1645), pp. 66-67.

33. Cotton, *The Way of the Churches,* p. 67.

34. I am indebted to my student Kyle Pedersen for the insights in his paper "A Mixt Assembly: Carnell Men and Pagans in John Cotton's Theology of Psalm Singing."

35. Spinks, *From the Lord,* pp. 76-84; Maxwell, *Liturgical Portions of the Genevan Service Book;* G. J. Cuming, "John Knox and the Book of Common Prayer" in *Liturgical Review* 10 (1980): 80-81.

36. See Maxwell, *Liturgical Portions of the Genevan Service Book,* pp. 177-79.

monies the English Church retained, and had phased out bishops, first using them as superintendents, and then allowing that office to lapse. In place was a presbyterian system of government. Many of the "godly" in England hoped that James would bring the English church into line with that of Scotland, and it was this hope that had inspired confidence in the instigators of the Millenary Petition. Assimilation of the two churches appealed to James, but unfortunately his desire was to conform the Scottish church to that of England. Bishops were gradually reintroduced, and in 1610 three were given the "historical succession" through ordination by three English bishops. In 1616 James set about to revive the observance of certain festivals and to replace the custom of sitting for Communion with kneeling. He also requested a new liturgy. Work on the latter was first in the hands of Patrick Galloway, who produced a draft. This was later expanded by William Cowper, bishop of Glasgow, and finally went into a third draft. The third draft used much more material from the English *Book of Common Prayer,* but was still Reformed in ethos and doctrine. Simultaneously, however, the king insisted on certain articles being adopted, known as the Five Articles of Perth, which imposed kneeling for Communion and observance of certain holy days in the traditional liturgical calendar. Opposition to the Articles led to banishment of a good number of ministers, and the troubles led to the abandonment of the plan for a revised liturgy. Knox's form remained the norm.

In the aftermath of the Five Articles a group of more radical ministers emerged whose emphasis was on preaching and inner conversion, with outward concern for the covenant ("federal theology") and a suspicion of set forms of worship. Two branches within this group can be identified, though they clearly knew and interacted with each other. First, a group of ministers fled imposition of the Five Articles by going to Ulster, where many Scots had been resettled, but where the episcopal system was weak and uniformity was not insisted upon. Ministers such as John Livingstone and Robert Blair were in this category. They encouraged more pious groups to assemble at times in addition to public worship for what might be described as more intense and personal forms of devotion, though they did not espouse separation from the Kirk.[37] Sometimes crowds gathered on the Saturday before Communion to hear a sermon and spent the Saturday and Sunday nights "in severall companies, sometimes an minister being with them, sometimes themselves alone in conference and prayer."[38] Linked with these ministers, who frequently revis-

37. See David Stevenson, "Conventicles in the Kirk, 1619-37: The Emergence of a Radical Party," in *Records of the Scottish Church History Society* 18 (1974): 99-114.

38. From R. Wodrow, *Select Biographies* 1, 142; cited by Stevenson, "Conventicles in the Kirk," p. 107.

ited Scotland, were David Dickson and Samuel Rutherford, both later to hold university chairs in divinity. Both favored private prayer meetings. They went further, however, and also began to attack certain customs and liturgical practices of the Kirk which were traditional, but which they claimed were recent innovations — such as saying the Lord's Prayer, singing the doxology at the end of the psalms, and bowing in prayer in the pulpit before preaching. There was also a growing preference for extemporaneous prayer. Samuel Rutherford, presumably trying to excuse John Knox for not sharing his views, wrote,

> Anent read prayers . . . I could never see precept, promise or practice for them, in God's word. Our church never allowed them, but men took them up at their own choice . . . it were good if they were out of the service of God.[39]

It was also from these movements that the growing custom of solemn Communions, which would become the open air Communion seasons, stemmed.[40]

Whereas James had had the wisdom not to push too far, his son Charles I did not, and the attempt to frame new canons in 1636 that prohibited extempore prayer and to introduce the 1637 liturgy led quickly to the National Covenant in 1638, when episcopacy, new canons, and the Five Articles of Perth were renounced. But the more radical parties renounced much more; they renounced a written liturgy.

The Westminster Directory

The immediate events after 1638 led to the English Civil War, the Solemn League and Covenant uniting nations and churches, and the Westminster Assembly of Divines. Although its initial task had been to revise the thirty-nine Articles of the Church of England, its intent eventually became to prepare a new confession of faith and to draw up forms of worship to replace the *Book of Common Prayer.* The compilation of the forms of worship were placed in the hands of a subcommittee chaired by Stephen Marshall, incumbent of Finchingfield in Essex, and a reluctant conformist until the civil war. Other members were Thomas Young, Herbert Palmer, Charles Herle, and one of the Dissenting Brethren, or Independents, Thomas Goodwin. They were joined by

39. Rutherford, *Letters,* ed. H. Bonar, p. 611; cited in David Stevenson, "The Radical Party in the Kirk, 1637-45," in *Journal of Ecclesiastical History* 25 (1974): 135-65, p. 141.

40. See Leigh Eric Schmidt, *Holy Fairs: Scotland and the Making of American Revivalism,* rev. ed. (Grand Rapids: Eerdmans, 2001).

four Scottish commissioners — Samuel Rutherford, George Gillespie, Robert Baillie, and Alexander Henderson. Goodwin co-opted his fellow Independent, Philip Nye — who set forth his dislike of set forms in his later work, *Beams of Former Light* — into the subcommittee as well. Herle offended his fellow Presbyterian-minded committee members because he frequently sided with the Independents. Of the Scottish commissioners, Rutherford and Gillespie were radicals of the Kirk. When the English Presbyterian Thomas Gataker reminded Rutherford that a particular proposal was already in the Scottish *Book of Common Order* of Knox, Rutherford replied "We will not owne this litturgy. Nor are we tyed unto it."[41] Thus of the membership of the subcommittee, Rutherford, Gillespie, Goodwin, Nye, and Herle disliked stinted prayer.

It is little wonder, then, that what emerged was *A Directory for the Publick Worship of God,* which was adopted by both churches for its standard of worship.[42] The *Directory* offered only an outline with suggested themes for prayers, allowing radicals in Scotland and Independents in England to pray "in the Spirit." It also contained detailed rubrics and instructions — in fact, the instructions were longer than the outline prayers and formulae. The instructions and material for Sunday morning worship included sections on solemn prayer, the public reading of Scripture, public prayer before the sermon, preaching the word (authored by Stephen Marshall), and prayer after the sermon. Directions were given for baptism, the Lord's Supper, marriage, visitation of the sick, and burial. The latter made no liturgical provision, but ordered that the body be interred without prayer or ceremony. Directions were also given for solemn fasting, singing of psalms, and days of thanksgiving. The English Independents challenged the sequence of prayers, arguing that Knox's sequence was unbiblical. There were also heated discussions over the inclusion of a creed at baptism and the posture for receiving the Lord's Supper. The Scottish practice — as also the Dutch — was sitting at successive tables. The Independents preferred to receive sitting in their pews.[43]

Of some significance, however, was the publication in 1645 of *A Supply of Prayer for Ships.* The *Supply* modified the Sunday morning *Directory* worship into set, formal prayer, for use on ships where no minister was available. This suggests that conceived or free prayer was regarded as a *ministerial gift,* not a general one. Lay-led worship could, and should, use set prayers.

41. Manuscript Minutes of the Westminster Assembly, Dr. Williams Library, London, vol. 2, p. 492.

42. See the extracts from the Directory on pp. 110-12 in this volume.

43. See Bryan D. Spinks, *Freedom or Order?: The Eucharistic Liturgy in English Congregationalism, 1645-1980* (Allison Park, Pa.: Pickwick Publications, 1984).

In the Scottish church the General Assembly adopted the *Directory*, though many were unhappy with it. David Calderwood made the plea, "Moderator, I entreat that the Doxology be not laid aside, for I hope to sing it in Glory." Instead it was decided to "let desuetude abolish it," and it fell out of use.[44]

In 1660 Charles II was restored to both thrones. Although hopes were high for accommodation between Presbyterian Anglicans and Episcopal Anglicans, the Independents knew that their time was up, and they prepared to depart. In England the *Directory* was deemed illegal and episcopacy restored. In fact, so few concessions were made that many Presbyterian Anglicans, such as Richard Baxter, also left to become tolerated dissenters. Baxter's views on set forms were set out in his work *Five Disputations of Church Government and Worship*, 1659. Although he allowed set forms, they were not his preference. He did of course author the Savoy Liturgy as an alternative to the *Book of Common Prayer*, but it was stillborn. In dissent, Baxter and most, if not all, his fellow ministers went the "Independent way" and abandoned set forms of worship.

In Scotland the restoration of bishops was problematic enough, and no attempt was made to revive and impose liturgy — though technically, with the Act Recissory, the *Book of Common Order* of John Knox was to be used. Some ministers used the new English Prayer Book, but most went the way of the *Directory*, and then even that was abandoned. On the other hand, surviving records show that Readers were supposed to read from set prayers, though what form was envisaged is not clear. With the ejection of bishops in 1689, the Kirk seems to have seen episcopacy and written liturgical forms as being almost synonymous. The Scottish Parliament of 1690, having heard the Westminster Confession read aloud, declined to hear the Catechism and *Directory*, and technically restored the use of the worship of the Church of Scotland to what had been established in 1592, namely, Knox's *Book of Common Order*. In reality, however, no forms, and not even the *Directory*, were used. Not until the nineteenth-century liturgical revival did English and Scottish Reformed churchmen contemplate authoring printed forms for public worship.

---

44. Cited by Stevenson, "The Radical Party," p. 159. See also David George Mullan, *Scottish Puritanism, 1590-1638* (Oxford/New York: Oxford University Press, 2000). It is unfortunate that Mullan has used the word *Puritan* with such a wide meaning. Also Bryan D. Spinks, *Sacraments, Ceremonies, and the Stuart Divines: Sacramental Theology and Liturgy in England and Scotland, 1603-1662* (Burlington, Vt.: Ashgate Pub., 2001).

The Revival of Liturgical Forms in the Church of Scotland[45]

Because of rifts within the Church of Scotland, by the nineteenth century there were three main groups: the Free Church of Scotland, the United Presbyterian Church (itself a union between the Relief Church and the United Succession Church) and the established Church of Scotland. All three of these churches witnessed in the nineteenth century a revival of printed forms of worship for use by the minister.[46] Influenced in part by the Catholic Apostolic Church in England and the Mercersburg Movement in the German Reformed Church in America, a number of leading Scottish ministers began to advocate provision of forms of public prayers in order to improve the standard of worship.[47] Already in 1802 the *Scotch Minister's Assistant* was published, re-issued in 1822 as *Forms of Prayer for use in the Church of Scotland*. In 1857 A. Bonar published *Presbyterian Liturgies with Specimens of Forms of Prayer for Public Worship,* and in 1865, Dr. Robert Lee published his *Order of Public Worship*. Of more significance was the founding of the Church Service Society in 1865, which was dedicated to publishing liturgical forms that drew on the classical and Reformed traditions of worship. In 1867 the Society issued the *Euchologion, a Book of Common Order,* which proved very influential, and went through a number of revised editions. The Society was the influence that led the United Presbyterians to found the United Presbyterian Devotional Services Association, which published *Presbyterian Forms of Service,* 1891; the Free Church formed the Worship Association, which produced *A New Directory for the Public Worship of God,* 1898. The latter two churches united in 1900, and in 1928 produced a *Book of Common Order.* In turn this United Free Church reunited with the old Church of Scotland in 1929. The (reunited) Church of Scotland produced a *Book of Common Order* in 1940, which represented a remarkable English-language liturgy, far superior to anything the Anglican churches had produced.[48] A new *Book of Common Order* was

45. Presbyterianism in England collapsed into Unitarianism, and very few congregations survived past the eighteenth century. The Presbyterian Church of England was refounded in the nineteenth century from Scotland. Congregationalism thrived in England, however, and its nineteenth-century recovery of liturgical formulae is described in this collection by Alan Sell.

46. See Duncan Forrester and Douglas Murray, eds., *Studies in the History of Worship in the Church of Scotland* (Edinburgh: T&T Clark, 1984).

47. Gregg Alan Mast, *The Eucharistic Service of the Catholic Apostolic Church and its Influence on Reformed Liturgical Renewals of the Nineteenth Century* (Lanham, Md.: Scarecrow Press, 1999).

48. Amongst the committee who prepared this liturgy was the liturgical scholar W. D. Maxwell, who himself had been the pupil of Richard Davidson, architect of the 1932 *Book of*

issued in 1979, though it was not popular. Finally, 1994 saw the publication of *Common Order* (revised 1996), which draws on contemporary liturgical and ecumenical scholarship, as well as Celtic spirituality.[49]

This list of liturgies witnesses to the erosion of the older "radical" suspicion or rejection of written (printed) forms of prayer, and re-establishes the older tradition of the sixteenth century. This does not mean that the radicals do not have their modern successors; there are still some ministers who insist that the true Reformed tradition is betrayed when printed forms are used. The printed forms, however, provide a standard. The book is available for the use of the minister as a guide and a resource, though the forms are not compulsory. Given the encouragement of congregational participation, some of these forms, where responses and congregational material require it, can be printed separately and can be in the hands of the congregation. Thus set prayers once more take their place alongside the tradition of free prayer.

Further Reading

Davies, Horton. *The Worship of the English Puritans.* Morgan, Pa.: Soli Deo Gloria Publications, 1997 [1948].

Forrester, Duncan, and Douglas Murray. *Studies in the History of Worship in Scotland.* Edinburgh: T&T Clark, 1984. Revised, 1999.

Maxwell, W. D. *The Liturgical Portions of the Genevan Service Book.* 2nd ed. London: Faith Press, 1965.

Spinks, Bryan D. *Freedom or Order?: The Eucharistic Liturgy in English Congregationalism, 1645-1980.* Allison Park, Pa.: Pickwick Publications, 1984.

————. *From the Lord and "the Best Reformed Churches": A Study of the Eucharistic Liturgy in the English and Puritan Separatist Traditions, 1550-1663.* Rome: CLV, 1984.

————. *Sacraments, Ceremonies, and the Stuart Divines: Sacramental Theology and Liturgy in England and Scotland, 1603-1662.* Burlington, Vt.: Ashgate Pub., 2001.

Common Order of the United Church of Canada. See Thomas Harding, *Patterns of Worship in The United Church of Canada 1925-1987* (Toronto: Evensong, 1996).

49. See the review of the *Book of Common Order* in *Scottish Journal of Theology* 52 (1999): 262-65.; Bryan D. Spinks and Iain R. Torrance, *To Glorify God: Essays on Modern Reformed Liturgy* (Grand Rapids: Eerdmans, 1999).

The Worship of English Congregationalism

Alan P. F. Sell

Congregational Origins and Geographical Spread

To begin with, a summary definition: Congregationalism (a polity shared by Baptists, some Pentecostalists, and others) is that form of church government rooted in the conviction that God graciously calls out a people for his praise and service, and that to be a member of the church catholic is to be a member of a local church gathered under the sole Lordship of Christ.[1] There are not many churches, but the one church in many places, and it comprises those who have by grace entered into a covenant, created at the initiative of God, whereby they are in fellowship with God and with their fellow church members. The church gathers under the sole Lordship of Christ, to whom, as a corporate priesthood, the members have direct access. In worship, united together, they praise God and receive the gospel proclaimed by word of mouth and enacted in the sacraments; in church meeting they seek the mind of Christ, and unanimity in him, concerning their corporate life and mission, ever aspiring to be a body disciplined for his service.

While the polity of the gathered church was deemed by those who promoted it to be in accordance with Scripture, it is equally the case that its outworking was influenced by the sociopolitical circumstances in which Congre-

---

1. For the history of the ecclesiology of Congregationalism and its Separatist harbingers see Alan P. F. Sell, *Saints: Visible, Orderly and Catholic: The Congregational Idea of the Church* (Geneva: World Alliance of Reformed Churches; and Allison Park, Pa.: Pickwick Publications, 1956). There is circumstantial evidence that the polity may have been influenced by Anabaptist refugees who settled especially in parts of East Anglia and the East Midlands. For this complicated matter see Alan P. F. Sell, *Dissenting Thought and the Life of the Churches: Studies in an English Tradition* (Lewiston, N.Y.: Edwin Mellen Press, 1990), chap. 20.

gationalists and their Separatist forebears lived. It will therefore be helpful to outline very briefly the course of events following Henry VIII's breach with Rome and the Anglican Settlement of 1534.

To those who sought a more thorough reformation of the English church, matters were by no means resolved by the settlement. Inspired by contacts with such continental Reformers as Bucer, Peter Martyr, and Ochino, the Puritans (as their name implies) sought purity of worship and church order according to the Scriptures and opposed what they regarded as the "trappings" of Rome. During the reign of Mary (1553-1558) many Puritans were persecuted, exiled, or driven underground. Under Elizabeth I (1558-1603) the drive, in the interests of national cohesion, for religious uniformity under an episcopalian system prompted the Puritans to adopt one of three main positions. Some sought a Reformed church-state on episcopalian lines; others, among them Thomas Cartwright (1535-1603), advocated a Reformed church-state along presbyterian lines; while others, the radical Puritans, despaired of achieving a truly purified church within an establishment structure. These last became known as Separatists, and they were the harbingers of Congregationalism.

In the early seventeenth century James I (r. 1603-1625) declared of all nonconformists, "I will make them conform, or I will harry them out of the land." Accordingly, many Separatists fled to Holland, and from there some, joined by others from England, went in 1620 as Pilgrims to the New World. Their counterparts at home went underground until, following a period of considerable unrest, the civil war broke out, Charles I was beheaded in 1649, and Oliver Cromwell (1599-1658) came to power in 1653. The Independents or Congregationalists now breathed more freely, and, indeed, assumed positions of authority during the Protectorate (1649-1660). But with the Restoration of the monarch in 1660 a harsh drive for conformity under episcopalianism was resumed. Between 1660 and 1662 nearly 2,000 clergymen were ejected from their livings because they would not give their "unfeigned assent and consent" to the *Book of Common Prayer* of the Church of England. Among these were 172 Congregationalists, about 1,700 Presbyterians, and 7 or 8 Baptists.[2] Once again nonconformist worship was strictly illegal, and a number of punitive laws (applied with varying degrees of rigor) were enacted against dissenting groups, with none suffering more than the Quakers. In 1689, following the accession to the throne of William of Orange, the so-called[3] Toleration Act be-

2. Some of the ejected ministers later conformed. See A. G. Matthews, *Calamy Revised* (Oxford: Clarendon Press, 1988 [1934]).

3. "So-called" because the word *toleration* appears neither in the title nor in the text of the Act.

came law. No earlier adverse legislation was repealed, but it was stated that henceforth it would not be applied against orthodox Protestant dissenters. (In other words, Jews, Roman Catholics, and Unitarians were not within the terms of the Act.) Nevertheless, for the first time worship other than that of the Church of England was legalized.[4]

While ever wary of formal subscription to creeds and confessions[5] — originally on the grounds that creeds and confessions were the work of men, not the word of God, and hence could not be binding upon the conscience — Congregationalists have not been slow to confess their faith. Indeed, they have done this in a variety of ways: individuals made their personal confession of faith and signed the local church covenant; ministers delivered a (sometimes lengthy) confession of faith when they were ordained and inducted; they all confessed the faith in their hymns; and they devised numerous statements of the faith commonly held among Congregationalists as a whole.[6]

As far as English Congregationalism is concerned, the Savoy Declaration of Faith and Order of 1658 may be said to have achieved classical status. John Owen (1613-1683), one of England's leading seventeenth-century theologians, was one of those responsible for it, and he and his colleagues were indebted to the exposition of Congregationalism propounded by John Cotton, formerly of Boston, Lincolnshire, latterly of Boston, New England. With certain modifications of wording, Savoy largely follows the Westminster Confession, in the preparing of which some prominent Congregationalists had been involved.[7] One reason for this was that the Declaration's authors wished to demonstrate their doctrinal orthodoxy in face of such scurrilous charges as that Congregationalism was "the sink of all Heresies and Schisms." Savoy does, however, omit Westminster chapters XXX and XXXI, concerning church censures, synods, and councils — Parliament having objected to these

4. See further Alan P. F. Sell, *Commemorations: Studies in Christian Thought and History,* (Eugene, Ore.: Wipf & Stock, 1998 [1993]), chap. 5.

5. Despite Congregationalists' refusal of subscription, it was nevertheless the case that during the eighteenth century it was the Presbyterians, not the Congregationalists, who became largely Arian and then Unitarian (even though Unitarianism was not legalized until 1813). See further Alan P. F. Sell, *Dissenting Thought and the Life of the Churches,* chap. 5.

6. See further Alan P. F. Sell, *Dissenting Thought and the Life of the Churches,* chap. 1. For a collection of Congregational statements of faith see Williston Walker, *The Creeds and Platforms of Congregationalism* (Boston: Pilgrim Press, 1960 [1893]). The most recent reprint of the Savoy Declaration is in David M. Thompson, *Stating the Gospel: Formulations and Declarations of Faith from the Heritage of the United Reformed Church* (Edinburgh: T&T Clark, 1990).

7. In turn, the Particular Baptist confession of 1677 drew heavily upon the Savoy Declaration.

as being too Scottish. It includes a new chapter, "Of the Gospel, and of the ectent of the Grace thereof," it adds to Westminster's statements on the civil magistrate, and it modifies Westminster's paragraphs "Of the Church." To the Declaration is appended the *Savoy Declaration of the Institution of Churches, and the Order appointed in them by Jesus Christ.* This comprises thirty paragraphs, the central message of which is that members of particular churches

> are Saints by Calling, visibly manifesting and evidencing (in and by their profession and walking) their obedience unto that Call of Christ, who being further known to each other by their confession of the Faith wrought in them by the power of God, declared by themselves or otherwise manifested, do willingly consent to walk together according to the appointment of Christ, giving up themselves to the Lord, and to one another by the will of God in professed subjection to the Ordinances of the Gospel.

Congregationalism Further Afield

Lest it appear parochial to focus upon the liturgical story of one strand of the Reformed family in its country of origin, it should be remembered that Congregationalism was carried to America by the Pilgrims of the 1620s; to the South Seas, China, India, Southeast Asia, Africa, and the West Indies by the London Missionary Society (LMS, 1795); and to Canada, Newfoundland, Australia, New Zealand, and South Africa by the Colonial (from 1957, Commonwealth) Missionary Society (CMS, 1836).[8] Although it was the "fundamental principle" of the LMS that the gospel, not Congregationalism, was to be proclaimed,[9] the polity, with culturally appropriate modifications, came to be present in all the places specified. The LMS and CMS united on 1 July 1966 to form the Congregational Council for World Mission, which was then enlarged in 1973 and renamed the Council for World Mission. The standard histories of the missionary societies do not discuss the forms of worship that were exported, and certainly the societies as such did not prescribe particular forms. The safest assumption is that the early missionaries — moderate Calvinistic evangelicals for the most part — took with them the free tradition of

---

8. See further John von Rohr, *The Shaping of American Congregationalism 1620-1957* (Cleveland: Pilgrim Press, 1992); Norman Goodall, *A History of the London Missionary Society* (London: Oxford University Press, 1954); Ralph Calder, *One Commonwealth for God* (London: Independent Press, 1966).

9. See R. Lovett, *History of the London Missionary Society* (London: Oxford University Press, 1899), vol. 1, p. 49.

worship they had inherited, and that in addition to singing and prayers, Bible teaching in the service of basic Christian proclamation was prominent in their services.

The Congregational family was further enlarged in the nineteenth century as a result of both American missionary work in Brazil and evangelical revivals and movements in Europe, from which emerged the Church of the Brethren (Czech Republic); the Mission Covenant churches of Sweden, Finland, and Denmark; and the Greek Evangelical Church. During the twentieth century a further Congregational union was formed in Brazil, and one was constituted in Argentina. The historic Dutch Remonstrant Church, which was not granted religious toleration until 1795, was, like the others mentioned in this paragraph, a member of, or in association with, the International Congregational Council (1891), which united with the World Presbyterian Alliance (1875) to form the World Alliance of Reformed Churches (Presbyterian and Congregational) in 1970.[10]

In what follows I hope to show that over the 450 years of its life the English Congregational tradition has manifested considerable variety in its understanding and practice of public worship. We shall see that much of this variety is attributable to the ever-changing sociopolitical and intellectual environment. I shall suggest that from this story there emerge some "matters arising" which have wider than English, and wider than Congregational, implications.

Congregational Worship in Context

Separatists and Early Congregationalists

At a time when the authorities in the land sought civil order cemented by legally required religious comprehension, those who sought a fuller reform, and who believed that it was not the prerogative of the monarch or government of the day to legislate upon matters of worship and church order, were necessarily Separatists from the church "by law established," and members of underground movements. While we know of their existence, their records are, for obvious reasons, scanty. We do, however, have news of a group of Christians meeting in London in 1567. They were members of Richard Fitz's "privie [that is, private] church," and what is especially interesting about them, given some

10. For the world families see Ralph Calder, *To Introduce the [Congregational] Family* (London: Independent Press, 1953); Marcel Pradervand, *A Century of Service: A History of the World Alliance of Reformed Churches 1875-1975* (Edinburgh: Saint Andrew Press, 1975).

within later Congregationalism who did not give the sacraments their due, is that among the objectives of Fitz's church was "To haue the Sacraments mynistred purely, onely and all together accordinge to the institution and goode worde of the Lorde Jesus, without any tradicion of inuention of man."[11] To the Separatist mind (and in a delightful mirror image of nineteenth-century Anglo-Catholic attitudes toward the allegedly "invalid" sacraments of the non-conformists) true sacraments are to be found only in the true church; the Church of England is Antichrist, and hence there are no true sacraments there. As the Separatist lawyer Henry Barrow (1550-1593) put it, "A false churche cannot have trewe sacraments, neither iz there trewe substance or promise of blessinge to false sacraments."[12] Another Separatist, Robert Harrison, declared that by baptism we are received into God's house, while the Lord's Supper, "which we are often to receyue," is "the foode wherewith our soules are nourished."[13] No Separatist expressed more clearly than Robert Browne (1550-1633) the relation between the church as the saints gathered and the Lord's Supper as the means and expression of churchly unity:

> The Lords supper is a Sacrament or marke of the apparent Church, sealing vnto vs by the breaking and eating of breade and drinking the Cuppe in one holie communion, and by the worde accordinglie preached, that we are happilie redeemed by the breaking of the bodie and shedding of the bloud of Christ Iesus, and we thereby growe into one bodie, and church, in one communion of graces, whereof Christ is the heade, to keepe and seake agreement vnder one lawe and gouernement in all thankefulness & holy obedience.[14]

From a deposition lodged in 1588 against a church comprising followers of Henry Barrow we learn something of their worship and use of Sunday, though there is no reference to the Lord's Supper:

> In the somer tyme they mett together in the fields a mile or more about london. there they sit down vppon A Bank & divers of them expound out

---

11. Champlin Burrage, *The Early English Dissenters in the Light of Recent Research* (Cambridge: The University Press, 1912) vol. 2, p. 13, quoting *State Papers Domestic, Elizabeth I, Addenda* xx, 107.I.

12. Henry Barrow, "Reply to Dr. Some's A Godly Treatise," in *The Writings of Henry Barrow 1587-1590,* ed. Leland H. Carlson (London: Allen and Unwin, 1962), p. 157.

13. R. Harrison, *Three Formes of Catechismes* (1583), in *The Writings of Robert Harrison and Robert Browne,* ed. A. Peel and Leland H. Carlson (London: Allen and Unwin, 1953), p. 140.

14. Robert Browne, *A Booke which sheweth the life and manners of all true Christians* (1582), in *The Writings of Robert Harrison and Robert Browne,* ed. Peel and Carlson, pp. 279-80.

of the bible so long as they are there assembled. In the winter tyme they assemble themselves by 5. of the clocke in the morning to that howse where they make there Conventicle for that Saboth daie men & women together there they Continewe in there kind of praier and exposicion of Scriptures all that daie. They dyne together. After dinner make collection to paie for their diet & what mony is left somme one of them carrieth it to the prisons where any of their sect be committed. In their praier one speketh and the rest doe groane, or sob. or sigh, as if they would ring out teares . . . there prayer is extemporall. In there conventicles they vse not the lordes praier, nor any forme of sett praier.[15]

What is interesting here is the insistence on extempore prayer as evidence of the determination *not to* be bound to a prayer book composed by men as well as a determination *to* be open to the Spirit. The Separatists were among the charismatics of their day, and this emerges also in their predilection for prophesying during worship — even though they did not expect the Holy Spirit to extend the gift of prophecy to women. As for singing, the psalms only were approved, and certainly not what Henry Barrow called "the apocryphal erroneous ballads in time-song" prescribed in the *Book of Common Prayer* of the Church of England.

Whether radical or not, all Puritans throughout the seventeenth century gave great place to the preaching of the word and to the observance of what they called the Lord's Day. Though by no means the humorless, pious prigs of caricature (at least the majority of them were not), they nevertheless repudiated traditional festivals and saints' days because of their associations with Rome, their superstitious aspects, and their overlooking of the fact that the saints are all those whom God gathers into his church. As already hinted, the *Book of Common Prayer* was weighed and found wanting, not least because it was deemed to uphold the hated doctrine of baptismal regeneration, and this further dissuaded the dissenters from adopting set forms of prayer. Nevertheless, in 1645 the Westminster Assembly (the members of which included some Independent or Congregational representatives) did produce its *Directory,* which, though not containing set liturgies, offered guidance on the order of worship to those called to lead it. Such guidance notwithstanding, the form and content of Congregational worship varied considerably. When Robert Kirk of the Scottish Episcopal Church visited London shortly after the pass-

---

15. C. Burrage, *Early English Dissenters,* vol. 2, p. 27. See further Stephen H. Mayor, *The Lord's Supper in Early English Dissent* (London: Epworth Press, 1972). Barrow, together with his Separatist colleague John Greenwood, was martyred in 1593. See Alan P. F. Sell, *Commemorations,* chap. 4.

ing of the aforementioned Toleration Act of 1689 (which for the first time legalized non-Anglican worship, but only that of orthodox Protestant dissenters), he attended a service conducted by the Congregationalist George
Cockain. Kirk records that there were

> no psalms before or after sermon. The people heard sermon with heads
> covered, and stood at prayer. . . . The preacher prayed not for the
> Protestant Churches, nor English, nor any Churchmen, only barely for the
> King and High Council, without naming the Queen. He did plead vehe-
> mently with God for a young man at the grave's mouth . . . saying, "Lord,
> 'tis rare to find a good man, more a good young man. Thou sparest
> 10,000ds of debauched youths, may not this dry but tender and fruitful
> branch escape the blast of thy displeasure. Save his soul. Spare his body.
> Sanctify all to the parents seeing though dost it, not theirs nor ours, but thy
> will be done." He had not the blessing at the end. The minister vested in a
> black coat.[16]

The narrowly focused pastoral concern in the prayer is noteworthy here,
as is the absence of singing, especially considering that many Puritans happily
used metrical psalms in worship.[17] It is more than likely that this reluctance to
sing resulted from the belief that since the apostolic exhortation was to sing
with grace in one's heart, it would be wrong for the grace-less in a "promiscu-
ous" congregation to join in.

Thus far we see, speaking generally, that in the worship of the Congregationalists and their Separatist harbingers, the preaching of the word is central,
the sacraments are given due place, metrical psalms are sung, extempore
prayers are used, and set liturgies are despised as cramping the Spirit, preventing earnest prayer relevant to local needs, leading to formalism in worship,
and, when officially imposed, denying that freedom under Christ which is an
essential gift of God to his church. Creeds are not used in worship on the
grounds that assent to them may be made a test of membership and that they
may fossilize the faith and overemphasize its intellectual aspects; they are

16. From D. Maclean, *London at Worship, 1689-1690,* quoted by A. G. Matthews, "The
Puritans," in *Christian Worship: Studies in its Hsitory and Meaning by Members of Mansfield College,* ed. Nathaniel Micklem (London: Oxford University Press, 1936), p. 180.

17. On Puritan worship, see further Matthews, "The Puritans," pp. 172-88; Horton
Davies, *The Worship of the English Puritans* (London: Dacre Press, 1948); and for the period
1690 to the present, Horton Davies, *Worship and Theology in England,* 5 vols. (Princeton:
Princeton University Press, 1961-75). For the Lord's Supper see Bryan D. Spinks, *Freedom or
Order? The Eucharistic Liturgy in English Congregationalism 1645-1980* (Allison Park, Pa.: Pick-
wick Publications, 1984).

manmade, whereas Scripture is the word of God, and for this reason Christians are expected to make their own confessions of faith.[18] Separatists and Puritans alike sought a form of worship in accordance with Christ's will and with apostolic practice, and there would have been widespread agreement with John Owen that the "chiefest acts and parts" of worship are *"preaching of the word, administration of the sacraments, and the exercise of discipline;* all to be performed with prayer and thanksgiving."[19] While it would take us too far afield to pursue the theme of church discipline here, we should note that the quest of a pure church inspired the fencing of the Lord's table so that church members only were permitted to receive what was, after all, a sacrament of the church.

Singing, Sermons, and Prayers in the Eighteenth Century

The gradual transition from exclusive metrical psalmody to paraphrases and thence to full-blown Christian hymns enabled the Congregationalists of the eighteenth century to offer some of their best gifts to the world church. I refer, of course, to the hymns of Isaac Watts (1674-1748) and Philip Doddridge (1702-1751), "When I Survey the Wondrous Cross" and "Hark the Glad Sound" among them. Isaac Watts also produced *A Guide to Prayer,* in which he advocates biblically grounded, orderly free or conceived prayer, the parts of which he summarizes in verse thus:

> Call upon God, adore, confess,
> Petition, plead, and then declare
> You are the Lord's, give thanks and bless,
> And let Amen confirm the prayer.[20]

For an example of a service of worship in eighteenth-century London we may turn to the Bury Street Independent Meeting:

---

18. See further Geoffrey F. Nuttall, *Congregationalists and Creeds* (London: Epworth Press, 1966); Alan P. F. Sell, *Dissenting Thought and the Life of the Churches,* pp. 57-58.

19. J. Owen, *A Discourse concerning Liturgies and their Imposition,* in his *Works* (1850-1853), ed. W. H. Goold (London: The Banner of Truth Trust, 1966), p. 10. Congregational teaching on these matters is summarized in *The Savoy Declaration of Faith and Order,* 1658, itself patterned closely upon the Westminster Confession of 1647, though with modifications of varying degrees of significance.

20. I. Watts, *A Guide to Prayer* (1715), abridged and edited by Harry Escott (London: Epworth Press, 1948), p. 50.

In the morning we begin with singing a psalm, then a short prayer follows to desire the Divine Presence in all the following parts of worship; after that, about half an hour in the exposition of some portion of Scripture, which is succeeded by singing a psalm or an hymn. After this the minister prays more at large, for all the variety of blessings, spiritual and temporal, for the whole congregation, with confession of sins, and thanksgiving for mercies; petitions also are offered up for the whole world, for all our rulers and governors, together with any particular cases which are represented. Then a sermon is preached, and the morning worship concluded with a short prayer and the benediction.[21]

When the Lord's Supper was kept at Bury Street it followed the sermon, though elsewhere, as recommended by Philip Doddridge, there was a gap between what we would later learn to call the liturgy of the catechumens and the liturgy of the table. It may well be that in Doddridge's mind was the desirability of ensuring that only church members partook of the Supper. But by the twentieth century the gap between the two services had become the occasion for wrapping up and distributing flowers and counting the offering — abominations from which that century's liturgical renewal did much to deliver us. It cannot be denied that the sermon gained increasing prominence during the eighteenth century, and to some it took precedence over all other parts of the service, which came to be regarded as preliminaries. Indeed, some people absented themselves from the lengthy prayer preceding the sermon, and if one cannot agree with this practice, one can at least understand it, when such prayers were, as Horton Davies has remarked, "occasionally Pentecostal" but "more frequently Purgatorial."[22] Consider Samuel Brewer of Stepney Meeting, London. We are told that he "was remarkable for great particularity in prayer" and that

> Having many seafaring people among his hearers, when a merchant ship was going to sail, he specified the captain, the mate, the carpenter, the boatswain, and all the sailors with great affection; and, it is said, that impressed with a belief of the benefit of his prayers, they frequently brought him home, as a token of gratitude, something of the produce of the country to which they went.[23]

21. *Transactions of the Congregational Historical Society,* VI, p. 334.

22. H. Davies, "Liturgical Reform in Nineteenth-Century English Congregationalism," *Congregational Historical Society Transactions* XVII, no. 3 (August 1954): 75.

23. David Bogue and James Bennett, *The History of Dissenters from the Revolution to the Year 1898,* 2nd ed. (London: Frederick Westley and A. H. Davis, 1833), vol. 2, p. 634.

Some Nineteenth-Century Developments

Perhaps not surprisingly in view of such pastoral prolixity, a number of moves were made during the nineteenth century to tidy up worship. Thus in 1812 *A New Directory for Nonconformist Churches Containing Remarks on Their Mode of Public Worship, and a Plan for the Improvement of It* was published, and as the century progressed numerous other liturgical handbooks followed. Not the least of the motives in all of this activity was the hope of making worship more palatable to the mercantile classes, from amongst whom the Congregationalists were increasingly drawing members. Robert Vaughan (1795-1868) was not untypical in explaining that "Distinguished laymen who take their place frankly among protestant dissenters, need not be apprehensive that the respect shown to their civil rank elsewhere, will be wanting on the part of their new friends."[24] There was also the influence of Anglo-Catholicism, with whose ritualistic extravagances (from their point of view) the Congregationalists had no patience at all, but from which they derived inspiration to seek liturgical propriety in their own way. Finally, under the influence of Romanticism, there was a greater concern for that which was aesthetically sensitive and pleasing — a motive that influenced Congregational chapel architecture away from the meetinghouse style and toward Georgian "opera house" and Victorian Nonconformist Gothic.[25] Even the Unitarians, under the distinguished leadership of James Martineau (1805-1900), were reforming their worship — could Trinitarians do less?

In 1856, with all of these influences swirling around him, Thomas Binney, one of Congregationalism's most distinguished ministers, reminded his co-religionists (whilst overlooking some negative examples) that their nonconformist forebears "had no objection to a Liturgy *as such,* but only wished some changes to be made in that which was in use, — that is it should not be *exclusively* enforced, that there should be the means of giving variety to the services, and the opportunity afforded for free prayer."[26] In 1847 an anony-

---

24. R. Vaughan, *Congregationalism: or, the Polity of Independent Churches Viewed in Relation to the State and Tendencies of Modern Society,* 2nd rev. ed. (1842), p. 181.

25. Concerning the Gothic, John Huxtable lamented that "Those who planned such places of worship did not consider carefully enough the question whether the building in which the Church gathers should be designed principally for hearing God's Word read and preached or for seeing the drama of the Mass enacted." See his "Worship in Contemporary Congregationalism," in *Proceedings of the Ninth Assembly of the International Congregational Council* (London: Independent Press, 1962), p. 130.

26. Preface to Binney's edition of Charles Baird's *Eutaxia,* which was originally entitled *A Chapter on Liturgies: Historical Sketches* (London: Knight, 1856), pp. ix-x.

mous work, *The Congregational Service Book,* was published in which a creed
was not included because it was deemed unnecessary (although the *Te Deum*
was admitted). Also absent were printed prayers, on the ground that free
prayer is more biblical and more ancient.

A number of nineteenth-century directories[27] accorded no place to the
Lord's Supper — this possibly in reaction against Anglo-Catholic ritualism.
The *Declaration of Faith, Church Order and Discipline* adopted by the Congregational Union of England and Wales in 1833 specified that baptism was
to be administered to all converts and their children, and that the Lord's Supper was "to be celebrated by Christian Churches as a token of faith in the
Saviour, and of brotherly love." This meager anthropocentrism (which was
to be rebuked by a Union Commission exactly one hundred years later)[28]
fostered an increasingly "memorialist" understanding of the Lord's Supper,
so that R. W. Dale of Birmingham regretted that "There is little doubt that
modern Congregationalists, in their extreme dread of high sacramental doctrines, have drifted into pure Zwinglianism."[29] In further reaction against
ritualism and sacerdotalist ideas of priesthood, some Congregationalists
emphasized the priesthood of all believers in such a way as to permit what
(somewhat unfortunately) we nowadays call the lay celebration of the sacrament — something which their forebears would by no means have sanc-
tioned.[30] They further chirpily proclaimed that they were as catholic — if not
more so — as anyone else, not least because they did not bar professed believers from the Lord's table.

As for baptism, the individualism flowing down from the evangelical revival of the eighteenth century, with its emphasis upon conversion as the way
into the saved community, devastated the concept of the local covenanted
church comprising believers and their children; in addition, the creation by
larger churches of "mission stations," while they undoubtedly permitted many
to hear the gospel, did little to foster the Congregational church order with its
emphasis upon the baptized community and the centrality of church meet-

27. For the variety of such directories see Bryan D. Spinks, "The Liturgical Revival
amongst Nineteenth-Century English Congregationalists," *Studia Liturgical* XV, nos. 3-4
(1982-1983): 178-87.

28. See *The Report of the Commission on the Sacraments of Baptism and the Lord's Supper*
(London: Congregational Union of England and Wales, [1933]), p. 11.

29. R. W. Dale, in *Ecclesia,* ed. H. R. Reynolds (London, 1870), p. 371. On the other hand
the celebrated leader J. Guinness Rogers was among many who were quite unperturbed by
memorialism. See his "Sacramentalism," *The Congregationalist* XIII (1884), pp. 980-89.

30. The prohibition of lay presidency at the Lord's Table is strongly worded in the Savoy
paragraphs *Of the Institution of Churches.* See Article XVI.

ing.[31] Hence Robert Mackintosh's sardonic observation that infant baptism "stands as the one bulwark against the destruction of the Church in favour of the evangelistic committee."[32]

In connection with evangelism we should note that from the nineteenth century until well into the twentieth, many Congregational churches held a more formal or traditional service on Sunday mornings and a more evangelistic service in the evenings. Further dissuasives to liturgical fullness included biblical higher criticism, which persuaded some ministers that Jesus had not after all instituted baptism and the Lord's Supper,[33] and the rise of a genial universalism that not only drew the sting of "hellfire and damnation" preaching but also blurred the distinction between those who were "in Christ" and those who were not — the very distinction upon which Congregational ecclesiology turns.

Among those who spoke out against the subjectivism of memorialism were R. W. Dale, whose oft-reprinted Congregational lecture on *The Atonement* first appeared in 1875 and, in the next generation, P. T. Forsyth (1848-1921), whose book *Lectures on the Church and the Sacraments* was first published in 1917.[34] The latter work, which contained the declaration that "mere memorialism" is "a more fatal error than the Mass, and a far less lovely,"[35] did more than any other theological work to prepare a number of Congregationalists for the liturgical renewal of the twentieth century. Also of considerable significance in this respect was John Hunter's widely circulated book of *Devotional Services,* which was first published in 1890. An order for the Lord's Supper was included in the third edition.

---

31. For the dramatic decline in local covenants after 1820 see Alan P. F. Sell, *Dissenting Thought and the Life of the Churches,* chap. 1.

32. Robert Mackintosh, *The Insufficiency of Revivalism as a Religious System,* bound with *Essays Towards a New Theology* (Glasgow: Maclehose, 1889), p. 28.

33. Robert Mackintosh felt that a stronger case could be made for Jesus' institution of the Lord's Supper than for his institution of baptism, but held that "a certain element of doubt exists whether Jesus literally founded either of the two New Testament sacraments." See his paper, "The living church . . . Its Sacraments," *Proceedings of the International Congregational Council* (London: Congregational Union of England and Wales, 1930), V, p. 139. See further Alan P. F. Sell, *Robert Mackintosh: Theologian of Integrity* (Bern: Peter Lang, 1977), chap. 3.

34. In subsequent reprintings the words "Lectures on" were dropped from the title.

35. P. T. Forsyth, *The Church and the Sacraments* (London: Independent Press, 1947), xvi.

The Twentieth Century: Freedom within Order

In 1933 the Council of the Congregational Union of England and Wales received *The Report of the Commission on the Sacraments of Baptism and the Lord's Supper.* The commissioners included the liberal theologian C. J. Cadoux, the middle-of-the-road principal Sydney Cave, the historian Albert Peel, and Bernard Lord Manning, another historian. They made no secret of the differences of opinion among them, some being more certain than others that Jesus instituted the sacraments; some were satisfied with a memorialist view of the Lord's Supper (though not a *mere* memorialist view, for it is the Lord who is remembered), while others were keener to emphasize "the Christ Who is present with us, the risen Lord, Who gives Himself anew to those who come to His table in humble faith."[36] Of them all, Peel was perhaps the most radical in holding that

> 1. No one today would claim categorically that the two Sacraments were instituted by Christ and that He ordered them to be perpetually observed. 2. No one can claim that the Sacraments are indispensable, in so far as the like grace can be otherwise mediated. 3. No one will deny that Christians have lived faithful and devout lives without the use of the two sacraments. . . . 4. No one will deny that our Lord stresses the spirit and not the letter, principles on which to act rather than acts themselves. . . . 5. No one will claim that it accords with the mind of Christ to exclude from His Church believers on Him, on the ground that they do not accept the perpetual obligation of sacraments and make no use of them. . . . Are the outward symbols essential? Has not the experience of the Friends and others shown there is proved religious value in worship without symbols . . . ? . . . Let us claim that there is a baptism of the Spirit

---

36. *The Report of the Commission,* 21. I have reason to think that this latter view was held by my teacher of Christian doctrine, the greatly loved George Phillips, a member of the commission. At this point we are far removed from that "liturgicial fusspottery" which overtook some of those influenced by the liturgical renewal of the twentieth century, and finds a number today in many-hued vestments whose relation to the heritage is not altogether clear. George, raised among the Strict and Particular Baptists, would have greeted this with benign amusement ("Bless my soul!" was one of his favorite expostulations), but would never have fallen for it. W. E. Orchard was a Congregational minister who tended ever Romeward and, indeed, reached that destination. His book of prayers, *The Temple,* appealed to a wider circle of Congregationalists than did his liturgies, for which see Bryan D. Spinks, *Freedom or Order?* chap. 7. His Romish rite may have been permissible by the Congregational polity, but it was far removed from the Congregational tradition.

which all Christ's followers must have, but that does not necessarily include baptism by water.[37]

The significance of Peel's words is that they represent a Quaker-Anabaptist-influenced strand of Congregationalism that has been present from the beginning, and they come from the most distinguished Congregational historian of that day. Looking forward, Peel cautioned that "If a reunited Church were to be formed which was to rule out the Friends because they did not use the Sacraments, many Free Churchmen, certainly I for one, would range myself with the Friends — outside a man-made Church, yet within the spacious freedom of the Church of God."[38]

By now, however, more international breezes were beginning to be felt. There is no doubt that Barth's theology of the word made an impact upon such Congregationalists as H. F. Lovell Cocks, John Marsh, Hubert Cunliffe-Jones, W. A. Whitehouse, and Daniel Jenkins,[39] while the more homegrown influence of Forsyth left its mark upon B. L. Manning, John Huxtable, and, above all, Lovell Cocks. John Whale's particular contribution was the recovery for Congregationalism of its Reformation heritage. On 12 March 1939 a letter was addressed "To the ministers of Christ's Holy Gospel in the Churches of the Congregational Order." It was drafted by Manning and revised by Nathaniel Micklem and Whale. The other signatories were J. D. Jones of Bournemouth, principals Lovell Cocks and E. J. Price, and John Short. It was a call to a deeper understanding of the church and of its life as utterly dependent upon the gospel of God's free grace. Because of their recourse to the faith of the ages, and especially because of their renewed emphasis upon the Reformed tradition, this group and their associates attracted the label "Genevan."

The burgeoning of the modern ecumenical movement, to which the Genevan party was committed, broadened liturgical horizons and cut a channel through which flowed continental liturgical influences.[40] The Church Order Group was formed in 1946 to stimulate liturgical renewal and a concern for good church order within Congregationalism, and while only a minority of ministers became active members of it, the group's influence was more widely beneficial in fostering the view that word and sacrament belong together, and

37. A. Peel, *Christian Freedom* (London: Independent Press, 1938), pp. 79-83.

38. Peel, *Christian Freedom*, p. 84.

39. Though none of them swallowed Barth whole, some being especially critical of his hostile attitude toward natural theology.

40. Not indeed that all ecumenists were necessarily Barthians. To one of Congregationalism's pioneer ecumenists, A. E. Garvie, the Barthian theology was "a minor evil product of the War." See his "Fifty Years' Retrospect," *Congregational Quarterly* VII (1929): 21.

that the pattern of approach, ministry of the word, and response to the word in the offertory and prayers of thanksgiving, or in the Lord's Supper, should be the norm as far as the local church's full diet of public worship was concerned.

One way of registering the changing attitude is by comparing service books. The book with which I was presented on leaving my home church for college was *A Manual for Ministers,* first published in 1936. This was the successor to the *Book of Congregational Worship* of 1920. It draws upon a number of sources, though its general theological cast is mildly liberal; it includes suggestions for the several parts of worship, as well as services of baptism and the Lord's Supper. It acknowledges much, but not all, of the Christian year (no Advent, no Trinity Sunday), compensating with services for Hospital Sunday, Peace Sunday, Choir Sunday, and the like. Of this book John Huxtable somewhat saucily remarked that it "had few redeeming features. Its liturgical formlessness found compensation in an appendix full of information about ministerial insurance; and there was an excellent order for the opening of a sale of work."[41] With this book may be contrasted *A Book of Public Worship Compiled for the Use of Congregationalists* by John Huxtable, John Marsh, Romilly Micklem, and James Todd (1948). This reveals the degree to which liturgical lessons had been learned, and the term *sale of work* is nowhere to be found. However, Geoffrey F. Nuttall, Congregationalism's leading historian of the Separatists and Puritans, and himself not influenced by the Quaker-Anabaptist strand of the Congregational heritage, observed in his review of this book that "Throughout Dr. Marsh's Introduction our traditional repudiation of such books is not discussed, while dependence on the Spirit's leadings is not mentioned at all."[42] Few strove more resolutely to hold the balance than W. Gordon Robinson, who chaired the committee appointed by the Congregational Union of England and Wales to produce *A Book of Services and Prayers* (1959), which appeared just in time for my ordination. In the contents the heritage of the faith of the ages is acknowledged, and the services are shaped in an orderly way, but space is left for *Our Heritage of Free Prayer* — the title of a pamphlet anonymously prepared by Gordon Robinson for the Union in the 1950s.[43]

Not all of public worship takes it cue directly from service books, however ill- or well-prepared they may be. I have in mind especially the children of

---

41. J. Huxtable, "Worship in contemporary Congregationalism," p. 131.

42. Geoffrey F. Nuttall, review in *The Congregational Quarterly* XXVI, no. 4 (1948): 367.

43. *A Book of Services and Prayers* is not accurately described by Bryan Spinks as a "neo-orthodox" book. See his *Freedom or Order?* p. 189. To my knowledge some fifty percent of the committee members would have declined to be so labeled.

the church and the way in which the traditional (that is, post–late-eighteenth-century) Sunday School gave way from the middle of the twentieth century onward to family worship in various permutations. In this matter the Congregationalists were pioneers, and the leadership given by H. A. Hamilton and his colleagues at Westhill College, Selly Oak, Birmingham, was widely influential. Increasingly, whole families gathered for the opening parts of the service, the children leaving at a certain point for worship and instruction appropriate to their age-groups. Sometimes they would return either to witness or (more rarely and more recently) to partake in the Lord's Supper. I shall return to this important segment of the church's membership in due course.

In 1972 the majority of the English and English-speaking Welsh Congregationalists united with the Presbyterian Church of England to form the United Reformed Church, and with this union my story ends. There could hardly have been a more fitting climax than the paragraphs on worship in the *Declaration of Faith* published by the Congregational Church in England and Wales in 1967. The first paragraph of this section is as follows:

> God calls the Church into renewed love and obedience to himself through its worship. The worship of the Church is expressed in many ways: through prayer and praise, through the reading of the Bible and the proclamation of Christ in preaching, through the sacraments of Baptism and the Lord's Supper, through many and varied acts of devotion and Christian ordinances, and through the fellowship and decisions of the Church. In all worship, God is present in his Word of Grace. Our part is to respond, in adoration and fidelity, by hearing and obeying him.[44]

I fear that I have been able only to distill the essence of a vast literature extending over 450 years. I trust, however, that it has become clear that the English Congregationalists, though always intending to ground themselves in Scripture, have been significantly influenced in their interpretation of the Bible by the ecclesiastical, intellectual, and sociopolitical environment in which they have lived. In the early decades they saw themselves as over against the Church of England, and there was a psychological tendency to do things differently on principle. The same thing happened during the Anglo-Catholic heyday in the nineteenth century. With the advent of modern biblical scholarship there has been less of a desire to adopt the earlier restorationist attitude to worship and church order; and in the twentieth century, openness to other

---

44. *A Declaration of Faith*, reprinted in *Reformed Witness Today: A Collection of Confessions and Statements of Faith issued by Reformed Churches*, ed. Lukas Vischer (Bern: Evangelische Arbeitsstelle Oukumene Schweiz, 1982), p. 142.

Christian traditions at home and abroad lessened the fear of utilizing liturgical material from elsewhere. After a somewhat patchy period during much of the nineteenth century, the sacraments have been restored to their former prominence, and, more often than not, are related in the liturgy to the preaching of the word — an activity which has never declined, however much it may from time to time have been abused (and even from time to time replaced among the *avant garde* by spontaneous dialogues, dramatic presentations, liturgical dance, and suchlike). In the last sixty years much more attention has been paid to the place of children in worship than hitherto. But for all the general increase of orderliness, there still linger (in my view rightly) echoes of the view that a minister who cannot pray without a book is somehow less than a complete pastor. And now that many churches have resorted to one service per Sunday only, the attempt in some quarters to marry the more formal liturgy with the more evangelistic type of meeting in such a way that the Te Deum rubs shoulders with banal jingles projected on the wall, and stockbrokers find themselves liberally bestowing the kiss of peace upon people from whom they hide behind the *Financial Times* on the train on Mondays to Fridays, may well offend the liturgically correct, confuse the babes in Christ, and vastly irritate the old hands.

Some Matters Arising

I turn now, and briefly, to some matters arising from the foregoing account. I suspect that some at least of these will have a bearing upon the entire Reformed family, not only upon those from the Congregational part of it.

Freedom within Order

The case study of Congregational worship shows that in different periods recourse has been had to the Bible for guidance on worship, but that what has been discovered has to a considerable extent depended upon the ecclesiastical and sociopolitical circumstances of the seekers and the attitude taken toward the question of biblical authority. If public worship is to be our own, it cannot be simply that of a previous age, but neither can it be something we invent anew each morning as we kick over the traces of all that has gone before. There are proper issues of the heritage of praise on the one hand and liturgical adventurousness on the other, and these need to be held in balance, if only on the pastoral ground of the proper security of the flock. The rhythm of the familiar is not altogether to be despised. But if pastoral sensitivity is to be prized, so is intellectual integrity, and this is a perennial challenge both in ordering worship and in preaching. I should, nevertheless, need a lot of persuading before I could agree that the full diet of Christian worship (and worship does not have always to be the "full diet" — it can take many forms) should be anything other than the holding together of the word and Lord's Supper in a liturgy in which the rhythm of approach, ministry of the word, and response at the table are clearly preserved. As the Congregational Union's Commission reported, "Our classic position is Calvinistic, and involves the belief that there is no difference of meaning between the preaching of the Word of God and the Sacraments; both of them alike 'hold forth and offer Christ to us, and in Him the treasures of heavenly grace.'"[45]

What seems quite clear is that the distinction between liturgical churches and nonliturgical churches is quite misplaced. *Liturgy* means service, and there are simply more and less adequate liturgies. Lest that sound elitist, let me hasten to point out that by *adequate* I do not mean in the first place "having liturgical propriety." That may well be a bonus, but by an adequate liturgy I mean one which enables people in diverse times and places to offer their praise to God and to hear and respond to his word. It is possible to be too liturgically precious — as if the kingdom will not come if the *epiklesis* is misplaced. It is possible, on the other hand, to be abysmally careless, as when we forget that it is God with whom we have to do. In this latter connection I recall an incident concerning the Jesuit theologian, Avery Dulles. It is said that during a service of worship he was horrified to see a banner hanging on the wall of the church proclaiming the sentimental heresy, "God is other people." When he could bear it no longer he went out to the vestry and returned with a marker pen, went to the banner and inserted a comma, so that it now read, "God is other, people."

At their best the Congregationalists strove for freedom within order. In their origins they were charismatic in the sense of being open to the Spirit's prompting and in freely addressing God in extempore prayers. Might it be that, for all the benefits to be derived from drawing upon the liturgical inheritance of the ages, the pendulum has today swung too far in the direction of liturgical scriptedness? In this connection I should like to pay tribute to the skill in conceived prayer of W. Gordon Robinson, author of the booklet *Our Heritage of Free Prayer,* to which I referred earlier. He was my college principal, and it was liturgically inspiring to experience six years of his prayers in college cha-

---

45. *The Report of the Commission on the Sacraments of Baptism and the Lord's Supper,* p. 20.

pel. The prayers were biblically grounded, orderly, rhythmically phrased, and ever fresh. One soon learned that what comes out in free prayer is directly related to what has previously gone on in terms of Bible study and personal meditation. There is nothing haphazard or "off the cuff" about it.

Again, freedom within order comes into view in connection with the attempt in some circles to marry the more traditional order of worship with the more evangelistic. I have already referred to this challenge, but now I add the thought that where the focus is on ever larger congregations, and where church growth methods and the corporate model are employed to this end, the question arises, Can a worshiping group be so large as to be a church no longer? With this question we come to the relation between worship and polity.

Worship and Polity: The Church Meeting

In the nineteenth century, during the period of expansion when nonconformists were building ever-larger chapels, one writer declared that "a chapel of over a thousand seats was a denial of basic nonconformist principles."[46] What did he mean? He had in mind the traditional understanding, now so frequently lost, that those who gather under the preaching of the word and receive the bread and wine together at the Lord's table then proceed to church meeting; there, under the guidance of the Spirit, their primary task is the creedal one of confessing the Lordship of Christ over all the work and witness of their church, and seeking his will in that matter. It is a Christocratic assembly where unanimity in Christ is sought (which does not mean that all agree with everything), not a democratic one in which there is one person, one vote, and government by the majority; and it should be conducted by the one called to lead the saints to the throne of grace, and not by some managerial type who is "good at meetings." Least of all should it be called the church's "business meeting." The critic of large buildings was therefore unable to conceive how one could have a church meeting of more than a thousand people. How much more would he have boggled at local churches of five or ten thousand or more members?

You will recall that in the opening paragraph of the section on worship in the Congregational *Declaration of Faith* of 1967, it is stated that one of the ways worship is expressed is "through the fellowship and decisions of the Church." The point is heavily underlined in the immediately following section on "Membership." The connection between the Sunday worship and the church

---

46. So J. H. Y. Briggs, *The English Baptists of the 19th Century* (Didcot: Baptist Historical Society, 1994), p. 13, referring to *The Patriot*, 11 January 1866.

meeting, though frequently obscured by Congregationalists themselves, is, I continue to believe, one of the tradition's great gifts to the church at large. It is also the point at which the Congregational tradition completes the Reformation on the side of polity, for whereas Calvin stopped at elders and deacons, the Congregationalists have sought to involve the whole people of God in ministry; and it seems odd, and possibly an indication of an individualistic understanding of ministry, that such a document as *Baptism, Eucharist and Ministry,* while it emphasizes the importance of the ministry of the whole people of God, does not recommend changes of church polity which would facilitate the common seeking of God's will by the corporate holy priesthood.[47]

Those whose polity does incorporate church meeting face a particular challenge at the present time. It used to be the case that a person's confession of faith, made at "years of discretion" — generally between sixteen and eighteen — would be followed by reception as a church member, admission to the Lord's table, and immediate participation in church meeting. Nowadays, with children receiving the Lord's Supper in many churches on the ground that they are baptized members of the church, and with professions of faith occurring at earlier ages, attendance at church meeting as part of the discipline of membership is delayed, and in some cases is never honored at all.[48]

Church, Ministry, and Worship

Every church order is open to abuse because the church comprises saints who are also sinners. And it must be confessed that Congregationalists have from time to time given the impression, and actually believed, that in the church anyone can do anything. In fact, of course, their position really is in the first place that it is the church, not the ministers, which preaches the word and celebrates the sacraments. Within this general understanding, those called to specific tasks are appointed thereto by the church, following whatever testing of the call and training of the person may be required. Their experience in the nineteenth century, when they were setting themselves over against Anglican ritualism and sacerdotalism, does, however, raise the question, Who may preside at the Lord's table? This question in turn raises that of the meaning of ordina-

---

47. See further Daniel Jenkins, *The Church Meeting and Democracy* (London: Independent Press, 1944); Alan P. F. Sell, *A Reformed, Evangelical, Catholic Theology: The Contribution of the World Alliance of Reformed Churches, 1875-1982* (Eugene, Ore.: Wipf & Stock, 1998 [1991], pp. 99-100; Sell, *Commemorations,* chap. 14.

48. Cf. Sell, *A Reformed, Evangelical, Catholic Theology,* p. 155; *Liturgical Group Report,* Congregational Union of England and Wales (1965), p. 16.

tion. I believe that at this point some sorting out needs to be done. On the one hand we have learned from the liturgiologists that word and sacrament belong together, yet often we permit all and sundry to preach, whilst prohibiting lay persons from presiding at the table. (I am not advocating laxity in this matter; all who conduct the Lord's Supper should be appointed to do so by the church.) But this seems to sunder word and sacrament once more. Again, while most Christian traditions will accept baptism with water in the name of the Trinity, even if performed by a lay person, some will not permit lay celebration of the Lord's Supper; and this seems to drive a wedge between the sacraments. I suspect that we may be holding to very un-Reformed doctrine if we think that God will not meet with his people if the Lord's Supper is conducted by a faithful lay person who has been called by the church to officiate. To say this is not to denigrate the ordained ministry; it is to honor the ministry of all, and to remind the ministers that they, along with all other members, are part of the people *(laos)* of God, and not members of a priestly caste.[49]

Children in Worship

We have seen that the Congregationalists took steps to ensure that children were welcome at the church's worship. They had always been welcome as candidates for infant baptism, and the propriety of the baptism of children of the covenant has never been in question. Unless, however, there is a strong grasp of the covenant idea, and a real attempt to teach and receive as members parents who have not professed their faith, it would seem that the justification that requests for infant baptism provide an evangelical opportunity for outreach to unchurched parents rings hollow. As for the presence of children in worship, great strides have been made in this direction, but there are still divergent views as to what should happen liturgically while they are present. The advice of the Congregational Union's Liturgical Group in 1965 was as follows:

> We regard an attempt to make the part of the service in which all share "suitable for the children" as mistaken. All are present to join in the church's corporate worship, not in a short children's service before adult worship begins. The service ought not to give the impression of beginning all over again after the children have left. What the church family has done together need not be repeated in the church or in the children's services.[50]

---

49. See further Sell, *A Reformed, Evangelical, Catholic Theology,* pp. 170-72.
50. *Liturgical Group Report,* 6-7.

It is, nevertheless, in some circles a brave minister who will banish the children's address.

Conclusion

Underlying the entire practice of worship in the Congregational tradition is the presupposition that we know who the gathered saints are; they have passed from death to life, made their profession of faith, and had their children baptized; they join in church meeting and are under the church's kindly gospel discipline. Ever since the evangelical revival question marks have been played against some aspects of this catalogue. Today, with increasingly mobile populations, with Congregational churches (or their united heirs) serving as quasi parish churches in some areas, and with the consumerist spirit that inclines many people to join in worship on grounds more aesthetic or emotional — or even on grounds of geographical convenience or the availability of ancillary facilities — rather than on ecclesiologically principled grounds, the question "Who are the church?" is sharply posed.

On the narrower question of the shape of the liturgy, the moral I draw from studying the worship of the English Congregational tradition is that one of the most important terms in the liturgiologist's vocabulary is the blessed word *normally.* This word, we may hope, both restrains the legalistic and leaves open a window for the Spirit.

For Further Reading

Davies, Horton. *Worship and Theology in England.* 4 vols. Princeton: Princeton University Press, 1961-75.

———. *The Worship of the English Puritans.* London: Dacre Press, 1948.

Forsyth, P. T. *The Church and the Sacraments.* London: Independent Press, 1953 [1917].

Mayor, Stephen H. *The Lord's Supper in Early English Dissent.* London: Epworth Press, 1972.

Micklem, Nathaniel, ed. *Christian Worship: Studies in its History and Meaning by Members of Mansfield College.* London: Oxford University Press, 1936.

Nuttall, Geoffrey F. *Congregationalists and Creeds.* London: Epworth Press, 1966.

Sell, Alan P. F. *Commemorations: Studies in Christian Thought and History.* Eugene, Ore.: Wipf & Stock, 1998 [1993].

————. *Dissenting Thought and the Life of the Churches: Studies in an English Tradition.* Lewiston, N.Y.: The Edwin Mellen Press, 1990.

————. *A Reformed, Evangelical, Catholic Theology: The Contribution of the World Alliance of Reformed Churches 1875-1982.* Eugene, Ore.: Wipf & Stock, 1998 [1991].

Spinks, Bryan D. *Freedom or Order? The Eucharistic Liturgy in English Congregationalism 1645-1980.* Allison Park, Pa.: Pickwick Publications, 1984.

Reformed Worship in the United States of America

Marsha M. Wilfong

Reformed Churches in the American Colonies

Reformed Christians immigrated to the American colonies in the seventeenth and eighteenth centuries from Great Britain and from continental Europe. Congregationalists were among the earliest immigrants. These English Puritans, some more radically Separatist than others, settled in New England in large numbers in the seventeenth century. Unlike later Reformed immigrants, the Congregationalist immigrants included large numbers of clergy. In fact, it was often the case that congregations followed the lead of their minister in immigrating to the new land in search of freedom to practice their religion free from the constraints of English political and religious authorities.

Presbyterians were the other group of Reformed Christians to immigrate from Great Britain. They arrived in waves throughout the colonial period — first English Puritans of Presbyterian persuasion, and later Presbyterians from Scotland and Ireland. Presbyterian immigrants settled throughout the American colonies. While the Congregationalists recognized no ecclesial authority beyond the local congregation, Presbyterian polity was connectional. The first presbytery in the American colonies was organized in 1706. In 1716, three additional presbyteries were organized, and the first synod was established.

In smaller numbers, Reformed Christians also immigrated from continental Europe. In the seventeenth century Dutch Reformed immigrants settled in the Dutch colony of New Amsterdam (later New York and New Jersey). More so than other Reformed groups, the Dutch immigrants maintained strong ties with their native church, the Dutch Reformed Church in Holland. German Reformed immigrants settled primarily in New Amsterdam and

Pennsylvania. French Huguenot refugees also arrived on American shores, but the vast majority were assimilated into the Dutch Reformed churches in New York and New Jersey or into the Anglican churches in the southern colonies. German-speaking Swiss immigrants were for the most part assimilated into the German Reformed churches.

All of these Reformed churches were committed to an educated ministry, but, with the exception of the early Congregational and Dutch Reformed colonists, they persistently experienced a shortage of trained pastors. This shortage eventually led to the establishment of educational institutions on the American shore. The problem of pastoral supply was also dealt with in other ways. Some congregations were served by pastors from a different Reformed group. For example, Dutch Reformed pastors from Holland were recruited to serve German Reformed and French Huguenot congregations. Some Reformed congregations joined in union worship with other Protestant groups. In many cases, however, congregations had to rely on lay leadership for worship, with only an occasional visit from an ordained pastor.

These various solutions to the pastoral shortage affected the worship practices of Reformed churches in colonial America. The order and elements of worship were influenced by cross-fertilization both among Reformed churches and more widely among Protestants. Worship traditions inherited from Great Britain and European countries mixed and mingled, and the variations from one local congregation to another did not necessarily follow denominational lines.

Worship Practices in Colonial America

Worship in Congregational and Presbyterian churches in eighteenth-century America was the product of their free-church heritage from Great Britain, in opposition to the state-imposed Anglican liturgy, beginning in the sixteenth century with the *Book of Common Prayer.* The Calvinist and Puritan view was that worship should be governed by Scripture and should include only elements specifically authorized by Scripture. Hence, the primary elements of worship were the reading of Scripture, prayer, the singing of psalms, and the sermon. The use of the Apostles' Creed and liturgical responses such as the *Gloria Patri* were rejected, along with set liturgical prayers. Even recitation of the Lord's Prayer in worship was rejected by many, especially the Congregationalists, who understood it as a model for prayer but not a prayer to be recited in worship. In consequence, Congregational and Presbyterian worship was clergy dominated. The only active participation of the people was the singing of psalms.

The Westminster *Directory for Publick Worship* (1644) reflected these Calvinistic and Puritan views, as well as the different nuances of interpretation between the Congregationalists and Presbyterians. The recommended placement of prayers conformed to the Presbyterian view, with the "Prayer Before the Sermon" being a brief prayer for illumination, while the "General Prayer" included elements of thanksgiving and petition and was followed by the Lord's Prayer. In Congregational practice, the worship service began with a long prayer of thanksgiving and intercession as described in 1 Timothy 2:1. This was followed by the reading of Scripture and the sermon, interspersed with the singing of psalms.

The Westminster Directory, as it is usually called, suggested the celebration of the Lord's Supper following the sermon. The frequency was left up to each congregation, but if the sacrament was not celebrated weekly, a preparatory sermon or midweek lecture was to be made preceding the Sunday of its administration.

In practice, Congregationalists in England and America encouraged the sacrament of the Lord's Supper once a month where possible. Among Scottish Presbyterians, however, another tradition developed. From the mid-seventeenth century onward in Scotland, the practice had been to celebrate the Lord's Supper only once or twice a year. These occasions were called "sacramental seasons." They were organized and publicized in advance and often involved participants from several neighboring congregations, with leadership and preaching shared by their pastors. The focus of the three-to-four-day event was the celebration of the sacrament by church members judged worthy to participate. While successive groups of communicants sat at the table to receive the Lord's Supper, other preachers addressed the remaining people present. This Scottish practice of annual "sacramental seasons" also became widespread among Presbyterians in the American colonies.

Early-seventeenth-century Dutch and German Reformed immigrants arrived in America with orders of worship that were more recognizably related to sixteenth-century Reformed liturgies. Puritan ideas about worship, however, affected Reformed churches in the Netherlands and Germany in the seventeenth and eighteenth centuries, through the Pietist movement. Later waves of Dutch and German immigrants, including pastors, brought with them worship practices consistent with this Pietist view. Because of changing practices in Europe, and under the influence of Congregationalists and Presbyterians in America, Dutch and German Reformed worship in the American colonies was also stripped over time of liturgical elements or fixed prayers, and focused on the reading of Scripture and preaching.

To give the reader an idea of the style and perspectives of the Westminster Directory, we reproduce here a few excerpts from this influential text. The full text can be most readily found in *Confession of Faith, The Larger Catechism, The Shorter Catechism, The Directory for Publick Worship, The Form of Presbyterial Church Government with References to the Proofs from the Scripture* (Edinburgh/London: Blackwood, 1969).

Directory for the Publick Worship of God

Established and put in execution by Act of the General Assembly February 3, 1645, and approved and established by Act of Parliament February 6, 1645.

In the beginning of the blessed Reformation, our wise and pious ancestors took care to set forth an Order for redress of many things, which they then, by the Word, discovered to be vain, erroneous, superstitious, and idolatrous, in the Publick Worship of God. This occasioned many godly and learned men to rejoice much in the Book of Common Prayer, at that time set forth; because the mass, and the rest of the Latin service being removed, the Publick Worship was celebrated in our own tongue: many of the common people also received benefit of hearing the Scriptures read in their own language, which formerly were unto them as a book that is sealed. Howbeit, long and sad experience hath made it manifest, that the Liturgy used in the Church of England (notwithstanding all the pains and religious intentions of the compilers of it) hath proved an offence, not only to many of the godly at home, but also to the Reformed Churches abroad. . . .

We have, after earnest and frequent calling upon the name of God, and after much consultation, not with flesh and blood, but with His holy Word, resolved to lay aside the former Liturgy, with the many rites and ceremonies formerly used in the worship of God; and have agreed upon this following Directory for all the parts of Publick Worship, at ordinary and extraordinary times. Wherein our care hath been to hold forth such things as are of divine institution in every ordinance; and other things we have endeavoured to set forth according to the rules of Christian prudence, agreeable to the general rules of the Word of God. . . .

Of the Assembling of the Congregation, and their Behaviour in the Publick Worship of God
. . . Let all enter the assembly, not irreverently, but in a grave and seemly manner, taking their seats or places without adoration, or bowing themselves towards one place or another. . . .

The publick worship being begun, the people are wholly to attend upon it, forbearing to read any thing, except what the minister is then reading or citing; and abstaining much more from all private whisperings, conferences or salutations or doing reverence to any person present or coming in; as also from all gazing, sleeping, and other indecent behaviour which may disturb the minister or people. . . .

Of Publick Reading of the Holy Scriptures
Reading of the Word in the Congregation, being part of the Publick Worship of God (wherein we acknowledge our dependence upon Him, and subjection to Him), and one means sanctified by Him for the edifying of His people, is to be performed by the Pastors and Teachers. . . .

How large a portion shall be read at once, is left to the wisdom of the minister; but it is convenient, that ordinarily one chapter of each Testament be read at every meeting; and sometimes more, where the chapters be short or the conherence of matter requireth it. It is requisite that all the canonical books be read over in order that the people may be better acquainted with the whole body of the scriptures. . . .

Of Publick Prayer before the Sermon
After reading the word (or singing the psalm) the minister who is to preach, is to endeavour to get his own and his hearers' hearts to be rightly affected with their sins, that they may all mourn in sense thereof before the Lord, and hunger and thirst after the grace of God in Jesus Christ. . . .

Of the Preaching of the Word
Preaching of the word, being the power of God unto salvation, and one of the greatest and most excellent works belonging to the ministry of the gospel, should be so performed, that the workman need not be ashamed, but may save himself, and those that hear him. . . .

Let the introduction to his text be brief and perspicuous. . . .

. . . In raising doctrines from the text, his care ought to be, *First,*

That the matter be the truth of God. *Secondly,* That it be a truth contained or grounded in that text, that the hearers may discern how God teacheth it from thence. *Thirdly,* That he chiefly insist upon those doctrines which are principally intended, and make most for the edification of the hearers. . . .

Of the Celebration of the Communion, or Sacrament of the Lord's Supper

The Communion, or Supper of the Lord, is frequently to be celebrated; but how often, may be considered and determined by the Ministers, and other Church-governors of each Congregation, as they shall find most convenient for the comfort and edification of the people committed to their charge. And, when it shall be administered, we judge it convenient to be done after the Morning Sermon. The ignorant and the scandalous are not fit to receive this Sacrament of the Lord's Supper. Where this Sacrament cannot with convenience be frequently administered, it is requisite that public warning be given the Sabbath Day before the administration thereof; and that either then, or on some day of that week, something concerning that Ordinance, and the due preparation thereunto, and participation thereof, be taught; that, by the diligent use of all means sanctified of God to that end, both in public and private, all may come better prepared to that heavenly Feast.

Of the Sanctification of the Lord's Day

The Lord's Day ought to be so remembered before-hand, as that all worldly business of our ordinary callings may be so ordered, and so timely and seasonably laid aside, as they may not be impediments to the due sanctifying of the day when it comes. . . .

Of Singing of Psalms

It is the duty of Christians to praise God publickly, by Singing of Psalms together in the Congregation, and also privately in the family. In Singing of Psalms, the voice is to be tunably and gravely ordered; but the chief care must be to sing with understanding, and with grace in the heart, making melody unto the Lord. . . .

Eighteenth-Century Developments

As the Pietist movement swept through the Netherlands and Germany, and the evangelical activities of John Wesley gained momentum in England, religious revivals also sprang up in the American colonies. The early revivalists were pastors concerned about the lack of vitality of their parishioners' faith. Genuine piety and moral Christian living were almost nonexistent. Churchgoers appeared to only go through the motions of faith and worship, without there being any impact on their hearts and lives.

The early, local revivals occurred under the leadership of Reformed clergy: Theodore Frelinghuysen, a Dutch Reformed pastor in New Jersey; William Tennent Sr., a Presbyterian pastor also working in New Jersey, along with his three sons, most notably Gilbert; and Jonathan Edwards (1703-1758), a Congregational pastor in Northampton, Massachusetts. The form these local revivals took reflected primarily a shift of focus in preaching: sermons were now less didactic and more fervently calling parishioners to deeper Christian devotion and a more dedicated Christian life. Although these early Reformed revivalists preached and prayed for a spiritual revival among their parishioners, they believed that any spiritual awakening would come only in God's time and at God's initiative.

What began as scattered local revivals in New England became a widespread revival movement throughout the American colonies with the arrival from England of George Whitefield, a colleague of John Wesley. Whitefield made numerous trips to the American colonies from 1738 until his death in 1770, traveling around the colonies and preaching at various churches as well as in more public gatherings. Following in his footsteps, Presbyterians Gilbert Tennent and Samuel Davies also took up itinerant revivalistic preaching.

This eighteenth-century revival movement, called the Great Awakening by historians, was marked by an emphasis on a heartfelt experience of conversion as the true beginning of Christian life and faith. Worship was understood increasingly as intended to touch people's hearts in order to evoke a conversion experience. It was directed primarily toward church members who had become spiritually indifferent, and only secondarily toward the conversion of the unchurched. While evangelical preaching was the primary vehicle of persuasion, the concern for an emotional, spiritual experience in worship also led to the introduction of hymns, particularly those of Isaac Watts, into the worship of some Reformed congregations.

This Great Awakening in the American colonies was not isolated from the various revival movements in Britain and Europe. The influence flowed in both directions across the Atlantic. Wesley and Whitefield in England, for example, were influenced by Jonathan Edwards's writings, just as Whitefield's itinerancy in the colonies helped spread the revival movement in America. News of Whitefield's visits to America, as well as Edwards's writings, eventually led to a spiritual revival among Presbyterians in Scotland.

But the Great Awakening also had a particular impact on the various churches, Reformed and otherwise, on the North American continent. The Great Awakening was in a sense an "ecumenical" movement, affecting all Protestant churches to some degree. Early revival preachers like Frelinghuysen, the Tennents, and Edwards knew each other and drew upon each other's ideas and methods. George Whitefield had contact in America with Edwards and Gilbert Tennent. What's more, Whitefield's more public revival preaching drew an audience from Anglicans, Baptists, and various Reformed churches, among others.

This ecumenical contact and experience contributed to the peculiarly American Protestant understanding of *church*. In a society where there was no state church, and no geographical parish lines drawn to define membership in a particular congregation, the various Protestant groups were seen as voluntary associations, in which individual Christians chose to participate. The different Protestant bodies were not viewed as "sects" with distinct and mutually exclusive theologies and practices, but as "denominations," subgroups of the overarching category "Christians." Clergy and laity alike often moved from one denomination to another — even across Reformation families. Theological emphases and worship practices were also exchanged across denominational lines, to the degree that it often became difficult to tell one American Protestant congregation (or even denomination) from another.

But the increasingly common denominator of American Protestant Christianity was not the only consequence of the Great Awakening. The revival movement, with its emphasis on the experience of conversion, had implications for both theology and worship practice, and these implications caused conflict, particularly within Reformed denominations. Presbyterians were divided into the New Side, which approved of revival measures, and the Old Side, which was opposed to the revival movement on both theological and practical grounds. This conflict led to an official Presbyterian division, which lasted from 1745 to 1758. Congregational churches and clergy, while not organizationally connected by polity, were also divided into two camps: the New Lights and the Old Lights.

Post-Revolutionary Tasks

By the 1770s the Great Awakening had waned. During the next several decades, the struggle for independence from Britain took up the energies of
clergy and church members alike, and took its toll on the well-being of American churches. Religious fervor and Christian commitment and lifestyle declined. Following the Revolution, Reformed churches, as well as others, faced
several important tasks: reorganization as independent church bodies in a new
nation; postwar rebuilding of church buildings and neglected congregations; a
shortage of available clergy; and the challenge of evangelizing a quickly ex-
panding western frontier.

Presbyterian reorganization, for example, included drawing up an
American church constitution, amending the Westminster Confession to conform to the American situation, and drafting an American Directory for Worship. The new American Directory was a revision of the 1644 Westminster Directory. The changes, in both the original draft and the final version approved
by the General Assembly in 1788, offer clues about worship issues and practices at the close of the eighteenth century.

The draft version included a preface that set forth the concerns of its
drafters, who sought to unify the worship practices of Presbyterian congregations. But unlike the Westminster Directory, which presupposed a devout congregation, the drafters of the American Directory saw the need for worship to
evoke devotion and dedicated Christian life in worshipers. The preface speaks
pointedly of this concern:

> It is absolutely necessary that something be done to revive the spirit and
> appearance of devotion. Where there is real devotion, there the appear-
> ance of it will be . . . and did we attend to the appearance, it might have a
> happy tendency to awaken and revive a devotional spirit.[1]

The idea that worship should function "to awaken and revive a devotional
spirit" reflects the influence of the Great Awakening.

The draft Directory also reflected other concerns. It offered pattern
prayers for study or use in worship, instead of Westminster's more general description of the content of various prayers. Following the Westminster Directory, it recommended the use of the Lord's Prayer at the close of the long

---

1. Presbyterian Church in the United States of America, *A Draught of the Form of Gov-
ernment and Discipline of the Presbyterian Church in the United States* (New York: S. and J.
Loudon, 1787), quoted in Julius Melton, *Presbyterian Worship in America: Changing Patterns
Since 1787* (Richmond, Va.: John Knox Press, 1967), p. 20.

prayer before the sermon. The draft also advised the celebration of the Lord's Supper at least quarterly, in the context of morning worship, and discouraged continuation of the custom of "sacramental seasons."

When the General Assembly adopted the Directory in 1788, the entire preface was dropped. The pattern prayers, as well as the suggested use of the Lord's Prayer, were deleted. Instead, a descriptive list of topics to be covered in various prayers was added, similar to but much shorter than in the Westminster Directory. The following comments were added:

> But we think it necessary to observe, that although we do not approve, as is well known, of confining ministers to set, or fixed forms of prayer for public worship; yet it is the indispensible duty of every minister, previously to his entering on his office, to prepare and qualify himself for this part of his duty, as well as for preaching. He ought, by a thorough acquaintance with the holy scripture; by reading the best writers on the subject; by meditation; and by a life of communion with God in secret; to endeavour to acquire both the spirit and the gift of prayer. — Not only so, but when he is to enter on particular acts of worship, he should endeavour to compose his spirit, and to digeil [sic] his thoughts for prayers, that it may be performed, with dignity and propriety, as well as to the profit of those who join it; and that he may not disgrace that important service by mean, irregular, or extravagant effusions.[2]

These comments seem to reflect a compromise between a concern for the quality — and dignity — of public prayers on the one hand, and a continuing suspicion of any fixed forms of prayer on the other. The enthusiastic excesses of the earlier revival movement and the long-standing rejection of the liturgy of the *Book of Common Prayer* formed the boundaries of what was acceptable.

A similar middle ground is evident in the final version of the section on the Lord's Supper. The original draft had advocated its celebration at least quarterly, and had discouraged the practice of sacramental seasons. The version adopted by the General Assembly stated only that the Lord's Supper was "to be celebrated frequently."[3] How frequently was left to the discretion of the ministers and elders of each congregation. As to sacramental seasons, the final version stated, "we think it not improper, that they, who chuse [sic] it,

---

2. *The Constitution of the Presbyterian Church in the United States of America: Containing the Confession of Faith, the Catechisms, the Government and Discipline, and the Directory for the Worship of God* (Philadelphia: Robert Aitken, 1797), p. 443.

3. *The Constitution of the Presbyterian Church*, p. 448.

may continue in this practice."[4] In addition, both the draft and the final version contained a statement acknowledging the presence of the unchurched at the celebration of the Lord's Supper: "It may not be improper for the minister to give a word of exhortation also to those who have been only spectators. . . ."[5] This statement reflects the view of the Lord's Supper as a converting ordinance, a view that had entered Reformed thinking through the revival movement.

One further change from the Westminster Directory also indicated the influence of the revivalists. This change had to do with congregational singing. The Westminster Directory had approved only the singing of psalms, and had conceded that, because of illiteracy, the psalms might be lined out by the worship leader. The American Directory acknowledged, without qualification, the singing of psalms *or hymns.* It also stated that the congregation should be furnished books, and that the practice of lining out should be abandoned "as far as convenient."[6]

The American Directory failed to achieve the purpose its drafters envisioned of unifying worship practices among Presbyterian congregations. For one thing, it was not viewed as binding on the church in the same sense as the doctrinal standards of the Westminster Confession. But even if it had been understood as binding, its directives for worship remained vague and allowed for great diversity in practice. The changes and tensions noted above not only reflect eighteenth-century worship practices, but also point forward to nineteenth-century developments — both among Presbyterians and in other Reformed churches.

Nineteenth-Century Revivals

The nineteenth century was marked by a series of revival movements. These various revivals began in different parts of the country and had somewhat different characteristics. Yet each affected Reformed churches and their worship practices in some way. In every case, Reformed churches (and/or individuals) were significant participants, although not to the exclusion of other Protestant groups.

The revival movement that historians call the "Second Great Awakening" began at the turn of the century and lasted for several decades. While it

4. *The Constitution of the Presbyterian Church,* p. 452.
5. *The Constitution of the Presbyterian Church,* p. 450.
6. *The Constitution of the Presbyterian Church,* p. 440.

was geographically widespread, and had significant impact on American Protestantism, it took somewhat different forms in different parts of the country.

The first phase of this "awakening" occurred at colleges founded by Reformed churches in Virginia and New England. In 1787, a revival began at Hampden-Sydney College, a Presbyterian institution in Virginia. The initial impetus for this revival was the attendance of several Hampden-Sydney students at neighboring Baptist and Methodist revivals. When they reported their experience of awakening to Hampden-Sydney's President John Blair Smith, he began meetings with students that led to a spiritual revival among them. In 1795, Timothy Dwight (1752-1817), grandson of Jonathan Edwards, became president of Yale College in Connecticut (which was Congregational). Concerned with the moral and spiritual state of Yale's students, Dwight's preaching and teaching efforts led to a revival among the students in 1802. The significance of both of these college-based revivals was that many students experienced not only a conversion but also a call to ministry. Their subsequent ministry as pastors spread the revival movement into congregations and contributed to the frontier phase of the Second Great Awakening.

Among Presbyterians in the South, the long-standing practice of sacramental seasons was the locus of the frontier awakenings in Tennessee and Kentucky. Initially, these sacramental seasons were no different from those annually celebrated by Presbyterians in both America and Scotland. But beginning in 1800 in Kentucky, the situation changed. The number of people in attendance who were not church members increased dramatically. (In some cases, total participants were estimated to be between ten and twenty thousand.) Methodists and Baptists joined Presbyterians, both as participants and as clergy leadership. Gradually the focus of the event shifted from preparation for the sacrament to the conversion of sinners. More emphasis was placed on preaching and exhortation designed to evoke an emotional experience of conversion — increasingly understood as the free will choice of individuals rather than the miraculous action of God.

These camp meetings brought together people of diverse backgrounds, with regard to ethnicity (Native Americans and slaves were among those included) as well as socioeconomic and denominational status. They generated new forms of religious music and resulted in increased membership, particularly in Presbyterian, Methodist, and Baptist churches. In some respects, they continued the eighteenth-century trends both of ecumenical interaction and cooperation and of the blurring of distinctions between various American Protestant denominations, particularly in worship. Preaching and praying were directed toward the widely assumed goal of individual conversion. The hymnody of Watts and Wesley, as well as the spirituals and choruses generated by the camp meetings, became for many the common "musical language" of American Protestantism.

At the same time, the camp meeting revivals caused conflict within the Presbyterian church, for reasons of both polity and theology. Eventually, schisms occurred that led ultimately to the formation of two new American Reformed denominations: the Cumberland Presbyterian Church and the Christian Church: Disciples of Christ.

In the northern part of the United States, the Second Great Awakening took a different form. The Congregational revival begun by Timothy Dwight at Yale spread primarily within established congregations rather than through the occasional camp meetings. Reformed efforts to evangelize the northern frontier resulted in 1801 in a Plan of Union between Congregationalists and Presbyterians. In effect, these two denominations agreed to pool their resources of ordained clergy in establishing new congregations in the West, beginning with western New York and Ohio. New churches, whether predominantly Congregational or Presbyterian, could be served by an available pastor from either denomination. In 1826, the American Home Missionary Society was established to oversee the Plan of Union.

This seemingly more orderly evangelistic effort was also focused on the goal of individual conversion. One such convert was Charles Finney (1792-1875), a lawyer and Presbyterian layman. Following his experience of conversion in 1821, he began an evangelistic tour in western New York. He was ordained by Presbyterians, despite his lack of college or formal theological training and his refusal to adhere to the standards of the Westminster Confession. Unlike the camp meetings of the South, Finney's revivals were held in towns and cities, at the invitation of churches of one or more denomination (including Presbyterian and Congregationalist). These urban "protracted meetings" would last at least three to four days, with preaching services morning, afternoon, and evening. Laity and clergy from the inviting churches were organized to hold local prayer meetings in advance of Finney's visit, and were trained to exhort and counsel those who experienced conversion following his preaching. Finney also hired a special musical assistant to lead the singing at his revival services.[7]

Finney's contribution to the revival movement went beyond his own itinerancy. In 1834-35, he published *Lectures on Revivals of Religion.* In those *Lectures,* Finney opposed the traditional Calvinist view that conversions and revivals were miracles due to God's sovereign action and that they awaited

---

7. William G. McLoughlin, *Revivals, Awakenings, and Reform* (Chicago: University of Chicago Press, 1978), p. 128.

God's time. Instead, he claimed that people, of their own free will, could choose conversion over sin, and that revivals could be produced by the use of particular means ("New Measures") designed to evoke conversion.

Some of these "New Measures" were simply idiosyncrasies — boisterous mannerisms and naming names aloud in public prayer. Others, however, were careful strategies — demanding on-the-spot conversions, having people "coming forward" to sit on an "anxious bench," and using "protracted meetings" to wear people into submission.[8]

Although most of Finney's "New Measures" had already been used by other nineteenth-century revivalists, his *Lectures* organized them into a systematic revival method, a method that was subsequently taken up by pastors and evangelists for generations to come. Finney was also the first notable example of a "professional revivalist," whose vocation it was to move from place to place holding extended revival meetings in the community.

Most of the professional revivalists who conducted protracted meetings did so for the particular denomination that had ordained them, but a few superstars (like Finney) conducted interdenominational meetings sponsored by all the churches in a town. Professional revivalists served principally as supplements to the regular ministry, appearing on call to provide a shot in the arm for a church, denomination, or city when religious life was at a low ebb.[9]

In this respect, Finney was the forerunner of later professional revivalist "superstars" such as Dwight L. Moody and Billy Sunday at the end of the nineteenth century, and Billy Graham in the twentieth century. It is interesting to note that all of these men emerged out of a religious background in Reformed churches.

Once again, the revival methods and experiences had implications for both theology and polity. Among the Presbyterians, this eventually caused a denominational split in 1837, between the New School and the Old School. The Old School Presbyterians held fast to Calvinist theology of the sovereignty of God, predestination, and election, and to a strict polity concerning educational and confessional requirements for ordaining pastors. The New School Presbyterians, driven by evangelistic concerns, leaned toward the Arminian theology (advocated by Finney and others) of universal salvation and individual free will, and were less strict about requirements for ordination. These distinctions also had an impact on their approaches to worship. The Old School maintained the Calvinist-Puritan tradition of decorum and a scriptural basis for every aspect of worship, while the New School advocates viewed evangelis-

8. Allen C. Guelzo, "Finney at 200," *Christianity Today* 36 (October 26, 1992): 17.

9. McLoughlin, *Revivals, Awakenings, and Reforms,* p. 127.

tic effectiveness as the primary criterion for worship and were willing to use the new revival measures to produce the desired effect.

Congregationalist churches and pastors were divided into two similar camps. Since Congregational polity was based on the autonomy of each local church, this division did not result in a denominational split. It did, however, produce "competing" Congregational churches in many locations.

The German Reformed Church was also troubled by the effects of revivals on theology and worship. No split occurred in that denomination, but resistance to the revival system led the German Reformed Church into the first serious conversations about Reformed theology and liturgy.

The American Sunday School Union

The evangelistic impulse of the nineteenth-century revivals emphasized not only the conversion of sinners. Those who were converted were also urged to involve themselves in the ongoing effort of evangelism. Initial efforts were local in nature. But soon national organizations were formed to coordinate and spread various aspects of this work. The work of these groups was for the most part organized, funded, and carried out by lay volunteers. While these voluntary societies were ecumenical in nature, their leadership and participants were predominantly Reformed, mostly Presbyterian and Congregational.

One such society was the American Sunday School Union, organized in 1824, with Presbyterians dominating its initial leadership. The American Sunday School Union was initially concerned with providing basic education and moral instruction for poor and immigrant children in urban areas, who had no other access to educational opportunities. Soon, however, the goal of the Sunday schools also was understood as preparing children for a conversion experience.

A new wave of immigrants from Europe had crowded the cities in the late eighteenth and early nineteenth century, and included a large number of Roman Catholics. The Catholic church had been only a small minority in the United States at the time of independence, but by the mid–nineteenth century it had become the largest religious group in the country. The Protestant reaction to this increase was strong. The early urban Sunday schools urged conversion to Protestant Christianity. The anti-Catholic sentiment also reinforced Reformed churches' negative views toward set forms of liturgy in worship. Sadly, this anti-Catholicism was also transferred to the mission fields, particularly in South America where the Roman Catholic Church had been dominant since the sixteenth century.

Eventually, Sunday schools moved beyond urban areas in the eastern United States and became a means of evangelization (and education) on the western frontier. In many communities, the lay-led Sunday school became the first, and for some time the only, religious institution present — for both children and adults. Hence, the only worship experience available was the opening assembly of the Sunday school, sometimes expanded to meet the needs of adult worshipers as well as the Sunday school children. Such worship consisted primarily of prayers, hymns, and Scripture reading, often responsive. In many frontier areas, a sermon was included only when an ordained minister visited.

Memorization was the primary pedagogical technique in the early Sunday schools. The texts used for memorization were Scripture verses, the Ten Commandments, and hymns. Where Sunday schools became tied to particular denominations in the Reformed tradition, confessional documents such as the Westminster Shorter Catechism or the Heidelberg Catechism were also used for instruction and memorization. Consequently, the Lord's Prayer and the Apostles' Creed were also memorized, and in some cases recited in the opening worship assemblies.

Effects of the Revival Movements on Worship

For the most part, the form and order of Sunday worship did not noticeably change during the nineteenth century. Certainly, there was no more uniformity in worship at the end of the century than at the beginning — perhaps even less. In most Reformed congregations, the primary elements of worship remained the same: prayers, psalms (or hymns), Scripture reading, and sermon. Participation of the laity was still limited to singing.

The sermon continued to dominate the worship service and to be geared toward the conversion of sinners. The length of the sermon, however, decreased as the century progressed, from one and a half hours at the beginning of the century to thirty minutes by the end.[10] Prayers were for the most part extemporaneous, and usually consisted of a brief opening prayer, a long prayer before the sermon (including confession and intercession), and a prayer after the sermon. In most Reformed congregations, the sacrament of the Lord's Supper was still celebrated infrequently.

The most marked change in worship was in the area of music. New

10. Ernest Trice Thompson, *Presbyterians in the South,* vol. 3, *1890-1972* (Richmond: John Knox Press, 1973), p. 342.

hymnody continued to make its way into worship — both from revivals and from Sunday schools. In addition, the use of organs and choirs (sometimes to lead congregational singing and sometimes to provide special music) gradually increased. In part, the impetus for musical changes was the evangelistic desire to stir up people's emotions as a means of conversion, but the changes also reflected a growing interest in active lay participation in worship, as well as increasing attention to aspects of worship other than the sermon.

Evangelism among Native Americans and African Americans

Evangelism among Native Americans began almost as soon as immigrants arrived in the American colonies. In the mid–seventeenth century, New England Puritans organized efforts to "Christianize" the natives. Their methodology included evangelistic preaching, catechism and dialogue, the organization of native churches, and the formation of Praying Towns, where Indian converts could be segregated from the influence of non-Christian Indians and whites.[11] The first Great Awakening of the eighteenth century brought about renewed efforts at evangelization by Presbyterians and Congregationalists. With the formation of the American Board of Commissions for Foreign Missions in the early nineteenth century (see below), work among Native Americans was viewed as a "foreign mission," and missionaries were recruited and supported under the auspices of that board.

As early as the colonial period, efforts were also made to "Christianize" African slaves. But where converted slaves were allowed to worship in white churches, they were segregated by seating in the rear of the church or in the gallery. Such segregation occurred in Reformed and other churches throughout the American colonies, and usually continued even after slavery was abolished.

The early–nineteenth-century camp meetings brought together blacks and whites in the South in a different way, but did not result in a noticeable increase in black membership in Presbyterian churches. Charles Colcock Jones, a Presbyterian missionary among the slave population, reported in 1848 that there were less than 300 black Presbyterians, while black Methodists and Baptists numbered almost 125,000.[12] The reasons for this numerical discrepancy

---

11. Henry M. Knapp, "The Character of Puritan Missions: The Motivation, Methodology, and Effectiveness of the Puritan Evangelization of the Native Americans in New England," *Journal of Presbyterian History* 76:2 (Summer 1998): 115-16.

12. Nathan O. Hatch, *The Democratization of American Christianity* (New Haven: Yale University Press, 1989), p. 102.

were twofold. First, Presbyterians, like other Reformed churches, stressed religious instruction in preparation for church membership. Catechumens were expected to learn the Apostles' Creed, the Lord's Prayer, and the Ten Commandments. Second, while an initial experience of conversion was emphasized, order and decorum were important in the practice of worship. Jones himself affirmed this solemn approach to worship:

> The *strictest order* should be preserved at all the religious meetings of the Negroes, especially those held on the Sabbath day, and *punctuality* observed in commencing then at the appointed hour. No *audible* expressions of feeling in the way of groaning, cries, or noises of any kind, should be allowed. To encourage such things among ignorant people, such as they are, would be to jeopardize the interests of true religion, and open the door to downright fanaticism. . . .
>
> The tunes should not be intricate but plain and awakening. One great advantage in teaching them good psalms and hymns, is that they are thereby induced to lay aside the extravagant and nonsensical chants, and catches and hallelujah songs of their own composing.[13]

By contrast, Methodists and Baptists allowed blacks freedom of expression in worship, including the singing of African-American spirituals.

At the same time, many Reformed Christians in the North were actively involved in the abolition movement, another of the many voluntary societies to grow out of the Second Great Awakening. And in the post–Civil War South, several Reformed churches were active in evangelizing blacks. All of these efforts, however, still resulted in some form of segregation of African-American Presbyterians. A good summary of some of these Presbyterian efforts as well as of these efforts' shortcomings is given by James Smylie:

> In 1874, the CPC [Cumberland Presbyterian Church] formed the Colored Cumberland Presbyterian Church (later the Second Cumberland Presbyterian Church). The PCUS was not too successful in its efforts, although it proclaimed that all God's children belong around the Lord's Table as members of one family. The denomination organized the Afro-American Presbyterian church, in 1898, which later became the Snedecor Memorial Synod with four presbyteries. The PCUSA evangelized blacks more aggressively, especially in the South. . . . The PCUSA segregated African

---

13. Charles Colcock Jones, *The Religious Instruction of the Negroes in the United States* (Savannah: T. Purse, 1842), quoted in Hatch, *The Democratization of American Christianity,* p. 105.

Americans in the synods of Catawaba, Atlantic, Canadian, and Blue Ridge until the 1950s, when the PCUS and the PCUSA did away with their racial and ethnic synods. In the intervening years, African-American Presbyterians fought against this segregation in Christ's body.[14]

While the southern Presbyterian Church in the United States was not very successful in evangelism among African Americans at home, it did support black missionaries sent to Africa. In 1890, William Sheppard, a black man, and Samuel Norvell Lapsley, a white man, were sent to establish the American Presbyterian Congo Mission. Through the educational institute in Tuscaloosa, Alabama (later Stillman College), the Presbyterian Church in the United States trained other black missionaries for Africa and black pastors for U.S. churches.

Worship on the Mission Fields

To my knowledge, no study of worship (Reformed or otherwise) on the mission fields exists. The literature that addresses nineteenth- and early-twentieth-century missionary activity includes official reports from missionaries, biographies and autobiographies of missionaries, and "historical sketches" of missions, published primarily for the consumption of American congregations who supported the missionary endeavor.

A sampling of these documents reveals few descriptions of worship practices *per se,* and then only in general terms. The writers were more concerned to describe the work and challenges of missionaries in a broader sense, and to report statistics such as numbers of converts, or of churches, schools, and hospitals established. Despite (or perhaps because of) the vagueness of references to worship, certain conclusions can be drawn.

What is clear is that the nineteenth-century missionary movement was the child of revivalism. The American Board of Commissioners for Foreign Missions, established in 1810 by Congregationalists along with Presbyterians and Dutch Reformed, was among the first of the voluntary societies organized in response to the Second Great Awakening. The evangelistic zeal for converting sinners, first on the American frontier and later in urban centers, was the impetus for foreign missions. Each successive wave of revivals continued to promote foreign missions, and encouraged converts to live out their new

14. James H. Smylie, *A Brief History of the Presbyterians* (Louisville: Geneva Press, 1996), p. 105.

Christian life by contributing to the conversion of others. Such contributions to missions took several forms: prayers for the missionary endeavor, monetary contributions to support missionary activities, and volunteers to serve on the mission fields.

Missionary work centered on three major activities: preaching, teaching, and healing. The primary goal, like that of the revival movement in America, was the conversion of individuals. Thus, preaching the gospel was viewed as the most important activity of missionaries. In many places, however, it was the educational and/or medical work that proved most effective in drawing people to the Christian faith.

Perhaps one reason for the absence of information about worship practice was that initially, as each new mission was established, formal Sunday worship was confined to the missionary community itself. The inclusion of native people in Lord's Day worship, and the establishment of native churches, occurred only later — when the mission had succeeded in making converts. This initial Sunday worship was undoubtedly the same as that experienced by missionaries in their American "home" churches.

Worship occurring in the course of the evangelistic work of the missionaries was less formal. It often took place with children and youth in Sunday schools or boarding schools established by the missionaries. Adults were reached through the "street preaching" of itinerant missionaries moving from village to village, or in established "street chapels," where preaching occurred on a daily basis.

The primary elements of this evangelistic "worship" were hymn singing, Scripture reading, preaching, and prayer. The worship in Sunday school and boarding school assemblies followed the same general pattern as that in American Sunday schools. The "worship" associated with daily "street" evangelism was less formal still. Hymn singing was regularly used to attract an audience. When a crowd was gathered, the preaching began, interspersed with prayer. Religious tracts were also distributed. In established street chapels, Scripture verses were posted on the walls and a room was set aside for conversation and prayer with "inquirers" who might have been moved by the evening's meeting.

During the first half of the nineteenth century in particular, reports from the mission field often speak of "revivals" occurring, especially beginning in boarding schools. During these times of revival, many people were said to have experienced conviction of sin and conversion.

All of these descriptions suggest that initial missionary efforts were very similar to the evangelistic strategies of the American revival movements. As in the revivals, preaching with the goal of conversion played a major part, as did hymn singing, which functioned both to attract potential converts and to stir up emotions. Where particular hymns are mentioned in reports, they include the hymns of Isaac Watts, Sunday school songs such as "Jesus Loves Me," and, later in the century, the gospel hymns popularized by the revivals of Dwight L. Moody.

Liturgical Renewal Efforts

The second half of the nineteenth century was also characterized by renewed liturgical interest within American Reformed churches. Yet the impact of liturgical renewal on actual worship practice, at home or on the mission field, remained minimal until well into the twentieth century.

The earliest liturgical discussions had begun in the 1840s in the German Reformed Church. Partly in reaction against the new revival measures, John Williamson Nevin (1803-1886) and Philip Schaff (1819-1893), of the German Reformed seminary in Mercersburg, Pennsylvania, spearheaded a liturgical exploration in the German Reformed Church which continued for four decades. The initial discussions were theological and emphasized the sacramental character of worship and the need to balance word and sacrament in worship practice. This led to the attempt to produce a liturgy consistent with a sacramental theology. A Provisional Liturgy was produced in the 1850s, primarily the work of Philip Schaff. This Provisional Liturgy was intended to be a prayer book for use by the laity rather than a manual for the minister. It offered significant opportunities for lay participation in worship, not only through congregational singing but also through various responses and liturgical forms. These proposals, however, produced such conflict between liturgical and anti-liturgical factions in the German Reformed Church that they were never approved. An eventual compromise was reached in the 1880s, with a revision of the German Reformed Directory for Worship, but, as Jack Martin Maxwell notes, it wasn't particularly effective: "There is evidence . . . that liturgically there was no real compromise, for the anti-liturgical congregations slipped back into the use of 'free worship' and the liturgical congregations got out the 'Order of Worship' again."[15]

During the second half of the nineteenth century, other Reformed churches engaged in less ambitious and/or less official discussions about worship. In 1853, the Dutch Reformed Synod appointed a committee to study revision of its liturgy, and a revised liturgy was eventually adopted in 1882. This

---

15. Jack Martin Maxwell, *Worship and Reformed Theology: The Liturgical Lessons of Mercersburg* (Pittsburgh: Pickwick Press, 1976), p. 332.

was for the most part only a modest updating of their 1767 liturgy, and it had little widespread effect on Dutch Reformed worship practices.

In 1894, the Presbyterian Church in the United States (the southern denomination born of the Presbyterian division at the time of the American Civil War) adopted a revision of the Presbyterian Directory for Worship. For the first time, sections were added referring to Sunday schools, prayer meetings, and foreign missions. In addition, the revised Directory contained forms for the administration of baptism, weddings, and funerals, as patterns to be used at the minister's discretion. The new Directory contained no liturgy for the Sunday worship service, however, and no form for the administration of the Lord's Supper.[16]

In the northern Presbyterian church, liturgical explorations were less formal and more diverse. In 1855, Charles W. Baird, a Presbyterian minister, published a book entitled *Eutaxia,* or *The Presbyterian Liturgies: Historical Sketches.* The book contained various sixteenth- and seventeenth-century Reformed liturgies, including those of Calvin and Knox, as well as liturgies of the French, Dutch, and German Reformed churches. In the introduction to the book, Baird stated his goal in presenting this historical collection of Reformed liturgies:

> It will be my object to demonstrate, first, *That the principles of Presbyterianism in no wise conflict with the discretionary use of written forms;* and, secondly, *That the practice of Presbyterian churches abundantly warrants the adoption and use of such forms.*[17]

Baird's book did spark discussion in Presbyterian circles (and in other Reformed churches as well). Unofficial prayer books, offering examples of fixed forms of prayer, were produced by both Old School and New School Presbyterians. Both clergy and laity produced liturgies for their particular congregations. It would be another half a century, however, before any denominational action was taken by Presbyterians in the North.

In 1903 the General Assembly of the northern Presbyterian Church in the United States of America appointed a committee to prepare, "in harmony with the Directory for Worship, a Book of Simple Forms and Services, proper and helpful for voluntary use in Presbyterian churches, in the celebration of

16. Ernest Trice Thompson, *Presbyterians in the South,* vol. 2: *1861-1890* (Richmond: John Knox Press, 1973), pp. 428-29.

17. Charles W. Baird, *The Presbyterian Liturgies: Historical Sketches* (previously printed under the title *Chapter on Liturgies,* 1856, and *Eutaxia,* 1855; reprint ed., Grand Rapids: Baker Book House, 1957), p. 5.

the Sacraments, in Marriages and Funerals, and in the Conduct of Public Worship."[18] In 1906, publication of *The Book of Common Worship* was authorized "For Voluntary Use in the Churches," as its title page clearly states. The following statement from its preface elaborates its intended use:

> This Book of Common Worship is, therefore, not to be taken in any wise as a liturgy imposed by authority. Nor is it a substitute for the Directory of Worship, but rather a supplement to it, wherein the instructions of the Standards are followed on all essential points, and aid is offered, to those who desire it, for the conduct of the Public Services of Religion with reverence and propriety.[19]

With this document, American Presbyterians for the first time in their history provided a liturgy, which contained examples of set prayers for worship (including the sacrament of the Lord's Supper) and offered opportunities for congregational participation beyond the singing of psalms or hymns.

This "voluntary" *Book of Common Worship* did not result in immediate, widespread changes in worship practice in Presbyterian congregations. It did, however, mark a significant change in attitude toward liturgy among American Presbyterians, at least in the North. The tension between freedom and form in worship remained. But the Reformed liturgical heritage of the sixteenth century was at least acknowledged as an appropriate and faithful option.

Twentieth-Century Influences

The diversity of worship practice evident in Reformed churches in the nineteenth century continued into the twentieth century. There was diversity in the use of free or fixed worship patterns, the singing of psalms and hymns, the frequency of celebration of the Lord's Supper, and the attention paid to the liturgical calendar. Worship practices varied not simply among Reformed denominations, but among congregations within denominations.

Many nineteenth-century developments continued to affect worship practice. For example, by the end of the nineteenth century the Sunday school movement was well established within Reformed and other Protestant churches. In some congregations, the Sunday school had become more impor-

18. Presbyterian Church in the United States of America, *The Book of Common Worship* (Philadelphia: The Presbyterian Board of Publication and Sabbath-School Work, 1906), p. iv.
19. Presbyterian Church, *The Book of Common Worship*, p. iv.

tant and better attended than corporate worship.[20] A survey taken by the Presbyterian Church in the U.S.A. following the 1903 General Assembly revealed that

> Sunday schools were often in advance of the worship services in using such classical liturgical materials as the Lord's Prayer, Apostles' Creed, or responsive readings. There are several likely reasons for this phenomenon. Sunday schools dealt with children, who were not habituated to sitting passively for long periods while someone else read, spoke, and prayed "in their behalf." Since recitation was an accepted pedagogical method, responsive or unison reading of Scripture was seen as valuable. So likewise was use of the Lord's Prayer, which for over two centuries had held an honored spot in the Westminster Shorter Catechism, Presbyterianism's traditional vehicle of religious instruction. Lay Sunday school leaders were seldom as adept as pastors in extempore conduct of worship periods; nor were they so well indoctrinated against liturgical procedures! In a short time "ready-made" services and readings began to appear in lesson literature and song books, to accelerate this "liturgical" trend in the Sunday schools.[21]

In addition, enthusiasm for foreign missions continued well into the twentieth century, and was reflected in popular, missions-oriented hymnody. The gospel music made popular by the late-nineteenth-century revivalist Dwight L. Moody and his song leader Ira Sankey also resounded in Reformed and other Protestant churches.

There were also new developments that affected the life and worship of churches in the United States. One such development was the Social Gospel movement. The impetus for the Social Gospel was the writings of Walter Rauschenbush, who urged that the nation's social and economic life conform to the gospel. Throughout the nineteenth century, Christian social concern had been directed primarily toward the moral reform of individuals, and expressed through voluntary societies focused on particular social issues such as abolition, women's suffrage, temperance, and education (through the early Sunday School movement) for poor urban children. The Social Gospel movement was concerned with the inequity and injustice systemic in social and economic institutions and urged Christians to work for institutional changes. This new perspective on social justice had an impact on the worship of Reformed churches, as Julius Melton points out:

20. Justo L. González, *The Story of Christianity*, vol. 2 (San Francisco: Harper & Row, 1985), p. 254.

21. Melton, *Presbyterian Worship in America*, p. 129.

Not only was this emphasis brought into the services through sermons and prayers; it also struck a blow at the notion of public worship as a time of escape from the world into the quietude of the spiritual realm. Sacrificial and confessional aspects of worship received more attention for this reason. And the churches began to wrestle with a problem still confronting them: How can worship become vitally related to the lives of Christians and to outsiders, and how can the reality of the Christian task in the world be made a vital part of worship?[22]

The institutional concerns raised by the Social Gospel movement also affected work on the mission fields, leading to a greater emphasis on agricultural, educational, and medical missions.[23]

Another development was the growing ecumenical movement. In the late nineteenth century, Reformed churches in the United States had been active in the establishment of world denominational fellowships such as the Alliance of Reformed Churches Throughout the World Holding the Presbyterian System (1875) and the International Congregational Council (1891). A primary impetus in the formation of these organizations was cooperation and coordination on the mission field. In the early decades of the twentieth century, numerous international organizations were developed that brought churches from different Protestant traditions into greater contact with each other. These ecumenical efforts culminated in the establishment of the World Council of Churches in 1948, and also led to the establishment of national councils, such as the National Council of the Churches of Christ in the U.S.A (1950). Ecumenical interactions would eventually result in new perspectives on the understanding and practice of worship. As Reformed churches were exposed to other Christian traditions, they had to look at their own practices in a broader context.

Furthermore, the necessity of knowing their own traditions, to say nothing of explaining them to others, prompted a flurry of research into church history and liturgics of the Reformed communion. The ecclesiological basis of many ecumenical discussions produced a new emphasis on the doctrine of the church, which in turn called attention to such churchly activities as worship. Vital study of the Bible — the common meeting place of all Christians — opened new avenues of approach to its viewpoints on worship. Persons touched by the idea of Christian unity soon became aware of how different worship traditions helped perpetuate divisions, and so they began to work to-

22. Melton, *Presbyterian Worship in America*, pp. 144-45.

23. Williston Walker, *A History of the Christian Church*, 3rd ed. (New York: Charles Scribner's Sons, 1970), p. 518.

ward removing nonessential differences. Others began to claim for their church valuable practices and approaches derived from the broader Christian scene.[24] Thus, the broader ecumenical contacts of the first half of the twentieth century paved the way for the liturgical reflection and reform that would occur in the second half of the century.[25]

The early twentieth century also saw the birth of a new tradition within Protestantism in the United States: the Pentecostal movement. It had its origins in 1906 at the Azuza Street Mission in Los Angeles, California. The movement quickly spread throughout urban centers in the United States and led to the emergence of numerous Pentecostal denominations. Pentecostal worship was marked by an outpouring of gifts of the Holy Spirit, such as speaking in tongues, prophecy, healing miracles, and ecstatic singing and dancing. It was also characterized by reliance on the Holy Spirit to guide both the content and the sequence of worship elements. While Pentecostalism initially had no direct influence on mainline churches, its impact would be felt later in the twentieth century with the rise of the charismatic movement.

The Decade of the 1960s

In many respects, the decade of the 1960s was a significant turning point not only in U.S. society but also in the life and worship of U.S. churches. It was a time of political and social turmoil on several fronts, most notably the Civil Rights movement, opposition to the Vietnam War, and the rise of feminist concerns. All of these movements contributed to the erosion of the authority and values of established social, political, and religious institutions. And all had an impact on churches in the United States, including Reformed churches.[26]

One example of an "official" Reformed response to the turmoil of the decade was *The Confession of 1967*, written by the United Presbyterian Church in the U.S.A. This Confession focuses on God's reconciling work in Christ and the church's mission of reconciliation, noting that "our generation stands in peculiar need of reconciliation in Christ."[27] It contains a lengthy section on "Reconciliation in Society," which highlights such issues

24. Melton, *Presbyterian Worship in America*, p. 146.

25. For a more detailed discussion, see Alan D. Falconer's chapter in this volume.

26. For further discussion, see Lukas Vischer's chapter in this volume.

27. *The Confession of 1967*, 9.06, in *Book of Confessions* [Part I of the Constitution of the Presbyterian Church (U.S.A.)], Study Edition (Louisville: Geneva Press, 1999).

as racial discrimination and poverty, as well as peace, justice, and freedom among nations.[28]

Reformed confessions of the sixteenth and seventeenth centuries had identified the "marks" of the church in terms of the true preaching of the gospel, the right administration of the sacraments, and (in the Scots Confession) ecclesiastical discipline. *The Confession of 1967*, however, identifies the church in terms of community and mission: "Wherever the church exists, its members are both gathered in corporate life and dispersed in society for the sake of mission in the world."[29] The function of corporate worship is understood as equipping the church for this mission in the world: "Jesus Christ has given the church preaching and teaching, praise and prayer, and Baptism and the Lord's Supper as means of fulfilling its service to God among men."[30]

There were also other religious responses to the social and political turmoil of the 1960s that were not tied to particular denominational institutions. A new wave of Pentecostalism arose among members of mainline Protestant and Roman Catholic churches. While most of these "neo-Pentecostal" charismatics remained within their respective denominations, a grassroots ecumenical fellowship eventually developed among them, distinct from the official ecumenical connections among established churches.[31]

At the same time, there was a rise in evangelical fervor among Protestants, which took a variety of forms. Parachurch evangelical organizations, such as Young Life, InterVarsity Christian Fellowship, and Campus Crusade, became increasingly prominent among high school and college students. In addition, many young people who had "dropped out" of societal and religious institutions were attracted to the more amorphous "Jesus Movement" as a means of meeting their spiritual needs. A number of independent evangelists gained a following and rose to national, and even international, prominence as TV evangelists by the 1970s and 1980s.

In some cases, this new evangelicalism was combined with charismatic expressions. Both the charismatic movement and evangelicalism reflected, on the one hand, concern over the ills of American society and, on the other hand, a distrust of established religious institutions.

Meanwhile, the Roman Catholic Church was experiencing a revolution of its own. At the instigation of Pope John XXIII, the Second Vatican Council was held from 1962 to 1965. In preparation for the council, Pope John XXIII

28. *The Confession of 1967*, 9.43-47.
29. *The Confession of 1967*, 9.35.
30. *The Confession of 1967*, 9.48.
31. González, *The Story of Christianity*, vol. 2, pp. 385-86.

had created in 1960 the Secretariat for Promoting Christian Unity, which opened the door for dialogue with other Christian churches. The *Constitution on the Sacred Liturgy* was produced by the council in 1963. The resulting changes in Roman Catholic worship included the use of vernacular languages and sensitivity to cultural expressions, the development of a new three-year Sunday lectionary, a new emphasis on Scripture and preaching, and the introduction of congregational singing. The increase of Protestant liturgical studies following World War II had greatly influenced these Roman Catholic reforms. In turn, the post–Vatican II reforms in the Roman Catholic Church would help to shape Protestant liturgical renewal in the decades to come.

Other Late-Twentieth-Century Influences

The final decades of the twentieth century saw further, or accelerated, developments in church and society. New waves of immigrants, particularly Asians and Hispanics, led to increasing ethnic diversity in the United States and challenged churches in terms of language and cultural expression in worship. Changing roles of women in church and society, which had been a century in the making, had a significant impact. Many Reformed and other Protestant churches now ordained women in increasing numbers. Concern for inclusive language about human beings became widespread and was evident in new biblical translations as well as official church publications, including service books and hymnals. The technological revolution moved swiftly from television to computers and the Internet, and significantly affected the way people learn, interact, and think. All of these developments, and others, have led to an increased fragmentation and pluralism in American society and have presented challenges for the church, particularly in the area of worship.

Worship in Reformed Churches in the Twentieth Century

The history of Reformed worship in the twentieth century can be officially traced through the production and revision of denominational service books, directories for worship, and hymnals. At the same time, one must take into account the actual worship practices of Reformed congregations. Both official liturgical resources and actual worship practice reflect (albeit sometimes in different ways) the influence of social, cultural, and religious changes that occurred in the course of the twentieth century.

The developments described below will focus primarily on the major

Presbyterian denominations. The present Presbyterian Church (U.S.A.) and its predecessors have been the most prolific of American Reformed churches in the production of liturgical resources, and have been at the forefront of changes in liturgical understanding and practice. Mention will also be made of other Reformed denominations as they have joined with Presbyterians in producing liturgical resources or have published their own.

The First Half of the Twentieth Century

The first U.S. *Book of Common Worship* was produced in 1906 by the (northern) Presbyterian Church in the United States of America, for voluntary use in congregations. In preparation for that service book, the 1903 General Assembly had set out four criteria to be followed:

> In the first place, the 1903 Assembly felt that for a service to be Christian it should be biblical; therefore it advised using biblical materials and forms and keeping the service firmly based on Scripture. Second, it thought a service for denominational use should embody the basic faith and experience of the denomination. In the third place, for the service to buttress Presbyterianism's claim to a place in the universal church it should express elements universal in Christian experience. Finally, the service should avoid being esoteric by relating itself consciously to the realities of the life of the church members.[32]

As the century progressed, subsequent revisions of the *Book of Common Worship* increasingly drew on the liturgical history of Reformed churches and on other Christian traditions — Protestant, Roman Catholic, and Orthodox. The first of these revisions occurred in 1932, and was a joint effort of the northern Presbyterian Church in the United States of America and the southern Presbyterian Church in the United States. Another revision was produced in 1946. This edition was modeled in part on the 1940 *Book of Common Order* of the Church of Scotland. The structure of the Sunday worship service was Morning Prayer plus the sermon, following the now centuries-old order of the Anglican *Book of Common Prayer*. The 1946 *Book of Common Worship* also contained a two-year lectionary, similar to that in the 1940 Scottish *Book of Common Order*.[33]

---

32. Melton, *Presbyterian Worship in America*, p. 136.

33. See Horace Allen, "*Book of Common Worship* (1993): The Presbyterian Church (U.S.A), 'Origins and anticipations'," in *To Glorify God: Essays on Modern Reformed Liturgy*, ed. Bryan D. Spinks and Iain R. Torrance (Grand Rapids: Eerdmans, 1999), pp. 13-29.

At the beginning of the twentieth century, the United Presbyterian Church in North America and a few other Reformed churches still sang only psalms in worship. For the rest, there were, in effect, two tracks of hymn-singing. In many churches, the nineteenth-century evangelistic gospel songs were popular in Sunday school and informal services, while more formal hymns were used in Sunday worship. The official hymnals produced by Presbyterians in the first half of the century (*The Presbyterian Hymnal,* Presbyterian Church in the U.S., 1927; and *The Hymnal,* Presbyterian Church in the U.S.A., 1933) did not include nineteenth-century gospel songs.[34]

In 1955, however, *The Hymnbook* was produced as a cooperative effort of five Presbyterian and Reformed churches: the Presbyterian Church in the U.S.A., the United Presbyterian Church of North America, the Presbyterian Church in the U.S., the Reformed Church in America, and the Associate Reformed Presbyterian Church. This hymnal included, on the one hand, a number of metrical psalms and, on the other hand, "a representative body of so-called 'gospel songs,' which properly have a place in the devotional life of the Church."[35]

Mid-Century Developments

In 1955 a joint committee of the Presbyterian Church in the United States of America, the United Presbyterian Church in North America, and the Presbyterian Church in the United States was formed to produce a new service book, in light of new developments in liturgical studies and post–World War II changes in church and society. They decided, however, that their first task needed to instead be a revision of the constitutional Directory for Worship. In 1961 a new directory was adopted by the United Presbyterian Church in the U.S.A. (the 1958 union of the former Presbyterian Church in the United States of America and the United Presbyterian Church in North America). The southern Presbyterian Church in the U.S. adopted its own new directory in 1963.

Following this endeavor a new service book was created. This ended up

---

34. Milton J. Coalter, John M. Mulder, and Louis B. Weeks, *The Re-Forming Tradition: Presbyterians and Mainstream Protestantism* (Louisville: Westminster/John Knox Press, 1992), p. 205.

35. Preface to *The Hymnbook,* published by Presbyterian Church in the United States, Presbyterian Church in the United States of America, United Presbyterian Church of North America, Reformed Church in America, and the Associate Reformed Presbyterian Church (1955), p. 5.

being a joint publication of the United Presbyterian Church in the U.S.A., the Presbyterian Church in the U.S., and the Cumberland Presbyterian Church. The Reformed Church in America and the United Church of Christ were also involved early on, but did not continue their participation in the project. The result was *The Worshipbook: Services,* published in 1970. This was an entirely new service book rather than simply a revision of the 1946 *Book of Common Worship.* It used contemporary language in its prayers and other liturgical elements (although the language remained gender exclusive). It set forth word *and* sacrament as the norm for the Sunday worship service. Consequently, the sermon was no longer at the end of the order of worship, but was followed by a creedal confession, intercessions, offering, and thanksgiving/Eucharist. At the last minute a three-year Sunday lectionary was also included in the *Worshipbook,* modified from the 1969 Roman Catholic three-year lectionary, which had been produced following Vatican II.

The final phase of the project was the production of the 1972 *Worshipbook,* which contained both the service book of 1970 and a new hymnal. In theory at least, this gave congregations access to the liturgy of the service book for the first time. The hymnal itself was innovative, including hymns from other Christian traditions as well as African-American spirituals. Meanwhile, beginning in the late 1960s, new forms of "contemporary" worship arose in the practice of many Protestant congregations. The impetus for these contemporary changes came in part from the "underground" folk masses that became increasingly popular in the Roman Catholic Church following Vatican II. They also reflected the more widespread changes in culture and society. Contemporary folk-style music was sung to the accompaniment of guitars, and visual elements such as balloons, confetti, and banners were used to reinforce or enhance certain elements of worship. Multimedia presentations (with slides or videos and music) often took the place of a spoken sermon. In Reformed and other Protestant congregations, this new style of worship did not replace, or even compete with, the traditional Sunday worship service. It was used primarily with and by the youth of the congregation, in youth meetings or retreats, as the format for the occasional "youth Sunday" worship service, or as a small, additional worship service in which youth were the primary participants (and sometimes leaders). While the style and expression of this contemporary worship were new, the ordering and basic elements of worship remained the same. In many cases, the involvement of youth in contemporary worship served to educate them about worship and to deepen their understanding of and participation in the traditional Sunday worship of the congregation.

Worship resources and practice in the 1960s and 1970s reflected the interplay of two different concerns: on the one hand, the desire for contemporary relevancy in language and music, and on the other hand, the interest in liturgical studies and the recovery of historical traditions. Two other Reformed hymnals published during this period exemplify these two concerns. In 1974, *The Hymnal of the United Church of Christ* included selections from the new contemporary worship music. Conversely, the Reformed Church in America published *The Book of Psalms* in 1973, which contained metrical versions for every psalm, but did not include hymns.

Liturgical Resources in the Last Decades of the Twentieth Century

The concern for contemporary relevancy and the interest in the recovery of liturgical tradition continued in the closing decades of the twentieth century. Both were "ecumenical" in nature. New denominational resources intentionally drew from other Christian traditions, and were often produced in consultation across the lines of denomination and tradition. In a different way, more contemporary liturgical practices and music spread across Christian traditions at a more grassroots level, and resources produced by other traditions, or by independent Christian groups or publishers, were increasingly used in many Reformed congregations.

The latest round of Presbyterian worship resources began in 1980, prior to the reunion of the United Presbyterian Church in the U.S.A. and the Presbyterian Church in the U.S. in 1983. These two churches were again joined in this effort by the Cumberland Presbyterian Church. The committee first published a series of seven Supplemental Liturgical Resources, beginning with *Service for the Lord's Day* in 1984. This effort culminated in the publication of the *Book of Common Worship* in 1993. The reunited Presbyterian Church (U.S.A.) also revised its Directory for Worship in 1989. In 1990 *The Presbyterian Hymnal* was published. The selections on this hymnal reflect both ecumenical and cultural diversity, including Native American, African-American, Latin American, and Asian hymns (often with texts in both English and the original language). A Psalter section is included, reflecting an attempt to recover the Reformed emphasis on psalm singing. The hymnal, as well as the Directory for Worship and the *Book of Common Worship,* also demonstrate sensitivity to inclusive language.

Similar resources have been produced by other denominations. The United Church of Christ published the *Book of Worship* in 1986, and the *New Century Hymnal* in 1995. The Reformed Church in America published its latest hymnal, *Rejoice in the Lord,* in 1984, and in 1987 published *Worship the Lord,* which contains both service book materials for worship and a Directory for Worship, as well as *Our Song of Hope,* the confessional statement approved by the 1978 General Synod of the Reformed Church in America. *Liturgy and Confessions,* the most recent Reformed Church in America service book, was published in 1990. It contains liturgies from previous editions (1987, 1968, 1906, and 1792), plus a new baptismal liturgy (added in 1994), as well as four confessional statements (Belgic Confession, 1561; Canons of Dort, 1618-1619; Heidelberg Catechism, 1563; Our Song of Hope, 1978) and the 1989 revisions of The Directory for Worship. The Christian Reformed Church published *The Psalter Hymnal* in 1988, and includes the 1993 Presbyterian *Book of Common Worship* in its catalogue of worship resources.

Into the Twenty-First Century

As the twenty-first century begins, there is still no consensus on worship practice in Reformed churches. In some congregations, the nineteenth-century order of worship, culminating in the sermon, still prevails, and congregational singing is from older denominational hymnbooks or from newer nondenominational hymnals that include a preponderance of nineteenth-century gospel songs. In other congregations, the most recent service books and hymnals are in use.

Increasing numbers of congregations celebrate the Lord's Supper at least monthly, but others still adhere to a quarterly celebration. For example, a 1989 survey of congregations in the Presbyterian Church (U.S.A.) revealed that 1 percent (101) of the congregations were celebrating the Lord's Supper weekly; 68 percent were celebrating it more frequently than quarterly, with nearly 44 percent celebrating it at least monthly; while 32 percent of the congregations still celebrated the sacrament quarterly or less frequently. Comparison with earlier statistics indicated a significant shift toward more frequent celebration of the Lord's Supper since the 1970s,[36] and this trend appears to be continuing.

The most recent development in worship practice is the increasing popularity of a new version of "contemporary worship." The basic order of worship is a preparatory time of singing (fifteen to twenty minutes), followed by the word (Scripture and preaching/teaching), with extemporaneous prayer interspersed. The music is primarily contemporary praise songs and choruses to

36. Harold M. Daniels, "Presbyterians at the Table of the Lord," *Reformed Liturgy and Music* XXV, no. 2 (Spring 1991): 60-64.

the accompaniment of a "praise band," whose members often double as worship leaders. The worship style is informal. The focus of worship is on evangelism — the goal being to attract unchurched "seekers" and/or younger people who are dissatisfied with the church's "traditional" worship.

The impetus for this style of worship comes from independent, evangelical "megachurches," which have attracted large numbers of worshipers by using this worship format. In an effort to counter a declining and aging membership, many Reformed and other mainline Protestant congregations are now offering a contemporary worship service as an alternative to the more traditional service, or are incorporating contemporary elements (particularly music) into their traditional Sunday service.

This new worship style presents numerous challenges for Reformed churches. On the one hand, there is a need to find ways to reach the unchurched in U.S. society and to make worship meaningful and vital. On the other hand, many of the underlying assumptions of this style of contemporary worship, and of its contemporary music, are contrary to a Reformed understanding of the church and its worship. In this model, worship is viewed as evangelism and is directed toward the individual and his or her needs and preferences; but there often seems to be little concern for growth in Christian faith or discipleship, and even less concern for ecclesiology — in terms of the incorporation of the individual into the Body of Christ, or any sense of the invisible, universal church. The divide between the desire for contemporary relevancy and a commitment to the tradition and unity of the church appears to be widening, and may well be the greatest challenge facing Reformed churches in the United States as the twenty-first century unfolds.

For Further Reading

Adams, Douglas. *Meeting House to Camp Meeting: Toward a History of American Free Church Worship from 1620 to 1835*. Austin: The Sharing Company, 1984.

Hageman, Howard G. *Pulpit and Table: Some Chapters in the History of Worship in the Reformed Churches*. Richmond, Va.: John Knox Press, 1962.

Maxwell, Jack Martin. *Worship and Reformed Theology: The Liturgical Lessons of Mercersburg*. Pittsburgh: Pickwick Press, 1976.

Melton, Julius. *Presbyterian Worship in America: Changing Patterns Since 1787*. Richmond, Va.: John Knox Press, 1967.

Nicholas, James Hastings. *Corporate Worship in the Reformed Tradition*. Philadelphia: Westminster Press, 1968.

Schmidt, Leigh Eric. *Holy Fairs: Scotland and the Making of American Revivalism.* Rev. ed. Grand Rapids: Eerdmans, 2001.

White, James F. *Christian Worship in North America, A Retrospective: 1955-1995.* Collegeville, Minn.: Liturgical Press, 1997.

Word, Sacrament, and Communion: New Emphases in Reformed Worship in the Twentieth Century

Alan D. Falconer

Throughout the twentieth century, patterns of worship and the understanding of worship in the Reformed churches, as in churches of every tradition, underwent extensive development and change. Such development has been a response to a variety of factors. Increasing social mobility and interchurch marriages, for example, have led to a greater awareness and appropriation of worship patterns of other traditions. In addition, while at the beginning of the century the church occupied in most societies a central place in the life of the community and the consciousness of the members, such a dramatic shift has occurred that now Sunday worship is for many the principal or only point of contact with the church community. As a result, Sunday worship now often has to assume the task of Christian nurture and education, unlike the beginning of the century, when Sunday worship was reinforced by worship in the home. Finally, while for most churches at the beginning of the century it was possible to assume that Christian symbols and language were immediately understood by the congregation, such an assumption seemed less tenable by the end of the century.

While at the beginning of the century, the normal Sunday worship in most Reformed churches was that of a service of the word, by the end of the century the sacrament of the Lord's Supper was being celebrated more frequently, and the occasion when the service of the word was celebrated was in many cases being seen as a service of ante-communion. Such a development was a response to movements of biblical and liturgical renewal that on the whole transcended the boundaries of Christian traditions. Within the sphere of liturgical renewal there was also a greater appreciation of the Jewish roots of Christian worship. As the twentieth century unfolded, new relationships developed between churches of the Reformed family, as churches in Africa,

Asia, Latin America, and the Caribbean became established and inculturated. Hymns and symbols from their cultures became more central to worship and these were shared with their partner churches, thus bringing new expression and experiences to the worship of the Reformed family. Perhaps for these reasons, among others, through the century there developed an important place for imagination in the creation of liturgies and the development of symbols, where previously there had been an emphasis on starkness and simplicity. As Reformed churches participated in the ecumenical movement, and particularly in international bilateral and multilateral dialogues, they have engaged in theological investigations of the nature and meaning of Christian worship, and this has led to new and renewed theological understandings, particularly in regard to the sacrament of the Lord's Supper. At the beginning of the century, children on the whole sat silently through worship, while more recently they have participated in the services and in some Reformed churches may also "communicate" in the sacrament of the Lord's Supper.[1]

Development and change in the worship of the Reformed churches, therefore, has been a response to social factors, the insights of biblical studies, the impact of the liturgical movement, and participation in ecumenical dialogue. With such a variety of factors, each of which has been shaped by the others, it is often difficult to determine the dominant influences on the changes in Reformed worship throughout the century. In this context, it is therefore important to emphasize that the role of theology as such has been a modest one. In many places in Europe and North America in particular, a division in the theological curricula between theology and practical theology has been evident. In many theological institutes, worship was almost a second-class activity — despite the basic definitions in the Reformed confessions of the church as the community of word and sacrament. Often the theology of worship, where it was explored at all (for example, under the theme "the theology of the sacraments"), was explored without any reference to the "ordo" or the content of worship, and was also not necessarily linked to Christology or Trinitarian theology. While that pattern may have been evident in departments of theology, the practitioners of practical theology often worked on the assumption that a theological foundation for their work had been laid. While this fragmentation of theology — a fragmentation evident also between biblical and theological sciences — was still evident at the end of the twentieth century, it is not necessarily the pattern that has developed in African and Asian theological colleges. It is therefore important to claim only a modest role for theological research in the change of patterns and understandings of worship throughout the century.

---

1. See Alan P. F. Sell's discussion of children in worship on pp. 104-5 of this volume.

Development and change in worship have varied in the different churches of the Reformed tradition, and at the beginning of the twenty-first century as at the beginning of the twentieth, diversity rather than uniformity remains a feature of the patterns of worship and the understanding of worship in the Reformed churches. It is therefore difficult to determine what is a specifically Reformed attitude or understanding of the nature of worship. Those theologians of the Reformed tradition who have reflected on worship and the sacrament of the Lord's Supper have done so in conversation with theologians of other traditions, and have drawn on their insights.[2] In such dialogue, however, there have been a number of themes, which have been offered as contributions to the shape, understanding, and event of Christian worship from and to the Reformed heritage. In identifying these themes, it is important to place them within the wider horizon of the developments in and influences upon the discussion of worship.

The Liturgical Movement

A major influence on patterns of worship and the understanding of worship has been the conversation among liturgical scholars and theologians throughout the twentieth century and into the twenty-first. Scholars of different traditions have sought to explore the roots of Christian worship in the attempt to understand better the "ordo" of worship, the significance of worship in the life of the church, and to develop appropriate prayers and symbols for the worshiping life of contemporary communities.

Already at the end of the nineteenth century, Eugène Bersier[3] of Paris had emphasized the centrality of the worship of the church in Christian life and the need for the Reformed churches to recover liturgical life. He himself produced a liturgy that emphasized worship as a fully corporate action and that balanced word and sacrament. Throughout the twentieth century, Bersier's work has been pursued in different Reformed churches by theologians and liturgical scholars who have engaged in dialogue with other scholars. It has also been pursued by churches through the establishment of specific committees and commissions. The Church of Scotland in the early part of the twentieth century, for example, established a Committee on Public Worship

---

2. To cite only three examples among so many: Donald Baillie, *The Theology of the Sacraments and Other Papers* (London: Faber, 1957); Jean-Jacques von Allmen, *Worship: Its Theology and Practice* (London: Lutterworth, 1965); Michael Welker, *What Happens in Holy Communion?* (Grand Rapids: Eerdmans, 2000).

3. For a more detailed description of Bersier and his work, see Bruno Bürki, pp. 46-48 in this volume.

and Aids to Devotion to address what many felt was "the unfettered freedom of ministers to conduct worship as they saw fit, allowing diversity and even idiosyncrasy."[4] The Reformed churches generally appointed to these commissions scholars and pastors who were also involved in discussions beyond the boundaries of their church on matters of worship. Although much work was done on the different roots and rites of Reformed worship, the developments in Reformed worship throughout the century have owed an immense debt to the conversation across the Christian traditions on the nature and meaning of Christian worship. This conversation has had an impact on the shape of Reformed worship, the prayers and texts of worship, the hymnody, the use of a lectionary, and the theological understanding of worship. Undoubtedly one legacy of the liturgical movement has been the more frequent celebration of the Lord's Supper within Reformed churches and in non-Reformed Christian traditions. While other contributors to this volume explore in greater detail each of these elements, it is important to note that this has been the context and one of the significant fora in which theological discussion has taken place. Reformed scholars have contributed to the wider debate, and Reformed churches have drawn on the insights of the liturgical movement.

Communities

In the course of the twentieth century, some communities have come into existence as a result of initiatives by Reformed pastors and theologians, and some of these have had a major influence on the practice and understanding of worship in Reformed churches and churches of other Christian communities. Perhaps the best known of these is the Taizé community in southeast France, which was founded by Roger Schutz and Max Thurian during the Second World War. This community developed a cycle of worship, a liturgy, liturgical music, and prayers that have become part of the worship materials frequently used in the worship of the churches and of ecumenical groups. Through the work of Max Thurian, the theological understanding of worship has also been enhanced, as we shall see. A number of "dispersed communities" have also been founded through the initiatives of Reformed pastors and theologians. Of these, perhaps the best known is the Iona Community, founded by Dr. George McLeod. This Scottish community, founded in 1937 to emphasize the connection between church and society, comes together once a year, at least, on the is-

---

4. See Duncan Forrester and Douglas Murray, eds., *Studies in the History of Worship in Scotland,* 2nd ed. (Edinburgh: T&T Clark, 1996), p. 177.

land of Iona, and maintains its community life during the year through a discipline of worship, service, commitment to peace, and common support. Its weekly cycle of worship on a different theme each day has influenced the pattern and understanding of worship in Reformed and other churches, and its hymns, compiled and composed by its "Wild Goose Group," have entered the hymnals of many churches.[5]

Historical Studies

While liturgical studies and the liturgical movement have contributed to the development of worship in the Reformed tradition, a number of studies by Reformed historians have created a climate that encouraged such change. The works of John T. McNeill, Ford Lewis Battles, Brian Gerrish, and Elsie McKee, for example, have through an examination of the writings of the Reformers and of the classic Reformed confessions of faith sought to move behind stereotypes to the main emphases in the thought of the fathers of the Reformed tradition. While a differentiation of thought among the Reformers has been evident, it is clear that the tradition's major confessions of faith have drawn on the insights of John Calvin.[6] Thus, while there was a plurality of voices in the Reformed tradition of the time of the Reformation, there has been an increasing focus on the life and thought of John Calvin, which has influenced the thought, life, and worship of Reformed churches in the twentieth century — creating a climate, for example, that has facilitated discussion on the frequency of the celebration of the Lord's Supper.

Biblical Studies

Central to the development of patterns of worship and the understanding of worship, within both Reformed circles and the liturgical movement as a whole, has been the contribution of biblical scholarship. The Reformed confessions of

5. See for example, Rex Brico, *Taizé: Brother Roger and His Community* (London: Collins, 1978); The Taizé Community, *The Taizé Liturgy* (London: Faith Press, 1960); Ronald Ferguson, The Iona Community, *Choosing the Wild Goose: The Story of the Iona Community* (Glasgow: Wild Goose Publications, 1998); and *Iona Abbey Worship Book* (Glasgow: Wild Goose Publications, 2001). For the first twenty-five years of its existence the worship of the community was regarded with suspicion by many in the Church of Scotland.

6. See Brian A. Gerrish, *The Old Protestantism and the New* (Edinburgh: T&T Clark, 1982), pp. 118-30.

faith invariably emphasize the central role of Scripture for understanding and articulating Christian faith, and the Reformed tradition in particular has therefore sought to develop systematic theology in relation to the testimony of Scripture. Reformed biblical scholars have contributed to the development of Reformed worship as well as that of other traditions. One such scholar is Oscar Cullmann, who assisted the churches in understanding early Christian worship and the prayers in the New Testament, and in recovering an awareness of the importance of both the resurrection meals of Jesus and the community for understanding the significance of the sacrament of the Lord's Supper.[7]

Out of all the influences on worship, biblical scholarship has, in Reformed churches, had the largest impact, so it is important to note that study of the Bible has undoubtedly been decisive in helping Reformed churches change their patterns of worship. Through preaching and teaching, the story of the road to Emmaus (Luke 24:13-53) raised questions about the separation of word and sacrament. In this narrative, the breaking of the bread and sharing of the cup led to an understanding of and appropriation of the word, which had been preached but not understood. A renewed appreciation of this incident led many to emphasize the inseparability of word and sacrament, and thus to begin celebrating the Lord's Supper more frequently. The Reformed churches in the Netherlands have even placed this text in the introduction to their new worship book.[8] Another question arising from biblical scholarship concerned the implications of the feeding of the five thousand (John 6:1-58). Many biblical scholars emphasized that this incident was for John's Gospel the principal meditation on the Lord's Supper. In congregations of Reformed churches in the Canton of Neuchâtel in the early 1970s, for example, a number of sermons explored the implication of the fact that children also would have received the manna in the wilderness, and therefore, since the Exodus experience was a "type" for interpreting the Eucharist, should not children also communicate fully in the celebration of the Lord's Supper? For a number of Reformed churches this issue has become an important one for the practice of the celebration and for the recovery of the emphasis on the sacrament as a community meal.

---

7. See Oscar Cullmann, *Early Christian Worship* (London: SCM Press, 1953), and *Prayer in the New Testament* (Minneapolis: Fortress Press, 1995).

8. *Dienstbook. Een Proeve. Schrift — maaltijd — gebed* (Zoetermeer: Boekcentrum, 1998).

The Ecumenical Movement

The participation of the Reformed churches in the ecumenical movement has also been influential in the development of the Reformed understanding of worship and, particularly, of the Lord's Supper. Initially that participation was primarily through membership in the Faith and Order Commission. In the first phase of multilateral dialogue, Reformed churches presented their understanding of the worship and the sacrament of the Lord's Super in the context of presentations by representatives of other churches. The methodology of dialogue in the first period of ecumenical encounter was comparative. Different positions were compared, differences noted, and a continuing agenda emerged in the attempt to resolve those differences. By the Third World Conference on Faith and Order in Lund (1952), it was apparent that the time had come to develop a different methodology. On the proposal of, among others, T. F. Torrance, it was decided to move to a methodology of convergence whereby scholars from different traditions would seek to offer a common understanding of worship and the sacraments. It was through the adoption of this methodology that the text on *Baptism, Eucharist and Ministry* was developed and eventually adopted at Lima (1982). For the study on the Eucharist, the contribution of scholars from the Reformed churches was fundamental — with Oscar Cullmann and F. J. Leenhardt in the background,[9] and Jean-Jacques von Allmen, Max Thurian, and Lukas Vischer as major contributors. While Reformed churches were appreciative of the final text of *Baptism, Eucharist, and Ministry* with regard to the Eucharist section, they raised a number of critical points, especially concerning the statement that the Lord's Supper is "the central act of the Church's worship." They also raised questions about the relationship between word and sacrament, feeling that not enough emphasis had been placed on the word. Many churches, however, sought to change their practice in light of the text.[10]

In the second half of the twentieth century, Reformed churches increasingly participated in bilateral dialogues with churches of other Christian traditions at regional, national, and international levels. In many of these dialogues, worship and especially the sacrament of the Lord's Supper were central subjects of conversation. These dialogues have led to an increased awareness of the importance of the Lord's Supper in the life of the church, and in many cases have led to the establishment of "pulpit and altar" fellowship, or "full communion," with other churches. Most of the themes evident in these dia-

---

9. See Oscar Cullmann and F. J. Leenhardt, *Essays on the Lord's Supper* (London: Lutterworth, 1958).

10. See *Churches Respond to BEM,* vols. 1-6 (Geneva: WCC, 1986-1988).

logues also are evident in the multilateral dialogues. For the international dialogue between the Reformed church and the Roman Catholic Church, however, the Reformed emphasis on Jesus Christ as Gift and Giver was particularly important.[11] The importance of this theme for ecumenical dialogue is that it challenges practices that exclude some from participating fully in the celebration of the Lord's Supper.

Ecumenical dialogues have been theaters in which Reformed theologians have been invited to offer their contributions to the wider Christian community, and they have provided occasions for Reformed churches to clarify and alter their understanding and practice of Christian worship. The attitude of some Reformed churches toward the ecumenical movement has unfortunately made it difficult for them to appropriate these developments and insights that have been embraced by other churches of the tradition.

Major Emphases in the Theological Debate

The liturgical movement, biblical scholarship, and ecumenical dialogue have, as we have seen, provided the occasion for discussion within Reformed and other churches on worship. From this work a number of major themes emerged from Reformed theologians which have had an impact on the practice and understanding of Reformed and other churches.

Recovery of an Appreciation of "Sacrament"

In the context of the Church of Scotland and the multilateral discussions of Faith and Order, Donald Baillie developed a theology of the sacraments that drew on the treasures of biblical theology, affirmed the Reformed emphasis on the "word of promise" as fundamental to the understanding of "sacrament," and sought to develop a wider idea of a "sacramental universe" than had been prominent in the Reformed tradition.[12] Whereas hitherto the understanding of sacrament had highlighted the nature of celebration as a "sign and seal" of the covenant, Baillie began to ask why material things should not be taken by the word and conse-

11. In "The Presence of Christ in Church and World" (1977) in *Growth in Agreement*, ed. Harding Meyer and Lukas Vischer (Geneva: WCC, 1984). See also Faith and Order Paper No. 108, pp. 433-63, for which the paper by T. F. Torrance, "The Paschal Mystery of Christ and the Eucharist," in T. F. Torrance, *Theology in Reconciliation* (London: Chapman, 1975), was important.

12. Donald Baillie, *Theology of the Sacraments*, p. 41.

crated to be instruments of divine grace. In developing this theme, Donald Baillie quotes Paul Tillich's *The Protestant Era* approvingly: Natural objects can become bearers of transcendent power and meaning. They can become sacramental elements. This is the basis for a Protestant rediscovery of the sacramental sphere, because of the relation of the material to historical divine revelation. In this understanding, Baillie reaffirmed Reformed themes such as covenant, promise, and the word as event and demonstrated the essential elements of an understanding of "sacrament" that maintained and strengthened the link between word and sacrament, affirming their interdependence and interrelation.

Anamnesis

A second major theme, which has been important for the development of the practice and understanding of worship and the sacrament of the Lord's Supper, has been that of "anamnesis" or memorial. While work had been done on this subject by Dom Gregory Dix and by Joachim Jeremias, it was the study undertaken by Max Thurian, a Reformed theologian and co-founder of the Taizé community, that has been particularly influential in Reformed churches. In the context of the Taizé community, Thurian was involved in shaping the ordo of the community's worship and in developing an understanding of the nature and meaning of that worship. In pursuit of this aim he provided a commentary on the movement and meaning of the liturgy — thus allowing those participating to engage in the celebration more meaningfully (a practice Thurian was to adopt again twenty-five years later when he drafted the Lima Liturgy and provided a commentary on it for the Faith and Order Commission).[13] He also produced for the community an extensive study on the meaning of the term *memorial* in the Hebrew Scriptures and the New Testament. While this drew on the work of other biblical scholars, it was also developed for the work of the Groupe des Dombes — a group of mainly Reformed and Roman Catholic theologians in southeast France who engaged in an informal dialogue, which had been initiated by Abbé Paul Couturier.[14] The Groupe des

13. See the Taizé liturgy in The Taizé Community's *The Eucharist* (London: Faith Press, 1962), and the Lima liturgy in *Baptism and Eucharist: Ecumenical Convergence in Celebration,* ed. Max Thurian (Geneva: WCC, 1983).

14. For the early history of the Les Dombes Group see Patrick Rodger's introduction to *Ecumenical Dialogue in Europe: The Ecumenical Conversations at Les Dombes,* trans. W. Fletcher Fleet (London: Lutterworth, 1966); and for the influence of the group on *Baptism, Eucharist, Ministry* see Alan D. Falconer, "To Walk Together: The Lima Report on Baptism, Eucharist, Ministry," *The Furrow* 34, no. 1, p. 83.

Dombes had produced a number of theses on the "Eucharist" in the 1950s and then began to work on a theological statement and statement of pastoral principles and practice in the 1960s. Max Thurian was a prominent member of that group, which had an immense influence on the development of the statement on the Eucharist of the Faith and Order Commission finalized at Lima in 1982.

In his extensive study *The Eucharistic Memorial,* Max Thurian emphasizes that the phrase "Do this in memory of me . . ." derives from the liturgical language of Judaism and is particularly associated with the celebration of the Passover.[15] The phrase appears frequently in the paschal rite, which, Thurian notes, is the framework for the Eucharist. As he indicates, during the Last Supper Jesus would have prayed, "Blessed art Thou, O Lord our God . . . who hast given to Thy people Israel this season of festivity for joy and for a memorial." Each item of food had its own significance, and as the Jews ate the food, they could re-live mystically, sacramentally, the events of the deliverance and exodus from Egypt. The celebration of the Passover enabled the concrete re-living of the deliverance of the people of God. Memorial is thus becoming one with the event and effects of deliverance and reappropriating the promises of God. Thurian emphasizes, however, that in one of the prayers of the paschal meal, we find that God is asked to recall the Messiah — a recalling to God in prayer of a promise he had made, asking him to fulfill it. Thurian concludes:

> In the paschal meal, we find a triple anamnesis, *a triple memorial:* of a past deliverance regarded as typical, of a present deliverance through the sacramental action of the paschal meal and of a coming salvation in the day of the Messiah. The post deliverance becomes a pledge of that which is to come, which will be perfect and definite.[16]

Through this study, Thurian addresses those within the Reformed family in particular who have wished to assume that memorial is simply the recalling of a past event. Thurian demonstrates that, on the contrary, the event of deliverance is present in the worshiping community, liberating them now and inviting them to live in the horizon of final and complete liberation.

In addition to his understanding of memorial as past, present, and future, Thurian's study focuses on four issues important for Reformed as well as for other churches. First, Thurian emphasizes the communal dimension of the celebration. Noting the importance of the fact that the Passover was also a meal offering, Thurian reinforces a constant Reformed emphasis on the corporate nature of celebration of the sacrament of the Lord's Supper. Within the Re-

15. Max Thurian, *The Eucharistic Memorial,* 2 vols. (London: Lutterworth, 1961-1962).
16. Thurian, *The Eucharistic Memorial,* vol. 1, p. 11.

formed tradition, while every effort was made to affirm the community-meal aspect of the sacrament, a countervailing tendency was also evident in the teaching and discipline of the churches which emphasized that the sacrament is "a means of grace." Because this latter point was invariably placed alongside other "means of grace" — regular reading of the Bible and personal prayer — it was often interpreted individualistically. The association between "being cate-chized" and "personal worthiness" prior to participation in the celebration fur-ther reinforced the tendency to focus on the celebration of the sacrament as an event for members of the church rather than for the community as such. Thurian's study — along with those of Oscar Cullmann and F. J. Leenhardt on the resurrection meals of Jesus and their relation to the sacrament — facilitated a renewed emphasis for Reformed churches on the Lord's Supper as a commu-nity meal to which all are invited and in which all participate fully.

The memorial is also an offering to God, and Thurian's second focus was on the intrinsic connection between the celebration of the sacrament and the forgiveness of sin. The meal is a thanksgiving to God that God has united himself with the believer; it is a peace offering signifying the community of life between God and the community of faithful servants, which involves a thanksgiving offering (sacrifice of praise) and a promise of salvation on the part of, and supplication for salvation and unity of, the people of God. And it is also an oblation and a sin offering, an act of reparation for sin committed, an expiation for sin that involved substitution. Thus thanksgiving and interces-sion are intimately connected.

In discussing the understanding of sacrifice, Thurian then turned his at-tention to the New Testament where *anamnesis* is used three times to designate the eucharistic memorial (Luke 22:19 and 1 Corinthians 11:24 and 25), and its synonym is used in a number of other passages. Because of Christ's sacrifice, Thurian argues, God remembers only his mercy. The memorial is thus not a repetition of Christ's sacrifice but a re-presentation of it. In Hebrews, anamnesis is paralleled with aphesis (remission of sin). Thus the eucharistic celebration is an event of forgiveness for individuals who truly repent, but also for the community. The Eucharist is a re-presentation of the whole life, minis-try, death, and rising of Jesus Christ. Through his study, therefore, Thurian helps Reformed churches to appreciate the language of sacrifice as a language appropriate to the sacrament.

Finally, Thurian outlines the link between Christ and the community through the power of the Holy Spirit. The sacrament of the Lord's Supper is the sacrificial presence of the sacrifice of the cross, by the power of the Holy Spirit and the word, and it is the liturgical presentation by the church of the Son's sacrifice, in thanksgiving for all his blessings and in intercession that he might grant them afresh. It is the participation of the community in the intercession of the Son before the Father in the Holy Spirit, that salvation may be accorded to all and that the Kingdom may come in glory. It is the offering that the church itself makes to the Father, united to Christ's intercession, as its supreme act of adoration and its perfect consecration in the Holy Spirit.[17]

In summary, throughout all of Thurian's emphases, the rhythm is that of the action of God and the response of the community.

Epiclesis

A third major theme in the understanding of worship in Reformed churches has been an emphasis on the epiclesis, the prayer to the Holy Spirit offered in the Eucharist. In Reformed tradition the prayer to the Holy Spirit, while it has been seen as safeguarding the community from assuming that it or its representative is responsible for the action of God, has also been important in describing the presence of Christ in and with the community. Reformed theologians during the Reformation emphasized the "spiritual presence of Christ" in the Lord's Supper. For many in the Reformed churches, this designation was understood as being opposed to "real," and in some circumstances for Reformed Christians that opposition was reinforced as an expression over and against Roman Catholic theology. While the intention of Reformed theologians was the twofold project of affirming the mystery of God and the priority of God's action through the Holy Spirit, this was not always understood in the tradition. Throughout the twentieth century there has been a recovery of the importance of the prayer to the Holy Spirit and the understanding of the role of the Holy Spirit in worship.

In the context of the Les Dombes conversations and of the multilateral conversations of the Faith and Order Commission, that Reformed emphasis on the epiclesis has been developed by, among others, Jean-Jacques von Allmen, Professor of Practical Theology at the University of Neuchâtel. Von Allmen became a member of the study commission on the Eucharist appointed by the Faith and Order Working Committee at its meeting in Aarhus (1964). The two principal themes to be explored were those of anamnesis and epiclesis, and out of this process eventually emerged the Eucharist section of the Lima agreement on "Baptism, Eucharist, and Ministry."

In his study *The Lord's Supper,*[18] von Allmen explores the relationship between epiclesis and anamnesis. By epiclesis he means the prayer that calls on

17. Thurian, *The Eucharistic Memorial,* vol. 2, p. 76.
18. Jean-Jacques von Allmen, *The Lord's Supper* (London: Lutterworth, 1969).

the Holy Spirit to act so that the Supper really becomes what Christ intended. Drawing on the words "It is the spirit that gives life; the flesh is of no avail" (John 6:63), he emphasizes that the mystery and the energy of the Eucharist are not at man's disposal, but must be sought in prayer. The character of the community is that of a praying church.

> When we try to gather together what the Church then prays for, two things must be emphasised. The Church first beseeches God to renew the event of Pentecost by freely offering to Him the purposes for which this eschatological event is above all desired; the people assembled to commemorate the history of salvation and the bread and wine brought by the Church because these were the elements of the meal which the Lord chose. In other words, the Church shows 'herself and her gifts' as an offering, so that, because of them, Pentecost may be renewed and remain a living experience, so that the eschatological condition, into which the members of the Church were initiated by baptism, may be confirmed, and that, in this condition, the recapitulation of all things in Christ may be lived out by those who take part in the cult.
>
> In the second place, this oblative prayer is supported by the certainty of its fulfilment. . . . The Church prays for the coming, not of a pedlar of dreams, but of the *pneuma tsoepaioun,* the Spirit which has power to confer eternal life, and to transform into eternal truth what is offered in blundering words here below. For this reason, the advent of the Spirit is invoked, not only on the baptised gathered for the Supper, but also on their gifts, so that the food may not belong to the order of the flesh which serves for nought but that it may be for them . . . spiritual food and drink, permeated with the Spirit and consequently with the presence of the Kingdom.[19]

Through the study, von Allmen examines in a dialogical context the significance of the role of the Holy Spirit and invites the Reformed churches to explore further their understanding of "spiritual presence." The work of the Holy Spirit enables the community to reflect that which God intends and thus to become a sign to the world of God's intention.

Intercession

The Christian community is invited not only to celebrate the gifts of God but to participate in God's intention for humankind. There has always been a

19. Von Allmen, *The Lord's Supper,* p. 32.

strong emphasis in the Reformed churches on the twofold meaning of *leitourgia* and the intrinsic connection between worship and the life of the community in the world. In many Reformed churches this has been evident through closing the church doors from Monday to Saturday as an expression of the fact of God's presence with the community as they live as the church in the world. In some contexts, the church building is simply called the "meeting-house" to stress this connection — it is the house where the community meets on Sunday to worship God, but otherwise the worship of God is to be experienced in the life of the church in society.

This link between worship and mission was in the course of the twentieth century stressed by Reformed theologians. In the context of his work in the Faith and Order Commission, Lukas Vischer published a study on intercession that has enabled churches, including the Reformed churches, to pray with each other meaningfully. This study provided a substantial basis for the Ecumenical Prayer Cycle, where churches throughout the world pray for each other in an annual cycle and express their communion in solidarity with each other. The study is an exploration of the nature of intercession in the Hebrew Scriptures and the New Testament. The links between intercession, anamnesis, and epiclesis are evident. Of particular interest is the strong Christological basis of intercession that Vischer identifies:

> The entire work of Christ can be presented from this standpoint, as intercession. In one sense, what he did was simply to intercede for all. He meets us with perfect love. He bears the burdens of others. He heals, he sets us free at the cost of his own freedom. He ends his life on a cross. By his life and by his death, he brings us into the presence of God in order that we may be welcomed into fellowship with him. His life and his death are an intercession, above all, for his disciples. By his intercession they are set free for a new life, united in a new fellowship, and called to bear witness in the world. But not just the disciples; also those who believe in him because of their preaching and action. He prayed for them and continues to pray: "that they may all be one; even as thou, Father, art in me and I in thou, that they also may be in us, so that the world may believe that thou hast sent me." He is the source of the fellowship which binds them to each other. When they intercede for one another with God, his intercession is there in the background. It leaves its stamp on what they are able to do for one another.[20]

20. Lukas Vischer, *Intercession,* Faith and Order Paper No. 95 (Geneva: WCC, 1980), pp. 5f.

In this study Vischer provides a solid basis for linking intercession with the celebration of the Lord's Supper and joins those biblical scholars who tentatively suggest that in John's Gospel the feeding of the five thousand and the high priestly prayer of John 17 may be eucharistic in character. In this the strong impulse of mission, of discipleship, is seen to be an intrinsic element of worship, thus reinforcing the double aspect of *leitourgia*.

Word, Sacrament, Communion

Throughout the twentieth century, theologians of the Reformed tradition developed their reflections on the nature of worship in the context of new social configurations in society, drawing on the insights of biblical studies, engaging in conversation with liturgical scholars, and participating in the dialogues of the ecumenical movement. The contribution of such scholars has facilitated change and development in the rites of worship and particularly in the understanding of the sacrament of the Lord's Supper, not only in the Reformed churches but in churches of other traditions as well. Indeed, it is important to stress that Reformed scholars have demonstrated that the Reformed tradition does not live to and for itself. Their work is placed as a contribution to the life, witness, and reflection of all Christian churches. In many respects it calls up the memory of C. H. Dodd, the Reformed biblical scholar who in the first part of the century wrote,

> In the sacrament we accept that which God gives, become that which he makes of us (by grace, not by merit) and render it up to him. . . . Indeed, in this Sacrament the whole of what our religion means is expressed. That which otherwise we apprehend piecemeal is integrated in a rite which presents it all as the sheer gift of God. On any one occasion we may be conscious only of this or that element in the meaning; but it is all there, because God in Christ is there. In dependence on Him for everything, we render it all back to Him in thankful adoration.[21]

For C. H. Dodd and for the Reformed theologians upon whom I have drawn above, the Lord's Supper is undoubtedly the central act of worship of the Christian community. In the twentieth century more Reformed churches have supported this view, moving toward more frequent celebration of the sac-

---

21. C. H. Dodd, *Christian Worship,* cited in F. W. Dillistone, *C. H. Dodd: Interpreter of the New Testament* (London: Hodder and Stoughton, 1977).

rament, as John Calvin himself desired; this trend has not been universal, however, and has been a matter of debate among Reformed churches.

While the classical confessions of faith of the Reformed churches speak of the church as the community of the true preaching of the word, the right administration of the sacraments, and (for some) the place where ecclesiastical discipline is uprightly administered, only a few of the twentieth-century confessions of faith mention worship at all.[22]

As C. H. Dodd and the other scholars cited earlier emphasize, however, at the celebration of the Lord's Supper, the whole drama of salvation in Christ is re-presented. The community is brought into existence through the event of God's action, and at each celebration is nourished and sustained by it. It is the totality of this drama that provides the "hermeneutical key" through which the community seeks to discern how to worship God in every aspect of its life. As the community celebrates "This . . . my body . . . ,"[23] its very identity as the Body of Christ is affirmed and appropriated. This is, and becomes again, the community committed to live in the light of the dying and rising Jesus of Nazareth. Through the action of the Holy Spirit, the gathering of Christians, who have become fragmented, is drawn into becoming a community, where the members, as John Calvin noted, are interdependent in Christ.[24] This community offers a witness to the society in which it is placed through its life of costly discipleship and its activity of building up and promoting that which is human and of pointing to that which dehumanizes in society — and always in the light of the attempt to discern God's will. Each community is nevertheless experiencing the presence of Christ in the church in that place. Each community is nevertheless also interdependent with other communities in different places who celebrate "This . . . my body" and seek to be faithful in their context.

The sacrament of the Lord's Supper is therefore a celebration of the fullness of the drama of salvation in Christ, an expression of the identity of the community (of how the community understands itself and the society it seeks to save), a confession to the world of God's intention and vision for humankind, and a charter for engagement with issues of humanization and dehumanization. Since the sacrament is celebrated in each time and place, the church,

22. See Lukas Vischer, ed., *Reformed Witness Today: A Collection of Confessions and Statements of Faith Issued by Reformed Churches* (Bern: Evangelische Arbeitsstelle Oukumene Schweiz, 1982). Notable among those who do are the Congregational Church in England and Wales (1967) and the Presbyterian Church (U.S.A) (1967).

23. As scholars remind us, Aramaic has no verb "to be," and thus I am using this expression for the words of Jesus.

24. John Calvin, *Institutes of the Christian Religion,* bk. IV, chap. 17, section 38.

through its various attempts to be faithful, affirms that unity in diversity, which is an essential witness in a divided and fragmented word.

The change and development that has taken place in Reformed worship has done much to reveal that indeed the sacrament of the Lord's Supper is central to the church's self-understanding and is the community of word-sacrament-discipline.

For Further Reading

Barkley, John. *Worship of the Reformed Church.* London: Lutterworth, 1966.

Barth, Markus. *Rediscovering the Lord's Supper.* Atlanta: John Knox Press, 1988.

Best, T., and D. Heller, eds. *So We Believe, So We Pray: Towards Koinonia in Worship.* Faith and Order Paper No. 171. Geneva: WCC, 1995.

Edwall, Pehr, Eric Hayman, and W. D. Maxwell, eds. *Ways of Worship: The Report of a Theological Commission of Faith and Order.* New York: Harper, 1951.

Forrester, Duncan, James I. H. McDonald, and Gian Tellini. *Encounter with God: An Introduction to Christian Worship and Practice.* 2nd ed. Edinburgh, T&T Clark, 1996.

Gerrish, Brian A. *Grace and Gratitude: The Eucharistic Theology of John Calvin.* Edinburgh: T&T Clark, 1993.

McCormick, Scott, Jr. *The Lord's Supper: A Biblical Interpretation.* Philadelphia: Westminster, 1966.

McKim, Donald, ed. *Major Themes in the Reformed Tradition.* Grand Rapids: Eerdmans, 1992. See especially pp. 273-310 (the essays by Nicholas Wolterstorff and LindaJo McKim).

Spinks, Bryan D., and Iain Torrance, eds. *To Glorify God: Essays on Modern Reformed Liturgy.* Edinburgh: T&T Clark, 1999.

Thurian, Max. *The Eucharist Memorial.* 2 vols. London: Lutterworth, 1961-62.

Vischer, Lukas. *Intercession.* Faith and Order Paper No. 95. Geneva: WCC, 1980.

Welker, Michael. *What Happens in Holy Communion?* Grand Rapids: Eerdmans, 2000.

Reformed Liturgy in the South African Context

Coenraad Burger

The Reformed Family in South Africa

Churches of Reformed origin form quite a large part of the Christian community in South Africa. According to the 1996 national census, the Dutch Reformed family is the largest denominational family in the country and constitutes 13 percent of the country's total Christian population. If the numbers of the other Reformed churches are added to those of the Dutch Reformed Church, the percentage rises to about 20 percent — compared, for instance, to the Catholics' 11 percent, the Methodists' 9 percent, and the Anglicans' 6 percent.

The Reformed family in South Africa consists of three large church groups and a vast number of smaller churches. All of these groups consist of both people who migrated to Africa and converts who joined the church as a result of missionary efforts.

The first of these groups and also, as we have mentioned, the largest, is the family of the Dutch Reformed churches. Sadly, these churches are still struggling to overcome the racial divisions between the predominantly white Dutch Reformed Church (DRC) and the Uniting Reformed Church (URC), which consists mainly of blacks and so-called coloreds. These two churches each have a membership of well over a million. The situation is further complicated by the existence of two smaller churches that also are connected with this family, the Dutch Reformed Church in Africa (the part of the black Reformed church that decided to stay out when, in 1990, the Uniting Reformed Church was formed) and the Reformed Church in Africa (which is predominantly Indian in membership). During the past decade several efforts have been made to bring these groups together, but the process has proved difficult.

As the name indicates, the Dutch Reformed family originated from the Reformed Church in the Netherlands. During the nineteenth century, however, a number of Scottish pastors were called to serve congregations in South Africa. These Scottish pastors, especially the Murray clan, had an immense influence on the Dutch Reformed Church. Through the influence of the Murrays — and through the influence of the *Nadere Reformatie,* the "Second Reformation" in the Netherlands — the DRC became a Reformed church with a definite leaning toward Pietism. Even today the brand of Reformed theology practiced by the DRC has a definitely evangelical nature. To a large extent this applies to all four groups within the DRC family.

The second largest Reformed group in South Africa is the Presbyterians, with a combined membership of over 700,000. Their churches are also divided along racial lines, though in September 1999 the two largest Presbyterian churches merged to form the Uniting Presbyterian Church of Southern Africa. The roots of this church are predominantly Scottish.

The third group is the Congregational churches. They came into existence through the work of the London Missionary Society (LMS). The largest denomination by far in this group is the United Congregational Church in Southern Africa (UCCSA) with a membership of almost 350,000.

Apart from these three large groups, there are a number of smaller Reformed churches that developed mainly through schisms within the larger churches. The most important ones are the Nederduits Hervormde Kerk van Suid-Afrika (NHKSA) (a predominantly white church with a membership of 170,000) and the Gereformeerde Kerk in Suid-Afrika (also a predominantly white church, based in Potchefstroom, with a membership of just over 100,000). The former president of South Africa F. W. de Klerk is an active member of the Gereformeerde Kerk. Both these churches broke away from the Dutch Reformed Church in the mid–nineteenth century. The NHKSA had ties with the Hervormde Kerk in the Netherlands and tended to be theologically more liberal, while the Gereformeerde Kerk tended to be theologically more conservative.

This chapter will focus on the liturgical developments in the DRC primarily because that body represents the oldest Reformed tradition in South Africa but also because it is the church of which the author has the best personal knowledge. After tracing the developments in the DRC, I will pay brief attention to the Uniting Reformed Church and then also to the developments in the Presbyterian as well as the Congregational churches.

Liturgical Developments in the Dutch Reformed Church

Origins (1652-1800)

When the Dutch East India Company (VOC) started the halfway station at the Cape they brought the Reformed faith, then the official Dutch religion, with them. For the duration of the Dutch settlement (1652-1795) the Dutch Reformed Church (or the Reformed Church, as it was then called) was effectively the official church and was supported by the political rulers of the Cape. This meant that the church was in effect under the authority of the government, who not only supplied the pastors or spiritual workers but also had the final say in all church matters.

The brand of Reformed liturgy that the settlers brought along was not Calvin's Genevan liturgy, but the Dutch version of Petrus Dathenus, which had been formulated at the Synod of Dordrecht in 1574 and confirmed by the important National Synod of 1618-1619. The order of service was the following: adjutorium, psalm or hymn, reading of the Decalogue (often responded to with a hymn), prayer, Scripture reading, hymn, sermon, hymn, prayer (called the prayer for the needs of all Christendom, concluding with the Lord's Prayer), hymn, benediction.[1] The center of the service was a strong and normally didactic sermon. Another characteristic of the Dathenian liturgy was the extensive use of long explanatory formulas to be read at baptismal services, the Lord's Supper (celebrated quarterly), and other occasional services. The 1566 Psalter of Dathenus was part of the package received from the church in the Netherlands.

For the duration of the Dutch political reign at the Cape (until 1795) the liturgical developments in the DRC followed the pattern of the church in the Netherlands to a very large extent. There were two reasons for this. First, all the pastors were educated in the Netherlands, and second, the Cape church was not allowed to form its own synod but was formally under the jurisdiction of the classis of Amsterdam. Although the French Huguenots and some Germans joined the church, the Dutch influence prevailed.

The liturgy did not change much during these years. There is reason to believe that the sermon became an even more important part of the service, overshadowing all the other elements. This was reflected in the fact that more and more of the other elements were moved to a position before the sermon. At one stage some of the elements were even moved to a position before the service. In some churches a reader performed a part of the service, including

1. Cf. W. F. Goltermann, *Liturgiek* (Haarlem, 1951), pp. 62-63.

Scripture reading, psalms, and a morning prayer, before the pastor entered and led the "real" service.

There are indications that the church was not spiritually strong during these years. Many of the members were apathetic and did not attend the services regularly. Not much attention was paid to missionary work: during the first forty years there were only four converts from the Khoikhoi and all of them, in some way or other, eventually denounced the Christian faith.[2] There was, however, an influx of so-called people of color into the DRC by way of baptism. Some of the settlers took slave women as wives or concubines and their children were allowed to be baptized, but the churches kept a separate list in the baptismal register for "slave children."

Two exceptions during these years — as far as pastors were concerned — were Helperus Ritzema van Lier and M. C. Vos. Fervent preaching that called for personal conversion and a life of dedication and holiness marked their ministry. They also shared a great concern for missions and reaching out to the poor and needy. This was an important development, because it was an early clear indication of the DRC's tendency toward an evangelical, pietistic brand of Reformed theology.

The Dutch Reformed Church under a New Regime (1795-1950)

When the British troops occupied the Cape in 1795 a new era began for the DRC. The Cape became a British colony until South Africa gained independence in 1961. The DRC lost its privileged position as the only official church and in the fifty years after 1795 most of the major denominations established congregations or missions in South Africa. Although this generally did not have a great impact on the DRC, a number of new developments evolved.

Due to the change in government it became more difficult for the DRC to induce pastors from the Netherlands to fill positions in the Cape region. As a partial answer to this problem, ministers of Reformed persuasion of the Church of Scotland were invited to serve in South Africa. The government, wanting to strengthen ties with England and to promote the English language, of course encouraged this move. Over the next fifty years a large number of Scottish pastors accepted positions in DRC congregations, and at one stage more than one-third of DRC pastors were of Scottish origin. This move did not have direct liturgical implications but was important in an indirect way.

2. Richard Elphick and Rodney Davenport, eds., *Christianity in South Africa: A Political, Social, and Cultural History* (Berkeley: University of California Press, 1997), p. 25.

One of the Scottish pastors who came to South Africa was Andrew Murray Sr. He was the father of Andrew Murray Jr., who would have a huge impact on the theology, life, and witness of the DRC. Through the younger Murray's influence (though not his alone) the evangelical leanings of the DRC were solidified and an assault of liberal theology on the Cape church (coming from the Netherlands) was averted. Murray was also part of a substantial group of pastors and members of the Cape church who were very positive about missionary work and who tried to promote positive racial relations.

A very important liturgical landmark in the history of the DRC was the beginning of the so-called Pentecostal services held daily for the ten days between Ascension and Pentecost. This custom started in Paarl in 1860 and engendered a huge revival in the DRC. The services, with their emphasis on prayer, may in fact be the most distinct characteristic of the liturgical developments in the DRC and had an immense impact on DRC theology, spirituality, and ethos. Even today most congregations in the DRC family continue to celebrate these services faithfully. For many congregations, both pastors and members, these meetings represent the climax of the church year — even more important than the Easter or Christmas cycles.

The evangelical character of the DRC's Reformed identity was further enhanced by the hymnbooks used in the church. For many years the Psalter of Petrus Dathenus, originally issued in 1566, was used. A new edition of this Psalter was introduced in 1773 and remained in use for the next 150 years. Along with the Psalter the Dutch *Evangelische Gezangen* was accepted for use in the DRC in 1814. During and after the revival of 1860-1861 several hymnbooks containing more popular revival hymns from England and the United States were introduced. Of these, the best known were the *Zionsliedere,* which eventually became the regular hymnal of the so-called Coloured Dutch Reformed Mission Church, and the immensely popular *Hallelujah-liederen,* which was reprinted and expanded several times. For many people in the DRC, including myself, one of the clearest and most moving childhood liturgical memories was the singing of these "hallelujah-liedere" during the Pentecostal services!

It was also in this period that the DRC was allowed — after more than 170 years — to form a larger, independent church convocation in the Cape, namely the Synod of the DRC in South Africa (officially to this day called the DRC's Western Cape Synod). This synod was convened for the first time in 1824 and played an important role in the subsequent history of the DRC. Through the new status the church gained, at least in principle, the freedom to make its own decisions regarding liturgy, but liturgical matters were seldom addressed by the synod (which is not untypical of Reformed churches in that era). Some interesting decisions were, however, made: a more relaxed view was taken with regard to liturgical texts for baptism and marriage, but the liturgy for the Lord's Supper was to be read in full; it was decided to terminate the role of the reader; and it was ruled that pastors were to preach on the Heidelberg Catechism.

It is worth noting that there are no references in the synod's annals to a prescribed order of worship. This should not be seen as an indication that total freedom was allowed regarding the order of the service but rather as a sign of relative consensus on these matters. Congregations were allowed some measure of freedom concerning minor details of the Communion service: two common features of the way the Holy Communion is still celebrated in the DRC that originated during these years are the distribution of the signs to the members in the pews and the use of tiny glasses instead of the chalice. This freedom is important because it was a point of contention in the schism that culminated in the establishment of the more conservative Gereformeerde Kerk. Another practice that developed during these years and that became a standard procedure in many Dutch Reformed congregations was the singing of a hymn as *introitus* when the pastor and the elders entered the church.

Two other liturgical practices became established during these years as well. Because many members were farmers who lived in rural areas, the custom of a quarterly "Holy Communion weekend" developed. During this weekend the preparatory service for Communion was held on the Saturday evening, the Communion service on the Sunday morning, and the thanksgiving service early that afternoon. In between, catechism took place, new babies were baptized, and the church council and women's organizations had their meetings. In many congregations this became an established practice that was followed until the 1980s. The second custom was daily personal or family devotions. Through the years this has been a treasured practice in many DRC homes.

One of the saddest occurrences in the history of the DRC took place in 1857 when the synod decided to legitimize the formation of separate churches for the different races "on account of the weakness of some." This was the result of a long-standing discomfort many white members experienced because of the presence of people of color in DRC services, especially in Communion services. As so often in the history of the church, the symbol meant to confirm and strengthen our unity as believers caused a new division. While this forming of a new church did not come as a total surprise, it is important to note that it was never a forgone conclusion. For two hundred years there had been only one DRC, and travelers have noted their experiences on many a white homestead where the black slaves and laborers were included in family

devotions.[3] Nevertheless, this sad decision of 1857 eventually led to the establishment of a separate church structure for so-called colored people, namely
the Dutch Reformed Mission Church (1881).

In a strange and ironic way one could say that the Calvinistic belief in the
intrinsic unity of liturgy and life was probably one of the reasons behind this
decision. The formation of the new church was a sad acknowledgment that
most people in the DRC could not celebrate the Lord's Supper, with its appeal
to unity and equal love, with a good conscience while they were sitting next to
a black brother or sister whom they knew they did not accept with the full love
of Christ.

The Modern Era (1950-2000)

Around the 1950s the first real signs of a greater liturgical awareness became
evident within the ranks of the DRC. The South African theologians involved
in this movement were G. M. Pellissier, H. D. A. du Toit, A. C. Barnard, and
B. A. Müller. Barnard was a practical theologian who specialized in liturgy and
who wrote the first extensive work on liturgy in Afrikaans.

The formation of a General Synod for the Dutch Reformed churches of
the various provinces in 1962 in many ways facilitated the further development
of this liturgical awareness. A Commission for Liturgy was formed at general
synodical level for dealing with important liturgical issues at this level of church
government. There were three particularly important achievements of this
commission. First was the publication of a report, approved by the General
Synod, called *Rondom die Erediens (Concerning the Liturgy)* on the theological
foundations of Reformed liturgy. It also contained a short historical section and
suggested orders for all the various services. Second, in 1976 *Die Kerkboek (The
Church Book)* was published, which contained all the different forms used in
the church and usually supplied not only the classical form but also alternative,
revised forms for the various services. A companion volume — in many ways a
sequel to *Rondom die Erediens* — was also published. Finally, in 1978 a new combined Psalter and hymnbook was published, almost doubling the number of
hymns. Part of the agreement concerning the hymnbook was that it would terminate the use of the more pietistic *Hallelujah-liederen.* It was a well-meant effort to counter the evangelical influence in the DRC and move toward a "purer"
Dutch expression of our Reformed identity, but with the present resurgence of
evangelical spirituality in the church (and the overuse of popular charismatic

3. Elphick and Davenport, *Christianity in South Africa,* p. 66.

"praise-and-worship" practices), many members are wondering whether the effort behind the new hymnbook was really a good idea.

It is ironic that this greater awareness of liturgy came about in the same period during which the schism between the white, black, and so-called colored divisions of the DRC was growing. In retrospect one has to acknowledge that this did not serve the cause of liturgy well: it had the effect of making many younger pastors and theologians suspicious not only of the liturgy but also of preaching as the means of grace that communicates the truth of the gospel.

I believe that the time is now ripe to add another perspective on the sad history surrounding apartheid. It is a common perception among some social analysts that the peaceful way in which the white rulers ultimately surrendered power to the new democratic government was to some extent engendered by the reality that, since 1980, the churches (and specifically the DRC) had begun to have second thoughts on apartheid. In a way I was part of that history and saw how it unfolded, first at the classis of Stellenbosch (the first official governing body of the DRC to admit that apartheid was a sin and to confess its part therein) and later at the Synod of the Western Cape. A few months ago a visiting theologian asked me what had prompted the DRC to revise its decisions concerning apartheid. While I realize that this is a loaded question with no easy answer, I do believe that our Reformed commitment to the word of God somehow played an important role. Apartheid was accepted and condoned by the church and its members as long as they were led to believe (obviously wrongly) that it was not necessarily in disagreement with Scripture. This standpoint had to be reviewed when more and more theologians and pastors started to admit that apartheid was definitely not compatible with the witness of Scripture.[4] Thus, hearing the word of God in the liturgy and in sermons ultimately did reach some people's hearts — albeit a bit late. Let us hope that it is not altogether too late.

At present the DRC is trying to adapt to the realities of the new South Africa. While in some ways it is a very painful process in which people are forced to deal with loss at many levels, it also is a liberating and invigorating experience. One of the most acute realities of the new situation is that the church (i.e., synods and synodical leadership) has in some way lost the tight control it had over its members and its congregations. I believe that the challenge of the present situation is to negotiate as well as we can the inherent dangers of independentism and voluntarism and to try to use all our positive energy and creative vitality toward responsible and constructive renewal.

4. Cf. Lukas Vischer's discussion of racism and the church, pp. 421-23 in this volume.

This also applies to the liturgy. Two trends — seemingly contradicting each other — have developed in DRC congregations during the last decade. On the one hand there is, as I already have mentioned, an upsurge of evangelical spirituality strongly influenced by American neo-evangelicalism and contact with some of the megachurches in the United States. In some congregations a choice for this kind of theology is having a huge impact on worship style. This is most evident in lengthy "praise-and-worship" sessions (using contemporary music from all kinds of traditions) before the actual start of the service. What is peculiar about these sessions is that there often seems to be a preference for English hymns (could this be due to feelings of guilt and be something of a denial of an Afrikaner identity?); in addition, music is supplied by a "band" (which is highly irregular for the DRC), and physical movement and the raising of hands sometimes take place (also irregular — and even alarming — for older members). No wonder there is widespread concern among older pastors and members that this is a distinct movement away from a Reformed ethos and spirituality.

On the other hand, a second distinct group in the church seems to be moving in the opposite direction, working toward an enrichment of the traditional liturgy. There is a conscious effort among this group to establish a connection with the ecumenical movement and to renew Reformed worship by making more ample use of the liturgical tradition of the early church. A liturgical study group formed under the auspices of BUVTON (an institute connected to the Theological Faculty at Stellenbosch) is playing an important role in this regard. One of the most meaningful projects of this group is the adaptation of the revised common lectionary (RCL) for use in the DRC and the URC. At present the group issues four publications annually around the lectionary: (1) a Lectionary for members with daily readings (the four weekly readings have been expanded to seven) and worship suggestions for families; (2) a preaching guide (like the German "Predigthilfen" or Dutch "Postille") with a full order of worship, directed at pastors, in which one of the four texts will be selected for the sermon; (3) a Bible study guide for small groups; and (4) a booklet for catechetical teaching following the lectionary. Representatives of this second group also campaign for a more frequent celebration of Communion, stronger emphasis on baptism and baptismal celebrations, and better use of symbols and rituals during the service. In some of these congregations there is a group of members who help the pastor plan and prepare the worship service.

It is not yet clear which of these two groups will be the most influential eventually. What is clear, however, is that there is much more variety in worship style within the DRC than there was twenty years ago.

Liturgical Developments in the Dutch Reformed Mission Church, the Dutch Reformed Church in Africa, and the New Uniting Reformed Church

For more than a century the congregations of the DR Mission Church followed, almost to the letter, the liturgy that was used in the DRC. The reasons were obvious. The DR Mission Church had very close ties with the DRC: not only was it strongly supported by the DRC, but the DRC also supplied its pastors. These pastors were trained at DRC institutions and therefore in the conventional Reformed liturgical practices. This means that what was said earlier about liturgical developments in the DRC up to 1960s would, to a large extent, also apply to the Mission Church.

One difference might be mentioned: in the Mission Church music and singing played a much more important role than in the DRC. I remember vividly that white people who attended a Mission Church service would always refer to the lively and spirited singing. The Mission Church used its own hymnbook called *Sionsgesange,* which resembled the *Hallelujah-Liedere* used in the DRC. There was, of course, one other important difference: whites were allowed at the services of the Mission Church, while blacks and "coloreds" were not always welcome in white DRC congregations.

All this started to change in the late 1970s when the Mission Church developed a stronger identity apart from the DRC. During these years the Mission Church and some of its leaders played an important role in the peaceful resistance movement that led to the end of the apartheid era. The Belhar Confession became the symbol of the DR Mission Church's new identity, and the liturgy and especially singing played an important role in sustaining the church life and the new identity. In the years 1980 to 1990 liturgical matters were a frequent point of discussion in these churches and at their synod meetings. In 1990 the synod adopted a resolution to work toward a new liturgy in which the following goals would be expressed:

- to motivate members to prepare themselves spiritually for the worship services;
- to constantly work on the close relationship between liturgy and life;
- to focus not only on God but also on the faithful;
- to encourage more active participation by the members;
- to introduce more meaningful and dynamic use of the liturgical forms (which, they acknowledged, would have to be rewritten for this purpose);
- to create a basic mood of joy, festivity, and friendliness in the services;

- to improve singing — "from the heart and to God's glory";
- to provide an opportunity for members to respond to the sermon;
- to involve children in a way that they would experience as meaningful;
- to ensure that the different elements of the worship service do serve their purposes.[5]

Shortly after this resolution was accepted the Mission Church would merge with the black Dutch Reformed Church in Africa.

Like the liturgy of the Mission Church, that of the DRC in Africa strongly resembled the traditional Reformed liturgy that was brought from the Netherlands. While the differences in language and culture between the white DRC and the Mission Church were minimal, it was clear from the outset that cultural differences in the DRC in Africa might require adaptations to the DRC's form of liturgy. The truth is that the missionaries were not too keen to promote, or even to allow, such diversity.

A member of a white or so-called colored Dutch Reformed Congregation, upon entering a worship service of a black congregation, would notice a number of distinct features. First, music and singing played an even stronger role than in the Mission Church. In a way, one could say that the service of a black congregation revolves around singing. They not only sing more hymns but these are also sung at more regular intervals — sometimes even during the sermon. A second difference is that during the offertory people often bring their gifts to an offertory table in the front part of the church. They do this in a joyful, dance-like manner while singing hymns. Third, the duration of the service could be substantially longer than in the white DRC or the Mission Church. A two-hour service would be quite normal in black congregations (compared to the sixty-minute service in white congregations). In addition, because of limited personnel and lack of transport facilities the black church developed a strong tradition of elders leading the worship and preaching, especially in so-called outposts of the congregation. It is during these services that singing sometimes functions as a kind of critique on the sermon. If some members feel that the preacher is deviating from the line of his sermon, they sometimes spontaneously sing a hymn to help him back to the point. A final difference concerns the church year. While the Mission Church has adopted the tradition of Pentecostal services, not many black congregations follow this tradition. It is customary in the black churches to emphasize Easter week, however, as is also the case with the Mission Church. In a way the liturgy of the black churches is a wonderful, strange mixture of a typical Western order of

5. Skema Werksaamhede NG Sendingkerk (1990), pp. 506-13.

service combined with a couple of African "interludes," for example during the singing and offertory.

There are signs that South Africa's new dispensation might also bring more questions to black congregations of the Reformed family. They are being challenged from many sides: the Catholics' colorful and mystical liturgy, the Pentecostals' ecstatic and expressionistic liturgy, and the African Independent churches' functional syncretism. The new government's emphasis on an African Renaissance is also promoting the rediscovery of African roots. The question many missiologists now ask is whether this could lead to a second round of indigenization in the black churches. Only time will tell.

After the unification of the so-called colored and black churches in the early nineties there was a strong awareness that they would have to deal with liturgical matters very urgently and wisely. While recognizing cultural differences, they clearly realized that the general synod would have to supply some kind of consistent framework for the liturgy.[6] In this regard a resolution was accepted and the commission was to report back in 2001.

Liturgical Developments in the Presbyterian Church

The Presbyterian Church in Southern Africa (PCSA) originated in the early years of the nineteenth century when George Thom, a missionary of the London Missionary Society, brought together Calvinist members of a Scottish regiment based in Cape Town into an small Presbyterian congregation. Although Thom later decided to join the DRC and the small congregation for some time was under the care of the LMS, the congregation persevered and formed its own official church in 1824, with the approval of the Edinburgh Presbytery. The arrival of the 1820 settlers increased the number of new congregations in the eastern Cape. Missionaries from Scotland also founded a number of mission stations in the eastern Cape — among them Lovedale, which was to play an important role in the training and formation of black Christian leaders in Southern Africa.

Although their initial policy was not to form separate churches for the different races, practical considerations and a difference of opinion within the ranks of the Free Church of Scotland's missionaries eventually led to the formation of two separate churches: the predominantly white Presbyterian Church of Southern Africa (PCSA) and the black Bantu Presbyterian Church (later called the Reformed Presbyterian Church in Southern Africa). In 1999

6. Cf. Skema Werksaamhede VGK (1997), p. 222.

these two churches merged to form the Uniting Presbyterian Church of Southern Africa.

The liturgy of the early Presbyterians was typical of the contemporary Scottish Church — and not very different from the liturgy used in the DRC. As one might expect in a frontier situation, there was not much reflection on the liturgy in the local church. The appointment of the well-known liturgical theologian, W. D. Maxwell, as professor in the theological faculty in Grahamstown signaled a new era for the liturgy in the Presbyterian church.

Since then there have been a few new developments in the Presbyterian liturgy. To begin with, many congregations have moved toward a more frequent (monthly rather than quarterly) celebration of the Lord's Supper. Holy Week is celebrated diligently in most congregations (compared to the DRC, where the emphasis is on Lent Sundays and Pentecost). In addition, there are some interesting differences from the DRC with regard to the order of service: the Entry of the Bible; no regular reading of the Law (Ten Commandments); more than one Scripture reading (usually both an Old and New Testament lesson); sharing of the peace; and regular congregational responses. At present the Presbyterian church also experiences a movement toward a more charismatic style of worship in some of its congregations.

Liturgical Developments in the Congregational Church

The work of the Congregationalists in Southern Africa started in 1799 when the London Missionary Society, an independent Congregationalist initiative, sent its first missionary, J. T. van der Kemp, to South Africa. Van der Kemp, his colleague John Philip, and others, such as Robert Moffat, played an important role in the growth and development of Christianity in Southern Africa. Their work grew steadily and in 1898 they reached a membership of 42,000 in the Cape Colony alone. In 1877 the independent congregations met to form the Congregational Union of South Africa (CUSA). Ninety years later, in 1967, another merger took place when CUSA joined forces with the Bantu Congregational Church (which had developed from the work of the Boston-based American Board of Missions) as well as a number of other smaller groups to form the United Congregational Church of Southern Africa (UCCSA). The Congregational church has a predominantly (90 percent) black and so-called colored membership.

The liturgy that the missionaries brought to the South African church was typically Congregationalist in that there were few fixed rules. There was a strong emphasis on freedom and practicality and on the idea that the congregation should be able to understand the service. The result has been that a great diversity of liturgical styles developed in the Congregational churches. This diversity of styles was increased even further by the cultural variety (thirteen different languages!) in the UCCSA.

In practice most of these churches have a free-church liturgy with strong leanings toward a Calvinistic order of service. Some of the black churches tend to be more structured in their services, almost leaning toward some form of Anglicanism. The UCCSA does have service books with formularies for Communion, baptism, induction, and ordination, and also other liturgical resources. The latter are more widely used in the Tswana-, Xhosa-, and Zulu-speaking churches. None of these liturgical forms or orders is obligatory, except the ones for the induction and ordination services.

In a 1996 publication ordered by the church, Roy Briggs postulated the following liturgical axioms as the governing principles of "free church" worship:

> The church gathers for worship on each Lord's Day.
>
> The church worships the triune God, Lord of heaven and earth.
>
> The church must make the structure and the content of the service the best it can devise.
>
> Worship must express the fact that members understand themselves to be a covenant people, meaning that the pattern of the service must portray the sequence of the covenant, namely, God's initiative and members' response thereto.
>
> Worship must have a definite structure — logical in its progression — so that those who take part in the service can follow intelligently.
>
> Being a Reformed church, the worship must be according to the word of God.
>
> The structure of the service must remain sacramental.
>
> The worship must be congregational in the sense that the whole congregation participates fully in the service.

The Assembly also approved an order for the Eucharist that is, to a large extent, a typically Reformed order of service for the Holy Communion. This is not obligatory but is recommended very strongly.

There are some concerns in UCCSA circles about the liturgy. Although they have a high esteem for congregational freedom, UCCSA churches do acknowledge the dangers and the detriment to worship that can be concomitant with this local freedom. Briggs emphasizes that this danger is heightened by the fact that UCCSA pastors are trained at ecumenical training centers where they do not receive adequate instruction in their own canons of worship. "Inevitably many of our local churches have become prey to the idiosyncrasies of their ministers who themselves lack liturgical expertise. This has also led to the almost total absence of liturgical understanding on the part of lay people who lead worship Sunday by Sunday in so much of the church. As a result, the worship of our churches has tended to degenerate into a mere haphazard mixture of hymns and prayers, scripture readings and sermon and offertory, with no discernable structure to it."[7] Briggs's exposition of Congregationalist liturgical axioms and the Assembly's approval of an order of service for Communion must be seen against the backdrop of these concerns.

Challenges for the Future

As the new century is dawning on us, the South African community is also entering a new era. It is an era of mixed and contradicting realities. Some commentators say that South African society is in the awkward situation that people have to learn to live with the realities of modernism and postmodernism at the same time. They are also asked to deal with growing globalization — while the president is calling for an African Renaissance. On the other hand, many white South Africans now realize for the first time that they are living in a third-world country and are discovering Africa as if for the first time.

For the churches this means facing challenges from three sides: dealing with modernity (and the threat of secularism), negotiating the negative elements of globalization (with the threat of Americanization), and rethinking their multicolored African heritage.

I believe that the Reformed tradition, maybe more than any other tradition, should be able to deal with these realities. Our chances to do this meaningfully and constructively will be enhanced if we give more attention than in the past to rigorous reflection on liturgical issues and are willing to rethink our Reformed tradition in a radical way. We also need to be humble enough to learn what we need to learn from the early church, the ecumenical tradition, and one another, and need to more sensitive than in the past to the world in which our members are called to be the Body of Christ.

7. D. Roy Briggs, *A Covenant Church: Studies in the Polity of the United Congregational Church of Southern Africa in Terms of Its Covenant* (Gaborone, Botswana: Pula Press, 1996), p. 114.

Further Reading

Bam, G. "Liturgiese besef en Liturgiese Ervaring by Kerkraads- en CJV-lede van die NG Sendingkerk." Pages 29-47 in *Apologia*. Vol. 1. Universiteit van Wes-Kaap, 1986.

Briggs, D. Roy. *A Covenant Church: Studies in the Polity of the United Congregational Church of Southern Africa in Terms of Its Covenant*. Gaborone, Botswana: Pula Press, 1996.

Cronjé, J. M. *Born to Witness*. Institute of Missiological Research (I.S.W.E.N.), University of Pretoria, 1982.

Die Erediens, 'n Handleiding by die Kerkboek. Kaapstad, 1976.

Die Kerkboek van die Nederduitse Gereformeerde Kerk. Kaapstad: NG Kerk-Uitgewers, 1983.

Du Toit, H. D. A. "Die Liturgie van die Ned. Geref. Kerk in Suid-Afrika." In *Jaarboek voor de Eredienst*. Kaapstad, 1965-66.

―――. *Laat ons dan Feesvier*. Kaapstad-Pretoria: NG Kerk-Uitgewers, 1969.

Elphick, Richard, and Rodney Davenport, eds. *Christianity in South Africa: A Political, Social, and Cultural History*. Berkeley: University of California Press, 1997.

Golterman, W. F. *Liturgiek*. Haarlem 1951.

Handboek vir die Erediens. Kaapstad: NG Kerk-Uitg ewers, 1983.

Handelinge van die Vergadering van die Sinode van die Nederduitse Gereformeerde Kerk in Suid-Afrika 36. Kaapstad: 1969. Pages 323-25.

Maxwell, William D. *An Outline of Christian Worship, Its Development and Forms*. London: Oxford University Press, 1936.

Muller, Julian. *Die Erediens as Fees*. NG Kerkboekhandel (Edms) Bpk, 1988.

Richter, Jannie. *Het ons hart nie warm geword nie . . . ?* Buvton, Riglyne vir 'n Gemeentelike Eredienswerkgroep, 1988.

Venter, E. A. "Aantreklike Eredienste." Pages 199-231 in *Jaarboek van die Gefedereerde Nederduitse Gereformeerde Kerke*. Kaapstad: Nasionale Pers, 1952.

A Survey of Reformed Worship in Indonesia

Ester Pudjo Widiasih

Indonesia is the largest archipelago nation in the world, consisting of over thirteen thousand islands, about six thousand of which are inhabited by 350 ethnic groups with their own cultures and languages. These cultures and languages vary so widely that it is difficult, almost impossible, to understand the cultures and languages of different ethnic groups. There is a national language, however, Bahasa Indonesia, which is based on the Malay language. Bahasa Indonesia unites us as a nation, for it has become the official language used in schools and business. In the big cities, where persons of many ethnic groups live together, Bahasa Indonesia is the common language among most of the population, especially the young. In Jakarta, for example, most of the youth cannot speak the ethnic language of their parents, or understand their ethnic cultures.

Since the sixteenth century, elements of foreign cultures and languages have been brought to Indonesia by merchants, missionaries, or foreigners who intentionally migrated to Indonesia. Many of these elements were accepted and incorporated into ethnic-tribal cultures, even into the Bahasa Indonesia language. Many words in Bahasa Indonesia are taken from Arabic, Sanskrit, Portuguese, Dutch, and Chinese.

In big cities like Jakarta, the culture is complex and impossible to delineate. People bring their tribal identities to Jakarta, yet their association with people from different ethnic backgrounds leads to cultural adaptation, adoption, or even assimilation. Thus, urban immigrants become anonymous and strangers to their ethnic cultures. This cultural anonymity is even more apparent among the youth who were born in Jakarta. Television, the Internet, and other media, as well as direct contact with foreigners, have introduced Indonesians to various cultures of the world. American commercialized culture has greatly influenced the younger generation, which prefers rock, jazz, R&B, and other American genres of music seen on MTV to traditional ethnic music. Some young people believe that American-style pentecostal or charismatic worship, complete with MTV-style music, is now more appropriate for the church. Thus, in big cities like Jakarta, there is a wide gap between the culture of the young generation and the culture of their parents. Youth accommodates and imitates "global" culture, while the parents strive to preserve traditional customs. Attempts to preserve traditional cultures are ambiguous, however, because everyone lives in a complex urban setting where all cultures are blended.

Economic factors add to the complexity of cultures in Indonesia. Society is divided into three economic classes — the rich, the poor, and the middle class — and the difference between the rich and the poor is obvious. Each class has its own identity and distinct customs. The rich and middle class go to shopping malls to purchase computers, cellular phones, and Internet access, while the street children go to malls to beg for coins. Slum areas sometimes stand side by side with the elite residences of the rich, with no interaction between the two. Children from rich families as well as some middle-class families are able to get a good education leading to a good job, while the poor who are able to go to school at all cannot advance beyond high school. Economic and educational factors determine and form the culture of Indonesian society, and thus become the social context of the church.

Indonesia is the largest Islamic country in the world; only ten to fifteen percent of the population is not Muslim. The government recognizes five official religions: Islam, Protestantism, Roman Catholicism, Hinduism, and Buddhism. Besides these religions, it is commonly recognized that Confucianism and some ethnic beliefs are "official" religions as well. The law stipulates that every religion has the freedom to exist in Indonesia, but in practice there have been some difficulties implementing the law.[1] Recently, the relationship between Muslims and Christians in some parts of the country has been disturbed by conflicts. It is generally held that these conflicts were provoked for political purposes, yet the rise of fundamentalism and militancy among both Muslims and Christians has aroused hatred between the two. Efforts to establish dialogue and to reconcile warring Muslims and Christians have had some success, but the situation is like a smoldering fire that can flare up at any time. This volatile situation does not exist in all areas of Indonesia, however. The bombings of churches and Christian cemeteries on Christmas Eve of 1999, for example, did not lead to conflicts in the affected areas because people were aware that it was done for political, not religious, purposes.

---

1. To build a new church, for example, the approval of neighbors is required. In many cases, neighbors have not given permission, or have even destroyed churches in their areas.

Because Indonesians have been so divided into different tribal groups and religions and have been subjected to so many foreign influences, it is not surprising that we cannot define a common Indonesian identity or a common Indonesian culture. Nevertheless, Indonesians differ from Europeans or Americans. We have our own cultures and customs, which should be respected and observed, since they provide the context in which Indonesian Christians live. Christians are about ten percent of the Indonesian population, and are distributed among the Catholic and Eastern Orthodox churches as well as a number of Protestant denominations and groups — Reformed, Lutheran, Baptist, Methodist, Pentecostal, and charismatic. The Reformed church is the largest denomination but is divided into tribal churches, such as the Javanese church, Sundanese church, Kalimantan church, Moluccan church, and so on. Each of these has its own synod, history, and church policy, making it difficult to present a common historical tradition of Reformed worship. There are similarities among the Reformed churches, however, since most of them originated from or had special relation with the Dutch Reformed Church.[2] Thus, I will make some general observations about Reformed worship in Indonesia, providing some specific examples from several churches.

Worship in Indonesia in the Seventeenth and Eighteenth Centuries

The Reformed tradition was brought to Indonesia by the Dutch East India Company (VOC). The Dutch came to look for spices in East Indonesia and to monopolize the spice trade. They arrived in Ambon, seizing the Spice Islands from the Portuguese in 1605. As a commercial company, it was not the purpose of the VOC to spread the gospel. Nevertheless, it supported Christians who had been baptized by Portuguese or Spanish priests, converting them to Protestantism. This approach was common at the time since church and state were inseparable. Governments were responsible for spreading the gospel, even through occupation of another country.

Not all VOC fleets had a pastor. During the first years of the VOC's occupation of Indonesia there was no pastor assigned to serve the sailors. They

2. In 1886 there was a great schism in the Dutch Reformed Church (Nederlansche Hervormde Kerk), when Dr. A. Kuyper founded Gereformeerde Kerken in Nederland (GKN). In addition to the mission boards of both churches, there were other mission boards that were not attached to a particular church. Which mission board worked in an area determined the church's polity, teaching, and worship. The ethnic background of a church, though not as influential, also affected its characteristics, especially after missionaries left.

had only a "comforter of the sick," who was responsible for leading morning and evening prayers each day, and for reading each Sunday a sermon written by a minister in the Netherlands. The "comforter" was not educated in theology, and his main task was to comfort sick sailors, not to serve Indonesian Christians.

The first Dutch minister came to Indonesia in 1612. He had to serve Christians in a vast area, including islands beyond Ambon. A shortage of ministers continued until the nineteenth century in every part of Indonesia, including Batavia (Jakarta), the seat of the Dutch colonial government. Consequently, worship was led by "teachers" or "comforters of the sick" who had no theological education. They were allowed to preach sermons written by Dutch ministers in the Netherlands that had been translated into Malay. Unfortunately, only a few sermons had been translated, so teachers or comforters of the sick had to read the same sermons repeatedly.

How did they worship? Sunday service was held in Malay for all Indonesians, even though only few people understood the language. Dutch missionaries could not speak tribal languages and thought that those languages were insufficient to express the gospel. Worship mirrored worship in the Netherlands: votum, greeting, congregational singing, reading of the Ten Commandments, prayer, Scripture reading, sermon, singing, the Lord's Supper (on certain Sundays), offering, prayer, more singing, and, finally, the blessing.[3] On Sunday evenings a Dutch minister led a catechetical service with preaching based on the Heidelberg Catechism. (Teachers and comforters of the sick were forbidden to preach on the Heidelberg Catechism.) In addition to Sunday worship, Christians had to attend evening prayer led by a local teacher or a comforter of the sick. These leaders read prayer formulas unchanged from those used by churches in the Netherlands, and memorized some Christian teachings together with school children. In this way, evening prayer meetings became catechism for the adults.[4] The VOC also required thanksgiving and intercession for the Dutch government, even though it was difficult for pastors to thank God for the unjust treatment of Indonesians by the colonial government. Moreover, the Dutch governor composed a form of intercessory prayer for the VOC to be used every night! When the church suggested praying for the Christians in Malaka who were suffering from wars, the government refused.[5] Pastors could not do anything without the colonial government's per-

3. Th. van den End, *Ragi Carita*, vol. 1 (Jakarta: BPK Gunung Mulia, 1980), p. 116.

4. Van den End, *Ragi Carita*, vol. 1, p. 119.

5. J. L. Ch. Abineno, *Sejarah Apostolat di Indonesia*, vol. 1 (Jakarta: BPK Gunung Mulia, 1978), pp. 66-67.

mission because they were government employees. The practice of worship imposed by the VOC was worship colonization.

The Lord's Supper was celebrated several times in a year, and only Dutch ministers could serve the sacrament. Churches in remote areas, without a minister, were able to celebrate the sacrament only on the infrequent occasions when a minister visited. Moreover, until the end of eighteenth century, 90 percent of Indonesian Christians could not receive Holy Communion, since the missionaries separated baptism from Communion. According to regulations of the Dutch Reformed Church in the Netherlands, an adult who converted to Christianity and was baptized was recognized as a mature Christian, fully welcomed to the Communion table. Nevertheless, missionaries did not permit Indonesian adult Christians who had been baptized to receive Communion until they passed catechism class, announced their intention to participate in Communion, and lived a pious life. This decision was the result of missionaries having baptized Indonesians without sufficient preparation, or with no preparation at all.[6] It was the practice of the missionaries to baptize Indonesian people as a group or a tribe. Except for Ambon and Batavia, where there were permanent ministers, missionaries were able to teach converted Indonesians for mere days or weeks. They baptized the flock as soon as possible in order to move on to other places. Catechetical instruction consisted of memorizing the Apostles' Creed, the Decalogue, the Lord's Prayer, and sometimes an abbreviated Heidelberg Catechism translated into Malay. The missionaries did not explain the meaning of these materials, or how the newly baptized were to incorporate them into their lives. As a result, Christianity could not penetrate deeply, and many "converted" Christians continued to live according to their old beliefs. For example, in Ambon Christians drank the water used for baptism since they believed that the water had magic power. Similarly, they bought Communion bread to be used as medicine. Europeans called Christianity in Ambon "the Ambon religion." Similar practices occurred throughout Indonesia.

European missionaries rejected all indigenous expressions, equating tribal religions with demon worship and regarding traditional customs — including traditional clothes, music, and dances — as inferior to Western tradi-

---

6. Many people converted for political reasons. When one tribe or a kingdom was in conflict with another, the weak one would ask the Europeans, who had modern weapons, to help them defeat their enemies. Then they converted to Christianity. Sometimes the Dutch forced their belief on the Indonesians, but this happened rarely. Tribal religious believers saw the status of Westerners and Christianity as higher, so converting to the Western religion enhanced their prestige. Some of them were also attracted to the personality of a missionary, causing them to leave their old religion (van den End, *Ragi Carita*, vol. 1, pp. 106-7).

tions. The missionaries did not try to understand the meaning and importance of Indonesian customs, and Indonesian Christians were forbidden to practice any traditional expressions in worship. Van den End concludes that, for Indonesian Christians, Sunday belonged to God's authority, but the other six days belonged to the spirits of the ancestors. Traditional customs controlled daily matters because Western Christianity could not provide answers to daily questions or guidance for daily living.[7]

The Bible was poorly translated into Malay because the missionaries did not master the language, and few Indonesians were able to explain the language in Western terms. Congregational singing was limited to Genevan psalms and some other hymns that had been translated into Malay. The complete Malay Psalter, translated by Werndly, was published in 1735. Singing was unaccompanied, led by the English lining-out method.

Worship in the Nineteenth Century

The VOC was dismissed as the representative of the Dutch government in 1799 when the Dutch government assumed direct rule over Indonesia. In 1807 the Dutch colonial government decreed freedom in religious life. The government became neutral, ending the era of the state church and state support of Christianity (i.e., Protestantism). Two obstacles blocked the government's policy, however. First, because the Dutch government would not abandon the VOC's churches, it encouraged the establishment of the Protestant Church in Indonesia. The second obstacle was the government's fear of Islam. Because Muslims were more difficult to conquer than Christians, the colonial government invited mission boards to evangelize all non-Muslims, that is, people who followed tribal religions. At the same time, under the influence of Pietism, churches in the Netherlands experienced a renewed interest in evangelization. They exhorted the government to provide missionaries who would work among the Indonesians. Some of the Dutch missionaries advocated studies of tribal cultures and religions. They did not compel Indonesian churches to conform to the worship of the Dutch churches, encouraging the incorporation of Indonesian culture in worship. Unfortunately, such "radical" ideas were not realized on a large scale, since the majority of missionaries rejected indigenous culture.

Evangelization was successful throughout the nineteenth century. Many missionary boards worked in Indonesia among the indigenous peoples, not

7. Van den End, *Ragi Carita,* vol. 1, p. 132.

only spreading the gospel but also building hospitals and schools. In 1874 the Dutch Mission Association directed that indigenous cultures be adapted and incorporated in worship and evangelization. Nevertheless, feelings of superiority prevented the Dutch missionaries from making meaningful changes. They compared their own civilized society to the shocking realities of headhunting and tribal wars. Because they were unable to be critical of Dutch society or to differentiate Western culture from Christian values, the missionaries were unable to discern the meaning behind indigenous practice.[8] For example, because the Europeans did not understand the Indonesian dowry system's social and religious function in society, they perceived it as mere "women trade."[9] Thus, the missionaries' approach to Indonesian indigenous culture remained the same as the VOC's. The Dutch continued to underestimate the local culture. The Malay language was commonly used because the missionaries considered the tribal languages too primitive to proclaim God's word, and missionaries consciously tried to Westernize the Indonesians in order to "tame" them.

Javanese Christianity was unique, however, in its use of traditional ethnic expressions in worship. For the most part, Christianity in Java was spread by individual Christians rather than by the Protestant Church in Indonesia. In East Java, a Dutch-Indonesian man named Coolen acquired Javanese arts from his mother, the daughter of a Javanese noble family. Coolen's method of evangelization was different from that of the other missionaries. He announced Christianity as a *ngelmu*, a new "wisdom of life."[10] In 1827, he established a new village named Ngoro where anybody could live without being forced to be a Christian. Although Coolen organized Ngoro with Christian principles, he taught Christian *ngelmu* only to people who wanted to know it. He incorporated Christianity into traditional ceremonies. In the festival to commence plowing of the fields, for example, Coolen would sing, "O Mount Semeru, O goddess Sri, bless our hand's labor. And above everything, we ask for blessing and strength from Jesus, whose power is incomparable."[11]

---

8. Van den End, *Ragi Carita,* vol. 1, p. 153.

9. Van den End, *Ragi Carita,* vol. 1, p. 175.

10. *Ngelmu* or *ilmu* means knowledge, a kind of wisdom of life. It touches not only the rational dimension, but especially the spiritual dimension, including magic. Javanese religion develops mysticism, which in the past was called high *ngelmu* (religious knowledge). It was developed in various mystical schools called Javanese *paguron* (discipleship system), usually under the leadership of a guru. See Sutarman Soediman Partonadi, *Sadrach's Community and Its Contextual Roots: A Nineteenth-Century Javanese Expression of Christianity* (Amsterdam: Free University of Amsterdam, 1988), pp. 22-23. A guru spread out his *ngelmu* through public debate. If he could defeat his rival, then the rival would become his follower.

11. Van den End, *Ragi Carita,* vol. 1, p. 200.

Coolen conducted Sunday worship in the front room of his house, praying and reading Scripture. The people responded by praying and singing in *tembang,* a Javanese musical style. Throughout the day people enjoyed *gamelan* (a Javanese musical ensemble), shadow puppets, and *dzikir* (a form of chanted prayer).[12] Coolen's community was quite distinct from the Protestant Church in Indonesia (GPI), the state church. In fact, Coolen did not like Western Christianity; he rejected baptism and the Lord's Supper, which he considered Western customs. Consequently, when any of his people requested baptism in the GPI, they were expelled from Ngoro. Ironically, many of Coolen's followers moved to the GPI because they preferred to be "Western Christians" rather than "Javanese Christians."

Emde, a German watch repairer in the East Java town of Surabaya, took a different tack, introducing thoroughly westernized Christianity. For Emde, being a Christian meant being a European. Consequently, he insisted that Javanese men cut their hair, discard sarongs in favor of pants, and take their kris off. He also prohibited traditional shadow puppet shows, playing or listening to *gamelan,* or participating in *slametan,* a ceremonial gathering.[13] He saw all of these Javanese customs as pagan practices to be avoided by believers in Jesus Christ. Even so, Emde respected the Javanese, considering them as human beings equal to Europeans.[14]

The first NZG (Nederlandsch Zendelinggenootschap) missionary in Java was Jellesma (1817-1858). He differed from Emde in not rejecting all Javanese customs. Jellesma believed that evangelization among the Javanese people should be done by the Javanese themselves, using means that were compat-

---

12. *Dzikir* is a kind of Muslim chanted prayer. People who do *dzikir* will repeat a religious statement (formula) many times until they experience an ecstatic state. The *dzikir* in Coolen's community repeated the Lord's Prayer and other short prayers. Coolen arranged the creed that was sung during the worship, adapting it to the Moslem syahadat:

> I believe that God is One.
> There is no God but God *(Lha illah lha illolah).*
> Jesus Christ is the Spirit of God *(Yesus Kristus ya Roh Allah),*
> Whose power is over everything.
> There is no God but God.
> Jesus Christ is the Spirit of God.

The phrase *lha illah lha illolah, Yesus Kristus ya Roh Allah* became the one of the *dzikir* formulas. See Partonadi, *Sadrach's Community,* pp. 134-36.

13. *Slametan,* derived from the word *selamet,* meaning "to save," is a Javanese social-religious ceremonial gathering to ask for blessing and to give thanks to God by praying and eating together.

14. Van den End, *Ragi Carita,* vol. 1, pp. 202-3.

ible with their society.[15] Thus, he welcomed Javanese culture selectively. He permitted Javanese men to keep their long hair and sarongs, and he adapted worship. During his ministry a number of spiritual songs and biblical stories were published in the Javanese language. But Jellesma also imposed church discipline when the elders of Mojowarno held celebrations with erotic dances.

In addition to Coolen, other Javanese lay evangelists tried to contextualize Christianity into Javanese culture: Paulus Tosari, Kyai Ibrahim Tunggul Wulung, and Kyai Sadrach Surapranata.[16] Kyai Sadrach Surapranata (1840-1924), who worked in the central Java area, was the most distinguished of these Javanese evangelists. He was introduced to Christianity by Jellesma and then became a student of Kyai Ibrahim Tunggul Wulung for several years. Many Javanese were attracted to his teaching and recognized him as a guru of the Christian *ngelmu*.[17] He organized his followers into independent churches and later affiliated with the Apostolische Kerk, in which he was ordained as an apostle.

Sadrach developed worship in the Javanese style.[18] His church was built in the Javanese *mesjid* (mosque) style from simple material found in the village. The structure was erected on the imam's[19] property both for practical reasons and as a theological acknowledgment of the imam's central role in the community. Instead of a church bell, the church used a big drum or a *kentongan* (hollow tube) made of bamboo or wood to call people to worship. The worshipers sat on the floor, which was covered with a mat. A small table was used as a pulpit, with the Bible laid on it like the Qur'an in Muslim services. Both men and women wore Javanese attire, although in areas where Islam was still strong, the women were required to cover their heads with a veil in keeping with Javanese Muslim traditions. These practices indicate that Christians did not want to be distinguished and separated from their fellow villagers. Worship services were held twice every Sunday and on the special Christian days of Christmas, Passover, Ascension, Pentecost, and the New Year. There was no fixed liturgy,

15. Van den End, *Ragi Carita*, vol. 1, p. 203.

16. A *kyai* is a traditional religious leader. The term is commonly used to address a Muslim religious leader. By addressing themselves as kyais, Ibrahim Tunggul Wulung and Sadrach identified themselves as religious leaders like the Muslim kyais.

17. By 1890 there were seventy communities consisting of 6,794 members. In the twenty-three year period (1907-1929), the total number of baptisms was 6,779 (Partonadi, *Sadrach's Community,* p. 128).

18. I am very much indebted to Partonadi's book for the explanation of Sadrach's worship style (Partonadi, *Sadrach's Community,* pp. 130-40).

19. An imam is a Muslim religious leader. Sadrach's community continued to use this term for the leader or pastor of their congregations.

so worship varied from place to place, prepared and conducted by the Christian imam. There were similarities in the worship style of Sadrach's churches, however, since the elders discussed worship during meetings with Sadrach in Karangjasa. Sadrach wrote a worship handbook containing the Lord's Prayer, the Ten Commandments, the summary of the Law in Matthew 22:37-40, and prayers for both individual and communal use. Unfortunately, no copy exists. Brief memorized prayers were used in rural, less educated communities — a familiar practice in Muslim services.

The Dutch missionary Heyting described worship in Sadrach's churches. He reported that women and men sat separately during worship. All stood when the imam and the elders entered, after which they sat to pray the Lord's Prayer or another opening prayer while the offering plate was passed. Then the worship service proper began with a prayer of thanksgiving by the imam, followed by a Javanese hymn, two Scripture readings with singing between them (the New Testament was read in the morning and the Old Testament in the evening service), a short exposition of the text or a personal testimony by the imam, and more congregational singing to close.[20] Another Dutch missionary, Adriaanse, reported similar worship services, with the addition of the Ten Commandments, the summary of the Law, and sometimes the Apostles' Creed following the imam's opening prayer.

Sadrach was impressed by Coolen's worship, employing some features of his liturgy. Among these was *tembang*, Javanese poetry composed in musical form. Sadrach set the Ten Commandments, the Apostles' Creed, the Lord's Prayer, and some other special prayers to various types of *tembang*.[21] The use of *tembang* to communicate the Christian message was especially significant, for it was commonly used in Javanese literature for moral or ethical teaching. Javanese communities observed rituals marking stages in life's journey. Both Sadrach's churches and Javanese Muslims performed these rituals. It was important to maintain the customs since the members of Sadrach's community did not live apart, but in the villages among the Muslims. Thus, Sadrach adopted and adapted the rituals so that Christian characteristics were integral. For example, to observe the traditional celebration on the fortieth day after a

20. As quoted by Partonadi, *Sadrach's Community*, pp. 132-33.
21. *Tembang* can be divided into three major groups with variation in each group: *Macapat, Ageng,* and *Madya* or *Tengahan.* The *Ageng* and *Madya* were used for the opening melody of a complete *Gending* (Javanese music of instrumental and vocal combination). *Macapat* was the most common and required no instrument. In the evening, especially on a special occasion, people gathered and chanted the *macapat,* which contained moral teachings suitable for the occasion. Sometimes they would invite a professional chanter. See Partonadi, *Sadrach's Community,* pp. 139-40.

child's birth, Sadrach developed a liturgy based on Jesus' presentation in the temple (Luke 2:22-23). Children were brought to the church to be presented to God. The imam used flower petals to sprinkle water on the child's head in the name of the Father, Son, and Holy Spirit. During the ceremony the incense was burnt, and the congregation chanted a Javanese *tembang*. Following the ceremony, a common meal, similar to the Javanese *kenduren* (religious meal) was provided in the home of the imam to give thanks to God.[22] But Sadrach did not adapt all rituals. He rejected the *slametan* that honored the spirits of the dead, as well as public celebrations that were identified with Islam.

A decade after the death of Sadrach, his successor Yotam decided to incorporate Sadrach's churches into the Zending van de Gereformeerde Kerken in Nederland (ZGKN), a mission board of the Reformed Church in the Netherlands (Gereformeerde Kerken in Nederland, GKN).[23] The worship practices and ritual ceremonies developed by Sadrach gradually disappeared due to GKN suspicions about Javanese culture. In the eyes of GKN ministers, converting to Christian faith meant leaving the old life, and that meant rejecting Javanese customs. This attitude became embedded in Javanese Christianity, causing a separation between the church and Javanese society, between worship and life. Sunday worship was Westernized, becoming more like that of the Dutch Reformed churches in the Netherlands. *Gamelan, tembang,* incense, and flower water no longer had a place in worship. *Tembang* was replaced by Genevan psalms, and Western hymns were translated into Javanese and sung to Western melodies.

Most of the Dutch missionaries underestimated Indonesian cultures and customs, even though the NZV encouraged the use of local cultures in evangelization. The missionary approach had implications for worship, of course. With the exception of Javanese Christian communities developed by

22. See A. G. Hoekema, *Berpikir Dalam Keseimbangan yang Dinamis: Sejarah Lahirnya Teologi Protestan Nasional di Indonesia (Sekitar 1860-1960)* (Jakarta: BPK Gunung Mulia, 1997), p. 75, and Partonadi, *Sadrach's Community,* p. 147. Partonadi describes some other rituals, such as those concerning marriage, pregnancy, childbirth, circumcision, death, New Year celebrations, and land cultivation and farming, and makes comparisons between the Javanese Muslim's customs and those of the Sadrach community (pp. 145-51).

23. ZGKN continued the works of previous mission boards in the Central Java: Nederlandsche Gereformeerde Zendings Vereeniging (NGZV). When Sadrach started his work, an NGZV missionary, Rev. J. Wilhelm, honored Sadrach and appreciated his Javanese-Christian beliefs. For this reason Sadrach invited him to be his colleague and pastor of his churches. The Reverend J. Wilhelm's approach to Javanese culture was very different from the other missionaries at that time and missionaries after him. Thus after Wilhelm's death, Sadrach refused to join with NGZV, because it did not want to recognize him as an equal partner. It even criticized Sadrach's beliefs and practices of Christianity as syncretism.

lay evangelists like Coolen and Kyai Sadrach, worship services were modeled on the Dutch style. There were some promising developments, however, that gave Javanese Christians the chance to be actively involved in worship. In some areas, where possible, the missionaries began to use tribal languages or the simple Malay language in sermons, education, and translation of the Scriptures. Rev. R. le Bruijn, for example, translated some evangelical songs into simple Malay because he wanted the Christians in Kupang to understand the meaning of the songs they sang. He did not use indigenous music, however. Efforts to make the gospel understandable to Indonesians were influenced by nineteenth-century Pietism's perspectives on education,[24] but native Indonesian perspectives on Western culture inhibited the contextualization of worship. Indonesians saw Western culture as "higher" than their own, and so they were reluctant to express their new faith through their old culture.

In addition to Sunday worship, many churches held prayer meetings and household services in the evening. Indonesian teachers or elders could conduct these services, whereas missionaries led Sunday morning worship. Of course, only missionary ministers were allowed to celebrate the sacraments, although some Indonesians were selected to be assistants to the pastor.

Worship in the Twentieth Century

Methods of evangelization and the approach to indigenous culture shifted at the end of the nineteenth century, especially among missionaries from the Oegstgeest school of evangelization. These missionaries were more open to Indonesian culture, trying to adapt it to Christianity. A. C. Kruyt, who worked in Poso, was especially notable. Impressed by Darwin's theory of evolution, he said that missionaries should not condemn and reject tribal religions, but rather adjust methods of evangelization to build on the foundation of tribal religion and advance to a higher level of understanding.[25] Instead of condemning the tribal religion in Poso, Kruyt studied it and adapted some of its traditions to Christian celebrations. For example, people in Poso cleansed the graveyard in order to gain a good harvest. Instead of objecting to the practice, Kruyt related the tradition to the Christian celebration of Easter. Kruyt's views were

---

24. Van den End, *Ragi Carita*, vol. 1, p. 229.

25. According to Kruyt, Christianity, which believed in one God (monotheism), was the highest religion and animism was the lowest. Thus, missionaries should guide believers from the lower religions to the higher one. See Th. van den End and J. Weitjens, SJ, *Ragi Carita*, vol. 2: *Sejarah Gereja di Indonesia* (Jakarta: BPK Gunung Mulia, 1999), p. 303.

influential among other missionaries. In Toraja missionaries permitted Christians to celebrate Torajan traditions as long as they did not involve idol worship or illicit sexual relations. To this day, Torajan Christians hold traditional celebrations to honor the dead.

Kruyt and other missionaries worked to adapt indigenous culture to Christianity, yet little was done to bring indigenous culture into worship as Sadrach had done. Generally speaking, although most worship was in the vernacular it followed the Western (reformed Dutch) pattern:[26] Churches were built in a simple Western style. Occasionally missionaries constructed churches in local architectural styles — a church in Malang was designed to resemble *pendopo* (the Javanese front house), and churches in Sangalla and Tator employed Torajan house architecture — but few others followed those examples. In addition, congregational involvement in worship was limited to singing; the order of service was simple, with the sermon as the central element; and Communion was rarely celebrated.

This situation continued through Indonesian independence. There were occasional attempts to create worship services that integrated Indonesian culture, but church members were not receptive.[27] Wayan Mastra reports a similar situation in Bali:

> The church became conscious of the fact that if it wants to win the people for Christ, it should take some steps in bringing the culture as much as possible to the church. This thought is especially strong among the younger generation of Christians. But these efforts have not always been welcomed by all Christians, particularly the older generation, those baptized in the 1930's. They well believe these things belonged to demons. They said: "Why should we try to use these cultural practices that we have tried to avoid and to leave behind?"[28]

Partonadi had a similar experience. When the Javanese church he served celebrated Christmas, the *gamelan* used to accompany Javanese dance was kept outside the church, for the senior elder of the church said the *gamelan* was not worthy of a place in a Reformed Christian church.[29] Christians of the older generation who had been baptized by the missionaries feared a return to the

---

26. Van den End and Weitjens, *Ragi Carita,* vol. 2, pp. 325-26.

27. Van den End and Weitjens, *Ragi Carita,* vol. 2, p. 359.

28. I. Wayan Mastra, "Contextualization of the Church in Bali: A Case Study from Indonesia," in *Gospel and Culture,* ed. John Stott and Robert T. Coote (Pasadena: William Carey Library, 1979), pp. 371-72, as quoted by Partonadi, *Sadrach's Community,* p. 232.

29. Partonadi, *Sadrach's Community,* p. 233.

old beliefs if traditional cultural expressions were permitted in the church, especially in worship.

J. L. Ch. Abineno observes that after the Protestant Church in Indonesia gained independence from the Dutch Reformed Church in 1935, imitation of the Dutch worship style endured because Indonesian church leaders thought the pattern was apostolic. The churches never questioned whether the adopted Dutch worship pattern was relevant to the situation in Indonesia or whether it communicated the kerygma.[30] Abineno urged the churches in Indonesia to evaluate their worship on three criteria: the liturgical pattern should be ecumenical, theologically responsible, and relevant to the local context.[31] But his call to renew liturgical patterns was not followed.[32] Dutch church traditions were deeply rooted, and the Indonesian churches were apprehensive about uncontrolled developments. Nevertheless, charismatic worship styles began to appear in the 1970s and have spread in the decades since, especially among younger generations.[33] The renewal of worship patterns takes time, and may have to start "from below."[34]

---

30. J. L. Ch. Abineno, *Liturgische vormen en patronen in de evangelische kerk op Timor,* a doctoral dissertation (Utrecht: Rijksuneversiteit, 1956), as quoted by A. G. Hoekema, *Berpikir Dalam Keseimbangan yang Dinamis,* p. 285. Abineno (1917-1995) was an Indonesian theologian who taught in the Jakarta Theological Seminary and was the president of the Communion of Churches in Indonesia from 1960 to 1980.

31. J. L. Ch. Abineno, "Tata Ibadah Kita Perlu Ditinjau Ulang," *Berita Oikumene* 180 (July 1991): 122-25.

32. There have been changes in the appreciation of our traditional heritage among the younger generation of Christians since the 1960s. On special occasions, such as the Christmas celebration, Javanese Reformed and Catholic Christians have welcomed traditional Javanese music and ballet, or have used shadow figures (*wayang*) as a medium to proclaim the gospel. These changes have not come without struggle, however. The effort originated with Javanese Christian artists outside the church. They ignored the church's opposition because they wanted to express their faith through their own artistic media, offering their talents to God. But in the 1970s the churches came to accept Javanese music, dance, and *wayang* as part of their worship services. The Javanese church in Jakarta included the Javanese ballet in Christmas worship for the first time in 1976. Since that time, congregational singing on Christian holy days often has been accompanied by *gamelan.*

33. The movement has caused some Reformed churches to adjust their worship style to meet the needs of young people. Many youth reject the "old" formal style of worship. They prefer freer worship consisting of contemporary gospel songs, praying, reading selected verses of the Bible, and a sermon discussing contemporary problems in contemporary language. They also like songs of adoration and personal conversion following the sermon. It is a kind of revival worship style.

34. Hoekema, *Berpikir Dalam Keseimbangan yang Dinamis,* p. 357, regarding his conversation with Abineno on May 26, 1983.

There has been some movement toward Abineno's call to examine liturgical patterns in terms of ecumenical breadth, theological grounding, and cultural relevance. In 1978, the Protestant Church of Western Indonesia (GPIB)[35] adopted an order of Sunday worship prepared by the Reverend H. A. van Dop, based on the reforms of the Second Vatican Council and the insights of the liturgical renewal movement.[36] A subsequent publication concerning the order for congregational worship showed appreciation for the Lima Liturgy of the World Council of Churches. Van Dop disapproved of worship led only by the preacher, encouraging more congregational participation. He differentiated the *ordinary* and the *proper* in worship, enriching the *propers* with contextual words and arts. He also encouraged the contextualization of liturgical music, though he still translated the Geneva psalms into the modern Indonesian language.

Other churches have tried similar reforms. Some churches in Bali have been built according to principles of Balinese-Hindu architecture. The color of the minister's robe has been changed from black to white because in the Balinese culture black represents evil spirits and white symbolizes good spirits. (Besides, white is more comfortable in a tropical environment.) A Toraja church in Jakarta was built in the traditional Torajan meetinghouse style. On special occasions, traditional musical instruments and songs are used to accompany traditional dances. Ethnic decorations may also be employed. Although this has not become routine weekly practice, the frequency is higher, and few people remain firmly opposed.

The ecumenical, liturgical renewal influence has also grown stronger. Some churches now celebrate Advent and Lent in addition to Christmas and Easter, and a lectionary based on the Christian calendar is commonly used in several churches.[37] Attempts are being made to shift the mood of worship from penitential-cognitive-educational toward celebrative-affective-meditative. The most important development may be increased interest in liturgical and church music courses among theological students. The curriculum of Jakarta Theological Seminary now has four areas of theological studies concentration, one of which is liturgy and church music. The department is still in its infancy and needs to learn from other school's experiences of liturgical contextualization.

35. This church belongs to the Protestant Church in Indonesia.

36. As related by the Reverend H. A. van Dop in November, 2000. Van Dop is a retired Dutch missionary who has worked in Indonesia since 1969. He is a hymn composer and hymnal editor, teaching liturgy and hymnology at Jakarta Theological Seminary. Some of his compositions were published in the *Kidung Jemaat (The Congregation's Hymnal)* and used materials from traditional Indonesian music.

37. The Communion of Churches in Indonesia (which includes most Protestant churches) has published a lectionary based on the Revised Common Lectionary.

Music is the central issue, because the first attempt to contextualize Indonesian worship is most often through music. Congregational singing has been an important activity in worship since Werndly translated Genevan psalms into Malay in 1735. In the eighteenth and nineteenth centuries, missionaries translated some hymns into the vernaculars. Most of the hymns came from Pietism and the revival traditions, except for the Gereformeerd missionaries who only permitted the singing of Genevan psalms. In 1908 Schröder published *Mazmoer dan Tahlil (Psalms and Songs of Praise)* for use in GPI churches, and in 1927 he collaborated with Izaac Tupamahu to published gospel songs in *Dua Sahabat Lama.* A new hymnal edited by I. S. Kijne, *Mazmur dan Nyanyian Rohani,* was released in 1947, consisting of some psalms, European hymns, and American gospel songs. Hymnals in tribal languages were also published, but only translated European and American hymns were included. No Indonesian compositions using traditional melody and structure can be found in these twentieth-century hymnals, with the exception of the 1927 Torajan hymnal that included three traditional melodies (and, of course, the Javanese *tembang* of Coolen, Sadrach, and other Javanese evangelists). Van den End notes that the Indonesians themselves discouraged the use of traditional music in worship, since it was closely identified with ancestor worship, and since it was not compatible with Western hymnic structures.[38]

Fresh wind blew in 1984 when the Church Music Foundation in Indonesia *(Yamuger)* released *Kidung Jemaat,* containing one hundred hymns by Indonesian composers. Even so, one of the editors acknowledged that not all of the songs in the new hymnal were contextual. Most reflect a European and North American heritage, making noticeable the Western flavor of *Kidung Jemaat.* But this was intentional, for Indonesian churches enjoy singing their faith in familiar terms. Moreover, congregations are enabled to experience the historical ecumenism of churches from all times and places,[39] since *Kidung Jemaat* also contains songs from Zambia, India, Sri Lanka, China, and Japan. In recent years, more Indonesian hymn materials have been composed with traditional music. They were compiled in the 1999 *Supplement to Kidung Jemaat,* which also included songs from Asia, Africa, the Pacific Islands, and the Taizé community, as well as contemporary European hymns and American gospel songs. The Creative Music Group of Jakarta Theological Seminary has encouraged the use of songs from Asia, Africa, and South America that were composed in

38. See van den End and Weitjens, *Ragi Carita,* vol. 2, p. 327.
39. H. A. van Dop, "Kontekstualisasi Musik Gereja," in *Apostole,* ed. Sularso Sopater (Jakarta: STT Jakarta, 1987), p. 119.

contexts similar to Indonesia's, and thus give voice to our struggles. The Group has also attempted to introduce songs that are not dependent on piano or organ accompaniment, using instead traditional instruments, guitars, and "garbage instruments" made of plastic jars, coconut shells, and other discarded materials. Organs and pianos are expensive instruments, and so the desire to use traditional music in worship is combined with a recovery of traditional instruments and instruments constructed from readily available materials.

Concluding Thoughts

For almost four centuries Indonesian Reformed churches worshiped God by using the Dutch Reformed order of worship. Long expository sermons were the central element in the Sunday service, while emotion and the arts were devalued, making worship more didactic and intellectual. Worship was also a means of implementing church discipline, as in the practice of the colonial era's separation of baptism and Communion, and today's fencing of the table of the Lord. The missionaries imposed a form of worship that was not grounded in tribal cultures, because those cultures were considered evil, unworthy of expressing Christian faith. Being a Christian meant being a Westernized person. At a more basic level, the very existence of colonialism prevented the colonizers from appreciating the goodness of Indonesian ethnic cultures. The efforts of Coolen and Sadrach to bring ethnic expressions to worship were greeted with suspicion by most of the missionaries. Efforts at enculturation were rejected, even branded as syncretism, with no consideration of the importance to Indonesians of their traditional cultures. On the other hand, Indonesian Christians often viewed Western culture as higher than their own. They also feared that worship using traditional elements could entice them back to their old beliefs.

The imposition of a particular culture as the only true way of worship has dislodged Indonesian Christians from their own societies. We have to struggle to be Christians and, at the same time, to be Javanese, Balinese, or Torajan. The rejection of indigenous cultures has restricted Christianity to the surface of people's lives, creating a division between worship and life, Christian community and society. In early 1960s when some artists and young people attempted to recover Indonesian culture for Christian worship, the older generation refused, because what they knew as authentic Reformed worship was the worship introduced by the missionaries.

Three paradigms indicate the current state of Reformed worship in Indonesia. The largest group has maintained the old Dutch Reformed liturgy, while at the same time being more open to accepting traditional cultural adaptation. For example, *gamelan* is commonly used in worship, and some new church buildings incorporate traditional styles of architecture. In contrast, Pentecostal and evangelical styles of worship, characterized by pop music and informality, have influenced the younger generation. Young people's attraction to this worship style has forced some Reformed churches to alter the style of their worship. Finally, the liturgical renewal movement has also had an impact on Indonesian Reformed churches, although it is still in its infancy. People influenced by this movement attempt to renew Indonesian worship by emphasizing the need both for contextualization and ecumenical convergence in worship.

Worship is at the heart of the Indonesian church's life. Many Christians, including the younger generation, worship diligently every Sunday. Many congregations have multiple services as well as Bible studies during the week, early morning or evening prayer meetings, household services, special youth and women's services, and more. Traditional Indonesian cultures do not separate worship and life. Life is worship, and worship marks the passages of life.

Reformed churches in Indonesia must contextualize their worship in order to make it relevant and valuable in people's lives. This is not an easy task, since the Dutch Reformed liturgy has been used for centuries. Furthermore, it is not a simple, straightforward matter to contextualize worship by using indigenous culture. The Indonesian context is highly pluralistic culturally, socially, economically, and religiously. It is almost impossible to speak about one kind of contextualized Reformed worship. Therefore, every church is challenged to seek its own path of contextualization while honoring the Reformed tradition and the ecumenical convergence in worship. The primary question is not merely how to worship God using traditional cultural elements, but how to worship God in the midst of a particular context so that people can live in harmony with their society and be empowered to show God's love for the world.

Further Reading

Abineno, J. L. Ch., *Liturgische vormen en patronen in de evangelische kerk op Timor.* A doctoral dissertation. Utrecht: Rijksuneversiteit, 1956.

———. *Sejarah Apostolat di Indonesia I.* Jakarta: BPK Gunung Mulia, 1978.

———. "Tata Ibadah Kita Perlu Ditinjau Ulang," *Berita Oikumene 180* (July 1991).

Hoekema, A. G.. *Berpikir Dalam Keseimbangan yang Dinamis: Sejarah Lahirnya Teologi Protestan Nasional di Indonesia (Sekitar 1860-1960).* Jakarta: BPK Gunung Mulia, 1997.

Mastra, I. Wayan. "Contextualization of the Church in Bali: A Case Study from Indonesia." In *Gospel and Culture,* ed. John Stott and Robert T. Coote. Pasadena: William Carey Library, 1979.

Partonadi, Sutarman Soediman. *Sadrach's Community and Its Contextual Roots: A Nineteenth-Century Javanese Expression of Christianity.* Amsterdam: Free University of Amsterdam, 1988.

Van den End, Th. *Ragi Carita.* Vol. 1. Jakarta: BPK Gunung Mulia, 1980.

Van den End, Th., and Weitjens, J., SJ. *Ragi Carita.* Vol. 2: *Sejarah Gereja di Indonesia.* Jakarta: BPK Gunung Mulia, 1999.

Van Dop, H. A. "Kontekstualisasi Musik Gereja." In *Apostole,* ed. Sularso Sopater. Jakarta: STT Jakarta, 1987.

Worship in the Presbyterian Church in Korea

Seong-Won Park

The Korean Presbyterian Church is basically a worshiping community, so worship is central to church life in Korea. People gather for worship not only in celebration of the Lord's Day on Sunday morning but also on Sunday evening for a service of praise, on Wednesday evening for Bible study, and on Friday evening for a vigil prayer meeting. Korean Christians put most of their faith activities in the context of worship. Being a Christian in Korea means attending worship services regularly. It is through worship that Christians' faith is kindled, their spirituality integrated, their church enlarged, and their witness to Christ borne.

The Korean Protestant church has grown astonishingly in the relatively short period of over one hundred years of mission history. No doubt, worship has made a major contribution to the growth of the church. This fact leads one to ask the following questions: What kind of contribution has worship made to such remarkable growth? What role has worship played in stimulating the vitality of Korean Presbyterianism? What then are the characteristics of its worship?

Transmission of the Reformed Tradition

The Reformed tradition was not transmitted directly from Geneva, or Bern, or Zürich to Korea. The Korean church received the tradition through the work of missionaries from Scotland, the United States, Canada, and Australia. It was a journey requiring three hundred years and spanning three continents.

In the course of its historical evolution, Reformed worship developed according to the historical realities and contexts in which it was celebrated. For instance, the much-reduced Reformed tradition in Europe is evolving in its own understanding of what it means to be Reformed. Earlier forms of Reformed worship in Europe have been largely reshaped under the influence of various movements: Puritanism, which was anti-liturgical; Congregationalism and Presbyterianism, which emphasized intellectual understanding of the word of God; Pietism and Moravianism, which insisted on personal experience. The Reformed tradition as transmitted to North America and Australia has developed its own rhythm and character. North American Reformed worship also developed under the influence of the Great Awakening, revivalism, and the missionary movement, which vigorously promoted a missionary aspect of worship. Likewise, Korean Reformed worship has been shaped by the Korean understanding of the gospel, which evolved out of the distinct cultural, political, historical, and social context in which Korean Christians have been living.

This does not mean that there is no line of continuity leading from Geneva, Bern, or Zürich to the Presbyterian church in Korea today. There is at least external continuity, but, at the same time, there is not necessarily a deep resemblance. Korean Presbyterian worship has developed its own Reformed character. The question then is how closely aligned the tradition is to that of its European forebears.

The experience of the Korean Presbyterian Church raises the following questions: To what extent and in what sense can the worship of the Korean Presbyterian Church be called Reformed? What kind of continuity or discontinuity has Korean Presbyterian worship with sixteenth-century worship in Geneva and with the historical development of Reformed worship elsewhere? What would all these developments mean in terms of the Reformed ethos of worship?

Historical Development of Korean Reformed Worship

Since it was missionaries from North America and Australia who brought Presbyterianism into Korea, their understanding of the Reformed theological tradition was in fact eponymous for Presbyterianism in Korea. Worship was no exception. The Korean Reformed worship that was celebrated in the early period, namely from 1884 to 1906, was an imported version of a much-reduced form of Reformed worship based on the beliefs of American missionaries whose understanding had been shaped by Puritanism, revivalism, and the missionary movement.

This form of worship began to be contextualized in 1907 in connection with the great revival movement that swept the Korean churches. It produced a number of unique characteristics like committed prayer, an emphasis on the presence of the Holy Spirit in worship, great value placed on feelings, story-telling sermons, dawn meditation, emphasis on the Bible, and mission-oriented worship. A kind of Koreanization of Reformed worship was achieved under the strong leadership of the Reverend Kil Sun-Ju, the most influential figure in the movement, whose personal background and spiritual experiences were rooted in Taoism and Buddhism.

Korean Presbyterians played a significant role in the independence movement after World War I, the so-called March First Movement that claimed sovereignty for the Korean nation. Their involvement also opened new dimensions of spirituality, and, through this experience, worship acquired a political dimension. Despite the depoliticization policy of the missionaries, Korean Christians had a strong sense of being called to respond to their political and historical reality. The liberating message of the Bible was the basis of their participation in political witness. Christians read the Exodus story in their own political context. They identified themselves with the Israelite people, and they confessed that the God who had liberated Israel from Egyptian bondage would liberate the Koreans from Japanese oppression and enslavement as well. The stories of the Bible were transposed into their own historical setting, and the biblical story was no longer simply a spiritual matter. The word of God was a living and active liberating word in their historical context.

The March First Movement was thus an Exodus paradigm for the oppressed Korean church. As the Israelite people acquired their distinctive historical consciousness and shaped their particular spirituality following the Exodus, the Korean people likewise acquired a spiritual vision in their concrete historical context and connected their spiritual belief with their historical situation.

In the face of frustration and harsh oppression following the failure of the independence movement in 1919, however, this vital understanding of worship came under the influence of otherworldly eschatological aspirations and mysticism. People thought that historical transformation could not be achieved by human efforts but only through the intervention of God. This notion led the Korean church to an otherworldly, eschatological faith that distanced the worship of the Korean Presbyterian Church from its historical and political context. During this period, the Korean church's worship and, more precisely, its revival meetings adopted one of the shamanistic ritual's characteristics: a ritual performed for obtaining blessings, but without ethical requirements.

From the second half of the 1930s until 1945, the Korean Presbyterian

Church had to face a deep crisis of faith. The Japanese colonial power imposed Shinto shrine worship on the churches as well as the mission schools. Even though the Japanese colonial authorities claimed that the Shinto devotion was not a religious practice but a patriotic ritual to unite the Japanese people, it obviously had religious implications and, moreover, was a form of emperor worship. Karl Barth once said that the first commandment was a foundational axiom of theology,[1] and worship of God alone was regarded by Korean Christians as an axiom of faith. Protestant churches, particularly the Presbyterian church, resisted participation in Shinto shrine worship because they thought it violated the first commandment and, in doing so, required participants to deny God. Through the struggle against Shinto shrines, Korean Presbyterian Church worship recovered political relevance, sharpening the meaning of the first commandment vis-à-vis worldly power. It was a confrontation between the war of the emperor and the peace of God, between the sovereignty of God and the sovereignty of the emperor. It was a confrontation between emperor worship and the worship of God. It was a matter of *status confessionis.*

After liberation of the country in 1945, the issue of readmission of those Christians who had lapsed in relation to Shinto shrine worship pointedly raised the question of forgiveness versus radical obedience. Throughout this dispute, Reformed worship began to be determined by a legalistic understanding of worship. Segments of the Korean Presbyterian Church were strongly influenced by this legalistic understanding, leading to an approach to worship that was strict, solemn, anti-cultural, anti-ritualistic, anti-political, and anti-festive.

Along with the effects of economic growth in the 1970s and 1980s, Korean Reformed worship responded to a strong pentecostal influence. The mission of the church was also considerably stimulated by economic growth. Adopting a popular ideology of economic growth, worship became a ritual of the "gospel of success." Worship in this period also reflects considerable influence from shamanistic ritual.

In the same period, Korean society was suffering under an oppressive military dictatorship. This situation challenged the Korean churches to witness to social justice as a historical mission task of the church, and *Minjung* theology was born in this context. *Minjung* is a Korean word for people. Sociologically speaking, *Minjung* indicates the people who are politically oppressed,

---

1. H. Martin Rumscheidt, ed., *The Way of Theology in Karl Barth: Essay and Comments,* Princeton Theological Monograph No. 8 (Allison Park, Pa.: Pickwick Publications, 1986), pp. 63-89.

economically exploited, and socially alienated. Politically speaking, the real subject of history is not the king, but this people. *Minjung* is equivalent to the Greek word *oklos,* which usually refers to people who were regarded by the religious as sinners (e.g., tax collectors, illiterate peasants, prostitutes, and so on). In the course of the 1970s and 1980s, in connection with churches' struggle for democracy and human rights, *Minjung* theology was articulated by theologians and the *Minjung* Church movement was initiated by pastors who committed themselves to witness to the liberating gospel as seen from the *Minjung* perspective. *Minjung* theology led to a movement aimed at making worship politically relevant and culturally contextualized. The *Minjung* theology and *Minjung* Church movement might be considered as a Korean Reformed theology and reformation movement. One of the most significant developments encouraged by the *Minjung* community in this process was recovery of the frequency and significance of the Lord's Supper as a communion with social implications.

Features of Korean Presbyterian Worship

What distinctive characteristics have been shaped throughout this historical development? Let me highlight some of the prominent features that have distinguished Korean Presbyterian worship in the process of its adaptation within the Korean social and cultural context:

1. Both in the past and today, the celebration of worship has been of central importance for the life of the Presbyterian churches in Korea. More than anything else, worship has played a decisive role in shaping Korean Presbyterianism.
2. The Reformed tradition was transmitted to Korea in a drastically reduced form. Through the adaptation to the religious and cultural context, important sixteenth-century themes were inadvertently and unintentionally recovered by the Korean churches.
3. The emergence of new forms of worship in Korea is, in fact, in harmony with the deepest intentions of the Reformers, who encouraged the adaptation of worship to the needs of the people.
4. The political struggles in which the Korean Presbyterian churches were successively involved in the course of the twentieth century have had the effect of rehistoricizing and repoliticizing the inherited ahistoricized and apoliticized forms and spirituality of worship. These aspects of worship were not introduced by missionaries but developed independently

in the Korean context in which Korean Christians were called to witness in their society to the liberating gospel.

5. Traditionally, the presence of Christ was the central theme in Reformed worship. The experience of the Korean church, however, emphasized the presence of the Holy Spirit much more than the presence of Christ in worship.

6. Within the context of the *Minjung* community, the Eucharist has acquired new significance and meaning. It is today celebrated more frequently than in the past, and the character of the Eucharist as a meal is being emphasized.

7. In contrast to the inherited Reformed tradition, with its strong emphasis on intellect and intelligibility, Korean worship gives much greater room to feelings.

8. In revival meetings and evangelism, singing and music have played an important role in revitalizing worship. This is closely related to the typically Korean feature of the people's love of singing and music.

9. A distinctive element of Korean Reformed worship is committed communal prayer (dawn services, etc.). This tradition has contributed significantly to Korean Christians' spirituality.

10. Mission is significantly emphasized in the worship of the Korean church. This theme was absent from the concerns of the sixteenth-century Reformation, but in the Korean church, worship celebration has been directly connected with missionary calling.

11. Korean churches developed a strong tithing tradition. This typically Reformed understanding of God's economy is more and more relevant in today's context, which is dominated by a mammonism promoted by neo-liberal global capitalism.

The experience of the Korean Presbyterian Church raises several questions and issues for further development of Reformed worship:

1. The new significance given to the Eucharist through the *Minjung* movement represents both a concern of the Reformers and a new departure. Calvin wanted to introduce the frequent celebration of the Eucharist. To what extent can the emphasis on the character of the Eucharist as community meal be considered to be Reformed?[2]

2. Intelligibility is a central criterion for the Reformed tradition. God's

2. For more in-depth discussions of the Eucharist, see the chapters by Alan D. Falconer and Joseph D. Small in this volume.

word needs to be preached and made known to the people, and the meaning of the sacraments needs to be made clear. But the primacy of the spoken word in Reformed worship has led to a neglect of experience and emotion. The Korean pattern provides a corrective in this respect; at the same time, it raises the question of the relationship between word and emotion.

3. Christianity has made a decisive contribution to women's emancipation from oppressive patterns in society. Though the majority of worshipers are women, their role in worship has been minimal. Only a small minority of churches ordain women to the ministry. With regard to the role of women, the Presbyterian churches are caught in the tension between tradition and renewal.

4. Political commitments expressed in worship have often led to tensions and splits. There is among Presbyterian churches no agreed understanding concerning the place of political commitment in worship. A thorough theological reflection on the political relevance of worship is needed for a common witness in united action.

5. The classical Reformed tradition restricted singing in church services to metrical psalms. In most Reformed churches, the role of hymns and music has been considerably enlarged. In Korea, originally, the classical view prevailed, and controversial debates on the legitimacy of music in worship continue to this day. At the same time, the claims of traditional Korean culture are increasingly being recognized. Criteria for evaluation are needed.

6. In the early days, ancestor rites were banned by missionaries, and even today attempts to revive a Christian form of respect for past generations cause bitter disputes. There is a legitimate place in worship for the recognition of a link of gratitude to past generations.

Relevance of These Reflections to the Reformed Theology of Worship

Reflection on the history of worship in the Presbyterian church in Korea and its implications draws attention to the following issues for the wider Reformed worshiping community.

Worship as a History of Church

Worship, like a mirror, reflects the faith and the identity of the church. The history of worship is at the same time the history of the church; worship both expresses the theological and the ethical convictions of the people and shapes those convictions. Faith is expressed in worship before it is expressed in creed, and it is learned in worship before it is learned in school. That is why the Reformed churches, from the beginning, defined the church primarily in terms of the action of God in word and sacrament, not in terms of structures or even correct doctrine. More attention, therefore, needs to be given to worship in order to make the church more authentic and relevant before both God and society.

Contextualization

Reformed worship cannot exhaustively be defined by referring to the Reformers, in particular to Calvin, and to sixteenth-century developments. Subsequent history has decisively shaped Reformed worship, and Calvin himself promoted the idea that worship should be relevant to its context and its moment in time:

> I mean that the Lord has in his sacred oracles faithfully embraced and clearly expressed both the whole sum of true righteousness, and all aspects of the worship of his majesty, and whatever was necessary to salvation; therefore, in these the Master alone is to be heard. But because he did not will in outward discipline and ceremonies to prescribe in detail what we ought to do (because he foresaw that this depended upon the state of the times, and he did not deem one form suitable for all ages), here we must take refuge in those general rules which he has given, that whatever the necessity of the church will require for order and decorum should be tested against these. Lastly, because he has taught nothing specifically, and because these things are not necessary to salvation, and for the upbuilding of the church ought to be variously accommodated to the customs of each nation and age, it will be fitting (as the advantage of the church will require) to change and abrogate traditional practices and to establish new ones.[3]

Karl Barth, too, argued that since worship is a human response, it should always be reformable according to context. Of course, freedom of reform

---

3. John Calvin, *Institutes of the Christian Religion* (4.10.30), ed. John T. McNeill, trans. Ford Lewis Battles (Philadelphia: Westminster Press, 1960), vol. 2, p. 1208.

should not be arbitrary; rather, it should be based on reasonable principles. The Reformers had some criteria, particularly biblical principles, for reforming worship. But those criteria, including their biblical principles, were not practical guidelines. They were, rather, a kind of vision.

Reformed tradition is not just one uniform reality. The frequently quoted phrase *ecclesia reformata semper reformanda* (the church that is Reformed and continually being reformed) indicates that the renewal of the church must continue, and this includes renewal of worship. The Reformation movement is by nature a movement that should remain open to the future on the basis of the experiences and perceptions of a worshiping communion. The movement initiated by the Reformers, therefore, must find its continuation today. The treasures inherent in various cultures must be brought to bear on the Reformed tradition, and the understanding of Reformed worship must be enlarged to include various cultural ways of praising God.

Communion

As for the significance and frequency of Communion, whereas mainline Korean Presbyterian churches emphasize a doctrine of atonement in the liturgy of Holy Communion, reminiscent of the understanding of Communion received from the nineteenth-century missionaries, *Minjung* churches celebrate the communal aspect of Holy Communion wherein the taking of bread and wine is a moment of Pentecost for the celebrants. This pentecostal moment empowers the participants to confront and endure the powers of this world as witnesses to the gospel of Christ in the world.

By more frequent celebration and emphasis on the significance of Communion, the *Minjung* community corrected the unbalanced celebration of the Reformed church, which put more weight on the service of the word than on the service of the Communion. In addition, the *Minjung* community renews the bond of the community of saints through Communion whenever the power of the Spirit is needed to bring the people together and empower them to act. By emphasizing in community the character of the Eucharist as a meal, the *Minjung* community recovers the unity of people in Christ as a community. Their celebration of the Eucharist also resonates with the importance that Koreans give to the building of community through the sharing of a meal.

Presence of the Holy Spirit in Worship

The place of Christ's presence in worship was one of the polemical debates between the Reformed and Catholic theologies of worship. Reformers argued that it was not in the elements of the Eucharist but in the word of God that Christ was present.

Korean Presbyterian worship went further. It places primary emphasis on the presence of the Holy Spirit. How is this emphasis to be interpreted? Traditionally, Reformed worship is Christocentric; in many Reformed circles, the pneumatological emphasis is considered to be pentecostal. In fact, however, since one can see the illumination of the Holy Spirit in worship that Calvin emphasized, the pneumatological emphasis is a legitimate dimension of the Reformed tradition.

Value of Feelings

Reformers such as Calvin and Zwingli were wary of emotion and divided the heart from the head. One unfortunate result of the Reformed tradition's negative view of "hysterical" emotionalism is that the tradition has exaggerated rationality to the point where faith is in danger of becoming mere rationalism, which is perhaps why Reformed or Presbyterian worship is sometimes criticized as being dry or even sterile. Although the tradition has often called into question the value of feelings, however, the Korean church sees an emphasis on emotion as a complement to the intellectual aspects of Reformed worship, which might easily become dry and without feeling.

The Reformed tradition traditionally emphasized the significance of intelligibility, so the Bible was translated to give people access to the word of God. But the value of feelings needs to be carefully examined as another form of intelligibility in contemporary worship. This is even more urgent in face of the growing challenge of festive celebration in the Pentecostal community. From the point of view of worship, the rise of Pentecostalism today and its appeal even to Reformed Christians could be seen as a protest against this sterility. In a sense, Korean Presbyterianism incorporated the festive and committed style of Pentecostal celebration without associating itself with Pentecostal theology.

People want to feel the meaning of the gospel directly as well as reflect upon what the gospel says. Korean Christians will not accept the division of feeling from thought, and Korean worship revivifies the whole person's relationship with God and with the believing community. True, there is a danger of falling into hysteria, as the Reformers warned. But the other danger, that of a worship life that denies the need to experience the intimate relationship between God and the world in one's soul, is just as pernicious. The Korean Presbyterian Church has achieved a synthesis between thought and feeling, rationality and action. They thereby set a model of worship as *praxis,* but one based on the high valuation of feeling, which Western models of *praxis* still degrade.

Political Implications of Worship

The primary aim of the Reformation was to restore the Lordship of Christ over the world. In worship, the life and witness of the church were to reflect God's grace and God's will in Jesus Christ. But the concern of the Reformers, especially Calvin, was not limited to spiritual things. It extended to the whole of society. The Reformation was a breakthrough not only with regard to the life of the church but to secular life, and the Reformers affirmed that God's will had to be obeyed in all spheres of life. True, there is a need to withdraw from the world — for moments of meditation and prayer, for example, or to gather for worship. But the movement of gathering leads in turn to a movement of being sent into the world. The benediction at the end of every worship service is meant to equip us for a renewed witness to that world.

Seen from this perspective, worship cannot bypass the demands of society. Rather, it must take into account the historical, political, and economic problems with which so many are struggling, from which they are suffering, and by which they are victimized. Worship needs to be a faithful echo of these struggles and of God's grace accompanying them in their struggle. No worship will be authentic, faithful, and relevant that bypasses the suffering and aspirations of people agonizing in their day-to-day situations. Worship needs to stir the real life of real people, because God is concerned with the whole life of God's people.

The Korean idea of discipleship is closely aligned to mission. Worship and mission go together. The Korean understanding of mission in worship involves the concrete practice of faith, as expressed in worship, and applies that practice to the problems of everyday life and to the task of bringing the gospel to the people. *Minjung* worship emphasizes the social dimension of that witness, which, as we have seen, has been regarded with suspicion if not outright hostility by Korean Presbyterian churches of the establishment. And is that not the case today among Reformed churches of the establishment in other countries?

Just as sixteenth-century Reformers criticized the elitist intellectualism of scholastic theologies and the ecclesiastical hierarchies to which they appealed for the word of God to be rendered to the people of God, so today's Reformed critique challenges theologies and ecclesiastical hierarchies — this time Protestant — to proclaim the word of God to the people of God and make it relevant to their social, political, and economic context, for these forces make life livable or intolerable.

Music and Art in Reformed Worship

It is not an exaggeration to say that music is a Korean's mother tongue. It, too, is a pentecostal event much like Holy Communion. It renews human relationships, empowers the people to endure life's difficulties, refreshes the spirit, and sets the atmosphere for worship. Not to recognize and honor the significance of music in the life of the Korean people is to distort their reality and demean their spirit.

This component of worship is increasingly becoming important in contemporary worship, not only in Korea but also in many parts of the world, particularly for the younger generation. The young are much more inclined to be moved and to respond to singing than to a sermon.[4]

This phenomenon might raise the whole question of the Reformed understanding of the role of art in worship. Is it not time to reconsider the value of art in worship since art is today becoming more important for spiritual communication?

Renewal of Worship

There is need for increased communication among the Reformed churches in order to promote a common movement of renewal. The revitalization of the church will start from a revitalization of worship, and it will most effectively be implemented through renewing worship. In sixteenth-century Europe, one of the most revolutionary worship renewals in Christian history was accomplished. Today, the worship tradition of the Reformed churches in the West stands in need of radical renewal. The renewal of worship will be a life and death question for the future and survival of the churches, not only in the Western part of the world, where the number of worshipers is drastically de-

4. Further discussion on this subject can be found in Emily R. Brink and John Witvliet's chapter in this volume.

creasing, but also in other parts of the world, which may face a similar situation sooner or later.

Concluding Thoughts

The experience of the Presbyterian churches in Korea can contribute to a deeper understanding of Reformed worship. Reformed worship in Korea has, on the one hand, accentuated tensions and contradictions inherent in the Reformed tradition, but, on the other, opened up new perspectives. What the Korean church received may not be the fullness of the Reformed tradition, but, nevertheless, the Korean experience has enriched worship in a truly Reformed spirit and may contribute to further developments in Reformed spirituality.

The *Minjung* challenge to Korean Presbyterian churches, for example, criticizes the artificiality of Korean Presbyterian forms of worship as inherited from the nineteenth-century missionaries. But this challenge is not limited to integrating social witness with personal faith. In the evolution of the Reformed tradition as expressed in Europe, America, and Australia, other elements in worship were gradually eliminated. The *Minjung* emphasis on the frequency and meaning of the Eucharist, for example, also presents a challenge not only to Korean Presbyterian churches but also to other Reformed communions around the world. The meaning of the Eucharist includes the theological dimension of community, binding people together in bread and wine. It is a universal communication of faith and community that goes beyond doctrinal, cultural, or linguistic differences, at least among Reformed and most other Protestant communions.

Minjung has its counterparts in other parts of the world. Worship among African, Indian, and Afro-American churches, to name a few, speaks to a gradual resuscitation of worship as a holistic experience rooted in the life of the people. What this suggests is that the intentional contextualization of worship may be expressing the heart of the sixteenth-century Reformers' aspirations. Afro-American music, for example, reaches to the heart of the people's misery and hope, cries out to God, and challenges mainline white American churches to find their own authenticity in worship. In the same way, *Minjung* churches challenge Korean Presbyterians to become more Korean by becoming more Reformed and more Reformed by becoming more Korean.

For Further Reading

Chung, Sung-Kuh. *A History of Preaching in Korean Church.* Seoul: The Chong Shin Theological Seminary Press, 1986.

Chupungo, Anscar J., O.S.B. *Cultural Adaptation of the Liturgy.* New York: Paulist Press, 1982.

Clark, Charles A. *Religions of Old Korea.* Seoul: The Christian Literature Society, 1961.

Kim, Yong-Bock. *Messiah and Minjung.* Hong Kong: Christian Conference of Asia, 1992.

Lee, Keun-Sam. *The Christian Confrontation with Shinto Nationalism.* Philadelphia: The Presbyterian and Reformed Publishing Co., 1966.

Min, Kyung-Bae. *A History of Korean Church (Han Kuk Ki Dok Kyo Sa).* Seoul: Christian Literature Society, 1979.

Park, Seong-Won. *Worship in the Presbyterian Church in Korea: Its History and Implications.* New York: Peter Lang, 2001.

Rafael, Avila. *Worship and Politics.* Maryknoll: Orbis Books, 1981.

World Alliance of Reformed Churches. *Testimonies of Faith in Korea.* Geneva: World Alliance of Reformed Churches, 1989.

World Council of Churches. *International Review of Mission, Korea.* Vol. LXXIV, no. 293. January 1985.

Reformed Worship in East Africa

Isaiah Wahome Muita

The Reformed Church of East Africa and the Presbyterian Church of East Africa exercise jurisdiction over congregations within the territories of Kenya, Uganda, and Tanzania. The Reformed Church of East Africa (RCEA) was founded in 1944 by the Dutch Reformed Church in the Netherlands with missionaries coming from South Africa. It was started among the Kalenijn and Luhya ethnic groups in Western Kenya. The synod of the RCEA holds for its doctrinal standard the historic confessions of faith: the Apostles' Creed, the Nicene Creed, and the Athanasian Creed. The Presbyterian Church of East Africa (PCEA) was founded by the Church of Scotland in 1891 among the Masai, Kikuyu, and Meru peoples of Central Kenya. For its doctrinal standard, PCEA takes the Apostles' Creed, the Nicene Creed, and the Westminster Confession and Catechism. The church also holds as a subordinate standard the statement known as "The Short Statement of Faith" adopted by the Presbytery of East Africa of the Church of Scotland.

Worship and liturgy have been able to bind the Reformed churches in East Africa together, and liturgical renewal has shaped the worship life of the church. Although there is not much difference in worship and liturgy, these Reformed churches have served to preserve the ethnic heritages of Europe. The Reformed Church in East Africa retains a decidedly Dutch ethos, while the Presbyterian Church of East Africa preserves a Scottish ecclesiastical ethos. Can the Reformed church in East Africa truly be the church of Jesus Christ today in its time and place and still remain Reformed?

208

The Challenges

The 1928 Controversy

The church in East Africa has faced many challenges. In the late 1920s, several members who were dissatisfied with the Presbyterian church broke away from it. Their source of dissatisfaction was the issue of female circumcision, a tradition the church opposed. Those who broke away from the Presbyterian church started the African Independent Pentecostal Church of Africa (AIPCA).

The AIPCA borrowed heavily for its liturgy from the Anglican and Roman Catholic churches but continued to use many of the translated Scottish hymns as well. It also added African tunes and concepts in some of the hymns and the liturgy. Over the years, many of these tunes and hymns were borrowed by the Reformed churches for their worship.

East African Revival Movement

The East African Revival began in Rwanda in 1936 and rapidly spread to the neighboring countries of Burundi, Uganda, the Congo, Tanganyika, and Kenya. The Holy Spirit moved through mission schools and spread to the Protestant churches and to the whole community, producing repentance and changing lives.

The East African Revival had great influence on the Reformed churches. It continued for fifty years and helped establish a new zeal for enthusiastic holiness in African Christianity. The message was that repentance of sin should be evidenced by total rejection and removal of everything associated with that sin. The revivalists believed this would allow the blazing light of God's holiness in their lives. The joy, peace, forgiveness, and liberation from the guilt and power of sin were received with singing and jubilation. Many Reformed church members joined in this movement.

The Reformed churches in East Africa therefore had to deal with this new phenomenon. At the beginning, many members of the church, especially the clergy who had joined the movement, were expelled from the church. But they opted to remain faithful to the church and to continue to go for fellowship and to publicly give testimonies of their experience. Many of the church leadership continued to join the movement. Slowly, people began to confess their sins publicly and to give testimonies in the church. In the 1960s the Reformed churches found themselves having adopted many tenets of the revival movement, singing hymns that came from the movement, for example, and accepting public confessions of sins and the putting away of doubtful habits. In a way, this changed the old Scottish and Dutch ways of singing and worship.

Pentecostalism

Connected with the East African Revival Movement is Pentecostalism, since both of them focus on charismatic renewal. Pentecostalism has perhaps had since the 1970s a greater impact on the Reformed churches than has any other movement. The growth of Pentecostalism in the West has been very impressive, and its influence has been felt all over the world. The Reformed churches in East Africa have not been unaffected by Pentecostal inroads.

Pentecostalism was looked upon as an inward power of the Holy Spirit helping the individual and the church to attain spiritual growth. The people who were not affected by Pentecostalism were regarded as lifeless, powerless, and ineffective. They were accused of sweeping around dusty dogmas instead of dealing with Scripture.

Many members of the Reformed churches in East Africa have accepted Pentecostalism but opted to remain in the church. Pentecostalism has slowly been accepted in worship, but the church has remained faithful to its Reformed tradition.

Worship and Liturgy

An important characteristic of worship in the Reformed tradition is that it centers on God rather than ourselves and our feelings. Worship should center on the triune God who creates and sustains all things, who is revealed in Jesus Christ the Lord, and who is at work among us through the Holy Spirit as the giver of life.

From the very beginning, African worship was designed as a service that would contribute to the church's renewal. The prayer book of the Presbyterian Church of East Africa expresses the Reformed belief about the church by describing it as a body called of God as a fellowship of believers, both local and catholic. As such the church is a community of faith and hope, embracing both the past and the future, and gathering to worship the triune God. Clearly, then, the African church's choice is not between worship that focuses on human needs and aspirations while ignoring God and worship that focuses on God to the neglect of human realities. It is a Christian faith that proclaims a God who is bound in love to all creation and to every person at all times.

During the early years of the church, there was fear in East Africa that Reformed worship was too exclusively focused on God and divorced from human realities, assuming an abstract, remote quality. The formation of the Africa Independent Pentecostal Church of Africa in 1929 was a great challenge to the churches in East Africa, especially the Presbyterian church. Most or all Christian teaching, ritual, and worship were set in patterns that were developed in countries of the North. As a result, there was an authoritative tendency to translate rather than to create new acclamation, songs, and prayers. African Christians from the very beginning wanted to contextualize worship and theological education in order to break away from the constraints of European theology and worship. There was a deep feeling among Africans that the missionaries had marginal knowledge of the African reality. For this reason, they wanted to have more African pastors and theologians within the African church, which would allow them to replace missionaries and their "expatriate values" and relieve them of writing liturgy and worship materials for a people they did not understand.

John Mbiti has described Africans as "notoriously religious," and he is correct; worshiping God was not new to Africans and it was something they wanted to do. Their life is centered on God and worship. In the Reformed church, they wanted to worship God and remember Christ from within their own imaginative and language pattern. At the same time they wanted a form of worship that would enable people to live their relations to kin, clan, and society without causing any disruption, either personal or social.

The praise and worship service is the single most important spiritual hour for African people. They come together to have a time when they can worship God in the way they choose. This is a time they speak a language they understand, through songs they know and stories they can relate to. The church draws the worship community into grateful celebration of God's grace and eager hope in the fulfillment of God's purpose.

Singing and Music

In more recent decades there has been a cultural shift that has helped achieve some of these goals. The imperatives of political independence attained in the early 1960s and the building of nationalism had a profound impact on the church's worship. There was the desire for liturgical and worship renewal within the churches, since hard pews, unsingable tunes, enforced silence in the church, and excruciating boredom were some of the ingredients that made up the common image of church worship prior to this time.

Before 1970, music consisted almost solely of hymns translated from European hymnals. Many churches did not have pianos or organs, and people had to learn to sing a cappella. The drum was introduced in the church for rhythm only in the 1970s. Young people were allowed to have guitars and other musical instruments that they could afford. African tunes were introduced and were expressed in the coordinated movement of the dance — dancing together rather than alone. The African sense of worship brought the entire body of people to be caught up in the dance. The reason behind this is that revering God requires that human beings have a personal wholeness. It requires respect for the human need to act in accord with the rhythms of nature. It requires harmony and oneness within the community.

Music in the Reformed churches has become the catalyst for drawing people to the experience of Christ. Music is emotional, spiritual, and physical, a way to worship God with mind, body, soul, and strength. Music is corporate; it is something that all people can experience together. It is also experiential. Music defines the God for whom people are looking. People hear God's word proclaimed through the songs. Praise and worship makes the church vital to the believers' experience. This kind of worship brings people together as participants to worship and praise God.

Music has also been used in Reformed churches in East Africa to communicate the message of the gospel to other people outside the church. This has opened the realm of evangelism. Christians are not the only ones seeking a relevant spiritual experience. All people have a deep spiritual craving. These other people are drawn to the church's worship before they are drawn to the message.

The implication of this shift is that people can come to worship where songs are sung anew, where new songs and the great hymns of faith are used in praise and worship of God. Worship in both style and content interacts with the culture in which it exists. It is not a spectator sport, but an action taken on our part and directed to God from where people live and the way they live.

Sacraments

The Reformed churches acknowledge two divine sacraments: Communion or the Lord's Supper and baptism. Often these sacraments are described as an outward and visible sign of an inward redemption by, and union with, Jesus Christ through grace. They are a sign and seal of the work of Christ, which is set forth to all believers in his gospel of salvation, so that believers might depend on Christ alone.

Communion

Communion is taken very seriously in Reformed worship. A whole liturgical complex of words, symbols, and actions constitutes Holy Communion or the Lord's Supper, and it is, first of all, the central act of Christian worship. It has the image of a joyful meal that is done with thanksgiving. Christians share the meal with joy and with one another and are united in that one meal. When they eat together they express the true meaning of community, a very pertinent concept for the African people.

Second, the Lord's Supper is taken as remembrance. The whole life and ministry, suffering, death, and resurrection of Jesus Christ are remembered in and through this meal. Songs like "Nothing But the Blood of Jesus" are very popular in the African Reformed churches. It is the blood that reconciles humankind to God. (This is a message of the Reformation.) Africans are not shy to speak of blood, sorrow, martyrdom, and death, and the heritage of such hymns continues to tell the biblical truth.

Third, to eat and drink together is to commune with and in the presence of the Lord. There is also emphasis on the eschatological meaning of the meal. It is a foretaste of the heavenly banquet.

According to the local custom, the elements of bread and wine are laid on the table at the beginning of the service. While the church debates whether to continue with the actual bread and wine, it is clear that there is need for participation by all believers using common elements for the celebration of the Holy Communion.

Baptism

Baptism embodies God's initiation in Christ and expresses a response of faith made within the Christian community. In baptism the new Christian identifies with Jesus Christ in death and in life.

Baptism in most churches is done by sprinkling, although members are given an opportunity to have baptism by immersion if they so desire. Each sanctuary therefore must have a baptismal font. Water from the rivers or just rainwater is used in baptism. Even where water is scarce, especially in arid areas, the church is careful to get water for baptism. Symbolism is very important. Both adults and children are baptized.

The manner in which baptism is administered becomes an aid in the spirit of worship. That is why baptism is done in places of worship in the presence of a congregation, unless there is an emergency that would not allow that to happen. Baptism is not administered as an emergency measure to ensure salvation, however, but as a means of showing forth the redemptive power of the word of God in Jesus Christ.

Since baptism cannot be separated from the word, it is ordinarily administered during the service at which the written word has been expounded, setting forth the promises and benefits the sacrament proclaims.

Revitalizing Worship

Reformed churches need to involve people in exciting exploration of God's word for our day. The African Reformed churches must be a place of encounter with the world outside their walls or worship will be increasingly irrelevant and preaching will be sterile. The church needs to make worship exciting, fulfilling, and experiential, so that people will be attracted to the church. Worship will help people reach out to God and to one another.

Another thing to note is that the African church, like churches in many other parts of the world today, can be described as literate, relatively affluent, and socially conservative as a privileged caste in society. It is made up of aging and many middle-aged people and youth. But the African church is biblically illiterate or misinformed. There needs to be more teaching and Bible studies so that the people may be deeply grounded in the word of God, which in turn will enhance their worship.

We also live in a multicultural, international, even shrinking world. We need to learn from one another and yet keep our identity. Christian ministry and worship, unless it is self-supporting financially and theologically, will not be effective in carrying out the mission of Christ in our situation.

Worship should form us and equip us to reach out to the culture around us with both words of the gospel truths and deeds flowing from gospel faithfulness. The way we worship and the way we communicate the gospel message must resonate with the culture of today.

New churches have emerged and they bring a whole new concept of worship. Many Reformed churches try to copy from them and import worship that sometimes does not look Reformed. Our times have changed and therefore we need to know where we are going as we continue to keep within the Reformed tradition.

We need to be learning from new churches, which have many attributes of established churches. These churches, especially the African Independent churches, are appropriating contemporary cultural reforms and creating a new genre of worship music. They also are restructuring institutional religion and democratizing access to the sacred by radicalizing the Reformed principle of the priesthood of all believers. These churches are attempting to reintegrate bodily experience into religious life. There are inherent strengths of the Reformed tradition that will continue to be significant, but there is need to keep learning the importance of religious experience. We need to bring life into our worship and personal lives. We also need to acknowledge that the Holy Spirit reflects the feeling and experiential dimension of religious life.

The method of receiving Communion needs to be looked at again. Communion is intended to build community, but there are currently obstacles to achieving this community, which we need to continue reviewing in an effort to eliminate them. Maybe we need to have movable chairs rather than fixed pews, or perhaps more singing would be helpful. This would lead to greater personal interaction and participation on the part of the congregation.

There is great need to bring joy into our worship. Joy and thanksgiving characterized New Testament worship because of God's gracious redemption in Christ. Early worship focused on God's saving work in Jesus Christ, and true worship was that which occurred under the inspiration of the Holy Spirit (John 4:23-24). The church today needs to learn from that early church in order to enhance worship. If the Reformed church were closer to the New Testament images, church services would be far from dull and boring. Worship would be very exciting. It would be near to heaven on earth!

Finally, worship is not about us but about God. The Reformed church's worship needs to be based on the fact that God is the center of worship. Worship needs to lead true worshipers to follow Jesus and to be committed to God's purposes of peace, justice, and the salvation of the world. Worship should form the congregation to be a genuine, inclusive community linked to all God's people throughout time and space in worship, doctrine, fellowship, the breaking of the bread, prayers, signs and wonders, communal care, and social involvement. Worship should equip us to reach out to the culture around us with the gospel, with words of the gospel truth and deeds flowing from gospel faithfulness.

For Further Reading

Kurewa, John Wesley Zwomunondiita. *Preaching and Cultural Identity: Proclaiming the Gospel in Africa.* Nashville: Abingdon Press, 2000.

Muita, Isaiah. *Hewn from the Quarry.* Nairobi: Jitegemea, 2001.

Mugambi, J. N. K., ed. *The Church and the Future in Africa: Problems and Promises.* Nairobi: All Africa Conference of Churches, 1997.

The Practice and Procedure Manual, Presbyterian Church of East Africa. Nairobi: Publishing Solutions, 1998.

The Worship Experience of the Reformed Family in Ghana/West Africa: The Cry and Quest for Liturgical Reform

Livingstone Buama

What this chapter seeks to spell out, briefly, is the fact that even though Christian worship, as it is presented and projected in and through our Reformed upbringing in Ghana/West Africa, can be said to be a rich legacy, nevertheless, it leaves the sons and daughters of the Reformed family in Ghana/West Africa crying for a liturgical reform that is culturally suitable, current, and existentially satisfying.

I will begin with an introductory section on the form of Reformed worship that reached Ghana; discuss the merits and demerits of these traditions and the extent to which they respond to today's situation; continue with a brief overview of the basic meaning and demands of Christian worship, which must inspire and guide reform; and conclude by describing the cry and quest for liturgical reform, with particular reference to the Ghanaian situation today.

The Arrival of Reformed Worship in Ghana

The advent of Reformed worship in the West African sub-region was due primarily to the activities of the missionary societies from Europe, the West Indies, and North America. The Evangelical Presbyterian Church in Ghana and the Eglise Evangélique Presbyterienne du Togo, for example, are the products of the missionary effort of the North German Missionary Society–Norddeutsche Mission (Bremen Mission) founded on April 9, 1836, and representing the Bremen Evangelical Church, the Lutheran Church of Oldenburg, the Evangelical Reformed Church, and the Leer and Lippe Church in Detmold, all from Germany. As a result of the outbreak of the First and Second World Wars, all the Bremen Missionaries working with the church had to

216

be replaced. This resulted in the arrival of the Scottish Mission in 1922, followed by the American Evangelical and Reformed Church, now the United Church of Christ, in 1946. Other missionary societies that helped with the planting of the Reformed tradition in West Africa include Basel Missionaries, the London Missionary Society, Moravians, and Wesleyan Methodists. There was, as a result, a multiplicity of strands or facets of Reformed worship within the established churches, mostly planted in specific ethnic settings which already had a clear concept of God, the Supreme Being, in their African worldview and cultural settings.

Nevertheless, the key elements built into Reformed worship — invocation, call to worship, exhortation, praise and adoration, prayers, affirmation of faith, singing of hymns, Bible readings, sermon (preaching), offertory, announcements, the sacraments, and self-dedication and benediction — could be found in most of the established Reformed churches in West Africa. Apart from the regular Sunday morning worship services, the members of the emerging mainline churches were also encouraged to participate in Sunday evening services, early morning weekday services, and prayer services, following well-prepared liturgies. There was great emphasis on the use of the Bible, the liturgy, and the hymn book.

The Merits and Demerits of These Traditions

The Merits

So far as the merits of our Reformed legacy are concerned, it must be said that the Reformed tradition is rich in content. This is generally seen in the key items that are built into the Reformed order of worship as already shown above.

In addition, the tradition presents and projects a worthy picture of God and a meaningful understanding of the church. During worship God is presented and projected as the pivot and focal point of every activity. The church is viewed, therefore, as an assembly before God — people summoned, called, or invited by God. Our coming together to worship is, in fact, our personal response to the call or the invitation of a personal God who meets us and deals with us personally as Father, Son, and Holy Spirit. As far as our Reformed upbringing is concerned, the church is a divinely instituted assembly. To borrow the words of Karl Barth, "The Christian congregation arises and exists neither by nature nor by historical human decision, but as a divine 'convocation.' Those called together by the work of the Holy Spirit assemble at the summons of their King."

Since God is the focal point of worship, the Reformed family does not fail to emphasize this. In all things, members of the congregation are expected to see, present, and conduct themselves in the most worthy manner possible. One of the cardinal statements repeated Sunday after Sunday as a call to worship is, "the Lord is in his holy temple; let all the earth keep silence before him" (Hab. 2:20). The full import of this statement can be outlined as follows:

> The God who has summoned us is the Lord.
> Because God is holy, in a holy house,
> and is personally present in our midst,
> we therefore need to be silent — we
> therefore need to give him due honor and reverence.

Another positive aspect of the Reformed worship, within the Ghanaian/West African context, has to do with the structure, organization, and conduct of worship. Worship, as it is carried out, is both an act and an art. It is not random and flippant, but is carefully structured to provide orderliness.

The Demerits

Notwithstanding its strengths, the Reformed tradition also possesses weaknesses. The critical observation of the Christian populace, especially the youth, is that traditional Reformed worship lays too much emphasis on the form of worship rather than on the spirit of worship. What is more, it is, sometimes, too rigid, too subdued and sober. The criticism is that the type of Reformed worship introduced by the missionary societies is too cerebral, a sort of classroom religion. As a result, a new convert who is being prepared to become a full-fledged communicant member of the church is said to be attending "class" and receiving "lessons."

Reformed worship has also often been presented in West Africa in a formal and dictatorial form that stifles the emotional expression of the believer. Geoffrey Parrinder echoes this when he states, "There was a general feeling that African customs, laws, dancing, family, marriage, language, clothing, court etiquette, sayings and philosophy, were decaying where they were not crushed."[1] On the whole, the missionary churches had paternalistic tendencies and an embarrassing reluctance to listen mutually to the voices and ideas from the Third World.

---

1. Geoffrey Parrinder, *Africa's Three Religions* (London: Sheldon Press, 1969), p. 150.

An Overview of the Basic Meaning and the Demands of Christian Worship

Before we can embark upon any concrete reform of Reformed worship within the Ghanaian/West African context, we need to examine what worship really entails. The word *worship* refers to the art and the act of acknowledging worth and giving worth. Religiously and theologically speaking, God is the most worthy and God alone deserves worship in the true sense of the word. Christian worship, therefore, has to do with the response of the total person, in the most worthy manner, to God who is the most worthy. All meaningful and authentic worship of God arises out of one's understanding of who God is and out of one's realization or experience of God's creative and redemptive activity in the world.

Those who worship God, according to the teaching of the Bible, are not expected only to do so in spirit and in truth. They are also expected to approach worship with faith, hope, love, humility, a contrite heart, and a cheerful spirit. According to Jesus Christ, God is spirit, and those who worship him must worship in spirit and in truth (John 4:24). True worship of God is made possible "not by might nor by power" but in and by the Spirit. Worship, however, is empty and futile without faith, for those who walk with God walk not by sight but by faith (2 Cor. 5:7). And "without faith it is impossible to please God" (Heb. 11:6). We need to recognize that God is the source and the power of every meaningful and lasting hope. He is our help, our mighty fortress and our eternal fountain of blessing. Our true fulfillment, joy, and peace can be found in him alone. Hope in God is what keeps us in the race of life and on the path of eternal life. It dispels the clouds of doubt, uncertainty, gloom, and despair. Those who worship God in hope and with hope worship him in a state of reasonable calm and joyful anticipation.

Worship that does not stem from love for God is no worship. God has made us in love and for love. When we come before God and speak in the tongues of mortals and of angels, but have no love for God and for our neighbors, we are nothing (1 Cor. 13:1). Whenever we come before God as Christians, we need to have the same humility that Jesus exhibited (Phil. 2:6-11). We also need to remind ourselves that worship cannot and will not be existentially satisfying or fulfilling unless it is approached with a repentant heart. If we come before God cherishing sin in our hearts or are party to injustice, God will not listen to us (Ps. 66:16-19). In worship, we are summoned to participate in the creative and redemptive activity of God, to rejoice in the victory of Jesus Christ, and to meet God through Christ and in the power of the Holy Spirit. As people who have experienced the power, the goodness, and the riches of

God's blessing, we need to come to his presence with singing and we need to "enter his courts with praise" (Ps. 100:4). Michael Ramsey asserts, "Praise of God is one of the most characteristic features of biblical piety."[2] The fact cannot be denied that "the whole Bible is punctuated with outbursts of praise. They rise spontaneously from the 'basic mood' of joy which marks the life of the people of God."[3]

All of the above need to be taken into consideration, to inspire and guide our theology and liturgical reflection, whenever we as a church community are led to address the issue of reform in the church's worship life.

The Cry and Quest for Liturgical Reform with Particular Reference to the Ghanaian Situation Today

As a result of the liturgical revolution that is unfolding in the African Initiated churches and in the charismatic ministries, many in the Reformed family, especially the youth, are crying for a similar revolution. They are crying for a liturgical reform that is culturally suitable, current, and existentially satisfying. More specifically, they want the structure, organization, and the conduct of worship to be free, simple, flexible, spontaneous, celebratory, and participatory. In the mainline churches not enough attention has been paid to religious experience, dreams, the manifestation of the gifts of the Holy Spirit, and, in particular, calls to prophesy and the importance of healing both body and soul within the African worldviews. Influenced by the independent churches and the charismatic ministries, therefore, many West African Reformed voices are calling for a liturgical revolution and practice akin to that of the New Testament or first-century church.

Christians within the Reformed family in West Africa are looking for Sunday worship that incorporates, among other things, Bible study, praise and worship (adoration), corporate prayer, preaching (ministry of the word), prophecy and the manifestation of other gifts of the Holy Spirit, witnessing, altar calls, healing and deliverance, anointing, thanksgiving through offering (which must be celebratory), and testimonies. According to Elom Dovlo,

> Though all these elements may be incorporated into Sunday worship, each of them can form the focus of a particular Sunday worship so that it may

2. Michael Ramsey, "Praise," in *Wycliffe Bible Encyclopaedia,* ed. Charles F. F. Pfeiffer, Howard F. Vos, and John Rea (Chicago: Moody Press, 1975), vol. 2, p. 1387.

3. R. S. Wallace, "Praise," in *The New Bible Dictionary,* ed. J. D. Douglas (Leicester, England: InterVarsity Press, 1977), p. 1019.

be designated as a Sunday devoted to a Healing Service, Anointing Service or a Service of Praise or a Prayer Festival, etc.[4]

In matters of faith and religion, Africans are not cold and casual. They are warm, serious, devoted, and enthusiastic. Africans do not hide their faith, lighting the lamp and then putting it under a bushel. They speak their faith, sing it, drum it, dance it, dramatize it, and manifest its power in a very concrete way. If there is anything that needs to be done in Christian life with spontaneity and resounding enthusiasm, according to the African outlook, it is worship. In this act we take our eyes from ourselves, as it were, and center our entire being — heart, soul, and mind — on the living God, affirming that "redemption has to some extent already taken place" and "we have already found it good to be part of the household of God."[5] The purpose of acts of worship, as Alan Richardson has rightly observed, "is to declare the saving power of God and to make this power a reality in the hearts and lives of those who participate in them."[6]

For the sons and daughters of Africa to worship God as Africans, they need to break the shackles of inhibition, repression, and suppression imposed upon them by foreign cultural accretions. Adrian Hastings, in his book *African Christianity,* underscores this fact when he observes,

> Africa is a continent of song, dance and musical instruments. It is a continent of language and languages. Here lies the heart of its communal artistic inheritance and nothing was sadder than the missionary failure to open a door whereby at least some of this wealth might pass across into the worship of the young churches. The drum was not heard in most Churches, only the harmonium accompanying carefully translated European hymns sung to the tunes of the West. The result was frequently deplorable.[7]

The following comments of John Stott are also worth noting:

> I remember the shock I felt on my first visit to West Africa and its churches. I saw Gothic spires rising incongruously above the coconut palms, and African bishops sweating profusely in the tropical heat, because they were wearing medieval European ecclesiastical robes. I hear

4. Elom Dovlo, "God's Spirit and Sunday Morning Worship: The Challenges of the Charismatic Movements" (an unpublished article, 1999), pp. 7-8.

5. Rachel Henderlite, *A Call to Faith* (Atlanta: John Knox Press, 1955), p. 165.

6. "Worship," in *A Dictionary of Christian Theology,* ed. Alan Richardson (London: SCM Press, 1968), p. 361.

7. Adrian Hastings, *African Christianity* (New York: Seabury Press, 1976), p. 48.

western hymn tunes being sung to the accompaniment of western instruments, and African tongues attempting to get round Jacobean and even Elizabethan English.[8]

Worship is the heartbeat of religion. It is also the wellspring of spirituality and, for that matter, the wellspring of the vitality of life. When worship is stifled or denied its authentic and native expression, life itself is stifled. When the finger of God touches us, through Christ and in the power of the Holy Spirit, all the hidden springs of our being are released to participate in God who is "the power of being that safeguards, preserves, renews, or rejuvenates existence, not only in human society, and humankind, but also in nature and the universe."[9]

Members of the Reformed family in Ghana/West Africa are calling for a more flexible and pragmatic, evangelistic approach to worship. A holistic worship is required that allows for greater involvement in the plight of the poor and in opposing sociopolitical oppression. We need a worship that will see the role of the healing ministry as good news for the sick, the poor, the afflicted, and the victims of evil spirits and sorcery and all other forms of systemic evil. Africans need a Reformed worship that does not dichotomize the "physical" and the "spiritual." We also need a church that is seen as a reconciliatory and participatory community where everybody is recognized and valued as a potential contributor to the liturgy. Our Reformed worship must be so structured contextually as to fully use the language, the music, and the cultural artifacts of the geographical setting in which it finds itself.

We need preaching and sermons that are culturally relevant and that fully address all issues related to the African cosmology, for Western cultural forms of Christianity are often regarded as superficial and out of touch with many realities of existential life.

Closing Remarks

Even as we look for ways and means of liturgical reform within the Reformed family in Ghana/West Africa, we need to be careful not to overlook the meaning and the demands of Christian worship.

While it is important to assert and affirm within the African context the

8. John Stott, *The Contemporary Christian: Applying God's Word to Today's World* (Downer's Grover, Ill.: InterVarsity Press, 1992), pp. 196-97.

9. F. D. Graeve, "Worship," in *The New Catholic Encyclopaedia* (New York: McGraw Hill Book Company, 1976), vol. 14, p. 1030.

need for the celebratory aspect of worship (the aspect which entails, among other things, free, spontaneous, enthusiastic, and joyous response to God), it is equally important to assert and to affirm the need for the quiet and reflective aspect. Whenever we come before God in worship, we need also to hear and to heed afresh the following words in Habakkuk 2:20: "But the Lord is in his holy temple, let all the earth keep silence before him." Silence before God gives us the opportunity, first of all, to listen to God, to hear his "still small voice" (1 Kings 19:12) and to meditate on his words. Second, silence before God gives us the opportunity to engage in critical soul-searching and sober reflection. Third, it helps us to engage in a heart-to-heart communion with God. Silence before God is golden. There is blessing and power in it.

> For thus said the Lord GOD, the Holy One of Israel:
> In returning and rest you shall be saved;
> in quietness and in trust shall be your strength. (Isa. 30:15)

Worship that is strictly solemn and reflective can be rigid, frigid, and inhibitive. Worship that is purely celebratory can become trivial and thus degenerate into mere merrymaking. The word of God that demands us to be reverent, sober, and reflective before God is the same word that summons us to come into his presence with singing and to enter his courts with praise, making "a joyful noise to the Lord." The two elements, the solemn and reflective on the one hand and the celebratory on the other, are complementary. While the celebratory element helps to lift up one's spirit, the solemn or the reflective helps to temper one's spirit and to deepen one's understanding.

Reformed Worship Taking Root in New Cultures: The Congolese Experience (Democratic Republic of the Congo)

Kasonga wa Kasonga

The Reformed family in the Democratic Republic of the Congo is comprised of a number of churches, all of which are members of the Church of Christ in Congo (ECC). The constituent churches include the Presbyterian Church in Congo, Presbyterian Church in Kinshasa, Evangelical Church in Congo (DRC), Evangelical Church in Congo (Congo Brazzaville), Disciples of Christ in Congo, Presbyterian Church in the Eastern Kasai, and Presbyterian Church in Western Kasai. This chapter deals only with the Presbyterian Church in Congo and the Presbyterian Church in Kinshasa, both of which are offspring of the American Presbyterian Congo Mission (APCM) that inaugurated its work in 1891 in Luebo station, Kasai province.

From the beginning, the heart of evangelization has been worship: singing, praying, offering, and proclaiming the word of God. The elements of worship have, however, undergone certain transformations. Because there have not been significant changes in the celebration of the sacraments, baptism and Eucharist, I will confine my analysis to music, prayers, and preaching.

In this chapter I will address three main questions:

1. What was the form of worship introduced through the missionary movement?
2. In what way was it transformed within the cultural and political context of the new church?
3. What is the present state of Reformed worship?

The Worship Taught by the Missionaries

The form of worship introduced by the Presbyterian missionaries at Luebo followed a familiar nineteenth-century pattern: opening prayer, first hymn, Bible reading, singing by choir(s), preaching, offering, announcements, second hymn, and benediction. Within this pattern, primary emphasis was placed on singing, offering, and especially on preaching.

Prayer

Missionary teaching on prayer was intended to develop in the new converts an intimate relationship with God. A deep personal relationship with God and the ability to pray intelligibly were mutually reinforcing. The Reformed tradition excelled in this teaching, while converts to the Roman Catholic tradition were trained only to listen to the prayers said by a priest or catechist. Prayer by the people was part of the openness that characterized Reformed worship in Congo. This was reinforced by access to the biblical text that all were taught to read and interpret under the leading of the Holy Spirit.

Hymns

Singing was one of the joyous moments in worship. The missionaries translated hymns into the language of the people, Tshiluba, teaching them to the growing community of believers. They insisted, however, that singing in Tshiluba fit American church melodies precisely. The Tshiluba Presbyterian hymnbook included references to the composer of the tune, the date of the tune's composition, the reference number in the American Presbyterian hymnbook, and the name of the Tshiluba translator (American or Congolese). Looking back on this hymnal, one admires the accurate rendering of the original tunes and themes. One also appreciates the fact that the missionary translators did a good job of communicating the hymns' meanings and sentiments to Congolese converts even though the classical Western melodies were so different from African music. In fact, the music of Congo was discarded as an example of evil practices that were considered to be incompatible with the gospel of Jesus Christ. Choirs were formed in the earliest days of the new church, and choral music was also imported from American churches. Needless to say, the missionaries did not allow the use of drums, xylophones, or hand clapping!

Bible Reading and Preaching

The missionaries were faithful to the Reformed tradition, placing emphasis on the reading and proclamation of the word of God. All of the Reformers — Calvin, Zwingli, and Luther — taught that genuine and faithful Christian worship must have the reading of the Bible and the preaching of the word at the center. For instance, Calvin wrote,

> We must hold to what we have quoted from Paul — that the church is built up solely by outward preaching, and that the saints are held together by one bond only: that with common accord, through learning and advancement, they keep the church order established by God (cf. Eph. 4:12).[1]

Thus we are reminded that the proclamation of the word has created and nourished the church from Pentecost through the primitive Christian communities to the contemporary church. Protestant missionaries to Congo, unlike their Catholic counterparts, succeeded in bringing African converts into close contact with the Bible in their own language. Literacy programs were instituted to consolidate knowledge of the Bible so that all men and women would be able to follow and understand preaching in the worship services. Church members were also expected to read and interpret the Scriptures in their homes.

Offering

In many respects, the new African churches were carbon copies of Euro-American churches, yet we should acknowledge that Protestant missionaries strove to build strong African communities.[2] Part of that effort was training new converts to give offerings to God in gratitude for what God had given to them. Early in the planting of the church, African Christians were taught to offer harvest produce, bringing it to the altar. Later, the practice was introduced of deacons going from pew to pew, collecting offerings of money. Collection

1. John Calvin, *Institutes* (4.1.5), ed. John T. McNeill, trans. Ford Lewis Battles (Philadelphia: Westminster Press, 1960), vol. 2, p. 1019.
2. The constant aim of the Protestant missions was to build strong African churches, though this outlook was subsumed by dominant colonialist motives. See two papers with the same title, "Building the African Church," by W. C. Willoughby and E. F. Spanton, in *International Review of Missions* 15 (1926): 450-75. The same idea is also developed by E. Bolaji Idowu in his book *Toward an Indigenous Church* (London: Oxford University Press, 1965).

of cash offerings was accompanied by a system of recording contributions (and announcing them in worship on the following Sunday). This was intended both to encourage new converts to give and to stimulate faithful giving by all members of the church. A faithful believer was one who made regular offerings to God. This evidence of faithfulness entitled one to come to the Lord's table. This control practice may not have been theologically sound, but it was a very good way of teaching self-reliance. Training in faithful stewardship enabled local Christian communities to become self-sustaining.

Prayers, hymns, Scripture and preaching, and offerings were thus the main components of the worship introduced by Presbyterian missionaries in Congo. The task now is to examine the ways worship was transformed in the cultural and political context of the new church.

The Context of Transformation

Congo gained political independence from Belgium on June 30, 1960. Because the struggle for sovereignty was coupled with the search for the religious and cultural dignity of the black people of Africa, changes in the political scene entailed changes in the church as well. Ethnic clashes erupted between the Ba-Luba and the Ba-Lulua, even though the two had enjoyed Christian fellowship since 1891, and the clashes threatened the Presbyterian church. Missionaries' lives were threatened and many, including medical doctors, were compelled to flee the country.

In order to protect the mission heritage, a decision was made in the early 1960s to have the American mission church (APCM) work separately from the Congolese church (Presbyterian Church in the Congo). This separation led to anger and the misuse of "mission church" properties, especially vehicles, which had previously been owned mainly by the missionaries. Since the separation was ill-conceived and was likely to destroy the church as a whole, reunion was celebrated in 1968. What was happening to the form of worship during the period of independence and separation? The following analysis will be limited to three aspects: preaching, singing, and offering.

Preaching

The experience of the Ndesha church, the main congregation in the city of Kananga (formerly Luluabourg), is typical. The minister of Ndesha church was trained at Luebo and then at Mutoto's Preacher School. He was not only a dynamic leader of the church, but also a powerful preacher. His preaching was enriched by the use of proverbial sayings. Proverbs are an important manifestation of African wisdom, especially when they are employed to impart specific moral standards. The missionaries taught preaching skills, but the use of African wisdom in ministry was an indigenous contribution. Especially at this period in the history of the Presbyterian Church in Congo, the use of proverbs was an affirmation of black African pride and dignity. The themes of preaching in Ndesha church and many others in Kasai and Kinshasa recalled the celebration of national independence: "We are free at last!"

At the Ndesha church, the moment of preaching was reminiscent of the chief addressing the assembly at a village gathering. The sermon was preceded by the beautiful sound of a traditional flute in the midst of reverent quietness. Within that silence a deep vibrant voice sounded, *Yehowa udi mu nzubu wandi wa tshijila, ba ha buloba bonso bahuwe ku mpala kuandi* (The Lord is in his holy temple, let all creatures be silent in his presence). The minister then preached the word of God with the pride and dynamism of a real village chief.

The traditional flute had not been used in the beginnings of Presbyterian evangelism in the Congo, and in fact did not appear in this church until after independence. The sound and message of the flute recalled the traditional way of praising and honoring a chief. When it was adapted for use in the Ndesha church, it became an enriching way of praising God.[3] The use of the flute did not continue, however, and it has never been emulated by other congregations. Perhaps the flute was introduced in worship without adequate preparation of the local communities. Even the other ministers did not see the traditional African flute as an important liturgical element. Nevertheless, I believe that a proper adaption can still be made in the context of enculturation.

Singing

A new style of singing appeared in the Ndesha congregation in the early 1960s to supplement the songs already introduced by the missionaries. The *Suivre la Lumière* (Follow the Light) choir employed melodies drawn from Luba-Lulua folk music. The rhythms expressed the African soul's religious aspiration. The choir used previously forbidden instruments such as xylophone, traditional drums, and flute, adding flavor to music in the church. The choir director, a young man who grew up in Luebo station, developed a way of conducting that did not follow the patterns taught by the missionaries. His whole body was en-

---

3. Though the question remains open whether it was praising God or the preacher.

gaged in leading, moving rhythmically like a palm branch dancing to the beat of the wind. Although the rhythm of the music fostered feelings of movement and the desire to dance, worshipers resisted out of respect for the "Presbyterian attitude." They remained still while "dancing in their hearts."

Most youth choirs in the Kasai adopted the *Suivre la Lumière* style. Among the themes employed in new music for worship was the declaration that "our ancestors knew God, they praised him with songs, they shouted to God to glorify him." This theme is a powerful affirmation of African culture. In the context of independence, it was a way of telling the white colonizers and the missionaries that our ancestors were not mere heathens, for they worshiped the living God before the advent of Christian missions. This attitude remains apparent in elements of worship today.

Offering

Another interesting aspect of singing is linked to the offering style. In the early 1960s people began singing a chorus during the offering — *Kuenzela Nzambi mudimu kudi kuimpe, nkulengela bushua* (To serve God is good, it is so wonderful). While singing, worshipers danced as they moved toward the altar to place money in a trunk or bowl. This style, which is still practiced today, was the beginning of an ongoing reaction to missionary worship. Africans do not wish to worship the living God as if they are sitting in a classroom; bodily movement accompanies spiritual sentiments.

In the early 1980s, preaching, singing, and offering continued to develop in worship. When internal conflicts split the Ndesha church, many members transferred to other congregations, while some members created new congregations. In both cases, they brought their new worship experiences with them. Some of the folkloric songs of the traditional society were recovered, then joined with words adapted from the Bible and Christian teachings. African names of God are employed to show God's power (something that was not allowed by the missionaries for fear of paganism). Today, congregations are more enthusiastic when singing indigenous music than when using Western hymns. Worshipers are fully engaged in worship, body and soul, when singing words of praise set to traditional African music.

In summary, the evolution of the liturgy was marked by the importation of traditional African elements such as folkloric melodies, drums, xylophone, flute, dance, and proverbial sayings. Throughout this evolution, African cultures were increasingly affirmed in opposition to the Western, and particularly American, culture of the missionaries.

The Present State of Worship

The Presbyterian church today is characterized by the reality that church members no longer live in isolated mission stations where respect for the Reformed tradition was easily induced. Presbyterians now live side by side with other traditions — Pentecostals, evangelicals, Methodists, Baptists, and others. Thus, we have learned that Western Presbyterian worship is not the only or the best way of celebrating our encounter with God. Presbyterians want changes that incorporate their Africanness while expressing elements that are biblically sound, including those that have been neglected. The critique of Western, missionary-shaped worship has led to specific changes that are experienced today.

Three areas of change are noteworthy: first, the emphasis put on the confession of sins; second, the use of praise songs or choruses accompanied by dance; and third, the explicit invocation of the Holy Spirit. The emphasis put on these elements in the liturgy is influenced by progressive believers who think the traditional liturgy is cold and detached, incapable of producing ardor in the hearts and souls of worshipers. More conservative believers do not see any problem with the traditional order of worship, content with worship practiced just as the Luebo missionaries taught. I will come back to this debate later.

Repentance

Those who want new attention to the confession of sin argue that repentance has been neglected in the past, so people fail to humble themselves before God by repenting and asking for forgiveness. We cannot come before God and listen to his word without attention to the crucial step of confession and cleansing by the precious blood of Jesus Christ. To overlook repentance is to fail to take God seriously. Calvin taught that *"The Lord requires the saints to confess their sins — and that indeed continually throughout life; and he promises pardon."*[4] This has been neglected since missionary times.

Songs of Praise and Worship

A new style of choruses and praise songs began to enter worship in the 1960s and remains an important part of the worship today. Pastors know that if they

4. Calvin, *Institutes* 4.1.23 (vol. 2, pp. 1036-37).

do not include praise music and choruses in the liturgy, people may leave for one of the new churches that mushroom everywhere. Proponents believe that new praise music, together with dance, speak to the African soul. They create joy and enthusiasm as well as peace and healing. In this perspective, choruses and songs of praise are not entertainment but an important manifestation of African culture. "No worship is culture neutral . . . It is cultural bound,"[5] stated the 1994 Geneva consultation on Reformed worship. Singing and dancing are part of African life in general, Congolese life in particular. Because life and worship are one, it is appropriate that these aspects of life are incorporated in worship. D. Maw has written,

> Life and worship are inseparable. Where faith is alive worship arises out of ordinary life and is in a certain sense the expression of this life. The most beautiful and most balanced liturgy is of no use if it is not related to the world in which the worshipers spend six of seven days.[6]

This must be taken seriously as an explanation of worship in the Congo and elsewhere in Africa. Singing and dancing are celebrations of life, so when they appear in worship they play an important role in the encounter with God.

There are two important dimensions in worship, the vertical and the horizontal. In worship's vertical movement, God reveals himself in the particular contexts where people are found. Maw shows that in these dynamics all the "ingredients" of worship, all the symbols, are vehicles of God's descent to worshipers:

> All elements of worship, all its components (silence, gestures, prayers, hymns, biblical lessons, preaching) can point to this movement into the world, to God's descent to us human beings.[7]

In the horizontal movement, the corporate character of worship increases as worshipers share the joy of the encounter with God. For a long time Presbyterian liturgy in the Congo did not incorporate the horizontal dimension. Today, many congregations have discovered its value.

5. *Reformed Liturgy & Music,* Special Issue 1995 (Office of Theology and Worship, PCUSA), p. 5.

6. D. Maw, "Le culte," *Manuel de Théologie Pratique, Colloque des Théologiens Africains* (Yaoundé, 1971), p. 26 (translated from the French by Lukas Vischer).

7. Maw, "Les éléments liturgiques du culte," *Manuel,* p. 40 (translated from the French by Lukas Vischer).

The Place of the Holy Spirit

The Presbyterian Church in Congo celebrated one hundred years of evangelization in 1991. Throughout those years, its worship had not given a prominent place to the Holy Spirit. Neglect of the Holy Spirit is the reason the Presbyterian Community of Kinshasa (CPK) lost a large number of members in the 1970s. They left to create the Assembly of God Church that has now become a member church of the Church of Christ in Congo.

The explicit invocation of the Holy Spirit reminds people that they have to surrender to the Spirit's leading and healing power. Unfortunately, this has not been officially recognized. The Presbyterian Church in Congo Book of Order, which gives guidelines for worship, contains nothing related to the work of the Holy Spirit.[8] This absence from the church's liturgical guidelines may explain why the Holy Spirit is vaguely or rarely acknowledged in worship or in healing practices.

These are a few aspects that characterize the present state of worship. Generally speaking, today's worship in the Presbyterian Church in Congo does not seem to respond fully to the problems that people face in daily life. The 1994 Geneva consultation was right in pointing out that "In other areas, the problems are more obvious: war, hunger, the daily struggle to survive, to feed children, to cope with disease or death or work which seems to serve no humane purpose, and more. What is the role of Christian worship in such situations?"[9]

Many pastors and worship leaders are not adequately equipped to shape worship that speaks creatively to situations of contemporary life. Today, people need spiritual accompaniment in situations of war and in the search for peace. Christians need spiritual nourishment as they experience desperate and miserable conditions of life arising from multiform crises. Presbyterian worship leaders in the Congo still disregard the potential for well-planned and intelligible worship to be an appropriate channel of God's healing and liberation for the people. This is why healing sessions are organized apart from worship by special intercessory groups of well-trained believers who dedicate their gifts to this ministry.[10] This is also why worship services are not focused on the ways and means to achieve peace.[11]

8. *Mokanda na Kobongisa Lingomba* (Kinshasa, n.d.), pp. 64-77.

9. *Reformed Liturgy & Music,* p. 5.

10. Healing practice is another important aspect of the Presbyterian ministry, besides worship, that needs to be addressed, but in a separate essay.

11. These ways and means can be fostered through education. Good education of the people of God can prepare them for significant worship.

Conclusion

There are two tendencies within the evolution of worship in the Presbyterian Church in Congo: conservative and progressive. Many of the changes mentioned above are resisted by a number of conservative believers and pastors. They argue that if we do not do things the way the missionaries taught us, we are no longer Presbyterians. The question is, "Can the Reformed tradition reform itself?" or "How much of the Reformed tradition can be reformed?" This question was addressed by the 1994 consultation.[12] I like the response that although "we are not seeking change for its own sake," the Reformed tradition is not re-formed once and for all. The Book of Order leaves appropriate room for any change to be thought through theologically before it is put into effect. My own experience as a Reformed pastor has taught me that all church councils, from the Session through the General Assembly, are prepared to examine carefully any new thought. If accepted, it is then adapted for practical use in local congregations. Because these councils meet under the guidance of the Holy Spirit, called to decide what is faithful to the will of God, I believe that the Reformed tradition can be reformed. Whatever change is faithful to the word of God must be welcomed.

For Further Reading

Bolaji Idowu, E. *Toward An Indigenous Church.* London: Oxford University Press, 1965.

"Building the African Church" (two articles with the same title), by W. C. Willoughby and E. F. Spanton, respectively).

International Review of Missions 15 (1926): 450-75.

Mokanda na Kobongisa Lingomba. Kinshasa: MKL, n.d.

Reformed Liturgy & Music. Special Issue 1995 (on Reformed Worship Worldwide). Office of Theology and Worship, PCUSA, 1995.

---

12. They asked, "What are the traditional aspects of worship that must be maintained in order to be faithful to God's revelation, and what are the aspects that can and should be reformed according to the historical needs of different times and places?" See *Reformed Liturgy & Music,* p. 4.

Reformed Worship in Brazil

Gerson Correia de Lacerda

Introduction

In writing an essay on Reformed worship in Brazil, it seems to me that the best way to proceed is to speak about my own experience in my ministry as a pastor in a small Brazilian Presbyterian denomination of about seventy thousand adult members and five hundred congregations. Our church is spread over all parts of the country, but it is mainly concentrated in the southern part of our national territory.

The church to which I belong (the Independent Presbyterian Church of Brazil, or IPI) arose from the first schism to take place in Brazilian Presbyterianism, in the year 1903. At the time of the division, Presbyterianism was still taking its first steps in Brazil. The first Presbyterian missionary, sent by the Presbyterian Church in the United States of America, had arrived here on August 12, 1859. The Synod of the Presbyterian Church of Brazil was organized in 1888.

The schism was not a break from Reformed doctrine or with the Presbyterian form of church organization. The Independent Presbyterian Church of Brazil preserves the same system of doctrine as the Presbyterian Church of Brazil (IPB), as well as the same organizational structure. The official doctrinal system of both churches is the Westminster Confession of Faith together with the catechisms produced by that famous assembly of theologians in the seventeenth century. At the present time, the two churches maintain a good mutual relationship. Perhaps the biggest difference lies in the area of ideology. The IPI of Brazil is a bit more open to change than the IPB. As a symbol of this openness, one can point out the situation of women in the two churches. The IPI of Brazil has been ordaining women to the office of deacon since 1934 and also, since 1999, to the offices of elder and pastor. The ordination of women has yet to take place in the more traditional IPB.

I have been a pastor of the IPI church for almost thirty years. Moreover, I belong to a family whose ancestors were among the first to be converted from Catholicism to Protestantism by the North American Presbyterian missionaries. When I analyze the story of my own life, I realize that I have, generally speaking, lived through every stage in the development of Reformed worship in Brazil. When I was a child, I was in a church where the worship services followed exactly the model that had been brought by the North American missionaries in the nineteenth century. In my youth, I lived through a time of dissatisfaction with this model of worship and of various attempts at renewal. At the present time, I am faced with the challenges of the impact of Pentecostalism and the new styles of worship produced or influenced by the Pentecostal movement. Because of this, the present study will have an existential character. It is more than a piece of research about Reformed worship in Brazil. In truth, it concerns my own spiritual biography, which I present with much emotion.

I do not think that this emotion will prejudice the academic or scientific character of this work. I make my own these words of Rubem Alves:

> Unforeseen events in my biography caused me to be deeply interested in Protestantism. . . . I do not believe that a science without emotion is possible. It is the affective relation to an object, which attracts or threatens me, that creates the conditions for concentrating my attention. . . . I agree with Gunnar Myrdal: "There never was such a thing as a disinterested social science and, for logical reasons, there never can be." It is an illusion to think that scientific knowledge, in opposition to common sense, is objective, whereas the latter is distorted by emotion.[1]

Original Characteristics of Brazilian Presbyterianism

The Presbyterianism that was implanted in Brazil was that which came from the United States in the nineteenth century, which means that its roots can be found in the development of Calvinism in England and in Scotland, and especially in Puritanism. From English Puritanism, Brazilian Presbyterianism still preserves "its view of the world and its way of living in it, its austere asceticism and its Biblical piety."[2] John Bunyan's famous *Pilgrim's Progress*, written in

---

1. Rubem Alves, *Protestantismo e Repressão,* pp. 15-16 (translation from the Portuguese by the author).

2. Antônio Gouvêa Mendonça, *O Celeste Porvir,* p. 38 (translation from the Portuguese by the author).

1678, was one of the first works to be translated into Portuguese and distributed by the Protestant missionaries who were active in Brazil. The picture entitled "The Two Ways" was distributed extensively and was a constant presence in the homes and the minds of Brazilian Protestants. In my childhood and my youth, I saw it every day, dominating the living room of my house, forming my way of understanding life and the world.

To this Puritan root are joined the characteristics of North American Protestantism, especially those of the Awakenings. As is known, the churches on the frontier of the United States were much influenced by the evangelical "Awakenings" of the eighteenth and nineteenth centuries. In the nineteenth century, with the so-called Methodist Period, practically all of the North American evangelical denominations acquired the same idiosyncrasies: emphasis on voluntarism, according to which the human being has free will and is able continually to perfect itself; establishment of the radical distinction between spiritual reality and temporal reality, with the church's space for action almost exclusively limited to the spiritual sphere; Puritanism in uses and customs; etc. As far as worship is concerned, there was a genuine break with the liturgical tradition of the Reformation. Worship became centered on the sermon, accompanied by the singing of hymns with strong emotional appeal.

This was the Protestantism brought to Brazil by the North American missionaries, and this was the worship implanted in our country by the first Presbyterian ministers. The service of this tradition was not liturgical — that is, it did not use previously elaborated liturgical forms. On the contrary, it placed great value on spontaneous prayer, it despised vestments and any other liturgical apparatus, and it placed its emphasis on preaching for conversion. Even the hymns that were sung served as a support for the sermon, with their appeals to accept Christ or to re-consecrate oneself to his service. In this context, the sacraments came to have an ancillary character. The Lord's Supper was considered a mere appendix to certain services.

A good illustration of this reality is the work carried out by Ashbel Simonton, the first Presbyterian missionary to Brazil, who came in 1859. He used the *Book of Common Prayer* of the Anglican Church for a few special ceremonies; the rest of the time, he developed an order of worship centered on preaching for conversion.

This was the worship I knew from the earliest years of my life and which I experienced throughout my childhood and youth, until the 1970s. There was, of course, some dissatisfaction with this kind of worship. At some moments, voices were raised against the poverty of a worship that, by giving high value to the sermon, gave high value to the preacher and de-valued the participation of the people. These voices, however, were suffocated and forgotten. Parachurch organizations from North America, by then active in Brazil, contributed a great deal to this state of affairs, reinforcing the conservative worship style of the earliest missionaries.

Attempts at Renewal

The catalyzing element in the kind of worship implanted in Brazil by the North American missionaries was anti-Catholicism.

Before sending its first missionaries to Brazil, the Presbyterian Church in the United States of America had made two important decisions regarding the Catholic church. First, in 1835, the General Assembly of the church "deliberated and decided that the Roman Catholic church has essentially fallen into apostasy from the religion of our Lord and Savior Jesus Christ and for this reason is not recognized as a Christian church."[3] In 1845 the same assembly, "after ample discussion, which lasted for several days . . . decided by a near unanimity in voting (173 in favor and 8 against) that the baptism administered by the Church of Rome is not valid."[4]

Since the Roman Catholic Church, the church of the majority in Brazil, is a liturgical church, the Brazilian Protestant churches developed the conception that any liturgical elaboration was to be repudiated as not being in accord with the Reformed tradition. This conception is based on an incorrect interpretation of the Reformed tradition, but it came to have the force of truth in Brazilian Protestantism.

The fact is that Brazilian Protestant churches have never had any contact with the Reformed worship of the sixteenth-century Reformation. On the contrary, all that the Protestant churches in Brazil learned about this subject was influenced by the style of worship of the Awakenings of the eighteenth and nineteenth centuries in the United States. The Protestant churches in Brazil therefore have the firm conviction that to use liturgical elaboration is to submit to the influence of the Roman Catholic Church and to cast aside the pure heritage of Reformed Protestantism.

Two significant examples illustrate this point: In the earliest Protestant worship services in Brazil, there was resistance to the practice of saying the Lord's Prayer together, with the participation of all, because it resembled a Ro-

---

3. Quoted in Carl Joseph Hahn, *História do culto protestante no Brasil,* p. 161 (translation from the Portuguese by the author).

4. Hahn, *História do culto protestante no Brasil,* p. 162 (translation from the Portuguese by the author).

man Catholic practice. And even today, in many Protestant communities the repetition of the Apostles' Creed (or any other creed) is looked at askance and actively resisted, as it is considered a Catholic practice.

This anti-Catholicism was (and still is) the great obstacle to a liturgical renewal in Brazilian Protestantism. Nonetheless, throughout the history of Protestantism in Brazil, there have been manifestations of dissatisfaction with the poverty of a service centered on the sermon. In 1932, the Reverend Erasmo Braga, a pastor of the Presbyterian Church of Brazil and an important leader working in favor of the ecumenical movement (he was known as "a prophet of unity"), wrote about the "signs of discontent with the kind of worship service which prevails, with a poverty of intellectualism of the pulpit."[5] In 1938, in the Independent Presbyterian Church of Brazil, Eduardo Pereira de Magalhães, a youth leader, expressed himself in these terms:

> In worship it is always the same thing, done the same way, with the very same words, the same ideas repeated over and over again, in the same place. Every meeting, regardless of its purpose, begins with a hymn, then a prayer, then reading from the Bible, then another prayer, etc. . . . The only thing on which value is placed in the service is the sermon. . . . It is, then, the important part, while the worship of God remains off to one side, despised.[6]

Thanks to these manifestations of dissatisfaction, there were some attempts at renewal. During the 1940s such attempts were put forward especially by the Evangelical Confederation of Brazil, an organization that was strong and active from its foundation in 1934 until 1964, and which brought together the major Brazilian historic Protestant churches. In 1942, the Confederation managed to produce and publish a text entitled *Liturgia: Manual para o Culto Público.* In 1945, the Confederation published a hymnal, the *Hinário Evangélico.*

In 1961, the Independent Presbyterian Church of Brazil approved and published a brief text entitled *Manual de Ofícios Religosos,* divided into three parts. In the first part, there was an orientation to public worship and two orders of worship (one brief, just giving the order, and the other elaborate, specifying what the officiant should say in each part of the service). In these two orders of worship, the celebration of the Lord's Supper was not included. In the second part of the *Manual* were the formulas for the so-called special ceremo-

5. Quoted by A. G. Mendonça, *Introdução ao protestantismo no Brasil,* p. 197 (translation from the Portuguese by the author).
6. Hahn, *História do culto protestante no Brasil,* pp. 319-20 (translation from the Portuguese by the author).

nies (baptism, profession of faith, organization of a church, etc.), all of them well elaborated and specifying what the officiant should say in each ceremony.

Also in the Independent Presbyterian Church of Brazil, two other attempts at renewal of worship should be mentioned. Both were connected with the work of the São Paulo Theological Seminary. The first of these attempts took place in the 1980s and resulted in the publication of a text entitled *Vida na Terra (Life on Earth)*.[7] This book was a result of the teaching of liturgy in the São Paulo Theological Seminary. It was used by students for worship and in several congregations of the Independent Presbyterian Church. This was really an attempt at a more profound renewal than the earlier efforts. First of all, there was an attempt to recover the historic Reformed liturgical tradition. For example, in *Vida na Terra* great value was given to the celebration of the sacraments, mainly of the Lord's Supper, according to the spirit of the reformation of worship accomplished by John Calvin. At the same time, there was an interest in the recovery of the singing of the psalms and other elements of church tradition. In addition, great value was accorded to elements of Brazilian and Latin American culture. For example, there was the use of contemporary religious songs, composed by Brazilian and Latin American musicians, with the rhythms of our country. At the same time, *Vida na Terra* included texts of contemporary creeds of the ecumenical movement. The dream of the seminary was to eventually reach the entire Independent Presbyterian Church of Brazil, as well as other denominations, little by little, in a genuine liturgical renewal.

The second attempt at liturgical renewal beginning at the seminary is still underway, with the elaboration and publication of a new *Manual do Culto (Worship Handbook)*.[8] The text was produced by a special commission appointed by the general assembly of the Independent Presbyterian Church of Brazil. It presents orders of worship that have been developed for the day-to-day life of the church, for special occasions, and for the liturgical year. It also contains liturgical texts for use in the service as well as information and orientation regarding the calendar and the lectionary. It ends by presenting sung responses. In general, the same concerns of *Vida na Terra* are in the *Manual do Culto*. The text was approved by the general assembly of the church and continues to be official. It represents an attempt at liturgical renewal which seeks to "conciliate zeal for a heritage which we have yet to appropriate completely, with the indispensable and concrete effort to incorporate such elements into Latin American and Brazilian culture."[9]

7. O. P. Mateus, ed., *Vida na Terra.*
8. E. G. Faria, ed., *Manual do Culto.*
9. E. G. Faria, ed., *Manual do Culto,* p. 6 (translation from the Portuguese by the author).

We have to ask what has been the impact of all these attempts at the renewal of Protestant worship in our land? I agree fully with the evaluation made by Antonio Gouvêa Mendonça, who wrote,

> The summary orders of worship are a dead letter, and, in most cases, the special ceremonies are performed according to the manual in the case of the rarer ceremonies; the sacramental rites, being more frequent, end up being done from memory or improvised, with simplifications and liberties being taken that frequently disfigure and banalize them. Many pastors think they are showing competence and independence by setting the manual aside.[10]

All this is to say that none of the attempts at liturgical renewal has been highly successful. The *Manual para o Culto Público* of the Evangelical Confederation of Brazil has enjoyed very little acceptance or use in the Protestant churches. The *Hinário Evangélico* was adopted only by the Methodist church. *Vida na Terra* seems to have been forgotten. The *Manual do Culto* is considered an excellent piece of work, but it is not being used frequently in the churches. Generally speaking, the worship services continue to be improvised and centered on preaching for conversion or for re-consecration.

What is the great difficulty that stands in the way of renewal? Why, if there is dissatisfaction with the poverty of worship in Brazil, are the efforts to enrich it not being accepted? On the one hand, the problem was and continues to be anti-Catholicism. The Brazilian Protestant mentality has developed and kept the conception that the use of any liturgy whatsoever that increases the role of the people of God is making the worship service more like a Catholic mass. This conception has impeded and continues to impede the successful renewal of Protestant worship in Brazil. On the other hand, a new element has arisen and created difficulties for liturgical renewal based on the Reformed heritage and Brazilian culture. I am referring to the great impact of the advent of Pentecostalism, to which I now turn.

The Impact of Pentecostalism

Modern Pentecostalism had its origin in the United States at the beginning of the twentieth century. We can locate its birth on January 1, 1901, when Agnes N. Ozman, a student at the Bethel Bible School in Topeka, Kansas,

---

10. A. G. Mendonça, *Introdução ao protestantismo no Brasil,* p. 165 (translation from the Portuguese by the author).

"spoke in other tongues," a phenomenon considered to be the baptism of the Holy Spirit and the return of the power of Pentecost.

Pentecostalism began to be transplanted to Brazil in 1910 with the establishment of two churches: the Assemblies of God, in Belém, in the State of Pará, and the Congregação Cristã do Brasil, in the states of São Paulo and Paraná. Their distinctive emphasis and characteristic was the so-called "gift of tongues."

We can talk about the arrival of the Pentecostal movement in terms of successive "waves." Each wave has its own characteristics, and each involves the implantation or organization of new denominations. That means that we have a different kind of Pentecostalism now than we did before. The first wave began with the transplantation of Pentecostalism in 1910. The second wave started in the 1950s, and the third wave in the 1970s.

Beginning in the 1950s, Brazilian Pentecostalism passed through a period of heightened activity and transformation. There erupted a movement of "tabernacles of divine healing." New denominations coming from the United States were implanted, such as the Church of the Foursquare Gospel (Igreja do Evangelho Quadrangular) in 1951. At the same time, new denominations were organized by Brazilian leaders of the Pentecostal movement, including O Brasil para Cristo (Brazil for Christ, 1956) and Deus é Amor (God is Love, 1961). New characteristics developed and were added to the emphasis on tongues, including a very high value attached to divine healing and to exorcism, and great use of radio stations for promotional purposes.

Starting in the 1970s, Brazilian Pentecostalism underwent a new development and another transformation. New denominations were organized, with the appearance of churches such as Igreja Universal do Reino de Deus (The Universal Church of the Kingdom of God), Igreja Internacional da Graça (The International Church of Grace), and Renascer em Cristo (Rebirth in Christ). These churches use modern marketing techniques in order to grow, and openly preach the so-called theology of prosperity.

The impact of Pentecostalism was felt in the traditional Protestant denominations. Many of them were going through processes of internal division. In the Independent Presbyterian Church of Brazil, some groups withdrew and organized the Igreja Presbiteriana Independente Renovada (Renewed Independent Presbyterian Church). But even in the part of the church that did not split off or join the Pentecostal movement, the impact of Pentecostalism was felt, especially in the matter of worship.

Among the examples of this impact, we would point out those that seem most important:

First, there was sharpened opposition to the use of anything prepared in a worship service. In the name of spontaneity under the orientation of the Holy Spirit, the reading of prayers or of printed texts in a church bulletin was repudiated. Everything was to be done in an improvised way, for only in this way, it is believed, is the Holy Spirit present and active.

Second, any attempt to recover the Reformed liturgical tradition was abandoned. This tradition is perceived as excessively formalistic and cold. It is taken to be a form of prayer that impedes the emotional involvement of persons in the act of worship. Even though we have not had a full experience in our churches of the riches of the Reformed liturgical tradition, any reference to it stirs up opposition.

Third, the appearance of the phenomenon known as *louvorzão* (praise time) must be noted. It has come to occupy the central place in the worship service, being more important than the proclamation of the word or the celebration of the Lord's Supper. It develops in more or less the same way in all communities:

- a group leads the singing of short songs, which become long ones as the words are repeated to the point of exhaustion;
- the song-leading style used by these groups is, generally speaking, the same one that is used by emcees to lead studio audiences on television programs — appeals are made to sing louder, with more enthusiasm, etc.;
- sophisticated electronic paraphernalia are used, with microphones, sound boxes, and musical instruments (electric guitars and drum sets are indispensable); the sound, even in the small worship spaces of smaller churches, is always loud;
- generally speaking, the words are not printed in a bulletin, and hymnals are not used; the preference is for the use of an overhead projector, with the words of the songs projected on a church wall so that all can sing them; improvisation is easier this way: with all the known songs ready on transparencies, the leader can choose any one of them on the spot;
- between the songs, those responsible for leading them repeat Bible verses and make brief comments, with emotional appeals, or they offer emotion-filled prayers; the songs that are sung generally praise God for creation, for salvation, and for all that has come to pass in the individual life of each believer; in other words, there are very few songs that serve as a confession of sin or that point to the social responsibility of the Christian.

A fourth impact of Pentecostalism is that attempts at indigenization are set aside. In this area, it is mainly the musical elements that are affected. It happens that, especially in the attempt at renewal that was made by the São Paulo Seminary and embodied in the book *Vida na Terra,* there was an attempt to use Brazilian and Latin American rhythms, with the use of words referring to Brazilian realities and problems. All this is disappearing, if it has not already disappeared. Contemporary "gospel" music is almost the only kind that is sung. As a symbol of the abandonment of attempts at indigenization, we see young people wearing T-shirts with inscriptions in English as well as driving cars with bumper stickers in English.

Fifth, there is a flight from the social problems that predominate in our world. There is a song much sung in our churches that goes so far as to make it explicit. The words are, "As we pray, Lord, come fill us with your love, that we might forget the agitated world and live your life each day. Come, then, transform our life, give us refreshment of soul. And now with other brethren, we unite ourselves to you in prayer."[11]

These practices are experienced in all the Protestant churches and even in the Roman Catholic Church. We can visit different Protestant denominations and see the same style of worship. The same songs are sung. The same kinds of groups playing guitars are present. The same value is given to praise time in all the communities. And now, in some of our churches, there is no pulpit. In its place, we see percussion instruments.

I do not deny that there is a positive contribution given by the Pentecostal movement to Reformed worship. Now worship in our churches is not so formal or cold, and the use of the body to praise the Lord is widespread. The worship is more joyful than in the past, and there is more emotion than in former times. Our great problem is to find a balance between the rich heritage of Reformed worship and the new contributions of Pentecostal worship. This is, at this moment, our great challenge.

---

11. Ao orarmos, Senhor,
      vem encher-nos com o teu amor,
      para o mundo agitado esquecer,
      cada dia tua vida viver.
      Nossa vida vem, pois, transformar,
      refrigério pra alma nos dar.
      E, agora, com outros irmãos,
      nos unimos a ti em oração.

Conclusion

In his analysis of Protestant worship in Brazil, A. G. Mendonça came to the following conclusion:

> Protestantism in Brazil constructed its essence not according to the standards of the Reformation but in accordance with historical circumstances which it has not succeeded in overcoming. It is for this reason that the introduction of forms that go back to the origins of Protestantism, which are historically more distant than the Age of Missions, find no echo: they are seen as having nothing to do with Protestantism and therefore as a denial of the Reformation. There is almost an essential difference between mission Protantism in Brazil and the Protestantism of the Reformation.[12]

That seems a somber conclusion. It seems to me, however, to be a correct conclusion. The worship of Brazilian Protestant churches has undergone changes: it has become more informal; it has become more joyful and lighter; it makes greater use of music; it facilitates a fuller participation by all. In the midst of so many changes, however, certain elements that were bequeathed to us by the earliest missionaries and that belong to the so-called missionary age continue immutable. We continue to encourage worship services that promote conversion and re-consecration. We have kept the anti-Catholicism.

In the face of this, the great challenge continues to be the same. We need, in Brazilian Protestantism, to discover and recover the richness of Christian worship, especially the worship of the Protestant Reformation of the sixteenth century. We are in want of a renewal of the serious study of the Holy Scriptures. And we need to have our consciousness raised about what is going on in the world today, so that worship may become the starting point and the endpoint of our ministry.

For Further Reading

Alves, Rubem. *Dogmatismo e Tolerância*. São Paulo: Paulinas, 1982.
———. *Protestantismo e Repressão*. São Paulo: Ática, 1979.
Carvalhosa, Modesto P. B. *Manual do Culto — formas compiladas e adaptadas ao uso da Igreja Presbiteriana no Brazil*. Rio de Janeiro: O Puritano, 1906.

12. A. G. Mendonça, *Introdução ao Protestantismo no Brasil*, p. 202 (translation from the Portuguese by the author).

Faria, Eduardo Galasso, ed. *Manual do Culto.* São Paulo: Associação Evangélica Literária Pendão Real.

Hahn, Carl Joseph. *História do Culto Protestante no Brasil.* São Paulo: Associação dos Seminários Teológicos Evangélicos, 1989.

Leonard, Émile G. *O Protestantismo Brasileiro.* São Paulo: Junta de Educação Religiosa e Publicações e Associação dos Seminários Teológicos Evangélicos, 1981.

Mateus, Odair Pedroso, ed. *Vida na Terra — a renovação do culto no Seminário de São Paulo.* São Paulo: Seminário Teológico de São Paulo da Igreja Presbiteriana Independente do Brasil, 1987.

Mendonça, Antônio Gouvêa. *O Celeste Porvir — a inserção do protestantismo no Brasil.* São Paulo: Paulinas, 1984.

————. *Introdução ao Protestantismo no Brasil.* São Paulo: Loyola e Ciências da Religião, 1990.

Worship and Community in the Pacific

Baranite T. Kirata

Introduction: The World of Pacific Christians

Traditional religious beliefs among Pacific people offered little opposition to Christianity. In fact, in each of them was an element of hope for some fulfillment coming from, according to Polynesian tradition, the *lagi* (the land beyond the clouds), or from *karawa* according to Kiribati mythology.

Let us begin with a brief reminder of the history of the churches in the Pacific. The Pacific region consists of three ethnic groups: Melanesia, Micronesia, and Polynesia. The beginning of Protestant Christianity was marked in 1797 by the arrival of missionaries from the London Missionary Society (LMS) in the islands of Tahiti, now part of French Polynesia. The London Missionary Society was made up of Congregational and Presbyterian churches. The late nineteenth century saw the arrival of other Protestant missionary bodies associated with the American Board of Commissioners for Foreign Missions (ABCFM), which concentrated on Micronesia, and the Methodist mission, which worked in Polynesia and Melanesia. Roman Catholic and Anglican missionaries came just before the turn of the century, when the Pacific had already become a stronghold of Protestant Christianity.

This brief study of worship and community will reflect on the above traditions in order to present a picture of worship in modern Pacific societies.

Becoming a Christian

Baptism

Initially, adult baptism was no doubt the norm used to receive new believers into the church. The practice quickly disappeared, however, once there were no more adults to be converted. Where the population is very small and people live in close-knit communities, religion often acquires communal aspects. Here, the baptism of infants replaced adult baptism. Although there is no explicit evidence of infant baptism in the Bible, the practice has been supported by the references to "household baptisms" in the New Testament (1 Cor. 16:15-18, the household of Stephen; Acts 16:15, the household of Lydia; Acts 16:33, the household of a Philippian jailer; Acts 18:8, the household of Crispus of Corinth).

The practices surrounding baptism were defined by the puritanical nature of the churches represented by the early missionaries. As in the churches of the Reformation in general, baptism was celebrated on the Lord's Day, not in the first place to underline its relation to Jesus' resurrection but rather to emphasize its public character.[1] Baptism was by the sprinkling of water on the foreheads of new converts. This writer's experience of the different Pacific churches with which he had contact, and especially those of the Reformed tradition, revealed that baptism by immersion was never a practice. Churches such as the Seventh Day Adventist, however, and the Church of God, which arrived in the Pacific in the mid twentieth century, practiced believer's baptism by immersion. At the time when many churches began to accept each other's baptisms and to find ways of working together as Christians, these twentieth-century newcomers were keen to break down such unity by proselytizing those who already belonged to a church. Disregarding the fact that people had already been baptized in their childhood, they insisted that true baptism could only take place when a person is old enough to make a personal commitment to be a Christian. The newcomers also claimed that baptism by immersion was the true form of baptism because it followed the baptism of Jesus himself. The Trinitarian formula of baptizing "in the name of the Father and of the Son and of the Holy Spirit" (Matt. 28:19), however, was never questioned.

---

1. James F. White, *A Brief History of Christian Worship* (Nashville: Abingdon Press, 1993), p. 109.

Confirmation

Although the Roman Catholic Church observes the rite of confirmation, the Presbyterian Church in Fiji is one of the few churches in Protestant Christianity to practice confirmation. This practice is known as a means by which a person can participate in the celebration of the Eucharist. Churches of the Reformed family, such as the Congregational Christian Church of Samoa, the Congregational Christian Church of the Cook Islands, the Kiribati Protestant Church, the Nauru Congregational Church, the United Church of Christ in the Marshall Islands, and the United Church of Christ in Micronesia (Pohnpei), require that a person become a communicant member after he or she has gone through a period of probation (communicant candidacy). The length of probation varies from country to country, but generally lasts two months. During this time a person studies under the guidance of his or her pastor important facts about the Christian faith, especially the Eucharist. At the end of the instruction period, the candidate is expected to make a public announcement at worship stating his or her intention to leave the "old life" and to "put on the new life" he or she finds in Christ. The congregation has the responsibility to voice its approval or disapproval of any candidate when the church council meets the Sunday before Eucharist Sunday.[2]

Living and Dying as a Christian

Although Christianity was a new religion to the Pacific people, its discipline in terms of worship was readily adopted. The Pacific people were already religious and they found Christian worship discipline not strange at all. What was found to be new and perhaps fulfilling was the active participation of members, especially at worship functions. In pre-Christian times, worship practices were often the task of pagan priests, since Pacific religions prescribed that only the priest performed acts of worship and acted as the intermediary between the divinities and the believers. The worshipers or believers were spectators. Hence, Christianity offered an exciting alternative for the majority of the people.

2. The Eucharist is only celebrated once a month.

Daily Public Prayer

The New Testament stresses the importance of daily prayer. The emphasis seems to center on the need for the churches to be ready for Christ's return (Phil. 4:5-6). Prayer also includes a missionary dimension since the church in Ephesus was urged to pray for the conversion of those who have not yet given their lives to God (Eph. 6:18-20). Jesus, being the initiator of Christian prayer, is the means through whom all prayers should be made: "If in my name you ask me for anything, I will do it" (John 14:14). Churches in Ephesus and Colossae were familiar with a prayer meeting that included Scripture reading, psalms, hymns, and scriptural songs (Eph. 5:19; Col. 3:16). The churches in the Reformation period aimed at "de-monasticizing and de-clericalizing"[3] prayer and bringing it back to its New Testament origins.

Pacific churches were in fact very much drawn to the New Testament period's practices of daily prayer. The command to "pray without ceasing" (1 Thess. 5:17) became a living practice in Pacific homes, and Protestant churches assigned men as leaders of daily family prayer meetings. The patrilineal nature of most Pacific societies was accommodated by this arrangement. Every morning and evening each family was expected to observe this pattern. I vividly remember the sound of the conch shell being blown all through the village in the early hour of the nights to tell all the villagers that prayer time had begun. Deacons patrolled the whole village to ensure that every home prayed. It was easy to tell that the village was praying because the favorite tune of "Jesus Keep Me Near the Cross" and other well-known hymns rang out into the dark hours of the night. The order of service was no different from that which the churches in Ephesus or Colossae used. To tell the village that prayer meeting had ended, another conch shell was blown. The next day would begin in the same way, with a twenty- to thirty-minute family prayer before sunrise. Often these took place before six o'clock.

The whole village community was expected to come together for midweek public prayer services, commonly held on Wednesday or Thursday mornings. These services came to be known as the *kaingabong* in Kiribati (the same word that is used for breakfast), reflecting the idea that after waking in the morning a person needed to fill his or her spiritual stomach with divine food that would provide support for the whole day. The forms these *kaingabong* (dawn prayer meetings) used were abbreviations of the forms of Sunday morning public worship services. What came to be understood as the focus of the Wednesday or Thursday *kaingabong* was prayer for the commu-

---

3. White, *A Brief History,* p. 116.

nity, and it really was a prayer for the community since every household in the village was named and prayed for.

Whether in daily family prayer meetings, Wednesday or Thursday *kaingabong,* or Sunday services, children were always a part of the praying community. I remember that as a child I had a distaste of family prayer meetings and used to find good reasons to escape them. The good thing about these family prayer meetings, though, was the preparation children got for their future life as adults. Another positive contribution was the trust given to the fathers of different families to act as leaders of their families' religious lives, and it should be noted that the use of the word *family* here means extended family and not just the nuclear family as in the Western sense of the word.

Eucharist

The Eucharist is often misunderstood as a feast of the privileged, with the disciples viewed as the "privileged few" to be admitted to the Lord's table. Writers of the New Testament seem to go into great detail explaining the sacredness of the meal so that only those who rightly understand it participate. Paul's words, "Examine yourselves, and only then eat of the bread and drink of the cup. For all who eat and drink without discerning the body, eat and drink judgment against themselves" (1 Cor. 11:28-29), spell out the criteria that should be met if one wishes to participate in the Eucharist.

The sacredness of the Eucharist came to be observed in various ways. The sacramental words of Jesus found in Luke, "Do this in remembrance of me" (Luke 22:19), and Paul's words of institution, "For as often as you eat this bread and drink the cup, you proclaim the Lord's death until comes" (1 Cor. 11:26), are strong calls for a frequent celebration of the Eucharist. Churches in the first century faithfully carried out that understanding. The book of Acts also makes reference to the celebration of the Eucharist on each Lord's Day: "On the first day of the week, when we met to break the bread . . ." (Acts 20:7).

The churches down the ages continued to celebrate the Eucharist on the Lord's Day, but the frequency of celebration has varied. By the medieval period, most lay people communed only once a year, although many devout medieval Christians practiced quarterly celebration of the Eucharist (Christmas, Easter, Pentecost, and the local patron festival in September).[4] Luther and Calvin both advocated weekly celebration of the Eucharist, but this was blatantly refused by the people. This may have been the people's way of giving

---

4. White, *A Brief History,* p. 122.

the Eucharist reverence by spacing out its practice. Here the common rule applies: the less often an event is celebrated, the greater the tendency for it to be revered.

The Protestant missionaries who came to the Pacific from Britain and the United States shared a similar conservatism. The Westminster Directory of 1645 influenced both mission organizations. The reference in the Westminster Directory concerning the frequency of the celebration of the Lord's Supper was understood by the American Puritans to mean the Eucharist was to be celebrated once a month.[5] Hence, the Eucharist was celebrated in the Pacific in the tradition best known by the missionaries, and the practice of monthly celebration continues to exist in many Protestant churches today, although the Disciples of Christ, for example, practice weekly celebration of the Eucharist. Most Presbyterian churches celebrate the Eucharist once a month.

The word *Eucharist* was not a term used by Protestants until the 1970s, when Pacific Protestant churches became involved in the ecumenical movement. *The Lord's Supper* and *Holy Communion* were Protestant terms, which Roman Catholics did their best to avoid. Roman Catholics and Protestants now use the terms Eucharist, Lord's Supper, and Holy Communion. It may seem insignificant, but the common usage of the word *Eucharist* has helped to bring Catholics and Protestants together.

The Roman Catholic and the Anglican Eucharist were weekly events, but for the religious communities (clergy and nuns), the Eucharist was a daily event. Prior to Vatican II, Latin was used in the Roman Catholic Eucharist, which worked well in cultures where oral tradition was very strong. Protestant churches, including Anglicans, used the vernacular of the people in all their services.

Both Roman Catholics and most Protestants agree that only ordained persons can preside over Eucharistic services. The Disciples of Christ and the Baptist Church are the only churches that allow laypersons to celebrate the Eucharist. Some time will pass, however, before the common celebration of the Eucharist will be realized. Pacific churches, including Roman Catholic and Protestant, have started talks on the issue of a common Eucharist celebration. At its general assembly held in Papeete, Tahiti, in January 1997, the Pacific Conference of Churches was challenged by the vision of its Program on Mission and Unity to make the dawn of the millennium the time that Pacific churches come together to celebrate the Lord's Supper. Despite the commitment and support of many church leaders in the Assembly for a joint celebra-

5. Horton Davies, *The Worship of the American Puritans, 1629-1730* (New York: Peter Lang 1990), p. 163.

tion of the Lord's Supper, the Roman Catholic delegation was not able to accept the proposal because of the official position of the Roman Catholic hierarchy. This stance from a single member of the predominantly Protestant Pacific Conference of Churches was influential in the decision that favored delaying a joint celebration of the Lord's Supper. It is sad that an important vision, which seeks to be faithful to the prayer of the Lord himself, was shelved because the "church systems" were not ready for it. But though there ought to be a common celebration of the Eucharist, it must be done in unison and in an approach that includes all.

The Preaching Service

Following the Reformation, Protestant churches developed a type of Sunday worship for those occasions when the Eucharist was not celebrated. These non-eucharistic services have often been described as "preaching services," since the emphasis of such Sunday worship was on the sermon. American liturgist James F. White has identified three possible historical sources for the preaching service.[6] One source was the Anglican service of morning prayer, with a sermon added at the end. A second source, derived from the Reformed tradition, was the service of the word (ante-communion) from the medieval eucharistic service. A third source was the nineteenth-century evangelistic camp meetings of the North American frontier, the goal of which was conversion.

White remarks that the form of Sunday service developed in North America "spread rapidly in mission areas overseas,"[7] and the Pacific Sunday worship followed this nineteenth-century American pattern. Pacific people greatly looked forward to such services not so much for the sermons that the missionaries had prepared but for the singing of hymns. Sunday services then became important occasions for conversions. Many people were moved either because of the hymn tunes, which the people saw as new, or because of the words of the hymns, which the missionaries had so carefully translated into native languages.

This pattern is still followed as Pacific Christians gather on Sunday mornings for worship. The order of service that was brought by the early missionaries continues to be used. In fact, that order had firmly established itself in the minds of Pacific Christians as something sacred and therefore something that could not be changed. The same order often finds its way into every

6. White, *A Brief History,* p. 159.
7. White, *A Brief History,* p. 161.

kind of activity. This arrangement provides for frequent preaching services, not only on Sundays.

Christian Time

The colorful development of the Christian year affects Pacific Christians in very minor ways. Roman Catholic and Anglican churches observe the Christian calendar in its entirety, but Pacific Christians have always marked only Good Friday, Easter Day, Christmas, and of course Sunday, in keeping with the tradition of the Puritans. In my childhood I witnessed Protestant Christians all gathering in one village to celebrate the known festive seasons, and this practice still continues. New Year's Day, interestingly, is ceremoniously a climax of the Christmas season, and also a time to seek God's blessing and guidance for the coming year.

Preaching from the lectionary was never a common thing for most Protestants. Ecumenism has introduced many Protestant churches to the use of a common lectionary, but many trained pastors of Protestant churches get very uneasy with a lectionary and prefer to select their own readings of Scripture. The only disadvantage of this method is that only a few of the biblical texts get preached, leaving a congregation that is not exposed to other scriptural passages.

Pastoral Rites

Most Pacific societies recognize old men to be counselors and advisors. Various societies give titles of respect to their old men — for example, the Fijian word *turaga qase,* which literally means "one who has grown to be wiser," or the Kiribati *unim'ane,* which literally means "anger of one who is old." These words represent a family of cultures that give prominence to old men as primary advisors to the nation. Traditionally, disputes between clans and families were arbitrated by old men, although there were cases where old men simply chose to ignore their mediating roles, and as a result led their people into regrettable situations.

Pastors started to be viewed in the same category as old men. In Kiribati society, pastors became even more important than the old men because they were seen as spiritual fathers. The fact that pastors were not from the village made them more balanced in their dealings with their clients, and their pastoral training had prepared them well to be more helpful than the old men of the village. This important shift corresponded well with the pastoral role the church played in the lives of the people.

Reconciliation

Confession remains the means to bring about reconciliation. Roman Catholics and Protestants do not agree, however, in their interpretation and practice of confession. Roman Catholics are better organized in that they have set instructions about confessions. Since Vatican II, for example, Roman Catholics have employed several methods of confession: individual confession to a priest in a reconciliation room, group confession, and general confession to priests. Anglicans used to have a process of confession, but now have dropped the practice altogether. Most Anglicans in the Pacific belong to the Low Church tradition, so their decision to drop the practice of confession is perhaps not surprising.

The Reformation shaped Protestant understandings of confession. Luther held that any baptized Christian was capable of pronouncing another person forgiven. Zwingli went further and declared — using the words of James 5:16-18 to show that Christians do not need priests to assist them in their confession — that a frequent confession to the Lord was all that mattered. In the Eucharist service, the saying of Jesus, "if you remember that your brother or sister has something against you, leave your gift therefore before the altar and go; first be reconciled to your brother or sister, and then come and offer your gift" (Matt. 5:23-24), is pronounced before the elements are distributed to communicant members. This can serve as an act of confession and reconciliation for the community. The disadvantage of this method is its failure to include the whole community: it may be possible that the persons we have wronged are not a part of the worship service in which the opportunity for reconciliation occurs.

Pacific societies celebrate reconciliations and treat them as public events. For instance, consider the case of a son who decides against the will of his parents to marry a girl of his choice. In some Pacific societies where arranged marriage is still the norm, the decision as to whom "Son A" marries belongs to Son A's parents as well as to his uncles and aunts. It is also important that the girl's parents, uncles, and aunts express their consent to a marriage proposal. Marrying the right partner is important, for this arrangement ensures support from all members of the extended family of the new couple; without such support, marriages are characterized by broken relationships between parents and sons or parents and daughters. The parents of the young couple would find it painful that a son or daughter is lost to them because he or she has decided to ignore their advice. If that separation continues for a number of months or years, then everyone in the village will start talking about Son A as a son who is "proud." Some members in Son A's family would encourage him to seek forgiveness from his parents. And if Son A listens, then great is the joy in the family. A feast is the most common way of celebrating restored family relations, and when those who aren't members of the family join in the celebration, then the happiness is even greater.

Confession and reconciliation are therefore an important part of life in Pacific communities. Like members of Son A's family, the Christian family needs to encourage every member of its community to see the importance of confession for healthy living. The Eucharist is Christ's feast for the church, a celebration of a restored relationship between God and God's people. At this celebration, Christ himself is the host and it is he who invites everybody to join him in the feast of reconciliation that he has prepared.

Healing

Roman Catholics used the "Last Rites" or "Extreme Unction" as part of ministering to the sick, but neither name was popular among the people because of the fear they projected to those in need of healing. Moreover, the laying on of hands and the practice of anointing with oil are considered by Pacific Protestants as abnormal and superstitious, and as practices done only by Roman Catholics. Proper worship, according to Pacific Protestants, must be free from anything abnormal or superstitious, and must be different from Roman Catholic worship.

This is the attitude of Pacific Protestants, but it is totally wrong. Protestant churches acknowledge that their worship patterns share the same history as those practiced by Roman Catholics but believe theirs are "pure and godly" because Luther or Calvin made them so. To talk about "extreme unction" is too Catholic. But what would Luther or Calvin have to say to Protestantism in the Pacific today? Perhaps the great reformers would not hesitate to point out with great enthusiasm that at all Sunday worship in Pacific churches the sick are named and prayed for. Would it not be more meaningful, even fulfilling the church's ministry, if all Pacific churches were to act out their commitments to those who are sick by extending the laying on of hands and the anointing of oil to them, particularly since most Pacific societies consider anointing to be a sacred practice? The fact is that many Protestant churches in North America and Europe administer "extreme unction" during home and hospital visitations to church members. Why should not Pacific churches do the same?

Christian Marriage

Marriage rites are as ancient as every society. For this reason, it is not surprising that Christian churches have modified the rites a number of times to reflect the different belief of societies. A few examples include John Wesley's removal of the "giving away of the bride and the exchange of rings" and the American Methodists' removal of the "bride's vow to obey" the husband.[8] In Pacific churches, including those of Australia and New Zealand, the vow of the bride has never been questioned. The Australian Prayer Book (Anglican) of 1978 still maintains as part of the bride's vow "to love and to obey." As in all Pacific churches, the words of the vow reflect a kind of mutual agreement, not an authority of the husband over the wife. In the agreement, husbands are also expected to obey their wives in love.

Christian Burial

Christian burials have successfully replaced all pagan burials in the Pacific. Some societies in the Pacific once practiced cannibalism, and burial practices were sometimes semi-cannibalistic: the dead were not buried but kept to decompose while family members underwent a period of mourning. The practice of keeping a corpse was discarded in Christian burials, but that of the family gathering was kept, and new meanings were given — that death was not the end, but the beginning of a new life in God's kingdom; that the feast was a foretaste of a heavenly feast of all people who have successfully won battles for God.

Living in Community

Leadership

Leadership in both Roman Catholic and Protestant churches has gone through a number of transformations to involve the laity in church leadership and life. The shortage of clergy in both Roman Catholic and Protestant

8. White, *A Brief History*, p. 165.

churches made it necessary to train catechists or lay leaders to be in charge of church life in local congregations. Catechists act as counselors and leaders at local churches' worship activities. The Eucharist is always problematic when it comes to the question of lay leadership. For most Protestants, the celebration of the Eucharist is almost always the function of an ordained person, but in extreme situations where the presence of an ordained person is not available, permission is given to trained lay leaders to celebrate the Eucharist. Roman Catholics are not as flexible as Protestants in this matter.

In the 1980s, the ordination of women became possible in a few of the Protestant churches in the Pacific. This important development in the life of these churches came about not because of the pressures for the rights and place of women, as in some Western societies, but as a result of enlightenment from Scripture leading to an acceptance of women as equal partners in God's ordained ministry.

Preaching

Protestant churches have inherited from their former missionaries an emphasis on the importance of preaching. It was mentioned earlier that fathers became preachers of the word to their families. In families where fathers are not available or are not "communicant members," however, mothers take up the roles of leaders and preachers at family prayer meetings.

Protestants have tended to shape their sermons to address life situations, that is, topically, while the Roman Catholic approach is more exegetical because of the use of the lectionary. For Protestant churches that have begun to use of the lectionary, the style has slowly shifted to that of exegesis. In addition, for Roman Catholics in the Pacific, freedom to celebrate the Mass in the vernacular meant that more attention was given to preaching. These developments brought out a lot of commonalities that Catholics and Protestants share in the interpretation of Scripture, and thus, preaching has become a common phenomenon in the churches' witness.

Church Music

Church music and architecture have gone through little change in most Pacific churches. Protestant churches are still singing hymns translated by the missionaries in the mid nineteenth century, and the theologies of these hymns reflect the European religious piety of that period. For them to be sung in the twentieth century in the Pacific makes very little sense at all. It therefore becomes imperative for Pacific composers to write hymns that are specifically Pacific.

The cases of the Cook Islands Christian Church and the Evangelical Church of French Polynesia offer interesting cases for study. Like most Pacific Protestant churches, the Cook Islands Christian Church and the Evangelical Church of French Polynesia were founded by the London Missionary Society. But unlike the rest, these churches still use their own traditional music in worship. In this way they are offering Pacific Christians unique church music that grows out of the experience of the peoples themselves.

Architecture

Church buildings in the Pacific are usually imitations of church structures that are found in Europe and America. They bear no cultural significance to the cultures of the peoples in the islands. Pacific people are often proud of building churches that resemble cathedrals or Western-style churches. Big, high pulpits, for example, which characterized the churches in the Reformation period, also abound in Pacific Protestant churches.

Before the arrival of Christianity, Pacific people had always viewed their wealth, skills, lives, and even their families as gifts of the gods they worshiped, in return for which they had to be prepared to do something for the gods. A visitor to any Kiribati village would be amazed to see one very big house in the center of a village. The big house is similar to other houses in the village, made of local materials but larger. In fact, the big house could easily accommodate up to five hundred people, the average size of a Kiribati village. This big house is the *m'aneaba,* the meetinghouse in which every kind of village activity, social or religious, takes place. The big house, according to Kiribati belief, is the spirits' house where the spirits of the totem gods of every clan and family in the village live and stay. In other words, the *m'aneaba* is the place where the worlds of the living and of the spirits meet and interact for the development and welfare of the life every person in the village. The size and beauty of the *m'aneaba* reflect the long hours given by and the expert workmanship of every villager. All these human efforts are the insignificant services the people of Kiribati offer to "house" the presence of their ancestors' spirits. The same mentality of commitment and service to a superior being is applied in all church activities in Kiribati. As in other Pacific societies, an *I-Kiribati* [9] will happily give his or her

9. *I-Kiribati* refers to both the language and the citizens of the country called Kiribati in the Pacific.

wealth or time to all church projects. Most common of these projects is the building of churches. Because foreign materials are often used to construct these churches, the cost of them is always high.

Despite the imposing frames of church buildings, with brick walls, corrugated iron roofs, splendid stained-glass windows, and high towers, their presence represents a different kind of Christianity that does not belong to the Pacific today. A meaningful church architecture for Pacific churches is one that enables a Pacific islander to worship like an islander. The architecture and concept of the *m'aneaba* is one that is traditional as well as rich in its religious meanings and one that *I-Kiribati* Christians could use to construct their church buildings. *I-Kiribati* Christians would better relate their faith with their environment once the *m'aneaba* became a place of worship each Day of the Lord.

Conclusion

Pacific Christians have celebrated two hundred years since the arrival of Christianity. The contributions that the new faith has brought into the lives of the Pacific people have been numerous. The Pacific is a region of many languages, and the familiarity of worship patterns, hymns, dress, and even the times for public or family prayer meetings has been a force that brought Pacific people much closer than ever before. The weekly Sunday public worship services and the nightly family prayer meetings have helped Pacific Christians overcome differences and barriers that cultures and languages had created. Through prayer and public or family readings of Holy Scripture, Christians in different islands of the Pacific are made a part of one universal community where the difficulty of isolation no longer hinders their celebrations of unity with each other and with their Pacific and global neighbors.

The Pacific is also a region that consists of more water than land. In this exercise I have been made to travel, to visit each of the churches to ask them how relevant worship is to their lives as communities with water surrounding. When liturgists talk about water, they engage in the discussion of baptism. The water of baptism and renewal is capable of challenging the existing patterns and practices of worship in the Pacific today. Pacific Christians should overcome what I call "denominational labeling" as the basis of deciding which worship patterns a church adopts and which it ignores. This attitude kills the Spirit's ability to nurture our lives through worship. My worship professor and mentor, Professor Horace T. Allen Jr., often reminds his students that Scripture is a canon; worship is not, so it should be open for revision and modification to suit the needs and interests of the community. Pacific Christians need to continue to remind themselves that they are a part of a Christian community that is bigger than their island communities. It is therefore imperative that they should not hesitate to learn from other members of the same community worship patterns that would help them live this unique communal life to its fullness.

Traditions and Principles of Reformed Worship in the Uniting Church in Australia

Geraldine Wheeler

If you have breath

Let everyone praise the Lord of life.
Let all things praise the Lord of love.

Give praise in your churches,
sound your praise in open spaces.
  with the grace of the great egret,
  with the ease of the eagle,
  with the tenacity of the turtle,
  with the courage of the crocodile.

Sound your happiness, bugling brolga.
Give praise, chirping crimson finch.
Come all who have ears to hear.
Come all who have songs to sing:
Let everything that draws breath,
praise our most wonderful God!

Bruce Prewer
(inspired by Psalm 146)[1]

1. Bruce Prewer, *Kakadu Reflections* (Adelaide, Australia: Lutheran Publishing House [now Openbook Publishers], 1988), p. 73. Bruce Prewer is a minister of the Uniting Church in Australia. He has published several books of prayers and modern psalms which draw upon Australian imagery. *Kakadu Reflections* includes fine photographs of the Kakadu National Park, the local indigenous people, and the park's flora and fauna.

Background

The Uniting Church in Australia was created on June 22, 1977, through a union of the Congregational Union of Australia, the Methodist Church of Australia, and the Presbyterian Church of Australia. It has the understanding that it is part of the universal Christian church, declaring in its *Basis of Union* that it lives and works within the faith and unity of the one holy catholic and apostolic church (para. 2). It also acknowledges as part of its heritage the "witness of the Reformation fathers as expressed in various ways in the Scots Confession of Faith (1560), the Heidelberg Catechism (1563), the Westminster Confession of Faith (1647) and the Savoy Declaration (1658)." From its Methodist heritage it holds the forty-four sermons of John Wesley in similar esteem (para. 9). Such a heritage allows the Uniting Church in Australia membership in both the World Alliance of Reformed Churches and the World Methodist Council.

This union of churches in Australia had been preceded by several other unions of churches across confessional lines elsewhere in the world. Churches from within the Reformed tradition were involved in the formation of the United Church of Canada, the Church of South India, the Church of North India, the United Reformed Church (U.K.), and the United Church of Papua New Guinea and the Solomon Islands. The union of churches in India included the Anglican tradition, thus making broader the liturgical heritage in the churches involved, but although the Anglican Church of Australia participated for a time in union discussions it did not proceed into the union. Other churches in the Reformed tradition in several countries have since united with others or are in the process of doing so at the turn of the twenty-first century.

This union made the Uniting church the third largest church in Australia, and it still holds that place although numbers are declining. According to government census statistics, the largest church is now the Roman Catholic at approximately 26 percent, having just topped the Anglican church (which is at about 25 percent). The Uniting church is less than 10 percent. The general culture is growing more secular and only a small percentage of the people claiming church allegiance worship regularly, though the Catholics do better than the Protestants. There continues to be a Presbyterian Church of Australia and a Reformed church of chiefly Dutch origin. On the world scene the numbers are not large, the total population of Australia being about eighteen million.

The Reformed Tradition: Lines of Historical and Cultural Transmission

Those European Reformed churches whose traditions were transplanted to Australia in the nineteenth century through migration were chiefly from the United Kingdom. A union of Presbyterian churches, predominantly Scottish, but also with Northern Irish and English background, took place in 1901. Welsh and English Independents brought forms of Congregationalism. With post–World War II immigration, Reformed Christians from the Netherlands arrived, and in recent decades immigration from many lands has resulted in an ethnically diverse church. Christians of the Reformed tradition from countries as culturally different as Korea, Indonesia, the Pacific Islands, South Africa, Hungary, and El Salvador worship in Uniting Church congregations. Many of the ethnic congregations, indigenous or immigrant, worship in their own language. Other immigrants join in the mainstream English-speaking congregations. Several indigenous communities whose contact with Christianity came through the Presbyterian and Methodist churches are also part of the Uniting Church.

Traces of the Reformed tradition in the Uniting Church are therefore far from uniform. They have arrived embodied in different cultural forms and are now being interwoven with influences from English Protestantism that have come by way of John Wesley and the Methodist movement. The *Basis of Union*, the document on which the three churches united, was strongly influenced by the ecumenical theology of the mid twentieth century in which Reformed voices were clearly heard. It is clearly, however, the document of churches whose vision was to transcend the inherited traditions, while holding to all that was seen as true and valuable in them, for the sake of the One whose prayer was and is "that they may all be one."

In the process of uniting, churches of the Reformed tradition again could see themselves as "reformed and always being reformed." The name "Uniting" rather than "United" was chosen to refer to the continuing process of growing into the unity of Christ. The church location is expressed as "in Australia" not "of Australia" in order to suggest a church that is part of the universal church, uniting in this particular nation, identifiably Australian yet quite independent of government structures.

In summary, the Reformed heritage is a major influence in the theology and worship of the Uniting church. But the fabric of worship, witness, and service of this church have patterns colored also by the Anglican/Methodist heritage, the contemporary ecumenical movement, the evangelical revivalist experience, and Pentecostal emphases of the last thirty years. There is a movement of people and ideas between churches and it is difficult to hold together such diversity. To aim to do so, however, is part of the Uniting Church commitment to the one Lord of the whole church.

Approaches to Worship in the Three Uniting Churches Prior to 1977

Christian worship in nineteenth-century Australia reflected the diversity and the legacy of the historical situation of the churches in Britain. (A British penal colony had been established at Sydney in 1788 and others followed in the early nineteenth century in other parts of the country. Gradually free settlers came in later decades.) These immigrant peoples found themselves in new frontier situations without the strength of established institutions. Many did try to re-establish the cherished church institutions they left behind, and for generations Australian Christians looked for leadership to home churches in the United Kingdom.

Approaches to worship in the three uniting churches may be characterized as representing one or other of the two major Protestant theological principles governing worship. Robert Gribben speaks of these as, first, that of Luther, Cranmer, and later the Methodist churches ("free to use any resources and activities in worship, excepting those things explicitly condemned by Scripture"),[2] and, second, that approach which approximates the Reformed position ("that nothing may be rightly used for Christian worship which is not explicitly laid down in Scripture").[3]

In practice, however, both Methodist and Reformed styles of worship in Australia can be described as fitting along a continuum. Some ministers and congregations would emphasize the "classical inheritance of the Kirk or Wesleyan Methodism (with its roots in Anglicanism),"[4] valuing the use of inherited forms, orders, and books of worship. Others valued freedom and greater spontaneity. Some Presbyterian congregations used the *Book of Common Order* of the Church of Scotland, following with interest the liturgical changes there. The Presbyterian Church of Australia adopted its own *Book of Common Order* in 1920 (revised 1929 and 1956) and used the Scottish *Psalter and Revised Church Hymnal*. Other ministers and congregations would use only

2. Robert Gribben, "A History of Worship," in *Worship in the Wide Red Land,* ed. Douglas Galbraith (Melbourne: Uniting Church Press, 1985), p. 90.

3. Gribben, "History of Worship," p. 91.

4. Gribben, "History of Worship," p. 91.

the Bible and the hymnal. Congregationalists, who were numerous in certain parts of the country, used books published in England. The *Congregational Hymnal* (1887), then *Congregational Hymnary* (1916), and finally *Congregational Praise* (1951) were in the hands of the people for singing. Ministers often used books of orders of service such as *A Manual for Ministers* (1936) and *Book of Public Worship* (1948), but there was nothing in the hands of the congregation apart from the hymnal. The Methodist church had the advantage of placing its major orders of service in the back of the hymnbook. Outside the main towns worship was conducted in very modest buildings or homes and "only those forms of worship which were mobile or could be created in new conditions could survive."[5]

All three churches were to some degree affected by movements of evangelical revival in the 1950s and '60s such as the Billy Graham Crusades and the Methodist Mission to the Nation. Those whose faith was so kindled generally had little time for books of order or written prayers. The Scriptures and the hymnbook were universally accepted, but there was strong suspicion of "the prayer book" in some quarters. This was true of many Presbyterians and Congregationalists as well as of some Methodists (for whom there was more of an expectation that at least some set orders would be used). The Reformed tradition of a directory of worship was often not understood. Except when the Lord's Supper was celebrated, the major difference between many Presbyterian, Congregational, and Methodist congregations at worship would have been the hymnbook used and the speed and gusto of the Methodist singing. Welsh Congregationalists, however, also had a fine tradition of rousing singing.

In 1977, the Uniting Church in Australia approved the continuing use of the books of worship used by the three uniting churches until such time as new worship resources were developed specifically for the Uniting Church. All three churches had been engaged in revising services of worship and preparing new resources using the language of the time, which included the change to addressing God as "You," "Your," and "Yours" instead of "Thee," "Thy," and "Thine." They also had been involved with the Anglican and Roman Catholic churches in the preparation of the *Australian Hymn Book*. When this hymnal appeared in 1977, it was readily adopted by many Uniting congregations (usually in the edition without the Catholic supplement) and it became the standard hymnal of the Uniting Church. This ecumenically prepared hymnal was extensively revised and expanded under the title *Together in Song* in 1999. Church of Christ and Lutheran contributions were now included also, and this

5. Gribben, "History of Worship," p. 92.

new hymnbook has again precluded the possibility of a book that contains both hymns and basic orders of service for the Uniting Church.

The Uniting Church in Australia has been structured through its inter-related councils in such a way that worship is the responsibility of the national body, the Assembly. Its Commission on Liturgy was first based in Adelaide, and for the first decade of its life, its work was centered on the preparation of new worship resources for the entire spectrum of the church's public worship.

The decade following the merger, 1978-1988, was a time of increasing awareness of liturgical work ecumenically. The context for the formal liturgical work of the Uniting Church was taken to be the worship of the churches in the English-speaking world and material from ancient sources in English translation, with special awareness of the Methodist and Reformed heritage. The network of contemporary discussion has expanded since that time with sharing across the Christian churches, locally, nationally, and globally.

Principles of Reformed Worship

Before considering in detail the worship of the Uniting Church in Australia and its Reformed elements, this summary of principles of Reformed worship is offered in order to provide the terms of reference for the material to follow.[6]

The longing for the renewal of worship should not be foreign to that stream of Christianity which is conscious of the church *reformata semper reformanda,* reformed and continually being reformed, through the work of the Holy Spirit. I offer the following groupings of ideas as the key principles of Reformed worship without suggesting that they are exclusive to the Reformed family of Christianity.

1. The worship of the church is shaped by God's self-disclosure. The unique, irreplaceable witness to this is the Scripture of the Old and New Testaments. Central to it is the event of the life, death, and resurrection of Jesus Christ. In it is the ever-dynamic meeting of God with the people of faith who are gathered to meet together with God, to listen and be

6. I have drawn material from the discussions about Reformed worship at the Twenty-Second General Council meeting of the World Alliance of Reformed Churches in Seoul, August 15-26, 1989, and the subsequent consultation on "The Place and Renewal of Worship in the Reformed Churches" held in Geneva, June 30–July 6, 1994. I have also consulted the *Directory of the Presbyterian Church of Aotearoa New Zealand* (1995) and the booklet *Ordered Liberty* (1999), prepared by the Uniting Church in Australia Working Group on Worship (formerly the National Commission on Liturgy).

nourished through word and sacrament, and to respond in praise, prayer, thanksgiving, confession, and the offering of their lives in love and service. All this is the work of the Holy Spirit. It is worship of God who saves by grace through faith and who is understood as triune.

2. The worship of the church must have integrity, a biblical and theological integrity. This is an integrity of what is prayed and what is believed *(lex orandi, lex credendi),* and of the hidden private life and its worship, which overflows into the corporate worship. It is also an ethical integrity, linking the worship with life in every secular place, loving God and loving and serving the neighbor.

3. The worship of the church must be that of the whole people, in the language and culture of the people, intelligible and edifying. The people of faith meet together with the One who is at the center of all life. They offer their adoration and praise, seek forgiveness and restoration, and offer supplications and intercessions for themselves, the church, and the world. The places of meeting are designed for this gathering for the worship of God. The people are then sent in mission, priests for one another and witnesses for the gospel to the world beyond the church. They are to live responsibly for God in the community and its institutions.

4. The worship of the church has characteristics of order (God is not a god of disorder) and liberty (because the Holy Spirit cannot be under the authority of human beings). People use their spiritual gifts as recognized and developed in the church for the offering of worship to God and the edification of all.

5. Characteristic of the Reformed understanding of God is that God is sovereign and must not be confused with the creation. Only God is to be worshiped. The worship of the church must be vigilant against idolatry, therefore, and must have a prophetic note that helps it to guard against its own possible idolatry and to recognize idolatry in the surrounding culture. (For much of its history this emphasis has meant that images in places of worship have been discouraged. There is, however, a revisiting of this question in relation to the use of the wide range of cultural and artistic forms through which people offer worship.)[7]

7. For a more detailed discussion, see my later chapter in this volume, "Revisiting the Question of the Use of Visual Art, Imagery, and Symbol in Reformed Places of Worship."

The Basis of Union on **Worship**

There is no one paragraph in *The Basis of Union* that gives a summary of the way the church is to worship, but, throughout, worship is spoken of as an essential mark and activity of the church. In every list of the essential characteristics of the life of the church worship is always placed first. For example, paragraph 15 states,

> The congregation is the embodiment in one place of the One Holy Catholic and Apostolic Church, *worshiping,* witnessing and serving as a fellowship of the Holy Spirit. Its members meet regularly *to hear God's Word, to celebrate the sacraments,* to build one another up. . . . [Emphasis added.]

In paragraph 18 we read, "She [UCA] prays God that . . . [God] will use her worship, witness and service to his eternal glory through Jesus Christ the Lord. Amen." Worship is thus centered upon the preaching of God's word and the celebrating of the sacraments. Baptism is referred to as being incorporation into the body of Christ (para. 7) and the Lord's Supper or Holy Communion as being the sacrament through which the risen Lord feeds his baptized people on their way to the final inheritance of the kingdom (para. 8).

Word and sacrament are spoken of as the action of Christ. The understanding is that Christ communicates and acts through word and sacrament. Verbs rather than nouns express what happens. There is giving and receiving, speaking and listening, feeding and being nourished. Such speaking is not first of all the language of the being and presence of God, although that is implied. Worship employs the language of acting, communicating, and relating rather than the language of materiality and substance. It is language that conveys the dynamic of relationship and dialogue. It may well be that this language is employed in order to avoid the problems seen in philosophies that identify God too closely with materiality in ontological terms. In the Reformed tradition it is important to keep clear the distinction between the divine and the creation.

The church is spoken of as a pilgrim people, and "on the way Christ feeds her with Word and sacrament . . ." (para. 3). The Lord is present when he is preached (para. 4), and he has commanded his church to proclaim the gospel in both words and the two visible acts of baptism and the Lord's Supper. "He himself acts in and through everything the church does in obedience to his commandment . . ." (para. 6). Christ is the active subject. The church's role is as witness, being obedient to the Lord who will therefore be faithful to the promises set forth in Scripture. (Had this document been written thirty years later, the language would probably be less Christocentric and more Trinitarian, speaking more explicitly of God in Christ through the Holy Spirit as the one who acts.)

According to the *Basis,* the church has received the books of the Old and New Testaments as unique prophetic and apostolic testimony[8] and its[9] message is controlled by the biblical message. Its ministers are to preach from the Scriptures and members have the serious duty of reading them (para. 5). The church receives the gifts of the Lord and acts in response in worship, witness, and service.

The Basis of Union does not include an overt discussion of prayer in the church. Although the *Basis* speaks of the church as praying, thanking, confessing faith, and in need of constant correction of that which is erroneous in its life, it makes no explicit reference to the prayer of the church as a central activity in its response of worship. In a church in which one traditional catechism spoke of the chief purpose of humanity as glorifying and enjoying God forever, perhaps more could have been said about the sacrifice of praise to God and the importance of prayer, spoken and sung.

The Uniting Church in Australia through its deliberate choice of ecumenical relationship across the Christian churches is also open to the living liturgy of other traditions. It is further open to finding afresh the relationship of its worship to its witness and service. The interrelatedness of worship and mission, or even thinking of worship as part of the total mission of the church, is one of the current issues of importance within the church.

The Preparation of Resources for Worship

The Commission on Liturgy, based in Adelaide, began to prepare new orders of service, which were urgently needed in the life of the new Uniting Church. Services of baptism, Holy Communion, ordination, and induction were first produced in small booklet form with permission to copy granted. Between 1980 and 1985 twenty services in eight booklets, entitled *UC Worship Services,* were produced as provisional services. They were widely purchased and used.

---

8. This is different language from that of the *Westminster Confession of Faith,* avoiding notions of inerrancy in the received text; for this reason, it was a concern for many, who chose not to enter the Uniting church from the Presbyterian church.

9. A more inclusive-language version of this *Basis* was issued for current use in 1991. In it the church is no longer referred to as "she" but "it." The version used when quoted in this paper is the revised version of 1971 upon which the churches united.

"The preparation of these provisional services," says D'Arcy Wood in the preface to *Uniting in Worship,* "gave the Commission opportunity to note new liturgical directions, ecumenically and internationally, as well as to reflect more deeply on the rich legacy of worship inherited from former denominational practice."[10] This turned out to be a process of trying different ideas and receiving comments that engaged many people across the life of the church. It was recognizing the important contribution of a wide group of the people of God.

The 1982 Assembly gave the Commission direction to begin work on the publication of a comprehensive collection of services and other resources for use in worship. At this time, new liturgical work was being done in the English-speaking churches and there was a network of correspondence established. The ELLC translations of traditional prayers and creeds of the church prepared by the English Language Liturgical Consultation (ELLC) were used with occasional adaptation.[11]

The diversity of sources for material can be seen in the following list of churches that gave permission for the use of their material: The Presbyterian Church of the U.S.A, The United Church of Canada, The Anglican Church of Canada, The Anglican Church of Australia, The Episcopal Church (U.S.A), The Church of England, The Methodist Church of Great Britain, The United Methodist Church (U.S.A), The Presbyterian Church of New Zealand, The Evangelical Lutheran Church in America, and the Roman Catholic Church (for material from its English Missal).

Uniting in Worship 1988 preceded the two major new books of worship in the English-speaking reformed churches of the 1990s, the *Book of Common Worship* 1993 of the Presbyterian Church (U.S.A.) and the Cumberland Presbyterian Church, and *Common Order* of the Church of Scotland, 1994, revised 1996. It, by then, had become part of the pool of liturgical resources consulted for those new books for worship. This is the nature of modern liturgical work, with the exchange and adaptation of the written worship books across the churches. *Uniting in Worship,* as is true of these later books also, is not in that tradition of the church that makes the book mandatory. It is a resource that some will use closely and others often ignore. It is much fuller than a directory of worship but is offered in the spirit of a directory, with suggested and sometimes recommended patterns, not prescriptions of words and rituals.

10. Preface to *Uniting in Worship,* Leader's Book (Melbourne: Uniting Church Press, 1988), p. 5. D'Arcy Wood was the first chairperson of the Commission on Liturgy and continued in this role until after the completion of *Uniting in Worship.*

11. That is to say, the decision was made to use the Nicene-Constantinopolitan Creed without the Western church addition of the "filioque."

Uniting in Worship 1988

Uniting in Worship appeared in two forms, the Leader's Book and the People's Book. The former contains the full wording of all services, collections of extra prayers and other resources for leaders, a calendar, a lectionary (the Common Lectionary), and a list of commemorations. The latter contains sufficient of the orders of service for the congregation to follow the main shape of the service and use all the responses. It also has the creeds, several statements of faith, litanies, a treasury of prayers through the ages, and most of the psalms, prepared for responsive reading. The leader of worship may need to use both books. The People's Book was designed for use both in the gathered congregation and for private devotion. In spite of the expressed opposition to the idea of a "prayer book," however, many members then expressed a preference to have full service words for the services of the sacraments. The People's Book was not as popular as anticipated.

The Commission on Liturgy saw *Uniting in Worship* as providing a framework for worship, with many varied resources and great flexibility. Given the diversity of the congregations of the Uniting Church, it met a mixed reception. The Leader's Book was widely used by ministers but many congregations refrained from buying the People's Book. The church commended *Uniting in Worship,* both the Leader's Book and the People's Book, for use in 1988 and recognized it as superseding the books of the former denominations as the official book in 1997. Apart from a few sets of words — those accompanying the action of baptism and the ordination vows — the form of words is not binding. In some places, other words with the same intent may be used, such as in the marriage vows. In general, *Uniting in Worship* is intended to offer the recommended shape of the service of worship.

The Service of the Lord's Day

The basic service in *Uniting in Worship* is the Service of the Lord's Day. Its major parts are the gathering of the people of God, the service of the word, the sacrament of the Lord's Supper, and the sending forth of the people of God. It is structured to facilitate the dialogue of God (in Christ through the Holy Spirit) with the people, through address and response. This is recommended as the basic pattern even without the sacrament (though not all congregations and ministers have departed from the other format, which places the preaching last before a closing hymn when there is no communion).

The gathering includes a call to worship (in words of Scripture or the simple "Let us worship God"), praise and adoration in song and/or prayer, a greeting, prayers of confession, and a declaration of forgiveness. This declaration is phrased in order to give the understanding that it is Christ's word of grace, "Your sins are forgiven,"[12] spoken by the minister or leader. It is Christ who forgives.

The service of the word allows for an Old Testament reading with psalm response and an Epistle and a Gospel reading. A responsive introduction to the reading of Scripture, one characteristically Reformed in its quoting of Scripture, may be used:

> Your word, O Lord, is a lamp to our feet:
> *a light to our path.*

Any specific children's talk is best placed here within the service of the word. The preaching follows the reading and then there is opportunity for response in many ways, including a creed or statement of faith, the offering, and the prayers of the people. These prayers include thanksgiving when the sacrament is not celebrated. Styles of preaching vary greatly and questions of enculturation impinge here. The sermon is frequently shorter than for previous generations, especially in settings such as schools or retirement villages where the powers of concentration of the worshipers may be limited. But there is more general concern that generations brought up on television have less ability to sit and listen and need also the visual to assist comprehension.

In the service of the Lord's Supper, both the "warrant tradition" and the "prayer tradition"[13] are possible for the placing of the words of institution. Gribben makes the assessment that this is "the only real difference in the liturgical customs of the three uniting churches."[14] The first great prayer of thanksgiving is an Australian one, with some Australian imagery, as in the line, "In time beyond our dreaming you set man and woman at the heart of your creation," with its reference to the indigenous understanding of the distant and mythical past as "the dreaming." The alternative prayer A came originally from an Australian Congregational minister, was adapted for the Australian Anglican prayer book, and then returned for use in the Uniting Church. Alternative B is strongly Reformed in wording and alternative G, from the Presbyterian Church (U.S.A), is a modification of Calvin's exhorta-

---

12. In *A Guide to Uniting in Worship* (Melbourne: Uniting Church Press, 1990), Robert Gribben compares this with Calvin's *Form of Church Prayers* (Strasbourg 1545), in which the minister retains the form "I declare . . . ," as being more fully in the Reformed spirit (p. 49).

13. Terminology used by Gribben, "History of Worship," p. 64.

14. Gribben, "History of Worship," p. 64.

tion.[15] The distribution of the elements is according to local custom, which may follow that of former churches or other modern practice. The sending at the close, with a word of mission, is to make explicit the link between the worship and the life of the people in the secular world.

A second departure from the inherited Presbyterian and Congregational traditions (the first being the use of the Nicene Creed without the "filioque"; see footnote 11) is the recognition that the Lord's Supper is the table for all the baptized, so that baptized children are welcome to receive the elements.

Baptism and Related Services

In the section "Baptism and Related Services," the first service is baptism and the reaffirmation of baptism called confirmation. This recognizes that the norm is the baptism of the adult and that this is set within the service of the Lord's Day, after the service of the word and followed by the Lord's Supper.

The shape and movement of the baptismal service, whether that of the adult or the child, express a Reformed emphasis more explicitly than the inherited Presbyterian and Congregational services. This is achieved by placing words of repentance and confession of faith (individual and creedal) before the baptism (or before the confirmation prayer with laying on of hands) but having the vows or promises following in order to show that baptism is not conditional upon these. Rather, they are a response to the love of God. The service of the baptism of a child includes a translation of the declaration from the French Reformed liturgy, "Little child, for you Jesus Christ has come . . . ," a brilliant expression of God's grace preceding human response.

The Uniting Church has reached an agreement with the Roman Catholic Church for the mutual recognition of baptism in which there are certain agreed steps in the baptismal service. This has also opened the Uniting Church to the possible use of new symbolism, understood with a Protestant emphasis. One such symbol is the baptismal candle, presented at the end of the service. The candle is pointing to Christ who is the light of the world and to the Christian life in which one's light is to shine so that all may see the good works and give glory to God.

Within this section of *Uniting in Worship* there are also services for congregational and personal reaffirmation of baptism and the covenant service, which derives from Methodism but which contains something of the Scottish and English Puritan understanding of covenant as it was transmitted with Wesley's evangelical emphasis.

15. Gribben, "History of Worship," p. 71.

Resources for the Christian Year

As with many churches in the Reformed tradition, the Uniting Church is re-admitting some previously excluded elements of Western tradition, now understood within a Protestant framework. The Christian Year receives greater emphasis, with recommended liturgical colors for the church and for liturgical stoles when ministers wear these.[16] The Revised Common Lectionary is now widely used and a list of commemorations is provided. The focus for the latter is upon God's faithfulness in the lives and witness of well-known Christians through the ages, apostles, people of prayer, pioneers in the faith, and social reformers. Several people of the twentieth century are included.[17]

Pastoral Services and the Ordering of the Church

Pastoral services include services and resources for marriage, reconciliation, a celebration of new beginnings, the reception of a member on transfer, healing, thanksgiving for the gift of a child (after birth or adoption), and services at the time of death. The service of healing allows for the use of anointing with oil, which, of course, has strong biblical warrant. The services for the ordering of the church have undergone many changes since 1988 as the Uniting Church has placed renewed emphasis on the diaconate, struggled to define the deacon's relationship to the minister of the word, and recognized new forms of lay ministry.

One important omission has been resourcing the people of the church for personal and family worship. There are no daily services for either church or home. The People's Book, by including a treasury of prayers and the psalms, has sought to meet this need to some degree. A local church in Sydney has for many years produced a widely used daily Scripture reading resource, *With Love to the World*. This contains a commentary on a lectionary or other passage, suggested prayer topics, hymns, a commemoration focus, and a discussion question. The Commission on Liturgy, based in Brisbane from 1990, has considered whether to prepare such material, but currently recommends the resources prepared by other churches to supplement those above.

---

16. A white ecumenical alb is the recommended form of liturgical dress for leaders of worship, ordained or lay. A sizeable proportion of ministers wear this, at least on some occasions. Only ministers of the word and deacons may wear liturgical stoles. There are preaching scarves and scarves of office that others may wear.

17. Gribben, *A Guide to Uniting in Worship*, p. 86.

Continuing Renewal and Enculturation of Worship under the Guiding Principles of Worship

D'Arcy Wood wrote in his preface to *A Guide to Uniting in Worship*, "The Uniting Church has many styles of worship which reflect diverse history, geographical location, size and age-range of the congregation and theological background."[18]

The Working Group on Worship, the successor to the National Commission on Liturgy, based in Brisbane, sees that its major task until the middle of the decade is to produce new worship resources for The Uniting Church in Australia in forms available readily in CD ROM and disk format, on the Web, and in small booklet form. It is not thought to be the time nor the church climate for the expense of a second large book. Several reasons lie behind this direction apart from the out-of-print status of the original Leader's Book and the fact that some of the material is out of date.

There are, to begin with, changing theological emphases. Some of these relate to the understanding and practice of ministry, the changing baptismal emphasis on the preparation of adults (and subsequent re-interpretation of the nature of confirmation), and the growing need for an upgraded service of thanksgiving and blessing of a child to be used when parents choose not to seek baptism for the child. Greater numbers of committed parents are choosing not to have their children baptized so that the children may seek baptism of their own accord when they are ready to make their own profession of faith. While rejecting the notion of dedication of children, the understanding is that parents can dedicate themselves to parenting, give thanks for their children, and ask for God's blessing upon their children. Material from the Churches of Christ (U.S.A) has been very useful in developing this service.

A wide range of questions relating to the cultures of the people must be considered. Questions of language include the issue of inclusive language and the differences between spoken and written language and language for formal and less formal occasions. There is also the matter of regional language differences, subtle differences in usage in different subgroups, and whether ethnic congregations would benefit from translations of Uniting Church worship resources. Worship in the vernacular was one of the major steps in the enculturation of worship at the time of the Reformation.

The seasons of the Christian year in Australia are celebrated "upside-down." Christmas is at the height of summer, in the middle of the summer holidays, and Easter is in autumn. The size of Australia from the tropical north of

---

18. Wood, preface to *A Guide to Uniting in Worship*, p. 7.

Darwin to the temperate south of Tasmania leads to the question of whether there are different relationships to be found between the Christian year and the natural seasons in different parts of the country.

There is also the task of envisioning worship and the words of worship in imagery that locates it within Australia. Uniting Church minister and poet Bruce Prewer has pioneered this through prayers and psalms written for worship over many years, which are now available in published form.[19] Visual artists and architects at times consciously design work that seeks to echo the creation's praise from within the Australian landscape.

Music, together with language, defines the cultural clothing of a people's worship. Again an ecumenical hymnbook, *Together in Song: Australian Hymn Book,* has been published just as the new liturgical work is undertaken. The congregations of the Uniting Church now use an enormous range of music, and generational differences are often paralleled by differences in music style. *Together in Song* has inclusive language for people, much modern material from various sources, approximately eighty works of Australian origin, and draws upon a wider range of Christian traditions — Reformed, Methodist, Anglican, Lutheran, Roman Catholic, and Church of Christ — than its predecessor. It includes several contemporary song traditions such as Iona, Taizé, Scripture in Song, and the work of popular songwriters like Geoff Bullock and Graham Kendrick. The music of worship no longer sings only the church's theology in extended poetic form, but it sings to remember verses of Scripture by repetition and to shout affirmations of faith. The words may well be of lament or refer to issues of social justice. The human voice may be accompanied not only by organ or piano but also by guitar(s), strings, a band, or a rock band. The singing may well be *a cappella,* particularly in congregations of Pacific Island origin.

An emphasis on mission is leading to a desire for worship that facilitates the movement from meeting with God in worship to being at mission in the world. Some call for the culture of worship to be friendly for those who enter the church for the first time, and for bridges by which the unchurched can cross into worship. Yet worship must not be turned into entertainment or become worship designed primarily for us to meet our perceived needs. Rather, worship is an offering to God and is to be shaped by God.

19. Bruce Prewer, *Australian Psalms* (Adelaide, Australia: Lutheran Publishing House, 1979); *Australian Prayers* (Adelaide, Australia: Lutheran Publishing House, 1983); *Kakadu Reflections; Brief Prayers for Australians,* vols. 1-3 (Adelaide, Australia: Openbook Publishers, 1991, 1992); *Jesus Our Future: Prayers for the Twenty-First Century* (Adelaide, Australia: Openbook Publishers, 1998); *Australian Psalms,* revised and expanded (Adelaide, Australia: Openbook Publishers, 2000).

Diverse personal experiences do have a bearing on the worship of the church. Women's experience of loss, grief, and violence has helped lead to a rediscovery of the place of lament, in Scripture and in worship. Resources for the tragic times of a stillbirth or the ending of a marriage have been produced. The Australian community still looks to the church to lead its public grieving and bring assurance in the face of a horror such as a community massacre or natural disaster.[20]

There is the question of using all the media of the culture, including the wide range of visual media, in the communication of the gospel and the interpretation of the Scriptures. This calls for a reconsideration of the iconoclastic nature of Reformed worship without losing the emphasis of vigilance against idolatry. *The Directory for Worship* of the Presbyterian Church of Aotearoa New Zealand (1995) has a section entitled "Other Forms of Proclamation" (2.2.8), in which it speaks of many art forms in which the gospel may be proclaimed. When it considers the use of "time, space and matter" in relation to worship it speaks of "the richness of colour, texture, form, sound and motion . . . brought into the act of worship."[21]

Appropriate contributions from indigenous culture are to be considered. The Uniting Church has begun to pursue this in relation to how an indigenous person may bring a blessing to another individual person (newly ordained or inducted) or to a whole congregation. A range of practices of enculturation may be suitable for indigenous communities and they are experimenting in many ways. Indigenous ritual may not simply be transposed, however, into congregations of non-indigenous people. The situation in New Zealand, where there is a much higher proportion of indigenous people, has led the Presbyterian Church to incorporate rituals in the home after death, drawing upon local custom.[22] Much more is to be done as part of the process of reconciliation between indigenous and immigrant peoples in the church.

The Uniting Church in Australia Working Group on Worship has taken the ecumenical context for its work very seriously as it has embarked upon the process of preparing new resources for the church's worship. It invited liturgists from the Anglican, Roman Catholic, and Lutheran churches to meet with it, to hear their insights about *Uniting in Worship* and the new directions they would

20. Dorothy McRae-McMahon and the Pitts Street Uniting Church Congregation, Sydney, have published resources such as *Echoes of Our Journey* (Melbourne: Joint Board of Christian Education, 1993) and *The Glory of Blood, Sweat, and Tears* (Melbourne: JBCE, 1996).

21. Presbyterian Church of Aotearoa New Zealand, *Directory for Worship* 1995, p. 8. See also my chapter entitled "Revisiting the Question of the Use of Visual Art, Imagery, and Symbol in Reformed Places of Worship" in this volume.

22. Presbyterian Church, *Directory of Worship* 4.12.7, 4.12.9, p. 42.

value in the Uniting Church. The work will be done with increased awareness of the treasures of East and West, ancient and modern, Catholic, Reformed, and evangelical, which form the pool of material for Christian worship.

What the Working Group on Worship aims to do is to provide an enriched understanding of the essential elements or framework for Christian worship, a wealth of suitable resources for worship in the congregations and councils of the church, and principles to guide suitable enculturation of that worship for the diversity of ethnic and cultural groupings. This encouragement of "ordered liberty" falls within the parameters of the principles of Reformed worship. In the final count it is only as the worship of the church is inspired by the Holy Spirit and offered in the name of the Lord, Jesus Christ, that it becomes the living worship of the living God.

Conclusion

The opening chapters of John Calvin's *Institutes of the Christian Religion*[23] recognize the place of the visible, created world in pointing people of faith to the God who created all things and to the praise of God, which all things are created to offer. When the church seeks to express itself within its landscape and the community in which it belongs, and in so doing to echo the praise of the psalmists, it is claiming a particular identity as part of God's people. Bruce Prewer's psalm based upon Psalm 146, with which this essay opened, stands within this Reformed emphasis, often neglected, but as old as the Scriptures. Another of the prayers he has written is used to close these reflections.

God of Space Shuttles

God of office towers and space shuttles,
of peak-hour traffic and the Milky Way,
   help us to seek you.

God of city hospitals and flying doctors,
of intensive care and desert sunsets,
   help us to find you.

God of noisy airports and outback tracks,
of control towers and red kangaroos,
   help us to know you.

23. John Calvin, *Institutes of the Christian Religion,* ed. John T. McNeill, trans. Ford Lewis Battles (Philadelphia: Westminster Press, 1960 [1559]), 1.5.1-3, pp. 51-55; 1.5.6-10, pp. 59-63.

God of pop concerts and country shows,
of violin concertos and cooing doves,
>   *help us to trust you.*

God of football crowds and lone yachts,
of protest marches and moonlit waves,
>   *help us to love you.*

God of cathedral choirs and corroborees,
of Lifeline counsellors and birdsong at dawn,
>   *help us to serve you.*

God of Mary's Son and Peter's Lord,
of a bloody cross and an empty tomb,
>   *help us adore you.*[25]

For Further Reading

Galbraith, Douglas, ed. *Worship in the Wide Red Land. Melbourne: Uniting Church Press, 1985.*

Gribben, Robert. *Guide to Uniting in Worship.* Melbourne: Uniting Church Press, 1990.

Presbyterian Church of Aotearoa New Zealand. *Directory for Worship,* 1995.

Uniting in Worship, Leader's Book. Uniting Church Press. Melbourne, 1988.

Uniting in Worship, People's Book. Uniting Church Press. Melbourne, 1988.

24. Bruce Prewer, *Jesus our Future.*

Part II

A Common Reflection on Christian Worship in Reformed Churches Today

What are the lessons we can learn from this survey of Reformed worship from the time of the Reformation to the present? In what ways can the worship tradition of Reformed churches serve as an inspiration for today's efforts to develop forms of worship that are both faithful to God's revelation in Christ and relevant to today's contexts? In the following chapter we wish to offer a few reflections that may provide some guidance in this respect.

Worship in the Perspective of History

What is it that makes Reformed worship Reformed? The historical survey gives a picture of wide variety of worship styles that at first sight is confusing. Throughout their history and still today, Reformed churches have adopted different understandings of worship and used a variety of forms and orders. Perspectives have changed from generation to generation. Even at the time of the Reformation approaches were not identical. As the impulse of the Reformation took root in the Anglo-Saxon world, new perspectives developed. Both Puritanism and Congregationalism can be regarded as new formative periods in the history of Reformed worship. The same is true for later periods — Pietism, the Enlightenment, the revival movement, etc. In each period new styles of worship were developed. Each of them continues in the worship life of Reformed churches, with the result that various ways of worship coexist in the family of Reformed churches to this day.

The process of further diversification also continues today. The accounts of the history of worship in different Asian, African, Latin, and African-American contexts show that the Reformed worship tradition continues to evolve as much as it ever has. Forms of worship are being appropriated, transformed, and enriched by new dimensions and elements. Through this process, many Reformed churches of the South may have new gifts to offer for the renewal of worship throughout the Reformed family.

How is the variety to be explained? Forms of worship are the result of a response to particular contexts. From the beginning, Reformed churches sought to discern styles and patterns of worship that were authentic — that were, in other words, faithful to God's revelation and to the situation in which they lived. They looked to Scripture for guidance and to set some parameters for what was acceptable worship practice. They relied on the Holy Spirit for an adequate answer, but their answer was, of course, influenced by the context of their time and place. Calvin's own answer, for example, bears the marks of the conflict with the legacy of the Middle Ages. The forms of Puritan and Congregationalist worship were in several ways determined by the opposition to the established church in England. Today's worship in Korea cannot be understood apart from Korean history. In each situation new insights are gained. At the same time, new forms of worship, once established, tended to develop into a fixed pattern, a tradition, which later could cease to be relevant. To remain faithful, new departures are often required.

What is it then that makes Reformed worship Reformed? From the beginning it was clear to us that no ready-made definition can be given. There is no normative time in history from which the nature of Reformed worship can be identified for all times and places. The Reformed tradition is a living tradition moving from horizon to horizon and acquiring new facets. We are therefore not simply looking back to the worship of the Reformation period, or to the period of the establishment of any particular Reformed church, as normative. What makes our worship "Reformed" in every time and place is, rather, the continued attempt to respond in worship, in the light of Holy Scripture, to the presence of Jesus Christ in the power of the Holy Spirit. Our primary concern is not that worship should be *Reformed* but that it should be truly Christian worship. As we engage in this effort, we will discover the validity of many aspects of the past — "with grateful hearts the past we own!" — and at the same time gain new insights, "like householders who produce from their treasure both the new and the old" (Matt. 13:52).

Like previous generations, our generation is called to give its answer to the question of authentic worship today. Each church has to respond to its own context. At the same time, churches increasingly face common challenges. Renewal is both a task of each individual church and of all churches together. We are a worshiping communion both in each place and in all places.

Searching for Authentic Christian Worship Today

A. General Considerations

1. Worship: Communion with the Living God

The scope of all worship is nothing less than an encounter with the living God. As the disciples were met by the risen Christ on the Sunday after his death, so we are met whenever we gather to worship. In worship God comes to us in self-revelation, so that we may experience the fullness of grace. God speaks to us and we dare to speak to God. As we worship, we trust that, through word and sacrament, God will come to us and be revealed to us in many different ways.

All signs, symbols, and rituals used in worship, in particular word and sacrament, are not means in themselves but point to God, to the presence of the living Lord and to the gifts and promises of the Spirit. They are not just helpful *memorabilia* to remember an absent Lord, but the sure signs of his presence with us. While various Christian traditions may differ in the way they perceive God's presence in worship, especially in terms of the Eucharist, all agree on the reality of God's presence in and through worship. The ultimate goal of all efforts at reforming worship is to lead the worshiping community into a deeper awareness of God's presence in our midst and to a deeper knowledge of the grace of the Lord Jesus Christ, love of God, and communion of the Holy Spirit.

Reformed worshiping communities have not always appreciated the fullness of God's presence in their midst or communicated this adequately in their worship services. The God we worship is the triune God — Father, Son, and Holy Spirit. The renewal of Reformed worship will involve a deeper understanding and a faithful reclaiming of the reality of God's faithful presence, expressed and experienced in the three persons of the Trinity — *God,* the creator of heaven and earth, the author of all blessings and protector of all created things; *Jesus Christ,* the unique Truth and Light of the World; *the Holy Spirit,* the source of true and eternal life. Worshiping the triune God means affirming God's love and faithful presence in the past, today, and for all times until the coming of the kingdom. Worship is not simply the expression of human religious feelings. It is an invitation to glorify God's name.

2. Worship: Celebrated in Community

We respond to the triune God in worship as the community of faith. The worshiping community is the community of the baptized, since baptism is the sacrament of incorporation into a community of God's new creation, uniting us to Christ in the power of the Holy Spirit. Too often, baptism is restricted to an isolated moment of ritual initiation, failing to encompass the wide, deep ocean of meaning proclaimed in Scripture. Within the range of New Testament baptismal texts, two are especially important at this time in the church's life. Romans 6:3-11 and Galatians 3:23-29 proclaim baptism as the sacrament of union *with* Christ and union *in* Christ that open us to new life in the world.

In baptism we are joined to Jesus Christ in his crucifixion and resurrection so that we are brought from death to new life. Our new life in union with the One who was and is and is to be incorporates us into the body of Christ. The union of each baptized person with Christ places us in union with the whole community of faith through time and across space.

This new community, as Christ's body, is a fully inclusive community in which distinctions are no longer divisions. Historical, cultural, racial, economic, class, and gender divisions are washed away by the waters of baptism that make us one in Christ. This new community of Christ's people does not exist for itself. Its union with Christ is union in God's mission in and to the world. The mission of God is not merely the activity of local or regional communities, but of the church catholic. As believers are united in local congregations and regional churches, so all churches are bound together in Christ's sacrifice and new life in the world.

3. The Role of Scripture in Ordering Worship

Reformed churches have always looked to Scripture as the primary (and sometimes the sole) guide for determining what is faithful Christian worship. But in their efforts to be guided by Scripture, various Reformed churches have asked different questions — and so come to different conclusions — about worship practice. For example, among other insights from Scripture concerning worship, Calvin was persuaded that the worshiping community should sing only biblical texts, primarily the psalms. Later generations, however, have embraced the singing of nonscriptural texts, while pointing to Scripture for their warrant: "psalms, hymns and spiritual songs" (Col. 3:16).

Some Reformed churches were of the opinion that Scripture provided guidance even for establishing the order of worship. They thought, for instance, to discern in Isaiah 6:1-9 a movement from encountering God (vv. 1-4), to confession of unworthiness (v. 5), to forgiveness of sin (vv. 6-7), to obedient response to God's call (v. 8), to proclamation of God's word (v. 9). Other Reformed churches limited the elements of worship to those mentioned in Scripture (e.g., prayer, singing of psalms, reading and proclamation of Scripture, almsgiving), but ordered those elements as they deemed fit. It is significant to note that both of these approaches led to an emphasis on the word read and proclaimed. Often, in discussing the scriptural basis of worship, reference is also made to the four elements mentioned in Acts 2:42, which leads to a stronger emphasis on the need for a balanced relationship between word and sacrament.

Concerning the sacraments, all Reformed churches, along with other churches of the Reformation, have agreed that Scripture makes clear Christ's institution of the sacraments of baptism (Matt. 28:18-20) and the Lord's Supper (1 Cor. 11:23-26, and Gospel parallels). Yet, on the basis of Scripture, differences of opinion persist over how these sacraments should be administered and what should be included in the sacramental liturgy.

So what is the role of Scripture in determining worship practice today? The fact is that the Bible contains neither one clear and complete order for Christian worship nor a complete and exclusive list of elements of Christian worship. It does not even contain a comprehensive "directory for worship," setting forth general guidelines and parameters for worship practice in every time and place.

In Scripture we encounter a community responding to the living God, and we are called to associate ourselves to this response. The pattern of the response will not at all times and places be the same. God meets us where we are, and we respond out of our particular situation; and always and everywhere, God is present and speaks to us through word and sacrament, in the community of faith, and we — the gathered community — communicate with God in prayer.

4. Form and Freedom in Worship

Calvin understood prayer to be the "common task" of the people in worship, whether prayers voiced by the minister on behalf of the people or psalms sung by the whole congregation. In fact, Calvin entitled his entire liturgy *La Forme des Prières*. Throughout the history of Reformed worship, different branches of the Reformed tradition have approached both the ordering of worship and the people's participation in the liturgy in different ways and have sometimes been at odds over those differences. In general, there have been two basic approaches to the order and content of worship as a whole and to the people's active participation in the liturgy. One might describe these approaches as "formed" worship and "free" worship.

"Formed" worship is often described as "liturgical." It provides many opportunities for congregational participation, not only through singing but also through unison or responsive prayers, including the Lord's Prayer, through affirmations such as the creed and/or Ten Commandments, and through sung or spoken responses such as the Doxology and the *Gloria Patri*. In addition, such liturgies (in the sense of the whole order of worship) include set forms for some (or all) prayers, particularly those during the sacrament of the Lord's Supper.

"Free" worship lacks most, if not all, of the worship elements in which the congregation obviously participates, with the exception of singing. Set liturgical responses (such as the *Gloria Patri*) and other fixed elements (such as the creed, or even the Lord's Prayer) often are not used. A particular characteristic of "free" worship is extemporaneous prayer. Historically, Reformed churches in England and Scotland developed a tradition of "free" worship, in opposition to the state-imposed liturgy of the *Book of Common Prayer*. In the present, however, there are many Reformed churches for which a "free" worship style is more appropriate for cultural reasons (e.g., the church is part of an oral culture, rather than a print-oriented culture) or simply because of a high rate of illiteracy.

Reformed churches whose tradition is "formed" worship usually produce worship books containing the order and elements of the worship service, as well as suggested prayers for use at various points in the order of worship and throughout the course of the church year. These worship (or service) books provide the minister with resources for the preparation of worship and in some churches have also been used by the congregation during the worship service itself. On the other hand, Reformed churches with a tradition of "free" worship sometimes produce directories for worship, which provide general guidelines for how worship should be arranged and what should be included as well as a simple description of the appropriate contents of various types of prayer.

Both "formed" and "free" worship have a long history within the Reformed tradition. At present, both "formed" and "free" worship are practiced in Reformed churches. Most congregations practice some mixture of the two — using more or less liturgical elements and/or including both fixed and extemporaneous prayers in worship.

5. Church Buildings

Although communities of Christians are able to worship in any place, not only in church buildings, it has been important throughout most of Christian history for churches to construct special places of worship, both to contribute to the sense of the community and as a visible witness to others in the wider society. While missionary movements brought with them architectural styles, part of the grounding of the Christian faith in new settings and cultures is for architects and artists to learn to express the theological and liturgical understanding of the faith using local cultural forms. While the Reformed tradition has always called for responsible stewardship of material resources and the avoidance of lavish expenditure and unnecessary luxury, there is validity in providing worship buildings that contribute through their style and beauty to the worship, the sense of community, and the ability of the church to build bridges into a non-Christian society.

B. The Worship of the Gathered Community

1. Worship as a Movement

How do Reformed Christians understand the presence of God in the worshiping community? God is present through the activity of the Holy Spirit where the word of God is read, preached, and heard, and the sacraments celebrated, in the community of God's people. The worship service of the community is to be understood as a *movement* leading from stage to stage. We gather and pray for God's presence through the Spirit. We sing God's praise and confess our sins to God and to one another. We hear anew the good news of forgiveness and reconciliation in Christ. We listen anew to God's word in the Bible and seek to understand what the Spirit is telling us here and now. We confess together the faith of the church and offer prayers of intercession for one another and the world. We receive the confirmation of God's forgiveness through the sign of the Lord's Supper; we recall God's great deeds in Christ and call upon the Spirit to assure us of Christ's presence in bread and wine. With God's blessing we are sent again into the world as witnesses of the coming kingdom. Each element has its own value and all are indispensable parts of the whole movement leading from gathering to being sent again.

2. The Word

God's gracious love for all creation and for us is revealed in the openness of divine self-communication. God speaks to us, and we are able to respond.

> For as the rain and the snow come down from heaven,
>   and do not return there until they have watered the earth. . . .
> so shall my word be that goes out of my mouth;

> it shall not return to me empty,
> but it shall accomplish that which I purpose,
> and succeed in the thing for which I sent it. (Isa. 55:10-11)

The word of God comes to us in terms we can understand, in human terms, in Jesus Christ the very word of God. The word's presence among us is a living reality, blessing and nourishing us: "Let the word of Christ dwell among you richly; teach and admonish one another in all wisdom" (Col. 3:16). God's word, spoken most clearly in Christ, invites our words. We listen to God's word together, and so we share with one another what we have heard. As we listen to each other interpreting the word, we hear the word anew. As the word dwells among us richly, it accomplishes God's purpose.

The Use of Scripture in Worship   Holy Scripture, the written word of God, bears witness to Jesus Christ, the living word of God, and so is at the center of all areas of life in the Reformed tradition, including its worship. Scripture points to Christ as the authority by which the church assembles in the name and presence of the triune God. This was given visual expression in the older Scottish custom of processing with the Bible into the sanctuary at the beginning of worship, representing Christ present in his word as Lord of his church. Scripture leads the church to confess its sins in penitence and faith, to hear that its sins are forgiven, to give praise and thanksgiving in prayer and song, to intercede for the church and world, and to celebrate baptism and the Lord's Supper. Scripture also provides much of the content of worship — the word in song (psalms and canticles) and the word read and preached. The Ten Commandments are featured in many of the forms of Reformed worship, serving as a warning against idolatrous or false worship and proclaiming the way of life of the church. The words of Scripture, its phrases and imagery, provide the main resource for both written and free prayer, and they are a touchstone against which other phrases and imagery may be judged for their authenticity and appropriateness.

One particular question that arises in regard to the use of Scripture in worship is *How should we determine what Scripture is read and preached?* Calvin's practice was the *lectio continua* method: reading and preaching through successive books of the Bible. This method has the advantage of presenting the worshiping community with the coherent biblical storyline of each book over a period of time. Many Reformed churches today, on the other hand, encourage the use of lectionaries to determine the Scripture to be read and preached. The advantages of this method include the reading and hearing of a broad scope of Scripture every Sunday and over time (lections from the Old Testament,

Psalms, Epistles, and Gospels); the coordination of Scripture readings with the significant events of the liturgical year; and a symbolic connection with the wider Christian community, as Christians gathered for worship in different places hear the same word read and preached. Both the *lectio continua* and the lectionary guard against our hearing and preaching only those biblical texts with which we are familiar or comfortable, and both remind us that God's word chooses us rather than our choosing the words we will listen to.

Challenges/Concerns for Preaching   In the Reformed tradition, the preaching and hearing of the word of God has always been considered a primary means of grace for the worshiping community. Through preaching Christ is made present to believers, strengthening their faith, deepening their devotion, and equipping them for Christian service in the world. Through preaching Christ is also made known to nonbelievers, leading them to repentance, conversion, and new life in Christ.

Reformed preaching is biblically rooted and grounded, giving witness to the triune God revealed in the Scriptures of the Old and New Testaments. Biblical texts read aloud in worship are also interpreted in the sermon, with special emphasis placed on proclamation that is clear, intelligible, and relevant for the hearers.

Yet if preaching is to be clear, intelligible, and relevant for people in the varied cultural contexts in which the gospel is being proclaimed in today's world, preachers must also attend carefully to the particular contexts in which they find themselves, and to the preparation of sermons which in theology, style, and form are both fitting and transformative for their particular hearers. Sometimes such proclamation requires the shedding of modes of proclamation forged in another era or another cultural context and the discovery of new styles, themes, and forms indigenous to a local culture (one example being the incorporation of African proverbs, flute music, and liberation themes in preaching in the Congo). Sometimes such proclamation requires experimentation with preaching practices that challenge traditional proclamation modes that are overly rational or authoritarian (as in the Korean church's emphasis on preaching that touches the feelings of people and the *Minjung* movement's emphasis on preaching that empowers the laity). And sometimes such preaching, when undertaken by relative newcomers to the pulpit (such as newly ordained women), challenges the very notion that one person standing in a pulpit addressing others is always the best way for the gathered community to experience gospel proclamation. In those cultures where the telling of the important stories takes place also through dance, music, drama, and visual art of various kinds, the communication of the word of God needs to make use of these forms in appropriate ways. Since preaching is inherently a theological act, the question for contemporary preaching in Reformed churches around the world is not *whether* contextualization will take place in the pulpit, but how, by whom, and in what manner. And in contexts where preachers are addressing multiple subcultures (or cultures) within one congregation, the challenges will be even more complex.

If, however, Reformed preaching is to be "local" in its address (for the sake of clarity, intelligibility, and relevance), it is also to be global in its concerns. Indeed, one of the hallmarks of the Reformed tradition has been its conviction that Christ is Lord of *all* life, and that consequently the pulpit must, on occasion, speak a prophetic word to any forces in society that threaten the well-being of God's people or God's world. The history of the Reformed tradition gives evidence that this prophetic "cutting edge" of the gospel has sometimes been blunted by an overemphasis on evangelism or a spirituality that is divorced from the political, social, and economic realities of the world. Yet at its heart the Reformed tradition has resisted such a divide, insisting that love of God and love of neighbor must go hand in hand in worship — as in the rest of life.

3. The Eucharist

The baptismal communion of persons, congregations, and churches is lived out in eucharistic communion. As we share the Lord's Supper we share in the body and blood of Christ, and as we share in the body and blood of Christ, we are one with all members of the body. Sharing in the Lord's Supper means communion both with Christ and fellow Christians.

As we receive the bread of Christ's body, we are re-formed as the body of Christ. As we receive the cup of the new covenant sealed in Christ's blood, we are re-formed as the people of the new covenant. Thus, the bread and cup we share are not for ourselves alone, but for the world. As the sinners with whom Jesus still eats and drinks, we are called to share the Lord's bread with the thousands.

It should also be noted that among the texts of the New Testament dealing with the Lord's Supper, 1 Corinthians 10:16-17 and 1 Corinthians 11:17-34 place particular emphasis on the communal dimension of the sacrament.

4. Relationship between Baptism and Eucharist

Our celebration of baptism and the Lord's Supper places us in the tension between the hope of sacramental calling and our continuing resistance to new life. Yet the sacraments are not in the first place our action, but the action of the living Lord who is present among us, bathing and feeding us. Our participation in the sacraments of Christ communicates Christ to us, making sacramental promise effective in the life of the church.

Baptism and the Lord's Supper are God's gifts to the whole church. They are not the possessions of one church or a family of churches. Our sacramental theology and practice, therefore, should be open to the church ecumenical. As we are made one with Christ, we are made one with *all* of Christ's people.

Baptism and Eucharist are integrally related. While each bears a distinctive stamp, neither can be known apart from the other. The interrelationship of the sacraments can be expressed in several ways:

- In both baptism and Eucharist the church is joined to Christ in his death and resurrection. Both sacraments bind the church and each believer to the crucified and risen Christ and to one another.
- In both baptism and Eucharist the church participates in the basic movement of grace and gratitude. It is not as if baptism were grace and Eucharist gratitude, but rather the fullness of the basic movement is central to each.
- In baptism we are born and in Eucharist we are fed. Eucharist follows baptism in a natural movement of new life in Christ.
- In baptism we are brought into God's covenant community, a community that has as its essential covenantal act the sharing of a meal with its living Lord. The new covenant, established in water, is sealed in Christ's blood.

5. Word and Sacrament(s)

Calvin believed that the true church is found where the word of God is purely preached and heard and the sacraments administered according to Christ's institution.[1] Reformed churches, however, have historically not fully appreciated or practiced the insight that the faithful church is marked by word *and sacraments.* They have attempted faithfulness by being primarily a church of the word alone. The sacraments — especially the Lord's Supper (Eucharist) — are only occasionally present in Lord's Day worship, and even then their significance is often restricted. While this does not mean that our worship has failed to be true worship, it may mean an impoverishment of worship and a narrow-

1. See Calvin's *Institutes* 4.1.9.

ing of the church's life. Some Reformed churches have sought to deepen the significance of the Lord's Supper through intensive "Communion seasons," while other churches encourage more frequent celebration. Similarly, some Reformed churches celebrate baptism whenever a person or family requests it, while other churches seek to celebrate all baptisms once a year, at Easter.

The relationship of word, baptism, and Eucharist points toward a sacramental theology and liturgy that is open to the whole of the Scriptures. Both theology and practice can be enriched by attending to the breadth and depth of the scriptural witness so that the sacraments can display the fullness of grace and the completeness of new life in the Spirit.[2] The word written (Scripture), the word proclaimed (preaching), and the word enacted (baptism and Eucharist) all bear witness to the completeness of God's saving action in history, centered in the Father's sending of the Son in the power of the Spirit.

Eucharist, baptism, and proclamation are thoroughly Trinitarian. In the Lord's Supper we proclaim the Lord's death until he comes, but this cannot be conceived in isolation from the full economy of God's salvation. Creation and redemption are joined in God's gracious movement in Passover and Pascha. Grace and gratitude are constitutive of all life lived in the grace of the Lord Jesus Christ, the love of God, and the fellowship of the Holy Spirit.

Baptism and Eucharist (not to mention preaching!) have often been understood in a narrowly Christological manner. Holy Communion and baptism are not sacraments of Christ alone, as if it were possible to be joined to Christ apart from the Father and the Spirit. The essential Trinitarian character of the sacraments is displayed in the prayers of baptism and the Great Thanksgiving of Eucharist that many Reformed churches have come to appreciate. These prayers display the sacramental movement of *anamnesis* and *epiclesis,* memory and hope, new life in the triune God.

The Trinitarian nature of word and sacraments, if fully appropriated in worship, protects the church's theology and liturgy from the following:

- splitting apart crucifixion and resurrection, either by preoccupation with sacrifice or by an easy theology of glory;
- splitting apart past and present, turning sacraments into historical observances and preaching into glib relevance;
- splitting apart atonement and sanctification, making the Eucharist into a penitential rite and baptism into an effortless entrance into new life;
- splitting apart Christ and the Holy Spirit, making Christ an object of memory and the Spirit a projection of human desires.

2. See Joseph D. Small's chapter in this volume.

The Trinitarian nature of word and sacraments joins the church's theology and liturgy in the fullness of doxology.

6. Prayer

The Nature of Prayer   All prayer emerges from the activity of God (Father, Son, and Holy Spirit). It is God the Father who seeks and enables our praying, who hears and responds to our prayers, and who speaks to us in prayer. It is Christ who teaches us to pray, and who intercedes with God the Father on our behalf. It is the Holy Spirit who prays our prayers, voicing that which we can only pray "with sighs too deep for words" (Rom. 8:26). Within this framework of God's activity, we give voice in prayer to our gratitude and our praise for the gracious acts and Being of God, to our needs and failings, and to our intercessions on behalf of the world. In prayer we also listen, seeking to hear and understand what God is saying to us. Christians engage in prayer in personal devotions, within families and other groups, on many occasions and at many times of the day and week. These more private prayers flow into and out of the prayers of the community gathered for worship.

Prayer in the Worship of the Gathered Community   The prayers of the community gathered for worship are corporate; that is, they are the prayers of the community as a whole. They are not simply the sum of our individual prayers, but rather our praying together with one voice as the body of Christ. Therefore, they are not simply the prayers of each visible community gathered in a particular place. Wherever a gathered community lifts up its prayers in worship, it does so in fellowship with the church of all ages and places and is joined to Christ the Intercessor.

There are certain types of prayer that characterize the corporate prayers in Christian worship (and that also characterize private prayers). These include adoration and praise, confession, thanksgiving, intercession, and dedication. While this list is not exhaustive, at least this range of prayers is usually included in our corporate worship.

There are also various ways of praying in worship. Our corporate prayers may be spoken, sung, silent, or even enacted in movement and dance[3] or embodied in visual art.[4] These various ways of praying may be led or per-

---

3. See the chapters by Ester Pudjo Widiasih, Kasonga wa Kasonga, and Baranite Kirata in this volume.

4. See the chapter by Geraldine Wheeler entitled "Revisiting the Question of the Use of Visual Art, Imagery, and Symbol in Reformed Places of Worship."

formed by a worship leader or group (such as the choir) on behalf of the congregation, by the congregation as a whole, or in a responsive interaction of leader(s) and congregation (e.g., "call-and-response" prayers).

For Calvin, the primary language of corporate prayer was the Psalms, sung by the congregation. Today, our prayers, whether voiced or sung, may draw on a variety of sources: psalms and other Scripture, the words of poets and hymn writers, or the rich heritage of prayers written by Christians in many ages and cultures. In terms of both the language and content of corporate prayers today, sensitivity to indigenous and emerging cultural forms is necessary for appreciating and discerning both the many ways communities and individuals may fittingly offer their petitions of praise and the ways they express their prayers of repentance.

Intercession and Offering: Bridges to the World

Prayers of intercession may be especially significant in today's world. They are a particular means for each worshiping community to relate to the worship of the whole church. When offering our intercessions, we are reminded that we are not worshiping alone, but join our worship and prayers to those of the church universal on behalf of the world. Through intercession, every worshiping community may lift up to God the needs and concerns of people and situations anywhere in the world, the concerns of neighbors and strangers, of situations both like and different from their own. In this way intercession gives voice not only to the unity of the whole body of Christ in every place, but also to the church's common vocation of ministry and mission in the world as a universal witnessing community.

Similarly, the act of receiving an offering in worship also forms a bridge between the church's worship and its vocation in the world. Through intercession, we acknowledge that, as a people created, chosen, and gathered by God, the church exists for the sake of God's mission to the world. Through the offering, we acknowledge that all we are and all we have are gifts from God, to be used for the purpose of God's mission to the world.

C. The Nature of the Worshiping Community

1. Unity in Christ

Because worship is about God's presence in the midst of God's people and the people's response, we must consider the nature of the community of God's people. In the creed we confess the oneness of the church. As the church gathers for worship, it seeks to give visible expression to this oneness. Worship is the occasion to bring before God what tends to divide us — feelings of enmity, hatred, and violence. Together we confess our sins, together we ask for forgiveness, together we celebrate reconciliation in Christ and prepare ourselves for the common witness in the world. Unity in Christ does not, however, mean uniformity. Commitment in faith to Christ enables us to accept variety and even to maintain communion in and through conflicts. Every effort must therefore be made to stay together in worship, and where division has occurred, occasions must be sought to renew the common celebration. There are limits. Where the authenticity of the gospel is at stake no compromises are possible. But separation on the basis of styles of worship, or differences of language, culture, age, or ethnicity, constitutes a counter-witness to the gospel.

2. An Inclusive Community

Jesus proclaimed God's love and grace to all races, ages, and social classes, and to both sexes, and he broke down the dividing walls of hostility among peoples and nations through his death on the cross. Following his example, the Reformed church has at its best sought to be an open, welcoming, and inclusive faith community. We believe in a God who welcomes adult believers and their children through baptism into a covenant community, in a Christ whose Communion table unites all peoples as one, and in a Holy Spirit who equips all believers with gifts for the various ministries of Christ's church. Thus, Reformed churches have wrestled — and continue to wrestle — with how to give visible expression through their worship to the new community Christ calls them to be.

Among the special challenges facing contemporary Reformed churches as they seek to express this unity are the following:

- In a world that is becoming more and more fragmented, intergenerational differences are a growing problem in society, and so also in the church. We should resist the tendency to ignore certain age groups in our worship (e.g., children or youth) or to offer different styles of worship for different generations. Rather, we need to see every generation as offering insights and gifts to the whole church, and the differences between generations as offering us an opportunity to learn how to deal with diversity in our midst. On the basis of their baptism, children and youth are an integral part of the Body of Christ, and they should be incorporated in the flow and activity of the worship service. The active incorporation of children in the service may help us move away from an overbearing formality and "uptightness" that sometimes marks Reformed worship services.

- Over the years racism has shown itself to be a very difficult and persistent problem in the Christian community and its worship life. While there have been some positive developments in this regard, we must admit that racism is still a huge problem in many churches. As we keep on working at this issue, we must not fail to see that other social divisions such as those caused by socioeconomic class, educational differences, and even differences in language and culture can be equally divisive and destructive for our common life and worship.
- Christian faith communities should give special attention to the inclusion of people and groups of people that have for some reason or another been forced to the fringe of society. In our day this includes, among others, persons with HIV and AIDS and people with other diseases or disabilities.
- Some of our churches are faced with extremely difficult and sensitive issues in regard to worship for which we do not yet see a consensus answer growing in Reformed circles. Among these issues are the position of people involved in polygamous or serial marriages and the place of gay and lesbian members of our faith communities.

Reformed churches generally profess an inclusive gospel and a church community open to all people who profess Christ as Lord and Savior. The challenges of how visibly and practically to become the one body we are called to be in Christ press the church in each new age to consider anew what it means to have unity in the midst of our diversity. Many congregations, because of their homogeneous makeup, do not visibly express this diversity. We need to think of creative ways in which liturgy can help us to remember that we are part of a larger and more diverse church, even as we also press toward its visible expression on the local level. We also feel compelled to warn against a tendency in some churches to see homogeneity as a positive principle in the formation of new congregations. In the long run the dangers and complications of churches formed in this way outweigh the benefits.

3. A Community of Care, Concern, and Mutual Accountability

The church, as it gathers for worship, is not only called to deepen its communion with God; it is also called to strengthen, build up, nourish, support, and celebrate the fellowship believers have with one another. Sometimes Reformed churches have been criticized for not being as warm, open, welcoming, and supportive as they might be. At times our evangelistic and outreach efforts have suffered because we have not evidenced in Christian community the same kind of love for one another that Christ has shown us (John 13:35-40). Renewal of worship has to do not only with renewing our sense of God's presence when the community gathers around word and sacrament but also with attending to one another in a new and more compassionate way. In preparing our worship services, we need to give special attention to hospitality and community-building aspects of our liturgies.

One of the ways we express care for one another is that we hold one another accountable to God and the gospel. The Scriptures encourage us to "speak the truth in love" to one another. In our modern and overly individualistic world, this aspect of our corporate care for others has become very difficult and even suspect. In the past, the Reformed tradition has exercised this responsibility in a variety of ways, often calling it "church discipline." In the time of Calvin this kind of discipline was the responsibility of the pastors and the elders and was done in pastoral meetings in the consistory (cf. recent publications on the meetings of the Genevan Consistory). In churches of the Congregational tradition, all those who have made their profession of faith exercise this responsibility corporately in church meeting. For a variety of reasons — some understandable — disciplinary practices like these have fallen by the wayside in many of our churches, and even the term "discipline" has taken on negative connotations. Nevertheless, the acceptance of mutual responsibility for one another is a vital part of our Christian fellowship and one that we cannot afford to lose or neglect. We need to look for new ways to express this mutual responsibility toward one another as an act of love that builds up community.

We should be encouraged by many churches and individual Christians who will boldly testify to the blessings and benefits of this kind of care. On an international level, the disciplinary decision of the World Alliance of Reformed Churches at its General Council in Ottawa (1982) on the two white Reformed churches in South Africa (in connection with apartheid) conveys a positive witness in this regard. Though one of them left the Alliance, subsequent pastoral conversations with the Dutch Reformed Church, the DRC's confession of apartheid as a sin, and their re-inclusion in WARC — after almost twenty years — stand as a reminder of the positive consequences of discipline.

Christians are not only called to care for one another; they are also called to love and serve the world. Our acts of love and compassion should not be restricted to our kin, but should flow freely over all boundaries to reach the needy — whatever their identity or faith may be. God's ultimate will is to create a new human community, and we are called to be a visible sign of this new creation on earth.

4. Ministry and Leadership

Worship involves the entire gathered Body of Christ. In the Reformed tradition different members of the body have exercised different functions in leading worship, though all are understood to participate equally in Christ.

In the earliest periods of Reformed worship ministers of word and sacrament had the office of expounding (and applying) the Bible and of administering the sacraments. Elders and deacons shared in distributing the Lord's Supper by offering the cup. Deacons were charged with collecting the money given to support the church's diaconal work, and sometimes also brought to the congregation specific concerns of those in need. The full congregation participated most actively through singing, which was usually understood as a form of prayer. While pastors ordinarily offered spoken prayer, the people also participated by following the printed liturgy, written in their own language.

In recent years there has been a movement within many Reformed churches toward greater participation of the entire worshiping community — both those ordained to offices of leader and those not — in the planning and leadership of worship. In some churches preaching and administration of the sacraments is exercised not only by ministers but also by other members of the congregation who have been selected, trained, and designated to carry out these roles. (This practice is especially common in areas where there is a shortage of ordained ministers, as, for example, in France, the Pacific, and rural areas of Canada and the United States.) Many local congregations are also seeking to discern the gifts of their broader membership in relation to worship, and are encouraging a greater representation of their membership (men, women, youth, and children) to participate in the planning and leadership of worship on the Lord's Day. While conflicts sometimes develop around such practices (as, for example, when lay preachers have had inadequate theological training for their task), many churches testify that their worship has been enriched through the gifts of the whole people of God, and that the benefits far outweigh the problems.

The Eucharist service in particular provides us with a special opportunity to witness to the powerful gift of collegiality in ministry. Collegial activity in the planning and the conducting of this service (between fellow pastors; between pastors, elders, and deacons; and between pastors and congregation) can thus be an important example and symbol of true Christian community and collaboration in the ministry of the church.

D. Worship of the Community
Responding to Contemporary Challenges

The community gathered for worship is also sent into the world to bear witness to Jesus Christ. This mission to the world has several aspects: evangelism, ministries of service and compassion in Christ's name, and witness to society at all levels as advocates for justice, peace, and respect for creation. The church community responds in mission to several contexts: the daily life of individuals, the local society and culture in which the congregation exists, the nation or region, and the global community.

The church no longer needs literally to *go* out into all the world to fulfill its mission to the world. The world is at our doorstep. We encounter a multicultural society in every place. This situation calls for a new assessment of what worship and witness *in context* might mean. While in each place there are social, cultural, political, and religious contexts characteristic to that particular place, one can no longer speak of a *unique* "local context," or of a local context without a universal, global outlook.

Today's new multicontextual situation has a significant impact on our search for authentic Christian worship. It affects our worship as a gathered community at every point — word, sacrament, community, and prayer. In the light of this multicontextual reality, we may need to read Scripture and preach God's word in new ways. The many aspects of Christ's gifts to us in Eucharist and baptism may be understood differently, with some aspects speaking more profoundly than in the past. Realizing unity in Christ within the worshiping community may be even more of a challenge as congregations and churches become more diverse in ethnicity, language, and culture. Our intercessory prayers for the world may take on new meaning and urgency.

The new multicontextual situation also affects our mission to the world, as we seek to respond to the tasks of evangelism and witness to society. And, as we gather for worship and go forth in mission, we face new opportunities and challenges in our relationships with other Christian traditions, as well as in encounters with people of other faiths.

1. Evangelism

The relationship between worship and evangelism involves both liturgy and life; in other words, it involves both the times the Christian community gathers for corporate public worship and those when it is sent out to love and serve the Lord.

Local communities of faith most often gather on the Lord's Day for services of word and sacrament. Some communities in the Congo and in Korea also meet daily for prayer in the early morning. In North America some churches are starting to explore small group worship as part of a larger community of believers. In times past, many more Reformed Christians attended midweek prayer meetings or Bible studies. But everywhere, Sunday morning has become the most important gathering time for the community, and for this reason it is also the most important time to equip the members for evangelism. An important dimension of preaching, and of singing and praying together, is therefore to equip all the members to give an account of their faith to others and to present the claims of the gospel to those who do not know Christ.

Worship services are also public events, and part of the joy of every Christian community is to welcome others to join with them. Particularly in post-Christian contexts, non-Christians may attend Sunday worship as part of their search toward or back to God. The genuine and heartfelt worship of the Christian community, in which love for God and for each other is manifest, is a witness to others and an important opportunity for evangelism.

To welcome truly those seeking God, the worshiping community needs to be sensitive to cultural forms, including those of language and music, that communicate to non-Christians. "In-house" language and action that unnecessarily prevent understanding (such as the use of acronyms) can turn a public event into a private one. It must be remembered that every local community owes its existence and its identity to the larger body of Christ. That connectedness in and of itself, shown in preaching, prayer, and song, can be a powerful testimony to "seekers" that the God who is worshiped is indeed a great God over all creation, in every time and place.

After the liturgy, when the community is sent out to love and serve the Lord, all members are challenged also to love their neighbors in word and deed. Part of that love for neighbor is to tell them in *word* about the love of God in Christ for them and for the whole world. In some parts of the world Christians may not be open to speaking of their faith. But all Christians can show in *deed* their love for God and neighbor. As faithful worshiping communities, we are to become salt and light in a dark world, showing love to all at home, in the church, in the workplace, and in every dimension of life.

2. Witness to Society

Mission includes concern for the public sphere. God who turns to humanity in judgment and mercy is the God of all things, so no aspect of human life is exempt from God's claim. Worship provides the occasion to point to this claim.

The quest for social and economic justice in society found powerful expression with the Reformers, especially in Calvin's preaching, writing, and public action. For him *Reformation* meant the transformation not only of the church but at the same time of the city as a whole.

Worship is the source of this witness. It serves to equip and re-equip the congregation for service in society. It provides the occasion to clarify the issues at stake, and to identify those whose voices are not heard. All parts of the liturgy contribute in their way to this task.

Vigilance is required to ensure that the churches' worship will not be misused by the powers of the world. By exclusively concentrating on spiritual themes, worship can involuntarily become a factor supporting injustice. There were good reasons to call religion the opiate of the people. Justice, peace, and reconciliation, as well as resistance against ecological destruction, need therefore to be central themes in worship, preaching, and intercession, and also in all other parts of the liturgy.

Social Justice   In the prophetic witness of the Old Testament, but supremely in the life and ministry of Jesus, we see God's concern for the poor, the weak, the marginalized, and all who are oppressed. At the heart of Jesus' teaching is the injunction that we have to love our neighbor as ourselves. In worship we hear anew the commandment "Love as I have loved you." This underlines the self-sacrificial love and service that the worshiping community is to carry into society.

Ministry to the poor primarily finds expression in generosity, openness, and hospitality, but it also requires solidarity with their struggle against oppression. Worship is an act of resistance against unjust powers.

Reconciliation and Peace   The worshiping community, reconciled to God and to one another, is compelled by the gospel to make a reconciling witness to society. The community will seek to identify in society points of tension and conflict and to provide opportunities to address them. It will call by their name issues that tend to be bypassed in silence and will seek to deal with the root causes of increasing violence today. Worship can become the context of acts of reconciliation.

Respect for God's Creation   In recent decades the problem of ecological destruction has become ever more manifest. A new awareness of the Bible's witness to God's creation has grown. More and more we are realizing that Western civilization has turned God's creation into an object for human domination and exploitation. We are rediscovering the deep meaning of the biblical affirmation that God created all things and that all things — mountains, oceans, even stars — praise God.

Creation is a fundamental biblical theme. The Bible is framed by the testimony to the creation "in the beginning" and the new creation "at the end of history." Turning to the New Testament we clearly see that the word of the Creator becomes flesh. In his ministry Jesus displays a deep concern for people who are sick, exploited, and ostracized, and in his teaching he constantly refers to the goodness and spiritual significance of nature: the lilies of the field, the birds, the grain of wheat. In instructing his followers how to pray, he exhorts them to ask that God's will be done on *earth* as in heaven. In his teaching following the feeding of the five thousand, he announces that he is the Bread of Life. At the Last Supper he took bread and wine — gifts of creation. We who gather at the *Lord's* Supper also bring gifts of creation, which we take as signs and seals of the covenant of grace. From all of this we infer the importance and dignity of creation and the necessity of an urgent witness on its behalf. The way we treat God's gifts is part of our worship of God. Just as at the Lord's Supper we should handle the elements reverently, so when we are sent forth from our corporate worship into the world, we should show similar reverence to the whole of God's creation.

Responding leads us to a critique of lifestyles of the industrialized countries and also to protests against obvious violations of nature such as bomb testing in the Pacific, deforestation, and the dumping of nuclear waste. The worshiping community is to be an ecologically responsible community.

In the classical Reformed confessions these themes are absent but this was because at the time they were written no threat to creation was perceived. It is highly significant, however, that the World Alliance of Reformed Churches has urged its member churches to consider resistance to the double threat of ecological devastation and "social and economic injustice" as part of our confession of Jesus Christ.

3. Relationships with Other Christian Traditions

In our search for authentic Christian worship today, we recognize that the Reformed churches are but one part of the whole body of Christ. We affirm that there is a fundamental unity in Christ cutting across all Christian traditions. Nevertheless, the variety in worship practice and theology only increases when we look beyond worship in Reformed churches to worship in other Christian traditions. This wider Christian diversity can be both a gift and a problem for Reformed churches in terms of the renewal of worship.

The identity of Reformed worship has always been positively and negatively affected by that of other Christian traditions. The Reformers did not intend to establish a new church, but rather to renew the church. They understood themselves to belong to the one holy catholic and apostolic church of the ecumenical creeds, and in their writings and practice drew on the insights of previous generations of Christians. In seeking to correct abuses of the medieval church, in particular in opposing the sacrificial character of the Mass, worship became one of the decisive factors in the differentiation of the Reformed community. In specific contexts further disputes over worship occurred that led to, or reinforced, the fragmentation of the church. Even though such division and fragmentation over worship occurred in the attempt to articulate authentic worship, Reformed churches also drew upon and adopted hymns, prayers, and forms of worship from other Christian traditions and movements.

In the course of the twentieth century, the interdependence of Reformed worship with that of other Christian traditions became in most places even more evident. Reformed worship has developed through the influence of the liturgical movement, the insights of biblical scholars from all traditions, and dialogue between representatives of different Christian traditions in the ecumenical movement. This development is reflected in hymnbooks and in the understanding of the order and meaning of worship, particularly baptism and the Eucharist. The constant intention of the Reformed churches through all this has been to manifest the unity of the whole church. The Statement of the Seventeenth General Council of the World Alliance of Reformed Churches (1954) concerning eucharistic hospitality is characteristic in this respect: "We invite and gladly welcome to the Table of our common Lord the members of all churches which, according to the Bible, confess Jesus Christ as Lord and Saviour. The Church has received the Sacrament of Holy Communion from Christ and He communicates Himself in it to the believer. The Table is the Lord's, not ours." Such recognition has been important as an expression of the Reformers' concern with the unity of the church and also as an expression of Christian and human reconciliation.

In particular, many Reformed churches in the twentieth century were engaged in discussions with churches of other Christian traditions to establish united churches. The United Church of Canada and the Uniting Church of Australia are unions of churches in the Reformed tradition with the Methodist Church. The Church of South India is a union that includes also the Anglican Church, and the Church of North India an even wider union including churches that do not practice infant baptism. The United Reformed Church in the U.K. came to include the Church of Christ (Disciples), and in the Netherlands the Together on the Way Churches (Samen op egkerken) bring together

Reformed and Lutheran churches. This process has led all of the churches involved to learn from each other as they have reflected on worship and crafted new worship books and hymnals. Other Reformed churches have sought to establish patterns of recognition with other Christian communities on the way toward a fuller realization of the unity of the church.

Even in the present, however, there are Reformed churches in many places that are unable to embrace fully the affirmation of unity in Christ with all parts of the wider Christian family — and so to welcome new insights about worship from other Christian traditions. In some churches, the problem is that their Reformed identity and worship practice were historically shaped over against another Christian tradition. In other churches, the difficulty has arisen out of a lived experience of persecution as a minority community in situations where a dominant majority church has made exclusive claims. And in some churches, there is today a perceived threat or competition from other Christian churches or groups with very different worship practices and theologies.

In our efforts toward the renewal of worship today, Reformed churches need to avoid the extremes of either defining Reformed worship practice over against other Christian traditions or appropriating worship practices indiscriminately from other traditions without theological and ecclesiological reflection. In order for the wider Christian diversity of worship practice to be truly a gift, we must seek both to learn from the heritage and insights of other Christian traditions and to offer our own unique heritage and insights — for the upbuilding of the whole church and for the sake of our common Christian witness in the world.

The Growing Influence of the Charismatic Movements   A particular example at present is the growing interest in and openness to the activity and gifts of the Holy Spirit within Christian churches and groups. This charismatic interest manifests itself in a variety of ways. The explosive growth of Pentecostal and neo-Pentecostal churches in many parts of the world is experienced as a particular challenge by many Reformed churches. In this regard, it is important to distinguish "historic Pentecostal" churches, which emerged from the early-twentieth-century Azusa Street experience in the United States, from "neo-Pentecostal" churches, which are at times found to be deliberately proselytizing from other churches. Reformed churches can be helped to think through these issues by consulting the report of the five-year Pentecostal-Reformed Dialogue sponsored by the World Alliance of Reformed Churches.[5]

5. "Word and Spirit, Church and World: The Final Report of the International Pentecostal-Reformed Dialogue," *Reformed World* 50, no. 3 (September 2000): 128-56.

In some countries, there is also a confluence of Pentecostal or charismatic streams with forms of evangelicalism. The megachurch movement in the United States is a good example of this. In many ways these charismatic/ evangelical churches have an even stronger appeal to people coming out of the Reformed tradition, since they tend to emphasize biblical teaching and preaching, have lively singing, and are to a large extent a modern version of the revival movements of previous centuries.

In addition, charismatic and/or evangelical movements have arisen *within* many Reformed churches, in part as an appropriation from these various other churches and groups. Pastoral concern for sisters and brothers in our midst and relationships with other churches require different (yet complementary) responses.

Reformed churches have been and can be both enriched and challenged by these charismatic movements and Pentecostal churches. Again, we must seek to avoid the extremes of reflexively opposing "Pentecostal" features in worship or of uncritically adopting "Pentecostal-style" worship. Rather, we need to be open to the gifts of these new movements and churches, asking ourselves, How can we hear afresh the good news of the Holy Spirit's gifts to the church? How can we appropriate the reality that the Holy Spirit gives gifts to everyone in the church for the sake of the whole church? How can we respond to the challenge of worship that engages the whole person and involves all people in the congregation? At the same time, we should search the Scriptures and our own experience to discover ways in which we can be open to the Holy Spirit's movement among us while resisting inauthentic "spiritual" experiences. Perhaps Reformed attention to the word of God will help us to "test the spirits to see whether they are from God" (1 John 4:1) instead of reacting to perceived competition from Pentecostal churches and charismatic movements.

4. Relationship with Other World Religions

Christianity has never been the only religion in the world, although, in some periods of European history, local communities have experienced their communities and culture as homogeneously Christian. Even then there was often a small Jewish presence. With the possible exception of some Pacific Island communities, members of Reformed churches since the Reformation have rarely found themselves constituting the total community in which they lived. Often they were minorities, in which case part of their identity was forged against the majority group, which in many cases was also Christian. In Asia and Africa, however, Christian faith was always held in a religiously plural situation.

In today's world, Reformed churches everywhere are experiencing contact with other world religions in new and different ways. The question of how to relate to people of other faiths takes on a new urgency — in terms of both our worship and our witness in the world.

There is no clear or single answer to the question of relationships with other religious traditions, and the ways in which Christians can relate to different religious traditions vary greatly. There is a certain relationship between the three great monotheistic religions (Judaism, Christianity, and Islam) that is quite foreign to the relationship between Christianity and Asian religions such as Buddhism and Hinduism. Nevertheless, the relationship of Christians with Jews and Muslims has frequently been that of suspicion and hostility. Each particular situation across the world has its own dynamic of not only religious but political, social, and economic factors that affect relationships between people of different religions. It is also true that no religion is monolithic in its structure or identical in its manifestation in each society. Islam, for example, manifests itself differently in different parts of the world. One important factor affecting relationships is the majority or minority status of the community.

What can be affirmed by Reformed churches in every situation is that we need to foster mutual respect among ourselves and with other peoples and communities. We do this out of our common humanity, created in the image of God, and for the sake of our own witness to society challenging injustice, working for peace and reconciliation, and caring for creation.

In particular situations, different issues are being raised and considered in the living out of that affirmation. For example:

- How is the Spirit leading us to pray for peoples of other faiths?
- Is there some sense in which we can "worship" together with people of other faiths while remaining faithful to the integrity of the Christian faith?
- Can we learn from the worship of other faith traditions and draw upon certain worship practices in faithful Christian ways? (For example, the Korean dawn prayer service has drawn on the model of a Buddhist devotion.)
- To what extent and in what ways can we work together with peoples of other faiths in common witness to society?
- What should be our response when conflicts arise between peoples of different faiths that result in violence and persecution? In particular, what should be the response when churches and congregations at worship are under attack — both the response of those directly involved and of churches who want to give support and encouragement to those experiencing persecution?

As Reformed churches reflect on such questions in their particular contexts, there will be a need to maintain a balance between integrity to our Christian faith and affirmation of and solidarity with the common human family. As each church seeks to discern how best to relate to other faiths, perhaps more conversations within the Reformed family would be useful to further understanding, gain perspectives, and share insights.

Conclusion

Worship is meant to glorify God and to communicate the gospel with which we have been entrusted. Worship is therefore a central task of the church, and every effort must be made to give to worship services their adequate form. But we are also aware that all acts of worship remain imperfect. As long as we live on earth we carry God's treasure in earthen vessels (2 Cor. 4:7). As little as we know "how to pray as we ought" (Rom. 8:26), we know how to worship as we ought. For our prayers to be acceptable in the eyes of God, we depend on the intervention of the Spirit. Often we have the experience that our worship efforts remain without effect. Often we have the opposite experience that services that lack coherence and beauty are blessed by God. Ultimately, therefore, it is not the form of worship that counts but the Spirit making use of our imperfect attempts to give God praise. Our confidence in all acts of worship is in God "who by the power at work within us is able to accomplish abundantly far more than all we can ask or imagine" (Eph. 3:20). To God be glory in the church and in Christ Jesus to all generations, for ever and ever.

Part III

Elaborations on Some Contemporary Issues

A Church of the Word and Sacrament

Joseph D. Small

The sixteenth-century Protestant Reformation led to unprecedented fragmentation within the Christian church. The unity of the "one holy catholic and apostolic church" had never been fully achieved or maintained, of course. Schism was a reality, most notably in the cataclysmic break between the Orthodox church of the Greek-speaking East and the Catholic church of the Latin West, but also in other divisions of longer or shorter duration. The Reformation changed everything, however. First there was Martin Luther and the Reformation in Germany. Then Zwingli and later Calvin in Switzerland, together with reform movements throughout the European continent and England — Lutherans, Reformed, Anabaptists, Anglicans, and more, all in a dizzying pattern of diversity, experimentation, and local expression.

The Reformation's centrifugal force was a matter of concern to the reformers themselves, and a cause of sharp rebuke from the Catholic church. Both the Catholic rebuke and the Reformation defense can be discerned in a remarkable section of the Second Helvetic Confession (circa 1566). The confession acknowledges that "We are reproached because there have been manifold dissensions and strife in our churches since they separated themselves from the Church of Rome, and therefore cannot be true churches."[1] The reformers took seriously the Catholic indictment that disunity signaled defect, and mounted a defense on two levels.

The first was to point to Rome's own history of conflict and factionalism, and even to strife within the New Testament church, concluding that "there have at all times been great contentions in the Church ... without mean-

---

1. Second Helvetic Confession, in *The Book of Confessions: Study Edition* (Louisville: Geneva Press, 1999), chap. 17, p. 126 (5.133).

while the Church ceasing to be the Church because of these contentions."[2] It all remained quite confusing, however. It was not sufficient merely to say that disunity was a fact of church life. The increasingly kaleidoscopic spectacle of a multiplying number of disputing churches caused confusion. How could believers make judgments about who was faithful and who was not? What was true and what was false? What communities claiming to be Christian were true churches? These were not casual questions, but matters of fundamental faithfulness to the gospel.

The reformers' second and more substantive response addressed directly the question of the "true church." John Calvin is typical: "Wherever we see the Word of God rightly preached and heard, and the sacraments administered according to Christ's institution, there, it is not to be doubted, a church of God exists."[3] The word of God rightly proclaimed and heard, baptism and the Lord's Supper celebrated in fidelity to Christ: these are the clear indicators of the presence of the one holy catholic and apostolic church. So central are these two marks, Calvin continued, that we must embrace any church that has them, "even if it otherwise swarms with many faults."[4]

Note that Calvin's "two marks of the church" center on lived faith within congregations. He does not speak in the first instance about a church's orthodox doctrine or its sacramental theology, but about the faithfulness of proclamation and reception, and the faithfulness of sacramental practice, within Christian communities. Calvin's marks of the true church point us to congregations, not academies; to churches, not libraries; to worship, not books. Theological purity and sacramental precision are not the primary issue. Calvin's marks are matters of fundamental ecclesial faithfulness that allows the gospel to be received, believed, and lived by ordinary men and women.

Perhaps it is because Calvin's marks of word and sacraments center on the lived faith of actual congregations that they do not work well if they are used only as boundaries to determine who is in and who is out. After all, how could we determine whether the word is *purely* preached, let alone heard, and whether the sacraments are administered *according to Christ's institution?* Calvin's marks of the true church are not really meant to function as boundaries, however. They are better understood as directional signs that point to the core of faithful church life. Any community claiming to be a Christian church must place proclamation of the gospel of Jesus Christ at the heart of its life, both

2. Second Helvetic Confession, in *The Book of Confessions,* p. 127.

3. John Calvin, *Institutes of the Christian Religion,* ed. John T. McNeill, trans. Ford Lewis Battles (Philadelphia: Westminster Press, 1960), p. 1023 (4.1.9).

4. Calvin, *Institutes,* p. 1025 (4.1.12).

through proclaiming and hearing the word and through faithful celebration of baptism and the Lord's Supper.

The identification of word and sacraments as essential marks of the church is not a sixteenth-century curiosity, confined to the recesses of historical memory. The recent Formula of Agreement establishing "full communion" between the Evangelical Lutheran Church in America and three Reformed churches — the Presbyterian Church (U.S.A.), the Reformed Church in America, and the United Church of Christ — is based upon mutual acknowledgment that the churches affirm an essential core, sharing a foundational understanding of gospel and sacraments. Moreover, agreement on the essential core of word and sacraments is sufficient to warrant full communion of the churches even though they are not fully agreed on all matters: "Both sides [Lutheran and Reformed] can affirm each other in the perceived unity of the fundamental understanding of word and sacrament and admonish each other in the richness of interpretive diversity."[5] Thus, the first article of the Formula of Agreement states that "full communion" among the churches means that the four churches "recognize each other as churches in which the gospel is rightly preached and the sacraments rightly administered according to the Word of God."[6]

The continuing application of word and sacraments as marks of ecclesial faithfulness is not mere nostalgia for Reformation clarity. Word and sacraments provide the church with foundational identifiers of ecclesial faithfulness. The question to be asked of any congregation or denomination is whether word and sacraments are found at the heart of common life. When we look at a Christian community, do we see — at the center of its life — proclamation of the gospel? Proclamation in word and sacrament is not the only thing churches do, of course. Congregations and denominations engage in a wide variety of activities that go beyond preaching and celebrating the sacraments. Designating word and sacrament as marks of the true church, however, means that other church activities must not bury word and sacrament, or push them to the periphery of church life. Furthermore, the whole range of church programs must remain subject to authentication by word and sacrament, for these crucial realities are the embodiment of the gospel in the life of Christ's women and men. Word and sacrament stand as the controlling core of church activities, the marks of a church's true life.

5. Keith F. Nickle and Timothy F. Lull, eds., *A Common Calling: The Witness of Our Reformation Churches in North America Today* (Minneapolis: Augsburg, 1993), p. 34.

6. Presbyterian Church (U.S.A.), "Official Text: A Formula of Agreement," *Book of Order* (Louisville: Office of the General Assembly, 2000).

The Presbyterian Church (U.S.A.) acknowledges this reality by calling its pastors "Ministers of the Word and Sacrament." Our *Book of Order* states that in the ministry of pastors, "primary emphasis is given to proclamation of the Word and celebration of the sacraments."[7] Too often, however, this "primary emphasis" is overlooked as pastors devote their time and energy to managerial tasks, multiplying programs to meet every need, and organizing the congregation to accomplish successful expansion. It is a sad irony that when pastors do take seriously their responsibility as ministers of the word and sacrament they often place *themselves* at the center of proclamation, leading to the dangerous supposition that word and sacraments — proclamation, baptism, and the Lord's Supper — are the *pastor's* business, with the congregation as mere consumers of religious goods.

Remember Calvin's formulation: A true church is where the word is purely preached *and heard.* Congregations are active participants in proclamation, for hearing the word requires discernment, response, and faithful action. A true church is where the sacraments are celebrated in Christ, and members of the congregation are central to the gospel's sacramental enactment. The really interesting question, then, is what it would mean for a congregation to be, truly and fully, a church of the word and sacrament. What would it mean for a congregation (or a presbytery or a denomination) to place proclamation and enactment of the gospel at the very heart of its life as the controlling characteristics of all that it says and does?

*   *   *

Reformed Christians are relatively comfortable talking about a church where the word of God is purely preached and heard. We have been conditioned to think of sermons as the most important thing in worship, the climax of the Sunday service. Yet most Reformed churches neglect the sacraments, relegating baptism and the Lord's Supper to the fringes of worship. Reformed churches tend to be not churches of the word and sacrament, but churches of the word alone. Ignoring the sacraments while exalting the word, we have become obsessed with words. James White says of Reformed worship that it is "the most cerebral of the western traditions . . . prolix and verbose."[8] Similarly, Brian Gerrish notes that the wordiness of the Reformed tradition can result in

---

7. Presbyterian Church (U.S.A.), *Book of Order* (Louisville: Office of the General Assembly, 1999), G-6.0104.

8. James F. White, *Protestant Worship* (Louisville: Westminster John Knox Press, 1989), pp. 58-78.

"an arid intellectualism that turns the worshiping community into a class of glum schoolchildren."[9]

The danger goes deeper than abstraction or even boredom. A church of the word alone is always in danger of becoming a church of *words* alone. And words are what we fight about, what we fight with. Reformed churches, so neglectful of the sacraments, so tied to words, are the churches that have divided and split more than any other ecclesial tradition, more than Lutherans, Anglicans, Methodists, Catholics, or Orthodox. It may be that our history of schisms, always growing from disputes *about* words, fought *with* words, is a result of our deficiency as a church, our failure to be a church of the word *and sacrament*.

If word and sacraments together are the heart of the church's true and faithful life, neglect of one leads inexorably to deformation of the other, for when either word or sacrament exists alone it soon becomes a parody of itself. We Reformed Christians are aware of how easily the sacraments can become manipulative superstitions in churches where sacraments are exalted and preaching is minimized. But we may be less aware of how easily preaching and teaching can deteriorate into institutional marketing or human potential promotion or bourgeois conformity in churches that magnify preaching while marginalizing baptism and Eucharist. Reformed neglect of the sacraments has led to a church of the word alone, a church always in danger of degenerating into a church of mere words.

The need for a church of the word *and sacrament* is not just a cure for our terminal wordiness. It is not a matter of supplementing left brain thinking with right brain feeling, or replacing sharp words with warm communal affections, or suppressing the word's judgment in favor of creating group ties that bind the church together. Word and sacrament are not contrasting aspects of church life: brain and heart, abstract and concrete. On the contrary, Calvin placed word and sacrament *together* at the core of the church's life because he took it as "a settled principle that the sacraments have the same office as the Word of God: to offer and set forth Christ to us, and in him the treasures of heavenly grace."[10] Calvin's view is remarkable in two ways. First, the purpose of the sacraments is the same as that of the word. Baptism and Eucharist have the same function as Scripture and preaching: to proclaim the truth of the gospel of Jesus Christ, giving us true knowledge of God. Second, the purpose of both is to communicate the presence of the living Christ to us, uniting us to him in the power of the Holy Spirit. The word is not for imparting information

---

9. Brian A. Gerrish, *Grace and Gratitude* (Minneapolis: Fortress Press, 1993), p. 86.

10. Calvin, *Institutes,* p. 1292 (4.14.17).

and the sacraments are not for imparting feelings; both are occasions for the real presence of Christ in our midst.

Calvin was confident that word and sacraments are effective: they give to us precisely what they portray. Preaching God's word imparts Christ himself to us, maintaining Christ's living presence among us. The sacraments represent the person and work of Christ, making real among us the very presence of Christ. "I say that Christ is the matter or (if you prefer) the substance of all the sacraments," says Calvin, "for in him they have all their firmness, and they do not promise anything apart from him."[11] Thus, the Lord's Supper and baptism are not occasions for the Christian community merely to celebrate its own life. The sacraments impart to the community the substance of its life in Christ.

Word and sacrament together are instances of the real presence of Christ. In baptism and Eucharist, *Christ* is present to the community of faith. In a way that is not dependent on the ability or predilections of preachers and teachers, the sacraments proclaim the gospel, depicting the good news in bold relief. Thus, Reformed neglect of the sacraments has muted the gospel's proclamation, both by an absence of Christ's sacramental presence and by a sacramental gap in union with Christ.

Overlooking the sacraments' transparent proclamation of the gospel is particularly harmful to the church when a meager sacramental life is coupled with an odd North American scarcity of the word written and preached. In far too many congregations the Scriptures have become strangers to church members. This "strange silence of the Bible in the church" is particularly dismaying when coupled with preaching that is too often about the people of the congregation and their activities instead of the One who is Head of the body. In a church that experiences a "famine of hearing the words of the Lord," the absence of baptism's water and Communion's bread and wine is perilously enfeebling.

*   *   *

Perhaps Protestants should avoid Latin phrases. We never seem to get them quite right, even when one is central to who we are. When we intone *ecclesia reformata semper reformanda,* are we saying that the church is reformed and always reforming? . . . always being reformed? . . . always about to be reformed? Few of us know Latin, our translations are usually secondhand, and it seems a bit pretentious anyway.

11. Calvin, *Institutes,* p. 1291 (4.14.16).

Lex orandi, lex credendi is a venerable Latin adage that can be construed in two quite different ways. Literally "law of praying, law of believing," it is usually taken to mean that the church's worship is a norm for its belief: *what is prayed shapes what may and must be believed.* Yet it is possible to reverse its force, making belief the norm for worship: *what is believed shapes what may and must be prayed.*[12] On a practical level, it works both ways. Clearly, the hymns we sing (and those we avoid), what we pray for (and what we ignore in prayer), the vestments we wear (or shun), the ways we participate (or remain passive), and the sacraments we celebrate (or neglect) all influence the shape of belief in the worshiping community. Just as clearly, however, how we worship is affected by conscious choices, some of which are theological. Theological convictions shape worship, which, in turn, shapes the faith of the worshiping community. The dynamic interaction between doctrine and liturgy is continuous.

The sixteenth-century reformers sought to establish doctrinal control over worship precisely because they were acutely aware of worship's power to shape the church's faith and practice. Subsequent developments within Reformed churches have tended to replace worship with doctrine, however. The Reformed approach seems to assume that proper theological formulations about worship are sufficient and that attention to the forms and practices of worship is distracting at best and corrupting at worst. Thus the widespread conviction that "understanding" the Lord's Supper is a prerequisite to participation and even the primary form of participation.

Because Reformed churches have tended to be acutely aware of the ambiguity of all human response to God's initiative, including the act of worship, they have insisted that biblical and theological norms should govern liturgical development. Perhaps, however, Reformed churches have been insufficiently appreciative of the lived experience of the Christian community. The church's piety can serve as a critical corrective to biblical and theological thought that may become divorced from the worshiping community. It would be naive to think that "right doctrine" can or should exercise exclusive control over the ways in which communities of faith worship. Similarly, it would be irresponsible to think that any and all liturgical practices are automatically faithful to the gospel. Theology cannot compel liturgy nor can liturgy proceed with indifference to theology. Instead, theological sensitivity to worship's faith-shaping capacity can lead to the shaping of worship that is faithful to the gospel. In this way the worshiping community can be shaped in fidelity to the gospel.

Reformed movement toward the fullness of word and sacrament de-

---

12. For an extended discussion of the *lex orandi, lex credendi* dynamic, see Geoffrey Wainwright, *Doxology* (New York: Oxford University Press, 1980), pp. 218-83.

pends upon the recovery of a vibrant sacramental theology *and* the grounding of that theology in vibrant sacramental practice. Thinking properly about baptism and the Lord's Supper is not celebration of the sacraments. Splendid liturgical texts for baptism and the Lord's Supper are not celebration of the sacraments. Thoughts and words are necessary, of course, but their sum is less than faithful sacramental practice. Pastors and elders must think deeply about the sacraments, and they must be discriminating in the selection of liturgical texts. Then, pastors and elders must shape congregational celebration with great care, for it is the *practice* of baptism and Eucharist that either discloses or obscures the presence of Christ, that either deepens or deflects faith and faithfulness. The experience of Presbyterians in North America is instructive.

*   *   *

In the not-too-distant past, baptism in North American Presbyterian churches was a customary rite, a routine act performed on babies as a matter of course. In recent years, however, baptism has been transformed into a chummy expression of congregational welcome. Everyone smiles as the family joins the pastor and an elder at the baptismal font. The congregation is poised in anticipation of the moment when something cute will happen so that everyone can coo and chuckle. The minister reads gracious words from Scripture and prays familiar prayers, well-known questions are asked and answered, and water moistens an infant head. Then comes the parade, with pastor bearing the baby up and down the aisle, introducing the adorable child to people who are rather arbitrarily identified as the "church family." The congregation may be reminded that the promises made to the newly baptized entail provision of quality childcare and a fully staffed Sunday school. Everyone enjoys this genuinely human moment in a too often impersonal worship service.

In typical baptism services, everything focuses on celebrating the incorporation of an infant into the life of the congregation. While the words of Scripture and prayers may describe a broader, deeper reality, the action itself narrows the sacrament to only one aspect of its significance. The folksy demeanor of the pastor, introductions of the family and friends, a hasty recital of brief readings and prayers, the minimal sight and sound of water, reminders of church programs, and the leisurely stroll through the congregation all combine to collapse meaning into the reception of a singular child into a particular congregation.

Baptism is the sacrament of welcome into the community of believers, of course. But it is not only that. Baptism's capacity to unite us to God in Christ through the power of the Holy Spirit is only hinted at in most actual baptismal services. A mere sample of New Testament baptismal texts reveals rich baptismal images cascading over one another in a stream of living water that sings of discipleship (Matt. 28:16-20), forgiveness of sins and the gift of the Holy Spirit (Acts 2:37-42), response to the good news and life in the community of faith (Acts 10:44-48), dying and rising with Christ and union with Christ (Rom. 6:1-11), a new exodus from slavery to freedom in Christ (1 Cor. 10:1-4), union with sisters and brothers in Christ (1 Cor.12:12-13), distinctions no longer divisions (Gal. 3:26-29), new circumcision (Col. 2:11-15), and new covenant, new community, and new openness to the world (1 Peter 3:18-22)!

In short, baptism is a sign of the fullness of God's gracious love and effectual calling that, in one moment, is poured over a single human being. The moment is not isolated, however, as a point in time that recedes into distant memory. Baptism is the sure promise of God's continuing faithfulness, inaugurating new life within God's Way. *The French Confession of 1559* puts it nicely:

> In Baptism we are grafted into the body of Christ, washed and cleansed by his blood, and renewed in holiness of life by his Spirit. Although we are baptized only once, the benefit it signifies lasts through life and death, so that we have an enduring testimony that Jesus Christ will be our justification and sanctification forever.[13]

It makes of it too small a thing if this ocean of meaning, deep and moving, is reduced to a chummy ritual of congregational welcome. It is true enough that baptism welcomes persons into the church, but it makes all the difference whether our sacramental action is polite introduction to a friendly gathering or incorporation into a community of faith, the very body of Christ. How can our baptismal *practice* begin to open us to the flood of significance for our very being as humans together before God?

Baptism does even more than present the fullness of the gospel. Baptism is a means of grace, *communicating and bringing about* the very thing it signifies. Baptism does not merely tell us about Christ, or point to Christ, or signify Christ. In baptism, Christ is present with us as we are made one with him in a death like his so that we will become one with him in a resurrection like his. How can an unabridged sacramental theology, expressed in rich liturgical texts, be incorporated in faithful sacramental practice?

The Presbyterian Church (U.S.A.) has in place two of the elements necessary for full and faithful celebration of baptism: theology and texts. The church's *Directory for Worship* includes comprehensive chapters on "The Sealing of the

13. *The French Confession of 1559*, trans. Ellen Babinsky and Joseph D. Small (Louisville: Presbyterian Church [U.S.A.], 1998), XXXV, p. 16.

Word: Sacraments" and "Baptism." These chapters set forth a theology of baptism that is biblically grounded, apostolically focused, and pastorally sensitive. The church also has biblically and theologically shaped texts that give voice to ecclesial convictions. The *Book of Common Worship* (1993) contains eighty-five pages of baptism liturgies, including six services of "Reaffirmation of the Baptismal Covenant" for a variety of congregational occasions. Theology and texts are present in and for the church. What is lacking is the third necessary element: a developed baptismal practice that enacts the fullness of the church's baptismal theology and animates the church's rich baptismal texts.

Enacting baptismal theology and animating baptismal texts in faithful baptismal practice is a contextual pastoral task. There are common elements required of all — the use of water in the name of the Father, of the Son, and of the Holy Spirit — but there are no universal prescriptions for ecclesially faithful baptismal practice. It is essential, however, that the actual practice of baptism display the full range of baptismal significance set forth in Scripture and draw upon the baptismal tradition of the whole church. Ministers and elders in each national or regional setting can work to craft baptismal practice that incorporates the community of believers in the grace of the Lord Jesus Christ, the love of God, and the communion of the Holy Spirit. While an international conference is not the place to propose particular practices, it may be the place to call for sustained contextual attention to the essential task of reforming Reformed sacramental practice.

*   *   *

"It would be well," wrote Calvin, "to require that the Communion of the Holy Supper of the Lord be held every Sunday at least as a rule."[14] Calvin failed in his efforts to convince Reformed churches to celebrate the Lord's Supper every Lord's Day, although this was the practice of the early church and remains the practice of many churches today. For centuries, "quarterly communion" was typical North American Presbyterian practice, although recent years have brought more frequent celebrations of the sacrament. The Lord's Supper may be on its way to becoming a monthly rite, but an arbitrary designation of the first Sunday of the month as "communion Sunday" indicates its institutional rather than ecclesial function.

The Presbyterian Church (U.S.A.)'s *Book of Common Worship* invites

14. John Calvin, *Articles Concerning the Organization of the Church and of Worship at Geneva,* in *Calvin: Theological Treatises,* ed. J. K. S. Reid (Philadelphia: Westminster Press, 1954) p. 49.

people to the table with the words, "Friends, this is the joyful feast of the people of God," but in many (most?) Presbyterian churches the Lord's Supper remains a gloomy exercise in silent introspection. This is not surprising, for we have been schooled to think of the Lord's Supper exclusively in terms of the *Last* Supper. On the night of his arrest, in an upper room with disciples (including one who would betray him and another who would deny him), Jesus shared bread and wine, body and blood, and then went out to die. If that is the sole model for our sacrament, it is no wonder that our corporate demeanor is sad. Remembering the prelude to tragedy is hardly the stuff of joyful feasts.

In the first centuries of the church, the community gathered every Lord's Day, sometimes at risk to liberty or life, to share eucharistic bread and wine. The church did not gather every Thursday night, but every Sunday morning; the church did not come together in remembrance of the Last Supper, but in celebration of life with the resurrected, living Lord. In the Gospels, eucharistic meals are dramatic features of Jesus' resurrection appearances. The risen, living Lord eats and drinks with his disciples. Perhaps the most familiar of these resurrection meals took place on the way to Emmaus: "When [the risen Christ] was at the table with them, he took bread, blessed and broke it, and gave it to them. Then their eyes were opened, and they recognized him" (Luke 24:30-31). The early church looked to resurrection meal texts more than to Last Supper texts because it recognized its own experience there. The community still ate and drank with the risen Christ, and in his presence they came to know him more fully and love him more deeply.

The church knew that eating and drinking with the Lord continued a pattern from Jesus' life. The narratives of the miraculous feeding of the thousands are explicitly eucharistic (Mark 6:30-44 par). The church also remembered that Jesus was notorious for eating and drinking with sinners, and so the community knew that Jesus eats and drinks with sinners still. In all of this the church hoped as well as remembered, looking to the great heavenly banquet when all the faithful would feast with God.

No wonder the early church celebrated the Lord's Supper every Lord's Day! They were not commemorating the tragic death of a hero or mourning the premature death of an inspiring teacher. They were gathering in the presence of the risen, living Christ to be joined to him in his death and resurrection and to be fed by him, receiving nourishment for growth in the love of God and neighbors. If congregations experience the Lord's Supper as a remembrance of Jesus' death, a re-creation of the Last Supper, it is little wonder that they do it infrequently and that when they do they are vaguely puzzled or dissatisfied by it all.

Memory alone is not enough to sustain significant corporate life. For citizens of the United States, July 4 is Independence Day, the remembrance and celebration of the 1776 signing of the Declaration of Independence in Philadelphia. Although everyone knows the reason for the holiday, it no longer marks our participation in the deep national and personal significance of American independence, a time of reflection on the foundation of our liberties. The Fourth of July has become just a long midsummer weekend. We may go to a fireworks display, or even take in a parade, but none of it binds us to our liberties in a deeply communal celebration of our national independence. Memory alone is not enough to sustain significant corporate life. Thus, celebrations of the birthdays of George Washington and Abraham Lincoln have been collapsed into an increasingly obscure "Presidents' Day," while Martin Luther King Jr.'s birthday is fast becoming one more three-day weekend. Remembrance alone is not sufficient to sustain significance, and so we reduce the number of times we try to force memory to do something new. Thus: infrequent communion.

Reduction of Eucharist to an infrequent memorial of Jesus' death is also a factor in the reduction of church to a voluntary assemblage of individual believers. Calvin notes three benefits of the Lord's Supper: first, we receive Christ himself and participate in the blessings of his death and resurrection; second, we are led to recognize the continuing blessings of Christ and respond with lives of gratitude and praise; and third, we are aroused to holy living, for by receiving Christ our lives are conformed to Christ. Calvin goes on to note that while conformity to Christ should be the reality in all parts of our life,

> yet it has a special application to charity, which is above all recommended to us in this sacrament; for which reason it [the Lord's Supper] is called the bond of charity. For as the bread, which is there sanctified for the common use of us all, is made of many grains so mixed together that one cannot be discerned from the other, so ought we to be united among ourselves in one indissoluble friendship. What is more: we all receive there the same body of Christ, in order that we may be made members of it.[15]

If the Lord is really present in his Supper, binding believers to himself and to one another, the absence of Eucharist may help to explain the fractured isolation that characterizes too many congregations and is a virtual description of denominational life. The risen Lord gives us himself in the bread and wine of communion, and yet we say "no, thank you" more Sundays than not. Merely increasing the frequency of Communion will be unsatisfactory, however, if eucharistic practice continues to promote silent introspection that distances believers from each other, the world, and even their Lord.

15. John Calvin, *Short Treatise on the Holy Supper of our Lord,* in *Calvin: Theological Treatises,* ed. Reid, p. 151.

The Presbyterian Church (U.S.A.) possesses sufficient theological resources to appreciate the substance of sacramental communion with the crucified and risen Christ. The *Book of Common Worship* sets forth full and faithful eucharistic liturgies for Lord's Day worship and other services, including more than twenty richly evangelical Great Thanksgivings. The church's theology and its liturgical texts envision individual hearers of an individually preached word becoming, in the Lord's Supper, a community bound in the grace of the Lord Jesus Christ, the love of God, and the communion of the Holy Spirit. Theology and texts anticipate that as believers are united to Christ, they are united to each other in a communion that is the body of Christ and so is no longer closed in upon itself, but open to "the thousands," including the "tax collectors and sinners."

Biblically faithful eucharistic theology and theologically faithful eucharistic texts are necessary, but hardly sufficient. For the Lord's Supper to nourish one holy, catholic, and apostolic community, Communion must be embodied in frequent eucharistic practice that enacts the fullness of the church's eucharistic theology and animates the church's rich eucharistic texts.

As with baptism, enacting eucharistic theology and animating eucharistic texts in faithful eucharistic practice is a contextual pastoral task. There are common elements required of all — bread and wine thankfully shared in the name of the Father, the Son, and the Holy Spirit — but there are no universal prescriptions for ecclesially faithful Communion practice. It is essential, however, that the actual practice of the Lord's Supper display the full range of significance set forth in Scripture and draw upon the eucharistic tradition of the whole church. Ministers and elders in each national or regional setting can work to craft Lord's Supper practice that incorporates the community of believers in the grace of the Lord Jesus Christ, the love of God, and the communion of the Holy Spirit. Again, an international conference is not the place to propose particular practices, but it may be the place to call for sustained contextual attention to the essential task of reforming Reformed sacramental practice.

*   *   *

Therefore, the sacraments have effectiveness among us in proportion as we are helped by their ministry sometimes to foster, confirm, and increase the true knowledge of Christ in ourselves; at other times to possess him more fully and enjoy his riches. But that happens when we receive in true faith what is offered there.[16]

---

16. Calvin, *Institutes*, 4.14.16, p. 1290.

Contemporary Developments in Music in Reformed Churches Worldwide

Emily R. Brink and John D. Witvliet

Music is a central concern for worshipers in the Reformed tradition. For nearly four hundred years, Christians have gathered to worship in congregations that self-consciously identify themselves with the Reformed tradition. Once gathered, these congregations have listened to sermons, offered intercessory prayers, given alms, and celebrated the Lord's Supper and baptism. Throughout these services, music has provided a primary (and at times the only) form of the people's action in worship — with the notable exception of Zwingli's era in Zurich, which banned all music in worship.[1] For two centuries, and to this day in some Reformed denominations, simple unaccompanied metrical psalmody formed the entire repertoire of music for the church. The Reformed tradition has not, therefore, produced as great a number of significant composers as the Lutheran or Roman Catholic traditions, but music is no less central to the experience of worship than in those traditions.

Music in the Reformation tradition is also a very complex topic. Understanding the practice of music in the Reformed tradition requires attention to multiple sources (Psalters and hymnals, theological treatises, printed liturgies, as well as social and cultural dynamics), multiple geographic contexts (beginning in Europe and moving to many countries on every continent), and multiple strands within the tradition (from mainline to evangelical, from Presbyterian to Congregational, from theologically conservative to theologically liberal). Music used in worship in Reformed churches today ranges from the exclusive use of unaccompanied psalmody in several conservative denomina-

---

1. For a summary of this research, see John D. Witvliet, "The Spirituality of the Psalter: Metrical Psalms in Liturgy and Life in Calvin's Geneva," *Calvin Theological Journal* 32, no. 2 (November 1997): 273-97.

tions to polyrhythmic music accompanying an offertory dance in African churches, from praise-and-worship choruses sung in large North American megachurches to a growing body of indigenous folk music in Reformed churches in southeast Asia, from stately hymns sung by a robed choir in a centuries old, tall-steepled European parish church to the vibrant, repetitive community chant of a congregation that gathers in a thatched hut in the Caribbean.

The first part of this chapter is descriptive, outlining the complexity of music in the Reformed tradition today. It will chart important musical trends and developments in Reformed congregations worldwide. Some of these trends can be observed from the music itself — from the development of published Psalters, hymnbooks, and other sources for liturgical song. Other trends can be observed from the liturgical and cultural contexts of the music. How churches understand worship makes a big difference in how they understand music.

The second part of this chapter is prescriptive. It probes what some leading Reformed voices are saying about the meaning and significance of music. This analysis will suggest some criteria by which all of these recent changes can be evaluated.

Current Trends in Reformed Liturgical Music

The last generation has seen a remarkable output of new Psalters, hymnals, and other music for liturgical use in Reformed churches. In many cases, these published sources are quite different than they were a generation ago. They reveal the influence of several simultaneous and often competing impulses that have reshaped worship in many Christian traditions in the past generation.

Psalm Singing

Ever since Calvin published the first, incomplete edition of the Genevan Psalter in 1539, congregational singing of metrical psalms has been at the heart of Reformed liturgical music. On the Continent, the Genevan Psalter remains at the center of the continental Reformed practice. The English and Scottish psalm-singing tradition was more musically diverse from the beginning. Reformed groups that eventually added the singing of hymns often experienced a decline in psalm singing, so much so that today many churches around the world are unaware of their heritage of psalmody. The ecumenical movement in the twentieth century and the liturgical reforms of Vatican II have been influential in helping the Reformed tradition to revitalize psalm singing.

This revitalization has come in two forms. On the one hand, there has been renewed energy in recovering the tradition of the Genevan Psalter — at least in printed Psalters and hymnals. In many cases, the Genevan tunes have been published in their original rhythms, replacing the nineteenth-century iso-rhythmic versions. Important historical studies of music in the Genevan tradition have supported and guided this renaissance, led by key studies of Pierre Pidoux, Edith Weber, Markus Jenny, Robin Leaver, and Jan Luth. On the other hand, there has been a remarkable experimentation with new forms of psalmody, including both new metrical psalm settings and responsorial forms.[2] Remarkably, denominations in both the liturgical and the charismatic traditions have rediscovered the importance of the psalms for worship. Psalms are now used in virtually *every* Roman Catholic, Lutheran, and Episcopalian service. Portions of psalms are also important sources of texts for praise choruses, and these new forms have also attracted attention in Reformed congregations.

Developments in each country signal a variety of approaches to balancing the old and new. In 1968 in the Netherlands, the interdenominational committee "Interkerkelijke Stichting" released a new set of metrical psalm texts to be sung to the Genevan tunes. The texts were prepared by an interdenominational team of the best poets in the Netherlands. The new texts for all 150 Genevan Psalms were included as the first 150 numbers in the 1973 *Liedboek voor de kerken,* an ecumenical Psalter hymnal used by several different denominations in the Netherlands, both Reformed and beyond, including Roman Catholics. The Genevan tunes in the *Liedboek voor de kerken* have all been restored to their original rhythms.

In Hungary, the progression of twentieth-century Psalters and hymnals has witnessed a steady increase in use of Genevan materials. In 1921 the Hungarian church issued a new Psalter hymnal that restored many older songs in addition to introducing new material. A Yugoslavian Psalter hymnal of 1939 led the way to more thorough reforms, and in 1948 the Hungarian church published a complete Genevan Psalter in Hungarian. The goal of the revision committee for the psalms was "to find a way to reinstall gradually the Genevan psalms — which had a deep and blessed effect on our Reformed church and nation — in a fresh, complete, and suitable form."[3] The most recent Psalter

---

2. Metrical psalmody refers to the placement of the psalm text in poetic meters, with given stanzas consisting of a number of syllables per line, often in a rhyme scheme. Metrical psalmody eventually gave rise to the development of English hymnody. Responsorial psalmody involves the congregation in singing a short refrain that captures a particular theme of the psalm; the refrain is sung intermittently after sections of the psalm are read or chanted directly from Scripture.

3. Translated from a 1948 document quoted in the preface to the 1988 psalter hymnal.

hymnal of the Hungarian Reformed churches, *Énekeskönyv — Magyar Reformátusok Haszználatára* (Budapest, 1988), is organized like the *Liedboek voor de Kerken;* the first 150 songs include the entire Psalter set to the Genevan tunes, restored to their original rhythms.

The great Hungarian composer and music educator Zoltan Kodaly took a keen interest in this project and selected several Genevan psalm tunes as bases for choral compositions. Many of his composition students also prepared settings. A collection of choral settings of seventy Genevan psalms, all by twentieth-century Hungarian composers, was published in *Magyar Zsoltárok* (Budapest, 1979).

In Switzerland, *Psaumes, Cantiques et Textes pour le culte* (1990) includes seventy-one Genevan psalms in additional to several responsorial psalms. In Germany, the complete Genevan Psalter with many new versifications was included in the 1996 *Evangelisches Gesangbuch,* which is used by all Protestant churches in Germany; the psalms were published separatcly in 1997 as *Der Psalter.*

In Scotland, the heritage of the 1650 Scottish Psalter continues; in 1992 The Free Church of Scotland published the latest musical update in a split page format; the texts remain those of the 1650 edition. In addition, the Iona community in Scotland has been a leading force in the revival of psalm singing; they have published some psalm settings from Eastern Europe and Africa, as well as a new collection of twenty-four metrical psalms: *Psalms of Patience, Protest, and Praise* (1993).

In North America, there is perhaps the greatest variety in approaches to the psalms. *Rejoice in the Lord* (1985) included a section of sixty-two metrical psalms in biblical order, nine set to Genevan or Anglo-Genevan tunes. Five years later the *Presbyterian Hymnal* (1990) included a section of one hundred psalm settings with great variety. In addition, the Presbyterian Church (U.S.A) published an entire Psalter of responsorial settings (*The Psalter,* 1993).

The history of congregational singing in the Christian Reformed Church in the United States and Canada also involves a gradual return of the Genevan repertoire; all editions of the *Psalter Hymnal* have included at least one setting of each of the 150 biblical psalms. The 1934 edition contained thirty-nine Genevan tunes with rhymed translations by Dewey Westra and others. The centennial edition of the *Psalter Hymnal* in 1959 contained thirty-seven Genevan tunes, some in the original "long-short" rhythm. The 1987 edition has forty Genevan melodies, almost all in the rhythm created by Calvin's composers.

The Canadian Reformed churches published *The Book of Praise: Anglo-Genevan Psalter* (Premier Printing, 1984), the only available complete Genevan

Psalter in the English language. The Presbyterian Church in Canada published a complete responsorial Psalter, *The Book of Psalms* (1995), and began their hymnal *Book of Praise* (1997) with 108 metrical settings, 8 to Genevan tunes.[4]

The new Japanese ecumenical *Hymnal 2000* includes several Genevan tunes; a report in 2000 from one congregation in the Reformed Church in Japan is that Genevan psalms are sung weekly.

It must be noted that this increase in published psalmody should not be equated in all cases with an increase in the singing of psalms. In some cases, psalm singing has been more an ideal of the publishing committees than a strong practice in congregations. Ironically, singing the psalms in many Reformed churches is likely to increase as a result of sources *beyond* the Reformed tradition, especially responsorial styles in the liturgical tradition recovered from the practice of the early church, and the Scripture choruses from charismatic sources. In any future editions of most Reformed hymnals, it would be quite safe to assume that the Psalter section would not be entirely metrical in style.

Also, it should be noted that psalms of lament, so much a part of the biblical psalms, have been missing from many hymnals that included portions of the Psalter. But after two World Wars, recent research on the psalms by such scholars as Patrick Miller and Walter Brueggemann, and the growing use of the *Revised Common Lectionary,* the psalms of lament are beginning to find their place once more in Reformed worship.

Hymn Renaissance

Though hymn singing is a relative latecomer in the Reformed tradition, it has nevertheless formed a significant part of Reformed music repertory for the past two centuries — at least since Isaac Watts for English hymnody. During the eighteenth and nineteenth centuries the hymn controversy was troubling in England, Scotland, and North America. The Scottish Presbyterians in particular objected to hymns of "human composition," exemplified by the freedom of Watts to move from versifying the psalms to imitating the psalms in New Testament terms to eventually writing hymns. The influence of Watts was great; however, some denominations, particularly those with conservative

---

4. See C. Michael Hawn, "A Survey of Trends in Recent Protestant Hymnals," *The Hymn* 42, no. 3 (July 1991): 24-32; George H. Shorney, *The Hymnal Explosion in North America* (Carol Stream: Hope Publishing Co., 1988); and Paul Westermeyer, *With Tongues of Fire: Profiles in 20th-Century Hymnwriting* (St. Louis: Concordia Publishing House, 1995).

Dutch and Scottish roots, rejected not only hymnody but Watts's treatment of the psalm texts, because the versifications were not close enough to the biblical text.

In most Reformed churches, however, hymns have been an important part of worship, and the past generation has witnessed a revitalization in hymnody in many parts of the world, both within and beyond the Reformed tradition. Since the mid-1970s, nearly every denomination has published a new hymnal. More than ever before, these hymnals were produced with cooperation among hymnal editors of various worship traditions. Several hymnals in the Reformed tradition also published companion volumes in the past generation.[5]

Recent hymnals have included a number of new texts and tunes, which has led to a small industry of related efforts: the publication of well over fifty single-author hymn collections, regular hymn-writing competitions, and workshops on hymn writing and hymn accompaniment.[6] Reformed hymnologists have had prominent roles in the Hymn Society in the United States and Canada, the Hymn Society of Great Britain, the European Internationale Arbeitsgemeinschaft für Hymnologie (IAH), as well as in major international conferences. (These three societies have met together every six years, beginning with the joint 1985 meeting in the United States. The recently formed Hymn Society of Korea has also attended some of these joint meetings).

In English-language hymnody, several Reformed hymn poets, tunesmiths, and editors have been among the most influential ecumenically. Erik Routley, a Congregationalist pastor of England, was the English-language hymnologist of his generation. Fred Kaan and Brian Wren, both from the United Reformed Church of England, have each published several volumes of hymn texts, many of which are now commonly sung throughout the English-speaking world.[7] In the United States, leading hymn text writers include Jane Parker Huber, Joy Patterson, and Thomas Troeger, and leading hymn tune writers include Roy Hopp, Alfred Fedak, and K. Lee Scott.

One of the most important issues for much of new English-language

---

5. See the *Psalter Hymnal Handbook,* ed. Emily R. Brink and Bert Polman (Grand Rapids: CRC Publications, 1998); *The New Century Hymnal Companion: A Guide to the Hymns,* ed. Kristen L. Forman (Cleveland: Pilgrim Press, 1998); *The Presbyterian Hymnal Companion,* ed. LindaJo H. McKim (Louisville: Westminster/John Knox Press, 1993); for a Dutch example, see *Een compendium bij de gezangen uit het Liedboek voor de kerken* (Amsterdam, 1977).

6. The Book Service of the Hymn Society in the United States and Canada is a good guide to the available literature in this area. Updated lists of books, recordings, and videos are included in every issue of *The Hymn;* for more information about the society, check their Web site: www.bu.edu/sth/hymn.

7. For more on Routley, Kaan, and Wren, see Westermeyer, *With Tongues of Fire.*

hymnody has been the nature of gendered language for both the human community and for God. One of the most progressive examples of inclusive language is in a hymnal in the broad Reformed tradition, the *New Century Hymnal* of the United Church of Christ.

Cultural Diversity

For several generations, Eurocentric psalmody and hymnody were exported by missionaries around the world. Many churches in Africa, Asia, and Central and South America now have developed their own indigenous hymnody and are starting to export it in publications and recordings. This diversity has led to the sharing of musical and textual resources among cultural traditions. The resulting diverse landscape has enriched worship for Christians of all backgrounds and traditions.[8] Hymnary revisions in Ghana, for example, have moved from contents greatly influenced by missionaries from the United Kingdom to larger and more ecumenical collections like the *Asempa Hymnary*. Another hymnal revision in Ghana increased the number of songs from 498 to more than 800, and at the same time removed some missionary hymns that, for example, spoke of going to heathen lands. Often, however, tensions still exist between those who wish to honor the heritage that brought the gospel from one cultural setting to another and those who wish to develop indigenous hymnody. For example, the Dutch Reformed heritage in Indonesia of unison singing of Genevan psalms accompanied by organ is too narrow for those who would be more open to using Indonesian texts, rhythms, harmonies, and instruments in worship.

Most hymnals in the past decade have greatly expanded their global offerings. Significantly, this musical diversity is expressed not just within the Reformed tradition as a whole, or even in specific Reformed denominations, but within congregations. Even ethnically homogeneous congregations are starting to become musically multilingual, singing songs and hymns from a variety of cultures. There are Scottish congregations singing songs from Asia, Asian congregations singing praise choruses written in England or the United

8. See Mark P. Bangert, "A Thousand Tongues: Babel or Pentecost," *Currents in Theology and Mission* 21 (1994): 85-92; John Bell, ed., *Songs of the World Church,* 2 vols. (Chicago: GIA Publications, 1990, 1992); C. Michael Hawn, "Vox Populi: Developing Global Song in the Northern World," *The Hymn* 46, no. 3 (July 1995): 28-37; Nora Tubbs Tisdale, "Worshiping Locally in a Global Way: Guidelines and Resources for Worship Planners," *Reformed Liturgy and Music* 30, no. 3 (1996): 118-24; and Mark R. Francis, *Liturgy in a Multi-Cultural Community* (Collegeville, Minn.: The Liturgical Press, 1991).

States, African congregations singing European hymns, and North American congregations singing songs from Africa and South America. So, for example, *Psaumes, Cantiques et Textes pour le culte* includes the African-American spiritual "Amen," and *Jubilate — Ergänzende Liedersammlung zum reformierten Kirchengesangbuch* includes "He's Got the Whole World in His Hands" and "Swing Low, Sweet Chariot," as well as a German translation of British songwriter Graham Kendrick's "Shine, Jesus, Shine." Worship resources from the Community of Taizé in France have also spread around the world. Beginning during the dark days of World War II, that monastic community with Reformed roots quickly became very ecumenical and international. Today many thousands of people, especially young people, visit the community each year and take home with them Taize's distinctive style of meditative worship.

Part of the international movement of worship resources has been fueled by congregations all over the world re-appropriating musical elements from their indigenous cultures. For years Reformed congregations in places as different as Korea and Costa Rica typically sang music produced in Europe or North America that was brought by missionaries. Increasingly, these kinds of congregations are experimenting with music that is based on indigenous melodies, harmonies, and rhythms, and played on indigenous instruments.[9] Examples include the Indonesian hymnal *Kidung Jemaat* (Jakarta, 1992) and other materials being developed at the Asian Institute for Liturgy in Manila. Scotland's Iona community has been another influential source both in promoting indigenous songs and in making them available widely.

The Charismatic Movement

Worship in nearly every Christian tradition has been influenced by the charismatic movement and the worldwide growth of Pentecostalism.[10] A series of revivals in the late 1960s, which resembled the earlier Pentecostal outpourings at the beginning of the twentieth century, soon led to important changes in

9. The entry on music in *The Historical Dictionary of Reformed Churches* (Lanham, Md.: Scarecrow Press, 1999) observes, "New songs have been written by pastors such as Tiyo Soga of South Africa, Joseph Andrianaivoravelona of Madagascar, and Trevor Rodborne of India" (p. 208).

10. See John D. Witvliet, "The Blessing and Bane of the North American Megachurch: Implications for Twenty-First Century Congregational Song," based on an address to the international conference on hymnody in York, England, 1997, and published in the I.A.H. Bulletin 26 (July 1998), pp. 133-56, as well as in *The Hymn* 50, no. 1 (January 1999): 6-14, which includes a bibliography of recent resources on contemporary worship

weekly congregational worship in many traditions. Closely related to (and perhaps a second generation of) the charismatic movement is the Praise-and-Worship (P&W) movement. Emphases of "P&W" worship include viewing exuberant praise as the basic act of worship, the use of several simple Scripture songs or praise choruses, the use of a sequence of actions that leads the congregation from exuberant praise to contemplative worship, and the use of a team of lay worship leaders often called a "worship team." This movement has resulted in the publication of Scripture choruses in many denominational hymnals or — more prominently — in the printed and projected replacements to traditional hymnals. It has also generated an independent industry complete with published and recorded music, copyright licensing procedures, magazines, and conferences.

Significantly, this movement has emphasized the importance of "experiencing God" in worship, signaling a shift from a rational toward an affective approach to worship. For some time already, language has shifted from expressions of "I think" to "I feel." Increasingly, people are expressing hunger for an experience in worship of encountering God. They desire worship that is nourishing to their whole being — mind and spirit, body and soul. That hunger is growing in all communions at the end of the twentieth century.

The shift is most easily seen in the exchange of the longer psalm and hymn texts, packed with theological content, for the shorter choruses that engage the emotions more simply and directly. Indeed, the lack of content or even traditional grammatical structure or correct punctuation is not considered an impediment so long as the music engages the heart. The shift can also be seen in the increasing role for drama in worship and in greater openness to visual symbols. The pendulum in some churches has swung very far, so that praise of God "just for who he is" is removed from recalling and reflecting on the mighty deeds of God. That pendulum is still swinging, drawing in more and more churches. The shift from rational to affective modes of communication is also evident in sermons, but not necessarily in terms of sermon length. In fact, some congregations that have introduced many short and contemporary choruses have longer sermons than a generation ago, often very expository and highly structured. The change comes more in the way the sermons are designed and delivered to communicate. People want to feel directly addressed and personally challenged, and pastors will continue to be challenged by people's hunger to encounter God in the word preached as well as in the songs sung.

The influence of this movement is felt worldwide. Music from charismatic and Pentecostal sources has emerged out of Latin America, England, Australia, and the United States. There are Reformed congregations everywhere from Korea to South Africa whose musical leadership is provided not by an organ but by a praise team. Reformed congregations in many contexts have been working to distinguish the musical forms associated with the charismatic and Pentecostal traditions from the theological orientation of the tradition in an attempt to forge worship practices that combine Reformed order with charismatic ardor.[11]

Post–Vatican II Ecumenical Reforms

The ecumenical liturgical movement has left its mark on nearly every worship tradition.[12] This movement has been spurred on by study of historical patterns of Christian liturgy and ecumenical encounters, and is symbolized by the changes promoted in Vatican II. It has led Methodists and Presbyterians to sing their eucharistic prayers, evangelicals to observe Advent and Lent, and Roman Catholics and Episcopalians to nurture congregational participation in liturgical music and psalmody. Much of this movement has been sustained by rigorous historical and theological scholarship, in which Reformed scholars have been active participants.[13]

Both *Psaumes, Cantiques et Textes pour le Culte* (Lausanne, 1990) and *The Presbyterian Hymnal* (Louisville, 1990), for example, include music that functions as part of the historic structure of the Great Prayer of Thanksgiving used during the Lord's Supper. It is not uncommon for Reformed congregations to sing a setting of "Kyrie eleison" or "Sanctus," just like their Roman Catholic, Anglican, and Lutheran counterparts.[14] Other examples include music associ-

11. See "Reformed Order with Charismatic Ardor," an interview with Henry Wildeboer, in *Reformed Worship* 20 (June 1991): 13-19. See also David A. Miller, *Contemporary Worship in the Reformed Tradition: Practical Approaches for Congregations* (Columbia Theological Seminary Press, forthcoming), as well as the appreciative treatments of some aspects of contemporary music by Brian Wren in *Praying Twice: The Music and Words of Congregational Song* (Louisville: Westminster John Knox Press, 2000).

12. John R. Fenwick and Bryan Spinks, *Worship in Transition: The Liturgical Movement in the Twentieth Century* (New York: Continuum, 1995).

13. Dutch Reformed liturgiologist Wiebe Vos was a founder of the international organization Societas Liturgica, and longtime editor of its journal, *Studia Liturgica.* Today there are over twenty-five active Reformed liturgical scholars who are members of the North American Academy of Liturgy. Another active group of scholars and practitioners is involved in liturgical studies groups in South Africa (per information from Coenraad Burger of the University of Stellenbosch).

14. Bruno Bürki explains that this historical pattern for eucharistic prayers is now common in the Reformed tradition in France, Germany, Switzerland, Scotland, and the United States. See his "The Celebration of the Eucharist in *Common Order* (1994) and in the Conti-

ated with the ecumenical Lima liturgy, as well as other music used at World Council of Churches Assemblies.

This movement has also led to the growth in popularity of responsorial psalmody (described above), as well as a significant amount of music associated with the Christian year. Nearly every recently published hymnal includes a section of hymns for the Christian year.

Worship as Evangelism

In many Reformed churches worldwide, there has been a growing movement to consider public worship a primary vehicle for evangelism.[15] This broad movement has encouraged congregations both to make worship services more accessible to non-Christians and to plan events specifically to address the needs and concerns of non-Christians. One result of this movement has been worship designed for specific groups of people, an approach that generated a whole new vocabulary for liturgical events: seeker-sensitive worship, seeker-driven worship, boomer worship, buster worship, etc. Church growth theorists — of both mainline and evangelical stripes — invite us to purchase subscriptions to *Net Results* and buy books entitled *Entertainment Evangelism.* The key thing to notice here, for good or ill, is the prominence of economic metaphors, including concern for a congregation's market niche and the way that music can function as a tool to appeal to a wide spectrum of people. In some cases, congregations have done away with any liturgical practices — candles,

---

nental Reformed Liturgies," in *To Glorify God: Essays in Modern Reformed Liturgy,* ed. Bryan D. Spinks and Iain R. Torrance (Grand Rapids: Eerdmans, 1999).

15. This movement is described and analyzed in Daniel Benedict and Craig Kennet Miller, *Contemporary Worship for the 21st Century: Worship or Evangelism?* (Nashville: Discipleship Resources, 1995); Marva Dawn, *Reaching Out Without Dumbing Down* (Grand Rapids: Eerdmans, 1995); Frank Senn, *The Witness of the Worshiping Community: Liturgy and the Practice of Evangelism* (New York: Paulist Press, 1993); Frank Senn, "Worship Alive: An Analysis and Critique of 'Alternative Worship Services,'" *Worship* 69 (May 1995); Patrick R. Keifert, *Welcoming the Stranger: A Public Theology of Worship and Evangelism* (Minneapolis: Fortress Press, 1992); Sally Morgenthaler, *Worship Evangelism* (Grand Rapids: Zondervan, 1995); Lester Ruth, "The Use of Seeker Services: Models and Questions," *Reformed Liturgy and Music* 30, no. 2 (1996): 48-53; Lester Ruth, "*Lex Agendi, Lex Orandi:* Toward an Understanding of Seeker Services as a New Kind of Liturgy," *Worship* 70 (1996); G. A. Pritchard, *Willow Creek Seeker Services: Evaluating a New Way of Doing Church* (Grand Rapids: Baker Books, 1996); and Thomas H. Schattauer, "A Clamor for the Contemporary: The Present Challenge for Baptismal Identity and Liturgical Tradition in American Culture," *Cross Accent* 6 (July 1995): 3-11.

robes, organs, even choirs themselves — that are perceived as foreign to the experience of the "target audience" of potential churchgoers. The typical argument suggests that though these things may be good in themselves, they are a hindrance to the church's attempt to minister to those unaccustomed to "in-house" church practices. Churches are paying more attention to creating a welcoming atmosphere so visitors will not stumble over unnecessary barriers, whether of facilities, dress, or the service itself, including language, music, and level of formality. The tension between using a learned vocabulary for the language of faith and a language that makes few assumptions about biblical knowledge or understanding of theological concepts will continue to grow. Many Reformed churches worldwide are exploring aspects of the seeker service as developed by the Willow Creek Association.

Priesthood of All Believers

The concept of the priesthood of all believers is taking hold in a new way in worship. The trend is away from sole worship planning by the pastor and, increasingly, away from sole spoken leadership by the pastor.

One of the principles of the sixteenth-century Reformation was for people to offer their own worship to God, not to have their worship done for them. The recovery of congregational song helped to shape the dialogic structure of worship: the minister spoke the word of God and the people responded in sung prayers.

In contemporary culture, listening is losing its power to count as an activity. People who listen are considered passive; only the speaker is active. The Danish philosopher and theologian Søren Kierkegaard (1813-1855) challenged Christians to think about what really happens in worship by using the analogy of drama. In worship, who are the actors? Who is the audience? The all-too-typical response was that the worship leader — pastor, organist, perhaps a choir — were the actors, and that the congregation was the audience. No, said Kierkegaard, the entire congregation forms the group of actors, the worship leaders are prompters, and the audience is God. It is the congregation that performs its "service" of worship.[16]

Kierkegaard's analysis does not do justice to a Reformed understanding of worship in which God is very much an actor in the rhythm of liturgy. But it does point out that if people consider themselves passive recipients, acts of lis-

---

16. For Kierkegaard's text and a commentary, see Emily R. Brink, "Who's the Host," *Reformed Worship* 33 (Grand Rapids: CRC Publications, 1994), p. 2.

tening and even singing congregationally no longer have the power to suffice as means of performing their service of worship. When different members representing the congregation read Scripture, lead songs, and offer prayers, the sense of the entire body of believers offering their worship to the Lord is greatly strengthened.

During the sixteenth century it was the passive role of the congregation that prompted the recovery of congregational song. It therefore should come as no surprise that during the second half of the twentieth century, the reforms initiated by the Roman Catholic Church moved beyond the recovery of congregational song. The documents of Vatican II promote the "full, conscious, and active" participation of the people. In some ways, the reforms for congregational involvement initiated by the sixteenth-century reformers in opposition to Catholic practices have now been carried forward by the Roman Catholics. Worship is what the people do, not what the priest does for them. Lay leadership, male and female, is involved in every Mass in leading the singing, reading Scripture, and offering prayer; lay preaching is also increasing. In fact, more Scripture is typically read in a Roman Catholic Mass than in many Reformed churches; similarly, more care is usually given to the preparation of the readings. Like the organist in the Reformed tradition, the team of musicians is often to the side, barely visible. Only the song leader, or cantor, stands at the podium, someone who is also trained as to the subtle but crucial difference between singing for the congregation and enabling the congregation to sing.

Today in Reformed churches, increasing numbers of lay people are involved in worship planning and leadership. The leadership role of the pastor is not diminished but becomes more complex and behind the scenes. Many churches are consciously nurturing the gifts within the congregation for leadership in prayer and music, among old and young, male and female. The older practice in many North American churches of inviting "special music" guests from beyond the local congregation is continuing to decline.

"Full, conscious, and active" participation is growing in many Reformed congregations, not as a result of denominational directives, as in the Roman Catholic Church, but through the broader and deeper cultural influences and theological reflection at work in virtually all Christian communions, and especially from the "Praise & Worship" approach to worship leadership. In contrast to current Roman Catholic practice, however, too often in Reformed churches the musicians are front and center, and the danger of performing for the congregation rather than enabling them to sing is much greater.

Summary of Current Trends

In sum, the worship practices in the Reformed tradition as a whole during the last generation have been anything but stagnant. The remarkable thing about all this change is how diverse and often contradictory it seems. Some say that worship has become irrelevant; others say that it has become irreverent. Many of these trends are the result of rethinking the purposes and meaning of worship. That is, many changes have arisen out of not only musical but also theological and pastoral concerns. No single vantage point allows any of us to really understand how profound and far-reaching these changes are. We might say that rarely, if ever before, has the church been revising its worship in so many directions at once.

Before moving on to more prescriptive statements, consider some brief observations about some underlying dynamics at work in these changes.

Each of the changes described above has been reflected in and shaped by the economic demands of the publishing industry. The changes in music and worship cannot be understood apart from the economic considerations involved. Through the first two-thirds of the twentieth century, many churches relied on denominational publishing outlets to provide worship resources, including music. Now most congregations look for worship materials from a large range of publishing companies. This movement may be most pronounced in North America, but there is ample evidence that it is spreading to many parts of the Reformed family worldwide. (In the church, as elsewhere, North America seems to be exporting a free-market mentality.)

Hand in hand with the economic factor is new technology that makes dissemination of worship materials to churches easier than ever before. Congregations everywhere are free to expand their repertoire beyond their hymnals. Whereas in times past, congregations relied primarily on printed sources for their repertoire, now they have access to recordings, photocopying and projection systems, and most recently the Internet. Some churches no longer use hymnals but rely completely on projected songs. An entirely new copyright management industry began in the last fifteen years to protect the economic interests of song authors and composers as well as of publishing companies.

At one level, these changes are an ecumenical movement of sorts. Individual congregations now learn from and are enriched by the musical contributions of a wide range of movements and churches. On another level, churches are subject to the influence of an aggressively market-driven publishing industry. As in any other industry, publishers respond to the market. They look for music that will meet perceived needs in all kinds of churches, music that will sell. The market pressures of the church music publishing industry are significant. Such pressures include fierce competition, rising costs (especially rising paper costs), widespread copyright infringements, and a fickle market. Somehow publishers must balance financial realities with musical and liturgical ideals.

Fortunately, many publishers do consider themselves both business people and stewards of the divine gift of music, both entrepreneurs and artists. Many publishers, in addition to providing a broad-based catalogue of music for worship, have singled out particular market niches for special attention. Some publishers, even at financial risk, have promoted particular music genres — hymnody, responsorial psalmody, music for children's choirs, etc. — in order to promote some of the best changes in worship music over the past few decades.

These economic and technological influences are even more pronounced in recent years with the growth of the Internet. Though many Reformed congregations worldwide do not have access to the Internet, many others use it as a primary means for distributing or finding musical examples for use in the worship — particularly music in a popular, commercial style distributed by large megachurches and related publishing houses.

Significantly, most of these developments have arisen from sources *external,* or much broader than the Reformed tradition, resulting in less distinctiveness for liturgical music in the Reformed tradition. Throughout its early history, Reformed congregations sang exclusively music generated by Reformed poets and musicians. Vernacular, metrical Psalters were in-house publications. The result was a clear delineation between Reformed liturgical music and the music of other traditions. This clear delineation was reinforced by political realities; most European communities had some form of a state church, in which the Reformed church would be the only established church in a city, canton, region, or country.

With the onset of hymn-singing, the Reformed tradition began to share music ecumenically — a move that has grown and increased for the past two centuries. Indeed, music has been one of the most tangible dimensions of ecumenical sharing, especially in the twentieth century.

Reformed congregations have responded to the growth of externally produced music in a variety of ways. Some have responded by embracing these changes wholeheartedly — at times with a bit of embarrassment about the Reformed heritage. In many Reformed congregations, worship services include a wide range of music, but noticeably ignore or even shun music of the Genevan tradition. Others have ignored or rejected some of these movements because they are not perceived to square with the Reformed tradition. Some Korean Presbyterian congregations, for example, have been reluctant to use music with distinctly Korean qualities, preferring instead to use music of North American or European origins closely associated with historic patterns of Reformed worship.[17]

Certainly none of these developments is isolated from the others. Worship in a particular congregation will likely reflect the influence of several of them. In fact, when historians look at us some day, they may identify "eclecticism" as the central feature of much public worship. This diversity is handled in several different ways. Some manage by multiple services in different styles. Some manage by multiple styles in the same service.

Theological Prescriptions for Music in the Reformed Tradition

All of these changes and areas of growth and development demand discernment. How can pastors, musicians, and their congregations make good choices in the midst of all these disparate movements? Providentially, along with all these changes have come a number of prescriptive statements about the nature of music in the tradition. Reformed leaders throughout the world have engaged in significant thought about the nature of liturgical music. Their insights have much to teach the thoughtful musical leader in today's church. There are four basic assertions that are especially important in recent writings.

Sung Prayer

First, all liturgical music must support the actions of the assembly in Christian worship. Its goal, its *raison d'etre,* is to serve the purposes of the gathered church. If the main point of Christian worship is to engage in a series of personal, relational actions between the gathered community and its Creator (e.g., confessing sin, praising God, interceding for divine intervention), then good liturgical music enables these actions to be accomplished. Liturgical music at its best embodies the purposes of liturgical action and is meant to carry out, to perform, to enact, to make real the shared actions of the gathered ecclesial community. Good liturgical music not only excels in the criteria of its own genre, but also enables the actions of corporate worship. Liturgical music, in other words, must be functional; it does not serve as an end in itself.

17. See James Moonyun Kim, "Historical Observations of Korean Hymnbooks" (Th.M. Thesis, Calvin Theological Seminary, 1998).

Music must serve the purposes of Christian corporate worship. Though worship songs have value for personal devotional use, for humming on the streets, for serving as the basis for elaborate compositions for choir and organ, their primary purpose is to allow a gathered community to thank God, confess sin, intercede for divine intervention, and express hope for the coming kingdom of God. Music is one means of expression, like speech or dance, by which people accomplish certain actions. Therefore, one of the most important roles for those that plan and lead worship is to understand why a given song is sung when it is sung.

From the start, the Reformed tradition has emphasized that music does not exist for its own sake. In exists in order to express, or even enact, the church's response to God. Calvin's "Epistle to the Reader," which prefaces the Genevan Psalter, reveals his theological and liturgical thinking on the sacraments and psalm singing. There Calvin calls congregational singing a "public prayer with song" that "has existed since the first origin of the Church." Calvin believed congregational singing "has great force and vigor to move and inflame the hearts of men to invoke and praise God with a more vehement and ardent zeal." Therefore the melody must not be "light and frivolous, but have weight and majesty" appropriate to the text. The best texts for religious usage, though "we look far and wide and search on every hand," are the psalms of David. "We shall not find better songs nor songs better suited" to praise God than those which the Holy Spirit made and uttered through David. "When we sing them we may be certain that God puts the words in our mouths as if he himself sang in us to exalt his glory."[18]

These root metaphors suggest viewing each liturgical act as personal and relational. In this view, hymns of praise, sermons, sacramental celebrations, and corporate prayer do not exist for their own sake but for the larger purpose of enacting a personal, relational encounter. They are means by which God speaks and by which the gathered community responds. This point suggests distinguishing the primary personal and relational actions of liturgy from the means by which they are enacted.

This point is extended by Nicholas Wolterstorff's use of speech-action theory. Wolterstorff's distinction between speech-actions and the means by which those actions are carried out finds a ready analog in liturgy. Liturgy, like all speech-acts, has both primary constitutive actions and means by which those actions are carried out. The primary actions of liturgy are those that establish and enact the personal, relational, self-giving encounter between God and the

18. In Oliver Strunck, ed., *Source Readings in Music History* (New York: Norton, 1988), p. 346.

worshiping community. These actions include confessing, blessing, proclaiming, interceding, and listening. These actions, to use the technical language of
speech-action theory, are illocutionary actions. The means by which those actions are carried out are manifold, including the actions of speaking, singing,
gesturing, and dancing. This set of actions, to use the technical language of
speech-action theory, comprises locutionary actions. They function best when
they serve the primary purpose of the liturgy, when they serve to enact a personal relationship encounter between God and the worshiping community.

Wolterstorff explicates this thesis further in conjunction with a fully developed aesthetic theory that is oriented to human action. He argues "that
works of art are objects and instruments of action. They are all inextricably embedded in the fabric of human intention. They are objects and instruments of
action whereby we carry out our intentions with respect to the world, our fel-
lows, ourselves, and our gods."[19] Wolterstorff points to liturgy as one primary
locus where art functions to support and enable particular human actions:

> Liturgy without art is something the church has almost always avoided. . . .
> But unless distortion creeps in, art in the liturgy is at the service of the lit-
> urgy. . . . Good liturgical art is art that serves effectively the actions of the
> liturgy . . . that the actions . . . be performed with clarity . . . without tending
> to distract persons from the performance of the action . . . without undo
> awkwardness and difficulty.[20]

The particular actions that liturgical art and liturgical music are called to support are actions of personal encounter or relationship. As Wolterstorff suggests, "The Christian liturgy is a sequence of actions: confession, proclamation of forgiveness, praise, and so forth. And works of art — passages of music,
for example — can be more or less fitting to these distinct actions.[21]

A similar view is reflected in the work of Swiss Reformed theologian
Jean-Jacques von Allmen. Von Allmen argued that "liturgical beauty is a protest, not only against all aesthetic self-centeredness, but also against negli-
gence, coarseness, casualness, and in general against vulgar familiarity." The
key to understanding liturgical art is "the very fact that the cult is an encounter
between the Lord and the Church." Von Allmen argued that the arts and other
liturgical media should aim at the "ennobling of this encounter and a glorifica-

19. Nicholas Wolterstorff, *Art in Action: Toward a Christian Aesthetic* (Grand Rapids:
Eerdmans, 1980), p. 3. Wolterstorff develops this theory more comprehensively in his *Works
and Worlds of Art* (Oxford: Clarendon Press, 1980).
20. Wolterstorff, *Art in Action*, pp. 184-85.
21. Wolterstorff, *Art in Action*, p. 16.

tion of the Lord who deigns to be present."[22] Liturgical art is offered not for its own sake, but as a means for realizing and enacting personal encounter. The approach of Wolterstorff and von Allmen suggests a criterion by which liturgical actions, gestures, rites, and texts can be evaluated: *liturgical actions are serviceable to the extent that they make possible and enable the experience of liturgy as a personal, relational, self-giving action.* Music, art, spoken texts, and gestures are not primarily valuable in and of themselves, but are functional means through which personal encounter is enacted.

Common Song

Second, from the start the unique Reformed impulse in music has been the value placed on unison, vernacular, congregational singing. Music in the Reformed traditions is of and by the entire congregation. Music is a corporate activity in the Reformed churches. Common song is a profound witness to and experience of *koinonia*. As Presbyterian theologian and pastor Craig Erickson argues, "We sing because it is a way of praying together. It shows forth our unity in Christ."[23] Von Allmen commends hymn singing in part because it is "a necessarily communal form of participation," which "favour[s] mutual edification."[24] One implication of this priority is that musicians and others who lead in worship function best not as *performers for* but as *representatives of* the community. This ecclesial vision calls for pastoral liturgical music that enables all persons to participate, that identifies the congregation as the primary choir, and that militates against the vision of the liturgical musician as solo performer. North American Reformed theologian Donald Bruggink argues

22. Jean-Jacques von Allmen, *Worship: Its Theology and Practice* (New York: Oxford University Press, 1965), p. 103. This point is also made in a wide range of popular writings on liturgical music, art, and architecture. Dean Thompson, for example, argues that "art in the liturgical context is not an end in itself. It is instead a servant of our chief end, which is the praise and glory of God.... Art in the service of liturgy is a winsome vessel for our celebration and understanding of God's self-disclosure as the One who comes to us in Jesus Christ" ("Art in Service of Worship," *Reformed Liturgy and Music* 21 [Winter 1987]: 63). See also John M. Frame, *Worship in Spirit and Truth* (Phillipsburg, N.J.: P & R Pub., 1996), pp. 114, 124; Willis Jones, "Five Perspectives on Music in Reformed Worship," *Reformed Review* 48 (1994-1995): 124; and Amy Van Gunst, "Five Perspectives on Music in Reformed Worship," *Reformed Review* 48 (1994-1995): 130.

23. Craig Erickson, *Participating in Worship: History, Theory, and Practice* (Louisville: Westminster/John Knox Press, 1989), p. 96.

24. Von Allmen, *Worship,* p. 170, and also "The Communal Character of Public Worship in the Reformed Church," pp. 1-12.

against architectural forms of "choirolatry," and argues instead that the architecture of the worship space should reinforce the choir's primary role as that of assisting the congregation in singing.[25] Further, this vision calls for music that invites the weakest members to participate along with the strongest, the youngest along with the oldest, and for the musical repertoire of a given community to include songs from worshiping communities in other times and places. In this way, music serves as an expression of solidarity and fellowship of the whole body of Christ.

Theological Integrity

Third, music should have theological integrity. The Reformed tradition has long been known for its emphasis on rigorous theological discourse. That same rigor has frequently been applied to examinations of recent innovations in liturgical music, particularly in books and articles that are critical of a given movement or development.[26] That rigor has also been evidenced in recent works on the theology of worship, works that challenge Reformed worship leaders both to portray God in ways consistent with scriptural teaching and to lead congregations in actions that fit with biblically based, theologically sound patterns for worship.[27]

Once the link between theology and worship is exposed, dozens of unsettling questions arise: Why do churches with a high doctrine of Scripture often feature so little Scripture reading in Sunday worship? What about a church that confesses the power of the word of God and then demands that its preacher use either high-gloss rhetoric or emotional manipulation to talk people into the kingdom of God? What about a church that holds to a Chalcedonian Christology, but whose hymns praise only the human Jesus? What about the church that proclaims a gospel of grace and then implies that

---

25. Donald J. Bruggink and Carl H. Droppers, *Christ and Architecture: Building Presbyterian/Reformed Churches* (Grand Rapids: Eerdmans, 1965), pp. 387-415. See also W. D. Maxwell, *Concerning Worship* (London: Oxford University Press, 1948), p. 108; Howard Hageman, "Can Church Music Be Reformed?" *The Reformed Review* 14 (1960): 19-28; and von Allmen, who is "very suspicious" of choirs that function as a "vicarious representative" of the congregation. Instead he calls for choirs to "become the mainspring of liturgical life and worship," by training "the congregation to fulfill their specific ministry" (*Worship*, pp. 196, 197).

26. See, for example, "It May Be Refreshing, But Is It Reformed?," by D. G. Hart, in the *Calvin Theological Journal* 32, no. 2 (November 1997): 407-22.

27. See, for example, James Torrance, *Worship, Community, and the Triune God of Grace* (Downers Grove, Ill.: InterVarsity Press, 1996).

true worship demands that one conjure up certain emotions? What about the church that confesses that God is both transcendent and personal but only sings songs that emphasize one of these attributes? What about churches with a high view of creation that nervously dismiss the contributions of visual artists? It turns out that Pelagianism, Arianism, dualism, and nearly the whole constellation of classic Christian heresies have liturgical correlates.

Worship and Inculturation

Fourth, music should be responsive to and critical of its own cultural context. One of the many contributions of Vatican II to twentieth-century Christian worship was its insistence that liturgical expression reflect the particular cultural patterns of local congregations. This insistence calls to mind Calvin's admonition that "the upbuilding of the church ought to be variously accommodated to the customs of each nation and age." Since Vatican II, a small cadre of liturgists have attempted to be self-conscious about how this accommodation — variously termed contextualization, indigenization, or inculturation — can best take place. Spurred on in part by postmodern concern for cultural particularity, this project has been approached enthusiastically by many ecclesiastical traditions. The Roman Catholic Church has produced a much discussed "indigenous rite" for Zaire. Protestants have eagerly encouraged the development of indigenous musical repertoires in Africa, South America, and Southeast Asia. And many traditions are exploring the stunning variety of cultural expressions that contribute immeasurably to the liturgies of the world church.

One unique feature of developments in the past decade or so has been that churches of very different types have become self-conscious and intentional about the way their worship practices mirror culture. On the one hand, church growth strategists have used sophisticated polling techniques in order to adapt worship practices to local cultural patterns. On the other, in an entirely different conversation, Roman Catholic and Lutheran liturgists have been studying the process of "liturgical inculturation."[28] This study is interested in how the ancient pattern of Christian worship is expressed in particular cultural environments.

Responses to these efforts vary dramatically. Some lament the notion

28. Typical examples of this work include S. Anita Stauffer, ed., *Worship and Culture in Dialogue* (Geneva: Lutheran World Federation, 1994); Anscar Chupungo, *Liturgical Inculturation: Sacramentals, Religiosity, and Catechesis* (Collegeville, Minn.: The Liturgical Press, 1992). For an overview of this discussion, see John D. Witvliet, "Theological and Conceptual Models for Liturgy and Culture," *Liturgy Digest* 3, no. 2 (1996): 5-46.

that cultural patterns, including musical preferences, should set the agenda for the church. Others assume that this process is inevitable and welcome. A mediating position contends that any given cultural feature has both good and bad aspects, and that Christian worship should arise naturally out of its cultural environment, but also critiques aspects of the culture that run against central tenets of the Christian faith. Some lament the rise of musical genres that mimic popular culture. Others welcome the change. Many attempt to find the best musical representatives of a variety of genres.

Work in this area has reminded us that all liturgical action is culturally conditioned. No circumspect attempt at liturgical reform, liturgical inculturation, or cultural critique can glibly assume that liturgy is not shaped by its cultural environment. All liturgical participants are products of a particular culture, with its patterns of communication and symbolization. Liturgical traditions are themselves products of earlier cultural contexts. Often this is most noticeable in the liturgical use of nonverbal communication (gestures, movement, dance), in extemporaneous speech (the style, rhetoric, and pace of homilies and spoken introductions), in the environment for worship (including color, symbol, and spatial parameters), and in music (including rhythm, harmony, the degree of improvisation, and other stylistic features). It is impossible for any ecclesial community, any church authority, or any liturgical reform to escape the influence of culture.

Significantly, the recent move toward inculturation has both promoted and limited indigenous forms of expression. It has encouraged developing indigenous forms only insofar as they complement the historic structure of Christian worship. Generally speaking, it has argued that Christian worship should arise naturally out of its cultural environment but also critiques aspects of the culture that run against central tenets of the Christian faith. The extremes of either complete identification with or complete rejection of a given culture are to be avoided at all costs. Identification with culture, among other things, threatens the meaning of Christian symbols. In the words of Langdon Gilkey, "Religious symbols that lose a special judgment and a special promise over against culture also lose their life and reality."[29] The denial of cultural ele-

29. Langdon Gilkey, "Symbols, Meaning, and the Divine Presence," *Theological Studies* 35 (1974): 253. Thus, the key question is "How the Church Can Minister to the World without Losing Itself," the title of Gilkey's early but influential book on the subject (New York: Harper and Row, 1951). This point is developed with respect to current musical practices in the Reformed tradition in Horace T. Allen, "Present Stress and Current Problems: Music and the Reformed Churches," in *Sacred Sound and Social Change: Liturgical Music in Jewish and Christian Experience,* ed. Lawrence A. Hoffman and Janet R. Walton (Notre Dame: University of Notre Dame Press, 1992).

ments, in contrast, fundamentally calls into question the very humanness of liturgy itself. The largest challenge is to both remain faithful to the gospel of Jesus Christ and be appropriately responsive to the cultural context. The twin dangers that cultural engagement seeks to avoid are "cultural capitulation" on the one hand and "cultural irrelevancy"[30] on the other. In every instance of cultural engagement, there must be a "yes" and a "no," a being "in" but not "of," a continuity and a discontinuity with accepted cultural practices.[31] Or, to use H. Richard Niebuhr's categories, "Christ against culture" and "Christ of culture" are unnecessary and harmful extremes that should be avoided.

Liturgical action must reflect common elements in the Christian tradition through the unique expressions of a particular cultural context. There must be a judicious balance of particularization and universality. As Geoffrey Wainwright phrases it, "While indigenization is necessary on account of the relevance of the Christian gospel to *every* culture, a concomitant danger is that this particularization may be understood in such a way as to threaten the universal relevance of the gospel to *all* cultures."[32]

Contextualization should serve to highlight, not obscure, distinctive elements of the Christian faith. In her contribution to the Study Team on Worship and Culture of the Lutheran World Federation, S. Anita Stauffer identified four basic dualities that define judicious liturgical inculturation: Liturgy must be both "authentic and relevant," "Lutheran [that is, oriented to a particular tradition] and catholic," "local and global," "Christocentric and anthropocentric."[33] Each of these parameters attempts to bring together universal and particular dimensions of liturgical experience.

Again, particularity and universality need not be conceived as irreconcilable opposites, for particular cultural contexts are the milieu in which common ("universal") liturgical actions are given expression. In fact, the most successful attempts at liturgical inculturation may be those in which the particularities of a given culture enhance universal elements of Christian worship. Kenyan congregational processional and offertory dances and Korean participational intercessory prayers are not successful because they are appealing; they are successful precisely because they express and deepen common

30. Kenneth Smits, "Liturgical Reform in a Cultural Perspective," *Worship* 50 (1976): 98.

31. Gordon Lathrop, "A Contemporary Lutheran Approach to Worship and Culture: Sorting Out the Critical Principles," in *Worship and Culture in Dialogue,* pp. 142-46. This point also questions the uncritical adoption of Bevans' Anthropological Model.

32. Geoffrey Wainwright, *Doxology* (New York: Oxford University Press, 1980), p. 366.

33. S. Anita Stauffer, "Christian Worship: Toward Localization and Globalization," in *Worship and Culture in Dialogue,* pp. 11-15.

Christian liturgical actions through unique cultural forms. The "universal" is expressed most clearly through the "particular."

*   *   *

In sum, several Reformed leaders have poured significant energy into reasserting the proper nature of music in Reformed worship. In their work, four basic insights stand out:

1. Music should serve to enact the relationship we have with God in Christ.
2. Music should be common to all the people.
3. Music should have theological integrity.
4. Music should be "in, but not of" the culture of the people.

These insights provide a rudder for negotiating the current sea of change.

Revisiting the Question of the Use of Visual Art, Imagery, and Symbol in Reformed Places of Worship

Geraldine Wheeler

The Present Context

During the last thirty years there has been a growing expression of dissatisfaction with worship in the Reformed tradition, certainly as experienced in the United States and other English-speaking countries. James F. White has summarized Reformed worship as "the most cerebral of the Western traditions . . . prolix and verbose . . . overwhelmingly cerebral."[1] As people of the Reformed tradition address this and seek ways for the total person to be engaged in the worship of God, there is need to engage in dialogue with the reformers, Zwingli and especially Calvin, and the tradition that developed from their theology and practice. There is need also to take into account the major forms of communication in any given culture.

Generally, churches in the Reformed tradition have followed the recommendations of Zwingli and Calvin and removed, whitewashed, or omitted works of visual art from places of worship, except, quite often, for the retention of stained-glass windows. The simplification of the issues into the Questions and Answers 96, 97, and 98 in the *Heidelberg Catechism*[2] illustrates the

1. James F. White, *Protestant Worship Traditions in Transition* (Louisville: Westminster/ John Knox Press, 1989), pp. 58-78.

2. *Question 96:* What is God asking for in the second commandment?

   Answer: That we should not make any kind of picture of God nor worship Him in any other way than He has commanded in His Word.

   Question 97: Is one then to make no pictures at all?

   Answer: God can and ought not to be depicted in any way. But as for the creatures, though they may be depicted, yet God forbids us to make or to have pictures of them for the purpose of worshipping them or serving Him by means of them.

stance usually adopted. Many voices are now reconsidering the matter. The South African theologian John de Gruchy, discussing Calvin's approach to idolatry, suggests that the approach should be as follows:

> The alternative to the misuse of visible symbols is neither to reject them nor to consider them as ends in themselves, but to use them properly as a means to worship.[3]

The first consultation on worship organized by the International Reformed Center John Knox, held in 1994, decided that one of the issues needing more attention in future discussions was "What are the roles of images and symbols in Reformed worship?"[4] Are there appropriate ways of including a greater emphasis on the visual?

During the twentieth century there was an increasing swell of voices calling for a reevaluation of the question. Historians became increasingly interested in questions of the Reformation and art. Some scholars and artists were keen to demonstrate that many important visual artists had Reformed allegiance and that skilled Reformed artisans and architects contributed to the arts and crafts. Thinkers in the Neo-Calvinist stream developed philosophies of culture giving a significant place to visual art in the general culture. The Reformed tradition did not reject visual art, they argued, only the attempt to depict God and the placing of images in churches and using them in conjunction with worship.

New churches in non-Western cultures have begun to express their faith and worship in their own cultural forms including their own styles of architecture and visual arts. Many leaders of worship in the West are now concerned to communicate with people whose education and daily news-gathering includes extensive pictorial as well as verbal communication. In addition, artists across the globe, tired of visually uninspiring places of worship, are persuading min-

---

> *Question 98:* But may not pictures be tolerated in the churches as the lay people's books?
>
> *Answer:* No. For we ought not to be wiser than God who does not want His Christian people to be instructed by means of dumb idols, but by the living preaching of His Word.

Quoted from Michael Owen, ed., *Witnesses of the Faith: Historic Documents of the Uniting Church in Australia* (Melbourne: Uniting Church Press, 1984), p. 103.

3. John W. de Gruchy, *Liberating Reformed Theology: A South African Contribution to an Ecumenical Debate* (Grand Rapids: Eerdmans, 1991), pp. 101-2.

4. *The Renewal of Worship in the Reformed Churches: Report of the Consultation on "The Place and Renewal of Worship in the Reformed Churches,"* International Reformed Center John Knox, June 30–July 6, 1994, in *Reformed Liturgy & Music,* Special Issue, 1995, p. 12.

isters to allow them to transform the places of worship. Sometimes the minister is also the artist. Some churches in the Reformed tradition happily embrace worship in conjunction with the visual arts, with art contributing to the setting and used in conjunction with the teaching and preaching.

The Reformed tradition is one in which theological integrity is valued across the totality of worship, belief, and the practice of the faith. A mark of this tradition is to grapple with the theological issues of its practice, and this needs to be done in relation to the questions of images and symbolism within the cultural contexts in which the church worships God. This chapter offers a dialogue with Calvin on the question of images and visual art in relation to the worship of the church. Then it will suggest areas for theological reflection, dialogue, and practice for theologians, philosophers in the field of aesthetics, liturgists, and artists within and beyond the Reformed tradition.

John Calvin on Visual Art in General and Images in Churches in Particular

> And yet I am not gripped by the superstition of thinking absolutely no images permissible. But because sculpture and painting are gifts of God, I seek a pure and legitimate use of each, lest those things which the Lord has conferred upon us for his glory and our good be not only polluted by perverse misuse but also turned to our destruction.... [O]nly those things are to be sculpted or painted which the eyes are capable of seeing.... [W]ithin this class some are histories and events, some are images and forms of bodies without any depicting of past events.[5]

John Calvin was adamant that it was unlawful to use a visual representational form for God, but he was not opposed to all visual art. The passage above details his view of what was permissible for the visual artist. Following this passage, however, he asked whether it was expedient for this permissible visual art to be used in the church, and he presented his several reasons for believing it to be inappropriate in the light of the human propensity toward idolatry. The home and public places, not churches, were suitable for placing works of art of the permissible sort, whether histories or decorative images. The other and major principle for Calvin in deciding about the place of art in worship was whether a particular aspect was commanded by Jesus and conveyed through Scripture.

5. John Calvin, *Institutes of the Christian Religion,* ed. John T. McNeill, trans. Ford Lewis Battles (Philadelphia: Westminster Press, 1960 [1559]), p. 112 (1.11.12).

The Development of Calvin's Thought in Book 1,
Chapters 1-12, of *Institutes of the Christian Religion*

The passage quoted above expresses Calvin's thoughts about visual art reached by the 1543 edition of the *Institutes* and retained in the final edition of 1559/1560. He begins the *Institutes* by discussing the knowledge of God the Creator, dealing with the interrelated knowledge of God and of self, granted by God's willing self-disclosure accommodated to the human ability to receive it (ch. 1). Faith is required for this knowledge of God in its fullness (ch. 2). Calvin states his conviction that there is a natural instinct or awareness of divinity, which has not been extinguished by the fall, and this includes the ability to distinguish between good and evil (ch. 3).

A major characteristic of Calvin's thought can be noted from this point onward when he gives his assessment of the human condition, the human falling away from God's original purposes. Here he speaks of superstition, deliberate turning from God, and making God after our own whims and hypocrisy. It is a way of understanding that moves back and forth, delineating God's gracious and glorious self-giving and then pointing to the human tendency of rejection of God and self-assertion apart from God (ch. 4).

Chapter 5, in sections 1-10, deals with God's self-disclosure in the creation and God's wisdom in the continuing rule of creation. In this chapter there are many references to the act of looking, the physical use of the eyes, in order to have knowledge of creation and therefore of its Creator. Calvin is not unaware of the parallels in gazing at a painting and regarding the visible creation. "We must therefore admit in God's individual works — but especially in them as a whole — that God's powers are actually represented as in a painting. Thereby the whole of mankind is invited and attracted to recognition of him, and from this to true and complete happiness."[6] The metaphor for God, unnamed by Calvin here, is that of artist. The viewer recognizes that there is, behind what is viewed, an artist with great creativity and skill to make, and make beautiful, what that artist (God) has chosen to create.

The human failure, Calvin argues, is the frequent inability to move from seeing the creation to giving praise and glory to its Creator. Instead, people tend to remain focused solely upon the creation as an end in itself. In this section is found Cavlin's polemic against the philosophers, particularly those of the ancient classical world, who exemplified that tendency.

"Knowledge of God" as used by Calvin has a breadth of meaning that is

---

6. Calvin, *Institues,* p. 63.

summarized by the translator as, in today's terminology, "existential apprehension."[7]

> [W]e are called to a knowledge of God: not that knowledge which, content with empty speculation, merely flits into the brain, but that which will be sound and fruitful if we duly perceive it, and if it takes root in the heart. For the Lord manifests himself by his powers, the force of which we must feel within ourselves and the benefits of which we enjoy. We must therefore be much more profoundly affected by this knowledge than if we were to imagine a God of whom no perception came through to us. Consequently, we know the most perfect way of seeking God, and the most suitable order, is not for us to attempt with bold curiosity to penetrate to the investigation of his essence, which we ought more to adore than meticulously to search out, but for us to contemplate him in his works whereby he renders himself near and familiar to us, and in some manner communicates himself to us.[8]

Calvin does not want to convey an idea of knowledge of God and self that is "arid intellectualism" or "overwhelmingly cerebral," I believe, but knowledge through which God is personally communicated and known.

Because of the perpetual human turning away from God, creation — the "mirror"[9] in which God is to be known, the "insignia whereby he shows his glory to us,"[10] and the "evidences . . . that declare his wonderful wisdom"[11] — is insufficient for people to come to this knowledge of God. Therefore, Scripture as a clearer communication is required. ("[I]t is needful that another and better help be added to direct us aright to the very Creator of the universe.")[12] Calvin speaks of two sorts of knowledge of God in the Scriptures, an intimate knowledge of God that distinguished the Hebrews from unbelievers and knowledge that leads to redemption in the person of Christ.[13] He deals with only the former in this section (ch. 6). Creation is described as mute,[14] and so Scripture as the word of God can communicate to us what the revelation in

---

7. Calvin, *Institutes,* footnote 1, pp. 35-36. See also the major study, E. A. Dowey, *The Knowledge of God in Calvin's Thought,* 3rd ed. (Grand Rapids: Eerdmans, 1994).

8. Calvin, *Institutes,* pp. 61-62.

9. Calvin, *Institutes,* pp. 52, 55.

10. Calvin, *Institutes,* p. 52.

11. Calvin, *Institutes,* p. 53.

12. Calvin, *Institutes,* p. 69.

13. Calvin, *Institutes,* p. 71.

14. Calvin may well be reflecting Psalm 19:3-4, where the mute creation still communicates the glory of God.

creation cannot. The visual world and all that can be known of God through creation need to be augmented by verbal communication and finally by the incarnation. All this becomes revelatory only to faith. The visual is not dismissed, and this may suggest for us today that while word and sacrament are at the heart of worship, the aesthetics of the place of worship are also important.

Chapter 7 speaks of the role and witness of the Holy Spirit in the conveying and receiving of this knowledge of God. In Chapter 8 there is a discussion of the priority of Scripture over the church and its post-scriptural tradition. Chapter 9 engages in the debate with the radical reformers whom Calvin sees as divorcing the work of the Spirit from Scripture. In chapter 10 he argues that the scriptural doctrine of God the Creator corroborates that knowledge of God whose "imprint shines"[15] in and through the works of creation.

Calvin is proposing that knowledge of God, recognized in faith, derives from Christ, from the Scriptures, and from the observation of creation. All this knowledge for the Christian presupposes faith, so this is not a sequential process with a natural "theology" as a preliminary to faith knowledge of God.

The focus for this chapter of mine is chapter 11 of the *Institutes*, in which Calvin critiques the church culture against which the reformers were protesting. The protest was over several matters, including images. Recent historical scholarship has drawn attention to what John Dillenberger describes as "[t]he intertwined foci of relics, indulgences and images, related to the increasing emphasis on Mary and the saints."[16] Added to this was the Catholic church's theology of the sacraments, particularly the Eucharist,[17] and liturgical rituals and practices. For the gathered worshipers, the *sight* of the elevation of the host was the climax of the liturgy and there was very infrequent reception. While much of the discussion in chapter 11 of the *Institutes* centers on images, there are these other aspects of the whole approach to the worship of the church about which Calvin had grave concern, and which are part of the complex background to his writing here.

The dominant theme of chapter 11, with its sixteen sections, is that it is unlawful to attribute a visible form to God. God does not have a form and Scripture forbids every pictorial representation of God. To do this is idolatry. The arguments that ensue, however, are also against the use of any images, particularly of the saints, in the churches because this is seen to lead to idola-

15. Calvin, *Institutes*, p. 98.

16. John Dillenberger, *Images and Relics: Theological Perceptions and Visual Images in Sixteenth-Century Europe* (New York: Oxford University Press, 1999), p. 5.

17. De Gruchy, *Liberating Reformed Theology*, p. 102, argues that Calvin's attack on idolatry was most fundamentally aimed at the doctrine of transubstantiation associated with the Roman Mass.

try. Images, as Calvin has known them in the Roman church, were so clearly linked with idolatry for him that the issues are all treated as part of this same question. The Heidelberg Catechism, Question 98, also treats images and idols as synonymous. The two serious difficulties that emerge for Calvin about idolatry — regardless of whether the idol is connected with part of creation (e.g., the sun or moon) or something made by human hands — are that the glory that is God's alone is attributed to another, and that human beings are trying to bring God close and under their control.

In the third section Calvin recognizes that from time to time Scripture speaks of God as giving definite, visible signs of his presence. There was the cloud, smoke, and flame (Deut. 4:11), the experience of Moses (Exod. 33:11), and the Holy Spirit as a dove (Matt. 3:16). All of these are fleeting and just for the particular occasion, he suggests. God's appearance as a man or messenger is explained as the prelude to the future revelation in Christ, and, against those who try to defend images of God and the saints with the example of the cherubim, Calvin reminds the reader that the outspread wings of the cherubim in Exodus 25:17-21 were designed so as to hide, not reveal, God's glory. This point is also made about Isaiah's vision of the seraphim. Calvin read Scripture meticulously and so was honest enough to recognize those commands that led to the making of images. But what he numbered as the second commandment, following Jewish precedence, is the governing principle. He refers to the "absurdity" of the bronze snake on the pole as a cure for snake bite in the desert, saying that it was more "suited to render the grace of God conspicuous than as if there had been anything natural in the remedy."[18] As a prefiguring of the cross (John 3:14) he sees it as "a symbol of spiritual grace."[19] Yet, one suspects, it is with delight that Calvin finds reference to the later need to destroy it, when it had become an idol. That only confirmed his point.[20]

As Calvin debates here with those who argue for images, he takes the Ten Commandments as binding, while relegating commands relating to the building of the mercy seat and the whole tabernacle as belonging to the "antiquated tutelage of the law."[21] It would appear that when it comes to his evaluation of human-made visual works, made at God's command, he evaluates them as never able to reveal God directly, as only negatively suggesting God's invisibility and ineffability. From our present perspective it is questionable whether

18. John Calvin, *Harmony of the Four Last Books of the Pentateuch*, vol. 4, trans. Charles Bingham (Edinburgh, 1853), p. 155.

19. Calvin, *Harmony of the Four Last Books*, p. 156.

20. Calvin, *Harmony of the Four Last Books*, p. 157.

21. Calvin, *Institutes*, pp. 102-3.

language reveals as clearly as Calvin supposes. The limitations of language also can suggest God's mystery, and we recognize a need for signs that point to the mystery rather than reveal clearly that which is beyond human grasp.

By the conclusion of section 4, it is clear that Calvin is equating both the images in the Western church and the icons of the Eastern church (three- and two-dimensional works) with idols. Sections 5-7 are his refutation of the often-quoted argument for images, first used by Pope Gregory the Great, that images are the books of the uneducated. He presents the arguments against idols as referring to all images and pictures from which the uneducated are taught (section 5). In section 6, he cites the Council of Elvira (ca. 305), which forbid "that what is reverenced or adored be depicted on the walls."[22] Section 7 carries comments about the immodesty and moral inappropriateness of some pictures of the saints. The teaching of the church should be sufficiently achieved through the preaching of God's word and the two sacraments, and if the church had properly carried out its work of teaching and worship that would have obviated the need for images.

Calvin works with the assumption that the visual cannot name God as Scripture can and that the saving knowledge of God in Christ can be conveyed only verbally. People infer knowledge of God from the visible creation just as knowledge of an artist or craft worker can be drawn from his or her work, but the direct communication of the Creator is verbal and then consummately in Christ, to whom the words of the New Testament witness. He does not seriously consider a possible partnership between words and images, though conceding that historical subjects for paintings may have some teaching value.

The next topic is the path to idolatry. Writing of the origin of idols, Calvin briefly considers that idolatry originated from conferring honor on the dead, but he concludes that it is characteristic of human beings to be uneasy "until [they] have obtained some figment like [themselves] in which [they] may fondly find solace as in an image of God."[23] He speaks of idols as symbols in which people believed God appeared before their bodily eyes. Idols are human ways of trying to make God present and under human control.

Once people believe that they look upon God in images, they worship God in those images, Calvin argues (section 9). They then believe that divine power resides in the image. Prostration in veneration is superstition. Calvin dismisses the explanation that it is not the image that is worshiped but that God is worshiped through the image and that a distinction is kept in the mind of the worshiper. Sections 10 and 11 critique the practice of the church, pil-

22. Calvin, *Institutes*, p. 106. See also p. 20, footnote 21.
23. Calvin, *Institutes*, p. 108.

grimages to some images, and the distinction argued between "veneration" or "service" and "worship." The critique of this semantic distinction is continued later in chapter 12. Others had claimed that there was a distinction between *dulia,* the respectful service of a slave, and *latria,* the worship due to a deity, but Calvin argues that the New Testament usage makes no such distinction. Kneeling and bowing constitute worship and should not be directed toward images.

This development of thought then provides the context for the passage about the permissible use of painting and sculpture. "And yet I am not gripped by the superstition of thinking absolutely no images permissible."[24]

Permissible Visual Art (*Institutes* 1.11.12)

Calvin describes the absolute prohibition of images as superstitious. Why? To make such a prohibition would surely imply a belief that divine or other power did inhabit images, and that only the total absence of images would protect people from that influence and danger. Calvin's strict ontological distinction between the divine and all created matter means that matter, the whole creation, is secular and not divine. This must hold true for every image made or drawn. The difficulty is in the human misunderstanding that makes an identification of the divine with matter, linking the power of God with the image itself and thus tarnishing the glory of God. The problem lies, on one hand, with the subject matter, when people believe they can depict the invisible God, and, on the other, when images of things that can be seen, such as saints (who were once seen), become objects of veneration. Any confusion of God with creation is at the heart of idolatry.

Calvin understands painting and sculpture to be exactly representational. The artist uses the two- or three-dimensional medium to make a visual representation recognizable from the original model. To do this for the invisible God is an absolute impossibility. The conclusion is therefore that visual art can convey nothing about God.

Calvin is also compelled by his understanding of God as creator to recognize the abilities of artists as gifts from God. "Sculpture and painting are gifts of God," he writes.[25] Does this have the second meaning that the works themselves can be considered gifts of God to others? These abilities and works are for the glory of God and human good. Permissible visual art may have as its

24. Calvin, *Institutes,* p. 112.
25. Calvin, *Institutes,* p. 112.

content things that can be seen, either historical events that have some didactic purpose or objects, persons, and scenes without narrative context, which are judged as merely decorative and for the pleasure of looking. The artist is to execute work to the glory of God. Typically, Calvin's thought moves to the possible misuse of this gift, and he reiterates his purpose to seek a pure and legitimate use.

Calvin's definition of historical subject matter can include biblical scenes. Protestant artists in the following century — perhaps most notably Rembrandt — would often paint biblical scenes either for patrons or for their own interest. But having made this statement about permissible subject matter for visual art, and conceding that some "historical" work may have teaching value, Calvin proceeds to ask not whether it is lawful, but whether it is expedient to place even such works in the church (section 13).

In the remaining four sections of the chapter Calvin produces arguments as to why it is not expedient to place any works of visual art in the church, all of which revolve around the idea that it is not expedient, wise, or useful to place images in the churches because of the dangers of idolatry.

First, he states his conviction that for the first five hundred years of the Christian church there were no images in places of worship. This, of course, can be challenged both historically and archaeologically. It is now known that Christians were using some images in places of worship in the third century. Such knowledge of new historical and archaeological material need not have altered Calvin's position, of course, except to reduce by three hundred years the period of time when, in his view, the church remained pure and free from images that were idolatrous.

Second, even if images were not dangerous in the church, Calvin states his preference for images that are

> those living and symbolic ones which the Lord has consecrated by his Word. I mean Baptism and the Lord's Supper, together with other rites by which our eyes must be too intensely gripped and too sharply affected to seek other images forged by human ingenuity.[26]

Elsewhere he would challenge ways of celebrating the sacraments that he linked with superstition and idolatry. He does not elaborate here on the other rites. As with the snake on the pole, even these dominical sacraments have not escaped misuse, but he is not at liberty to recommend that they be discontinued because they have been specifically commanded. The rituals of celebra-

---

26. Calvin, *Institutes*, pp. 113-14.

tion can, however, be greatly simplified. His tendency is to argue that unless something is required by Scripture — which, in the case of worship, means the Scripture of the New Testament — it is unnecessary.

The third argument relates to church decisions, directives that Calvin finds abhorrent. He discusses the Second Council of Nicea in 787, which decreed that the church should use and reverence images.[27] He had become aware of the *Libri Carolini,* prepared at Charlemagne's direction, which presented both supporting and opposing arguments at the council. Calvin writes contemptuously of the misuse of scriptural texts in support of images and in horror at those who would compel the use of images. The final thoughts of this section make for the first time explicit reference to an image of Christ and devotional behavior toward it:

> [A] clause is added: let those who, having an image of Christ, offer sacrifice to it, rejoice and exult. Where now is the distinction between latria and dulia. . . ? For the Council accords, without exception, as much to images as to the living God.[28]

This criticism is leveled at both the image and the accompanying devotional behavior. It clinches the argument that images attract the behavior of worship and that it is therefore not expedient to place them in churches. It is not clear to this point whether Calvin would consider any images of Christ to be idolatrous in themselves. His acceptance of historical subjects should allow works that depict the "historical" Jesus.

Chapter 12 is the final one to deal with the matter of idolatry before Calvin moves on to the doctrine of the Trinity. In seeking to define how God is to be distinguished from idols, Calvin reiterates "that nothing belonging to [God's] divinity is to be transferred to another."[29] His perception is that both Jews, as depicted by the prophets and other Old Testament writers, and the church have interposed series of lesser gods between humanity and God, and that the saints were "elevated into co-partnership with God, to be honoured, and also invoked and praised in his stead."[30] He dismisses as inappropriate use of language the distinction between *latria* and *dulia,* arguing that the words and the concepts are not distinct and different. He argues that honoring images is dishonoring God and critiques reverencing behavior, such as kneeling

27. Calvin, *Institutes,* p. 114, footnote 27. The editor points out that while bowing in veneration is enjoined, actual worship *(latria)* is forbidden. Calvin did not accept this distinction.
28. Calvin, *Institutes,* p. 116.
29. Calvin, *Institutes,* p. 117.
30. Calvin, *Institutes,* p. 118.

and bowing, and a way of thinking that makes verbal distinctions in order to argue that reverencing is not the same as worshiping, which is fitting for God alone.

When explanation is required for biblical anthropomorphisms — references to God's mouth, ears, hands, and feet — Calvin draws upon the idea of God's condescension.

> For who even of slight intelligence does not understand that, as nurses commonly do with infants, God is wont in a measure to "lisp" in speaking to us? Thus such forms of speaking do not so much express clearly what God is like as accommodate the knowledge of him to our slight capacity.[31]

While Calvin has no difficulty in taking such a nonliteral approach to verbal communication, in the church context of the time he would find a parallel approach to visual communication impossible. Images were not seen as forms of communication or as metaphorical in parallel to metaphorical language, I suggest, but as attempts at literal re-presentation, literal presence within matter, with associated powers.

Questions and Insights at the Beginning of the Twenty-First Century

In the dialogue with Calvin and the tradition there are now questions that arise from Reformed churches in very different contexts as they seek to worship authentically using their own cultural forms. Those living in cultures that place great importance upon communication by visual means will read Calvin with interest for his understanding, often neglected, of the place of the visual in self-understanding. Questions are asked afresh because of the changes in contexts, over these five centuries and on different continents, which lead to a reevaluation of the issues.

The Act of Seeing and Worship

The importance of the visual and the part played by the physical act of seeing does not escape Calvin in developing his understanding of the knowledge of ourselves (and creation) and knowledge of God through the creation. It is a

31. Calvin, *Institutes,* p. 121.

given in the way human beings have been created. Calvin's own gazing at the works of creation lies behind what he writes about the viewing of the creation; he understands it to communicate something of its Creator and so to draw the viewer into the praise and worship of the Creator. The role for creation is thus as witness to the existence of the One who created it, the powers of that Creator, and the character of the One whose good purposes were to bring it all into existence as good, ordered, and beautiful. He describes creation as a theater in which human beings may behold God's glory.[32]

In contemporary society, which seeks to recognize the wholeness of the human person and to realize a balance between different facets of human living and communication, a new perception of human wholeness in the relationship with God is required. This includes an openness to what is seen. We find Calvin in some ways to be aware of this.

Beholding God's glory leads to the inward response of praise to God. A Reformed view of worship is that it is essentially of the spirit, the work of the Spirit of God with the spirit of the people of God through the mediation of Christ. The inward response is important, but there are other dimensions. The world is not bypassed in Calvin's view of worship, but provides vehicles for the means of grace God has chosen to use. Scripture, with its sacraments using actions with water, bread, and wine, provides these means, understood to function so as to maintain the ontological distinction between divine and creation. A response in words and song, prayer and music, has also usually been part of worship.

Many people of the Reformed tradition are now seeking to offer a response to God that makes an extended use of all human faculties. Included in this view is the proposal that the artist can draw upon the creation to make works that touch people inwardly and then lead them to offer worship to God. There is here a question of God's freedom to meet people in ways other than those specifically written about in New Testament times.

Artistic Talent and Mental Images: God-Given Abilities and Faculties

As already noted, abilities for engaging in the visual arts are also gifts of God in creation, granted to and developed in certain people in particular, and to be used rightly for God's glory. The Reformed tradition is not one in which there is a thoroughgoing ascetic denial of the world. God's creation is good; the ma-

---

32. Calvin, *Institutes,* p. 61; and many other references cited in footnote 27.

terial world is thus not evil, and visual artists generally work with products made from the God-given earth, employing eye, mind, and hand as they work.

In addition, humans (or at least the majority of humans, those with the ability to see) were given the ability to store images in the mind. Some have also the gift of presenting those images in ways that make them accessible to others, either in visual form or by verbal description. The term "imagination" may be used for this with its positive meaning, not its sometimes pejorative meaning of constructing that which is not true or fabricating lies. Imagination, then, is also to be understood as a God-given faculty that the artist uses. The use of the imagination became a matter of serious debate in the seventeenth and eighteenth centuries for people in the Reformed tradition, or at least those in its Puritan wing. The tension for the Puritan Christian revolved around the question, "If mental images are natural products of the imagination, how can a mental image of Christ be condemned as idolatrous?"[33] In addition, why could not the visual artist express this in image when the speaker or writer is free to use words for the same expression?

The created world itself gives glory to God by being itself and so offering praise. This notion finds its basis in many of the psalms, and Calvin's sense of the small creatures offering praise is in keeping with it.[34] The human person of faith, recognizing creation's mute acts of praise, joins his or her praise with that of creation and all the small creatures. Calvin is himself doing this as he writes these ideas and reflects on his own praise of God as he beholds creation. Is the visual artist prohibited from doing this through art? Or only from doing it through art placed in a church? The fear of idolatry prevented Calvin from recognizing that people, viewing images that point to God as creator and redeemer, may respond as to the creation itself with the praise of God. He emphasized the difference between words and images, fearing the power of images to draw people into idolatry, without perceiving parallels in their function and a complementarity in their use for human understanding.

The Ontological Distinction between Creator and Creation

The firm distinction Calvin makes ontologically between the divine and creation must mean that matter and God do not co-mingle. Therefore, there should be no confusion about worshiping the created world instead of God.

---

33. John K. La Shell, "Imagination and Idol: A Puritan Tension," *Westminster Theological Journal* 49 (1987): 305.

34. Calvin, *Institutes*, p. 69, text and also footnote 44.

Idolatry, belief that God is the world (or part of the world) or that part of the world is worshiped as God, arises from human misunderstanding or from a misguided desire to control and manipulate God. Images in any medium cannot be divine. In theory this gives freedom for image-making provided the images are not worshiped or believed to be divine.

Changed Understanding of Images and Visual Art

Calvin's objection to images in churches centered on the fact that people offered devotion to them and treated them as somehow containing or being channels for the effective power of God. They became idols. Images today, however, are generally regarded quite differently.[35] Representational visual art with the employment of realistic perspective is only one of many options for artists, and the understanding of the relationship between the image and the subject has changed. Artists are interested in many things — in conveying message and meaning, for example, and in drawing attention to the vast array of texture, color, shape, and other qualities in the material they use. With information technology, many of the viewed images are virtual, fleeting, not able to be permanently housed and regularly viewed. The church has images of many different sorts from which to draw to enhance its worship.

The Use of the Scriptures

Calvin gave to the Scriptures a central and determining role on all matters of faith and worship. While the Bible still has a central place in the worship of churches of the Reformed tradition, there is a greater awareness of the diversity in the biblical witness. The New Testament church and its worship was not uniform, and while the Bible gives essential insights on worship, there is no to-

---

35. Jérôme Cottin, *Le Regard et la Parole* (Geneva: Labor et Fides, 1994), part 1. Unfortunately I was able to read this study, not yet available in English translation, only after having concluded this chapter. I believe that it succeeds in addressing positively the main theological issues at stake. Drawing upon modern theories of language, sign, and symbol, Cottin shows in the first part how image and word are inextricably related. The second part is theological, both biblical and systematic, concluding that while God's relationship with the image is not direct, images stand as complementary to language in the whole hermeneutical process in which the Holy Spirit interprets the word to us. The third section is historical, looking at the understanding of the image rejected by the reformers and the openings in the thought of the reformers, particularly Luther and Calvin, that invite later development.

tal prescription for it. Calvin's view that what was done in worship must have biblical warrant did not allow for all questions to be addressed properly.

The biblical texts that became the governing ones for Calvin in relation to idolatry and to the placing of images in the church were Exodus 20:4-6 and its counterpart in Deuteronomy. Calvin was a very careful exegete but, of course, a person of his time. His application of this commandment to the church situation he knew led to his equating image, when in a church, with idol. Today, exegetes are more likely to recognize the diversity of Scripture rather than choosing only one determining principle, as Calvin did with the second commandment. The interpretation of Scripture in the present context will not always provide the same conclusions reached by Calvin, either with regard to meaning or with regard to application.

From the New Testament, where the cultural milieu included the worship practices of Israel, the discussion of John 4, between Jesus and the woman at the well, is seen as a key passage. John 4:23 is central, stating that true worshipers will worship the Father in spirit and in truth. Jesus is shown both as fulfiller of the law and as transcending the law. Worship in spirit for Calvin did not mean a worship that abolished either the Bible (its exposition and its psalms of praise) or the sacraments of baptism and the Lord's Supper, which are recorded as required by Jesus. The inwardness of worship, not located in the intellect alone, was also related to outward components, even though much of the ritual of the church was removed.

Perhaps Calvin's vigilance against idolatry, as he saw it in the practices of the Roman church, and other issues of that contemporary church debate, precluded fuller attention being given to these considerations of human experience of God and God's self-accommodation into means of communication appropriate to human capacities. Later philosophical developments, which emphasized the human being as a thinking being, no doubt influenced the Reformed tradition in further emphasizing words and thinking in worship to the detriment of other human faculties.

The Church and Cultural Context of the Reformers

Historical studies placing the reformers in their setting — sixteenth-century northern Europe and the inherited practices of church life — help us to be aware of the part played by context.

It may be argued that the faculty of sight had come so to dominate the worship life of Christians of western Europe (and perhaps of much of eastern Christendom as well), that the Reformation was a movement to recall the vital importance of the word, in Scripture and in Christ, the Word made flesh. Philip Butin points to several new emphases that began to influence culture and scholars at the turn of the sixteenth century. These were the influence of humanism, leading to a fresh valuing of ancient texts, including the Bible; a rediscovery of rhetoric, placing value on the spoken word and hence a revival of preaching; and the development of printing and rising literacy rates, both of which increased access to Scripture. "For the Reformed, both spoken and written forms of verbal expression came to be invested with greater authority and value in worship than its visual aspects, which were perceived as the source of so many problems."[36]

An emphasis on communication through one of the senses, sight, changed to an emphasis on another, hearing, particularly hearing the spoken word. Sight in worship was not eliminated. Reformed worshipers saw other human beings, understood to be made in the image of God, and the sacramental actions using water, bread, and wine. They used their eyes to read the written words of Scripture, including the psalms and, later, hymns, and to see the architecture of the church buildings, which at some times and in some places was uplifting if plain. The senses of touch, taste, and smell were occasionally engaged in the sacraments. Nevertheless, the strong emphasis was on hearing the word.

In the present context, idolatry is far more likely to be perceived in institutions, secular social structures, and indeed secular images than in anything placed within the church building. It must be acknowledged that human beings are God's creation, that they receive knowledge of the world and themselves through all the senses, and that knowledge of God is available only as God chooses to be accommodated to these created means for self-communication; the faculty of sight cannot be dismissed as having a place in worship.

The Reformed tradition has placed constraints on what is seen in the worship space out of the fear of idolatrous practice, but the reader of Calvin can be surprised to discover Calvin's delight in being human within the richness of creation. There is opportunity through parts of his writing about creation to rediscover some of this delight today, in a world where the idolatries of the time are different from those of sixteenth-century western Europe.

The worship of God happens wherever people of faith offer praise and worship to God; it is not able to be confined only to places designated as churches. It can happen in any place. On a mountaintop or by a lake, wonder at the creation leads to praise. By taking into consideration Calvin's theolog-

36. Philip W. Butin, "Constructive Iconoclasm: Trinitarian Concern in Reformed Worship," *Studia Liturgica* 19, no. 2 (1989): 134.

ical positions on creation, his understanding of the range of God's chosen ways of communication with humanity, and his hints about the valid, non-idolatrous use of works of visual art, one can argue that there is not an a priori prohibition of images within places of worship, except images which purport literally to depict God who, being invisible and beyond human perception, cannot be depicted. While taking seriously the second commandment, there is no need to identify images with idols as Calvin regularly did. It is a question of expediency, of practical judgment in the light of human factors of the time.

Suggested Areas for Reflection, Dialogue, and Practice for Theologians, Liturgists, and Artists

What is required is a consideration of appropriate images and ways to use visual art and symbol that are compatible with the central theological tenets of the Reformed tradition. I suggest the following possibilities for immediate implementation and/or further study.

1. The architect and visual artist have a contribution to the praise the church offers to God. This may be termed a doxological role.
Given the acknowledgment that human beings can receive some knowledge of God through the sense of sight, the visual creation's potential to lead into a response of worship calls for study. The story of Moses, attracted by the sight of the burning bush, may be taken as a paradigm for the role of what is seen in leading to the encounter with God. From this may follow a recognition that the visual setting for worship is important. It may for many people evoke the inward response that flows into the praise of God. A function of art is to open the inner person to a transcendent meaning, a relationship of spirit. The role of both the seen natural world and the human built and decorated world in shaping human self-understanding needs study. Both the architect and the visual artist have a role in providing settings for worship that draw the worshiper into doxology and the possible encounter with God, which God, however, always determines.[37]

Those churches (congregations, ministers, and artists) that have already decided there is a legitimate Reformed iconography and placed visual art in the worship space may provide fruitful insights. By the end of the nineteenth cen-

---

37. John W. Dixon, *Art and the Theological Imagination* (New York: Seabury Press, 1978), takes seriously the role of the seen world in shaping self-understanding.

tury, Mansfield College Chapel in Oxford contained stained-glass windows and large wooden carvings of God's people, ranging from biblical figures to the reformers to recent notable Christians. Le Temple de Carouge near Geneva, which contains frescos of biblical scenes, stained-glass windows, and wooden carving, most completed in the period after World War I, presents a total visual impact. The Christian Protestant Church in Bali has reinterpreted Balinese architecture and art forms to express Christian insights.

2. The visual artist may be an interpreter of biblical stories and images.
There is a role for the visual artist as interpreter of the stories of Scripture. The Reformers have always known this, but in the past the artists' works were not allowed to be placed in the churches. Modern questions of the whole hermeneutical process of interpretation of the ancient texts, the place of the imagination, the interpretation of the material into contemporary forms, and theories of the reception of the communication all call for the attention of the Reformed tradition. The primary paradigm for communication in the Reformed tradition is found in language, but the expansion of this into the realm of visual communication holds many possibilities. Visual art can be employed for a re-telling of the stories of Scripture, both the historical and the parabolic stories. It may complement the preaching and the teaching of the church even if an image, used alone and out of context, is often ambiguous and open to incorrect interpretation.

Finding parallels between words and images rather than placing them in opposition is important. Gabriele Finaldi uses a telling phrase in discussing the early shepherd images in Christian catacomb art. "The Good Shepherd images should not be understood as representations of the person of Christ but as visual renditions of the metaphor employed by him to cast light on his nature and mission."[38] For many indigenous Australians, storytelling without visual "diagram" is very difficult. This is not a pictorially representational art. There is the whole interplay of image in language and image in visual form for discourse about God and the worship of God that this opens up. Modern understanding of visual art, which does not aim chiefly to "describe" faithfully what is seen, could bring freedom from the notion of the presence of the material in the image.

38. *The Image of Christ: The Catalogue of the Exhibition Seeing Salvation* (National Gallery Company Ltd., London, distributed by Yale University Press, 1999), p. 12.

*3. Visual art may present aspects of the world
for which the church is to intercede.*
Images in printed or painted, screened or projected form can show to the worshiper aspects of the world for which the Christian is to intercede. This may be
one point where much of what Paul Tillich said about art and theology touches
the worship of the church. Tillich placed great limits on the style of visual art
that he considered able to carry the weight of religious meaning. But art, which
both documents the human condition and expresses its depths, can remind the
church of the larger world and cause it to intercede for the world. The work of
George Gittoes, Australian war artist with peacekeepers in places such as
Rwanda and Vietnam, which often hangs in the Paddington Uniting Church in
Sydney, evokes the human depths of tragedy, courage, and turmoil that enter
the prayer of the church and remind of the Spirit who prays where the prayer is
only articulated in groans beyond words.

*4. Studies to understand human wholeness and
authentic worship can draw upon several disciplines.*
The fullness of being human requires the Reformed tradition to give wider recognition to the possibilities of God's self-accommodation in communication
with human beings. This may be recognized first by searching the Scriptures
themselves, and second by drawing upon insights from other disciplines that
provide understanding of the human reception of communication and development of self-knowledge. Such disciplines would include aspects of philosophy,
aesthetics, and other fields in which the range of human communication is the
focus. An expanded use of the visual may lead to the enrichment of preaching
and the prayer of the church. This may also provide a balance to extreme individualism. Where there is only inwardness there is a diminution of community.

*5. The idea of the image of Christ as the image
of the invisible God must be considered.*
An important question for the Reformed tradition, which a few of its theologians have just begun to explore, is the place and theology of icons in Orthodox worship.[39] This includes questions of the nature of Orthodox worship, the
theology of color, and the underpinning Christology, which believes in a ne-

---

39. Alain Blancy, "Protestantism and the Seventh Ecumenical Council: Towards a Reformed Theology of the Icon," and Georg Kretschmar, "The Reformation and the Theology of
Images" in *Icons: Windows on Eternity,* compiled by Gennadios Limouris (Geneva: WCC Publications, 1990). See also D. J. C. Cooper, "The Theology of the Image in Eastern Orthodoxy
and John Calvin," *Scottish Journal of Theology* 35, no. 3, pp. 219-41; and Jérôme Cottin, *Le Regard et la Parole,* pp. 135-38, 164.

cessity for images because Jesus is the image of the invisible God. The Orthodox church came to believe there is a Christological imperative that overrides the perceived imperative of the second commandment. The reformers rejected this because of what they saw as idolatrous developments from the use of icons, not only of Christ and many biblical figures but also of later saints. Part of the ecumenical dialogue surely requires the Reformed tradition to revisit the arguments on both sides of the iconoclastic controversies.

6. Is it still expedient to exclude all images from places of worship?

Whether to place images, works of visual art, in places of worship is a question of practical judgment, depending upon how several other factors are understood. Calvin recognized this by asking the question, "Is it expedient . . . ?" Today, when the forms of media communication and education are so filled with images that have a very different status from the images in medieval churches, it is expedient for the church to look at its possible communication through images. The power of the image on the television or computer screen does not reside in an understanding that links a material object with the presence and power of the divine. These images exercise power differently. They can be idolatrous when misused to communicate falsely and invite worship of things other than God, but the context is different when the question is asked today, "Is it expedient . . . ?" Communication in worship can be enhanced through the use of these common cultural forms to express the content of the faith and point toward God.

7. What visual art is suitable for Reformed places of worship? What symbols and actions are suitable?

In order to make congruous the relationship of theology and art, word and image, it may be necessary to define the features of visual art — images and symbols — appropriate to Reformed worship. Bernard Reymond, in concluding that churches today need a greater emphasis on the visual, suggests that, with vigilance against idolatry still in mind, such works should not be permanent; rather than frescos and fixed two- or three-dimensional works, objects of visual art in the church should be changeable and rotating.[40] The artist and the church will need to act in partnership so that the visual will lead to doxology and the clearer communication of both Scripture and world.

The test to separate symbol and symbolic action from simple image could be whether they point to Christ. The lighting of a candle to point to Christ as light of the world is one such example. Karl Barth hung a reproduc-

---

40. Bernard Reymond, *Protestantisme et les Images: pour en finir avec quelques clichés* (Geneva: Labor et Fides, 1999), pp. 121-27.

tion of the central crucifixion panel of the Isenheim Altar Piece in his study, to be viewed from his desk, so he could regularly gaze on that depiction of John the Baptist pointing to Christ. This visual work reflected his theological emphasis, even as he argued a congregation out of having a new stained-glass window in the local church. All is to point to Christ and the One who sent him.

The *Directory for Worship* of the Presbyterian Church of Aotearoa New Zealand (1995) has a section, "Other Forms of Proclamation" (2.2.8), in which it speaks of many art forms in which the gospel may be proclaimed. It summarizes as follows the principles for their use:

> The Reformed heritage calls upon people to bring to worship material offerings which in their simplicity of form and function direct attention to what God has done and to the claim that God makes upon human life. The people of God respond through expressions in architecture, furnishings, vestments, music, dance, drama, language and movement. When these artistic creations awaken us to God's presence, they are appropriate for worship. They are inappropriate when they call attention to themselves, or are present for their beauty as an end in itself. Artistic expressions should evoke, edify, enhance, and expand worshippers' consciousness of the reality and grace of God.[41]

I see every reason to add works of visual art to this list.

Conclusion

A Reformed theology will always seek to use the categories and emphases that have been central for its tradition. These have been primarily concerned with language, word, hearing, and acting rather than image, seeing, presence, place, and being. But new departures will emerge from the framework of the old. Christian worship of God calls for the engaging of the whole person in relationship with God, through Christ, in the power of the Holy Spirit. What was rejected by way of images and symbols, when reintroduced, will be reinterpreted within the dominant theological emphases. The reforming of worship needs to be open to using all God-given faculties and ways to which Scripture points, which can include usages that have been underemphasized in the past few centuries. The continuing recognition, however, that human beings can turn what is God-given and good into idols is a Reformed emphasis that is healthy for a faith that aims to keep God and humanity in the right perspective.

41. Presbyterian Church of Aotearoa New Zealand, *Directory for Worship,* 1995, p. 8.

370   *Geraldine Wheeler*

Further Reading

Begbie, Jeremy. *Voicing Creation's Praise: Towards a Theology of the Arts.* Edinburgh: T&T Clark, 1991.

Benedict, Philip. "Calvinism as a Culture? Preliminary Remarks on Calvinism and the Visual Arts." In *Seeing Beyond the Word,* ed. P. C. Finney. Grand Rapids: Eerdmans, 2000.

Calvin, John. *Institutes of the Christian Religion.* Ed. J. T. McNeill. Trans. F. L. Battles. Philadelphia: Westminster Press, 1960. 1.1-12.

Cottin, Jérôme. *Le Regard et la Parole: Une theologie protestante de l'image.* Geneva: Labor et Fides, 1994.

Dillenberger, John. *Theological Perceptions and Visual Images in Sixteenth-Century Northern Europe.* New York: Oxford University Press, 1998.

Limouris, Gennadios, compiler. *Icons: Windows on Eternity.* Geneva: W.C.C., 1990. (See the articles by Blancy and Kretschmar.)

Miles, Margaret R. *Image as Insight; Visual Understanding in Western Christianity and Secular Culture.* Boston: Beacon Press, 1985.

Reformed Liturgy & Music. Issues 19:3, 1984; 28:3, 1994; Special Issue, 1995; and 31:3, 1997.

Reymond, Bernard. *Protestantisme et les Images.* Geneva: Labor et Fides, 1999.

Women, Worship, and God's Reforming Spirit

Leonora Tubbs Tisdale

During the past century a number of Reformed churches around the globe have begun ordaining women as ministers and as elders. Some churches — such as the Protestant Church in Indonesia, the Church of Christ in Japan, and the United Church of Canada — have now experienced at least three generations of women in ordained leadership. Others have more recently moved to ordain women, while still others continue to debate the issue. Currently almost three-fourths of the churches that are members of the World Alliance of Reformed Churches ordain women as ministers, elders, or both, and the numbers continue to rise.[1]

The testimony of these churches has been overwhelmingly positive regarding the gifts women bring to all dimensions of church leadership. Despite the many years of debate that frequently precede a decision to ordain, it is notable that none of the churches that have voted to do so have subsequently revoked that decision. Rather, their testimony has been one of gratitude for the positive contributions women have made to the life of their churches, celebration of the unique perspectives and competencies women have brought to their vocations, and thanksgiving for the new opportunities for partnership and collegiality between women and men afforded them through women's ordination.

One of the consequences of the rise in numbers of ordained women is

---

1. For a discussion of the biblical, theological, and cultural issues at stake in women's ordination, and for a complete listing of the churches that are members of the World Alliance of Reformed Churches and their status regarding women's ordination (including dates for the ordination of deacons, elders, and ministers), see "Women and the Ordained Ministry," *Reformed World* 49, nos. 1 and 2 (Spring–Summer 1999).

that women are now more involved in the design, planning, and leading of public worship than ever before. Worship in Reformed churches is being re-shaped, re-formed, and re-envisioned as women take on the full mantle of leadership afforded them by right of their ordination, including the opportunity to preach, to administer the sacraments, and to lead the public worship of the people of God on a regular basis.

While ordination has afforded women greater opportunities for worship participation, however, it is also important to note that women were involved in worship leadership long before the churches decided to ordain them. Many women through the centuries have led worship in their own homes, in women's organizations, and in more informal church worship settings. Women have also long contributed to the corporate public worship of God through their musical and artistic offerings, their prayers, their Bible teaching, and their testimonies. Although ordination has certainly helped to "mainstream" and to expand women's worship leadership roles in the church, Christian women have been leading in the worship and praise of God ever since the Holy Spirit was poured out upon them at Pentecost.

It is also important to note that historically women's proven gifts and competencies as worship leaders have often played a significant role in pressing the churches toward their ordination. The very first woman ordained as a Presbyterian minister in my own country, the United States, was ordained in 1889 by a presbytery of the Cumberland Presbyterian Church, a small denomination forged during the nineteenth-century western frontier movement. During the years of westward expansion, when it was difficult to find enough trained male pastors to preach, women frequently had the opportunity to serve as evangelists, preaching and leading worship as they traveled by horseback from village to village. One such woman, Louisa Woosley from Caneyville, Kentucky, was licensed by her presbytery as an evangelist in 1888. During the following year, primarily because of her enormous success as a preacher and worship leader (in that one year she had "won more souls to Christ" and raised more money than any man in her presbytery!), her presbytery voted to ordain her. While the presbytery's action sparked a storm of controversy, Louisa Woosley nevertheless continued riding horseback and serving as an itinerant preacher until her death.[2]

If truth be told, more hearts have probably been changed about women's ordination by people experiencing firsthand a gifted woman preaching or leading worship than by all the theological and biblical debates and arguments

---

2. See Louisa M. Woosley, *Shall Woman Preach? Or the Question Answered* (Memphis: Frontier Press, 1989 [1891]).

the church has mustered. More than a few Reformed parishioners have found themselves asking after experiencing a woman's gifts in the pulpit, "How can I deny that the Holy Spirit has also been poured out upon *her?*"

Nevertheless, the church *has* often resisted the Spirit's winds, and therein lies the pain and struggle for many women who have long felt called to ordained ministry but have been too long been denied access to it. In a recent edition of *Reformed World,* authors from countries as diverse as Malawi, Brazil, Poland, Mexico, Zambia, and Greece spoke of the ongoing cultural and theological resistances to the ordination of women in their contexts, many citing the fact that women are still considered "unclean" (by virtue of menstruation or childbirth) in their contexts, and therefore unfit for worship leadership.[3] Consequently, a part of what women bring to public worship leadership in Reformed churches is a history of oppression and subjugation at the hands of the Christian church that has shaped their view of God, of the church, of the Bible, of theology, and of the very rites and rituals they are now increasingly allowed to lead. Women, because of their long history of being marginalized — not only in the church but also in the larger society — sometimes view worship differently than their male counterparts. That difference affects in subtle and not-so-subtle ways the manner in which women lead worship, and challenges the church to continue to reform its worship in ways that are more inclusive of the whole people of God.

In this chapter I will explore three different areas in which ordained and lay women are challenging Reformed churches to re-vision their understanding and practice of worship: women's leadership styles and worship, women's theology and worship, and women's ritual practices and worship. While these three focal points for discussion are not exhaustive, they are suggestive of some of the spheres in which women are challenging the church to expand its worship horizons.

Admittedly my own observations are shaped by my own social location as a white clergywoman of privilege, who has served as a pastor and a professor in Reformed congregations and seminaries in the United States. I have also, however, consulted with ordained women from Reformed churches in Africa, Asia, Latin American, the Pacific, and Europe while preparing this chapter. Their insights, observations, and stories related to women's ordination and worship have been invaluable for broadening my own limited horizons and for opening my eyes anew to the manifold ways in which "women's ways of worshiping" are sparking worship change and renewal in the larger church of Christ.

---

3. See "Women and the Ordained Ministry."

I am also aware that it is always dangerous — and especially dangerous in the context of a global church where so many different cultures, races, nationalities, and life experiences are represented — to talk about "women's ways" of doing anything. Women are a diverse and varied gender (as are men), and there is always the peril in discussions like this one of "universalizing" women's experience, or of dealing in an overly facile way with the significant differences that exist among and between women and men.[4]

Yet it is also the case that when women gather across national and international boundaries to talk about the problems that confront them in the life of the church, common themes and concerns often emerge. And frequently, despite their vastly different life experiences, cultural backgrounds, and socialization processes, women do find encouragement in sharing with one another the ways in which they — in their own contexts — are seeking to address those concerns.

This chapter, then, represents an attempt to name the challenges *some* women in *some* cultures are experiencing in the worship arena, and to identify *some* of the changes that are taking place in the worship of Reformed churches because of the increasing involvement of women as worship leaders, planners, and teachers. While I am well aware that my observations are not universally shared by all women, I do believe that the issues raised here are common enough to warrant ongoing reflection and consideration by the larger church. It is my hope that by recognizing and celebrating the contributions of some, all might be made more open to the Spirit's reforming and renewing winds.

---

4. Reformed theologian Mary McClintock Fulkerson challenges altogether the notion that "something is common to or shared universally by all women" or that there is any such thing as generic "women's experience." Noting the vast cultural, racial-ethnic, national, and socioeconomic differences that exist among women, Fulkerson warns against adopting a perspective that blurs or minimizes those differences. Fulkerson's concern is also voiced by other women — including African-American "womanist" theologians in my own context — who are quick to point out that while they may share a history of oppression (based on gender) with white U.S. women, they also share another history of oppression (based on race and class) that unites them in solidarity with black men and children. These differences significantly shape how they view worship, and the type of the reforms they would bring to it. See, for example, Delores S. Williams, "Rituals of Resistance in Womanist Worship," in *Women at Worship: Interpretations of North American Diversity,* ed. Marjorie Proctor-Smith and Janet R. Walton (Louisville: Westminster/John Knox Press, 1993), pp. 215-23. Williams writes, "A womanist recognizes her tie with both feminism and the black community. She liberates her sisters, her people (including males), and herself. She loves the spirit. . . . Womanist worship is family worship because it is also seriously inclusive of the experience of black men and black children" (p. 216).

Women's Leadership Styles and Worship

One of the challenges women frequently face when moving into church leadership roles previously denied them is how to develop their own leadership styles in a church culture long dominated by men. Frequently, women experience enormous pressures (both spoken and unspoken) to "lead like men" if they want to be accepted in their ordained roles as ministers and elders. A clergywoman from southern Africa (Botswana) speaks for many when she says that women who are in church leadership positions "have a constant fight to measure up against the dominant male imagery of ministry and leadership presented in the Church."[5]

Yet women, because they are socialized differently than men and afforded different gender roles in society, are often accustomed to exercising authority and leadership very differently than their male counterparts. Participants at a 1999 Reformed consultation on the partnership of women and men in the church, held in Togo, West Africa, observed that in many African cultures "men are regarded as active progenitors," while "women, for their part, are thought of as passive recipients. The woman gives life but does not have authority." Consequently, when it comes to role differentiation in church and society, "The men (those with the authority) generally make the decisions," while "the women always play a secondary role, such as seeing to the church's welfare, cleaning, looking after and decorating the premises."[6]

Gender-role assumptions such as these affect not only women's confidence in their ability to exercise church authority but also the ways in which women define and exercise the authority they are afforded. It is not uncommon, for example, in my own North American context to hear church women talk about the differences they observe in leadership styles between themselves and some of their male colleagues. Frequently women experience male leadership styles (especially those of men who are not accustomed to working collegially with women) as being more authoritarian and directive in nature than their own preferred collaborative and democratic style. Rather than viewing authority in terms of exercising power *over* people, many of these women view authority as exercising power *with* people. Relationships in such an operating style are as important as ideas, and the processes by which decisions are reached can be as important as the outcomes. Authority is exercised in com-

---

5. October 2000 correspondence to the author from Rev. Cheryl N. Dibeela, an ordained minister of the United Congregational Church of Southern Africa.

6. "The Togo Workshop," *Reformed World* issue on "Gender Awareness and Leadership Development," 50, no. 1 (March 2000), p. 10.

munity and has as one of its primary goals the empowerment of others for faithful Christian living. The leader's goal is not so much to convict and to convince others of her point of view as it is to initiate conversation, to invite new reflection and action, and to encourage others to discover and use their own God-given gifts faithfully and creatively.

Reformed theologian Letty Russell has re-visioned church authority from a feminist perspective not as "domination" but as a collaborative and mutually enriching partnership exercised in God's "household of freedom."[7] She contends that in the church, leadership should be exercised "in the round," where "power is not understood as a zero sum game that requires competition and hoarding in order to 'win.' Rather, power and leadership gifts multiply as they are shared and more and more persons become partners in communities of faith and struggle."[8]

When women bring such understandings of authority to worship leadership, they inevitably challenge commonplace practices and assumptions in Reformed churches. Some women, for instance, are questioning whether the mode of preaching currently employed by many of our churches — one person standing and addressing others for an extended period of time — is a mode we should continue to exercise in the future. Noting, in part, the harm that has been done to women at the hands of male pastors who have interpreted Scripture in ways that have kept women in submission and even caused them bodily harm (by pressuring women to remain in abusive domestic relationships, for example), these women are asking whether we need to rethink the whole model of preaching we employ. A clergywoman from Kenya writes,

> I consider preaching a poor methodology of educating people about their faith in God and their relationship with people and all creation — especially, in a patriarchal-colonial context where the leader or the teacher is supposed to know it all and not to be questioned. . . . Many sermons only help people to remain ignorant, passive, and lack critical reflection of their faith. This is more so when the majority cannot read for themselves. The educated can easily take advantage of the non-literate. In fact well-articulated and constructed hymns and songs can be more effective than half an hour of a sermon.
>
> Churches in Africa must think of better ways of educating the people in

---

7. Letty M. Russell, *Household of Freedom: Authority in Feminist Theology* (Philadelphia: Westminster Press, 1987).

8. Letty M. Russell, *Church in the Round: Feminist Interpretation of the Church* (Louisville: Westminster/John Knox Press, 1993), p. 56.

the whole liturgy, from the prayers, hymns, readings, Bible studies. If I had my way, I would experiment holding Bible studies in small groups instead of sermons in worship. This is actually happening in Ghana, where I recently witnessed a whole congregation wrestling with the text and the preacher only summarized the discussion. . . . With proper training in Bible study methodologies that take seriously African ways of communicating — story telling, proverbs, musical theatre — I believe this would reduce ill-prepared sermons or distorted messages and more people would participate in interpreting the scriptures as well as their cultural, social, and historical reality.[9]

Other women, while maintaining the traditional practice of preaching, challenge its authoritarian tendencies by their modes of proclamation. For example, studies of the North American context indicate that women, instead of using speech and communication patterns that signal to a congregation that the preachers' words are identical with the "Word of the Lord," tend to use more qualifiers, hedges, and questions in their preaching than men, thus inviting the congregation to ponder and reflect upon their own (admittedly limited) interpretations of Scripture.[10] Some women are moving out from behind the pulpit when they preach — choosing instead to stand behind the Communion table or in the midst of the congregation — in order to signal that they do not stand "over against" or "above" the faith community in the preaching event but "with" them as they engage in interpreting the Scriptures. And still others are engaging members of the congregation in Bible studies before the preaching event itself, thereby incorporating the wisdom of the larger faith community into their Sunday morning sermons.

Lucy Rose, a Reformed preacher and teacher of preaching from the United States, has encouraged Christian churches to re-envision the preaching event itself as a "roundtable" conversation in which the preacher places her own interpretation of a text on the table during the Sunday morning sermon in an effort to initiate and facilitate a conversation that will engage the whole community of faith throughout the week. Rather than adhering to a more traditional view of the preacher as a "herald" (through whom the eternal word of God is funneled toward rather passive hearers), Rose envisions preaching as a "wager" in which the preacher risks bringing her own (admittedly biased and

9. October 2000 correspondence to the author from the Rev. Dr. Nyambura Njoroge, the first woman ordained by the Presbyterian Church of East Africa.

10. See Leonora Tubbs Tisdale, "Women's Ways of Communicating: A New Blessing for Preaching," in *Women, Gender, and Christian Community,* ed. Jane Dempsey Douglass and James F. Kay (Louisville: Westminster/John Knox Press, 1997), pp. 104-16.

limited) interpretation of the word into the midst of a diverse community of equals for ongoing conversation, correction, and consideration.[11]

But preaching is not the only juncture at which women's leadership is changing or challenging Reformed worship practice. Women also bring their unique gifts and perspectives to bear as liturgical leaders. Women, for example, who have long been comfortable welcoming people to dinner tables or holding babies in their arms, bring to their observance of the sacraments in Reformed worship an ease and a grace that can be especially welcoming and hospitable. Since the early days of the church when Lydia welcomed Paul and other apostles into her home, women have practiced the grace of Christian hospitality. When they bring that grace into the arena of liturgical leadership, worship frequently becomes a more welcoming and inviting place for all.

Furthermore, because women have known oppression and marginalization in their own lives, they are often quick to reach out and embrace others the church tends to marginalize: children, gay and lesbian persons, the elderly, the poor. This embrace occurs not only within the context of worship, but also without. Jane Dempsey Douglass, former president of the World Alliance of Reformed Churches, has noted that women's spirituality — nourished through worship and Bible study — is often integrally connected with their activism in the world. In Togo, West Africa, for example, the Presbyterian women's organization engages in grassroots development work in which women help other women improve their agricultural efforts through literacy training, the pooling of resources to buy seeds and other needed tools, and leadership training. In Kenya, church women created the Council of the Shield in order to help end the practice of genital mutilation of girls. In Asia, Presbyterian women have taken the initiative in developing ecumenical groups to put an end to child prostitution.[12] For women, care for the body and care for the soul are integrally interrelated. Connections between spirituality and service, worship and justice, are often emphasized in sermons, prayers, litanies, and hymns written by women.

This preference for an "embodied" spirituality is also reflected in the ways in which women structure and conduct worship services, including their design and arrangement of worship space. When worshiping among themselves, women in my context frequently rearrange the space in which they find

11. Lucy Atkinson Rose, *Sharing the Word: Preaching in the Roundtable Church* (Louisville: Westminster/John Knox Press, 1997).

12. Jane Dempsey Douglass shared these perspectives in her address, "Reflections on Women in the World Church," given at a Princeton Theological Seminary Conference for Women, Princeton, New Jersey, March 2, 1998.

themselves so that they can be more visually and physically engaged with one another during the worship experience. In the process straight rows of chairs become curved or rounded, and the room is reconfigured to foster a greater sense of community and intimacy. Women also bring to their worship services candles, flowers, colorful cloths, or other visual symbols that can assist them in worshiping in a way that appeals to all the senses, not just to the ear alone. While the Reformed tradition, at its worst, has tended toward an iconoclasm that robbed sanctuaries of all objects of beauty and art, women have frequently been leaders in reintroducing art and sensual experience into services of public worship. Engaging the senses is essential if embodied worship is to occur.

In like manner, it is often women who are urging Reformed churches to reintroduce more bodily movement into services where it has been discouraged or inhibited. A clergywoman from Kenya writes,

> Lay women (including elders) have demonstrated creativity in composing songs and drama but unfortunately . . . they usually do not reach the regular Sunday worship but [occur] in social gatherings and women's organizations. Only here are women free to dance their hearts out and swing their bodies without any fear of being reprimanded for not being "decent and orderly." Slowly, worship services allow some body movements and thought provoking choir songs, use of drums and other instruments, but it is not unusual to find Scottish worship in the middle of a rural [Kenyan] congregation.[13]

Symbolically, the wearing of traditional European Reformed vestments in worship leadership also poses a dilemma for some clergywomen. While, on the one hand, traditional vestments signal to the larger church that women are now ordained and authorized to wear the "mantle" afforded their male colleagues, the fact cannot be denied that most vestments were originally designed for male clerics,[14] reflect male dress of a prior period,[15] and also symbolize for women a church patriarchy that only recently admitted them to its ordained ranks. In some countries of the South, whose churches were founded by Western European powers, those vestments bear the double stigma of colonialism *and* patriarchy.

---

13. October 2000 correspondence from Nyambura Njoroge.

14. Witness, for example, the way in which the neck opening of the black "Geneva gown" — probably the most common Reformed pulpit vestment in the United States — is designed for use with a shirt and tie.

15. A number of the Reformed European liturgical garments were derived from specifically masculine "street dress" of a prior day.

In response to this dilemma, some Reformed clergywomen are abandoning traditional European Reformed vestments altogether, donning instead vestments more representative of the church universal (such as the alb, with roots in the white baptismal garments worn by the newly baptized in the early church), or vestments more representative of their own cultural heritage (such as the use of African kinte cloth in vestments worn by African-American clergy in the United States). Still others are attempting to "feminize" traditional vestments in various ways (such as wearing feminine collars with Geneva gowns, redesigning vestments for female bodies, or wearing stoles that reflect feminine design and themes). One African pastor commented that even the practice of wearing vestments and changing colors for liturgical seasons or festival days is a luxury many women in her country could never afford. Others have noted that the symbolism of liturgical colors and vestments varies from culture to culture, and that women need freedom to create and use meaningful symbols that reflect their experiences.

Women's Theology and Worship

During the last decade of the twentieth century, the World Alliance of Reformed Churches, under the leadership of Dr. Nyambura Njoroge (the first ordained clergywoman in the Presbyterian Church of East Africa), gathered church women and men together for regional meetings under the PACT program (Program to Affirm, Challenge, and Transform the Relations of Women and Men in the Mission of God in Church and Society). Interestingly, the first priority to emerge from those conversations was not that of opening church offices, including the office of pastoral ministry, to women. (That was priority number two.) Rather, the general consensus that emerged from these local gatherings was that the first priority should be "to gain full respect for women and for women's perspectives in theology."[16] And, frankly, that may be an even harder task to achieve.

Even when women are admitted to ordination, they are not always allowed access to leadership of worship on the Lord's Day — a primary place in which the local congregation's own theology is shaped and re-formed. Dr. Sang Chang, President of Ewha Women's University in Korea, writes that 191 women have been ordained in the Presbyterian Church of Korea since 1995, accounting for 2 percent of the church's total ordained pastors. Only 37 of the women, however, are pastors of local congregations. The remainder are vice-

16. Douglass, "Reflections on Women in the World Church," p. 11.

pastors (81), administrators (54), or are preparing for missionary work abroad (18). That reality affects women's opportunities for worship leadership.

> If a woman pastor takes charge of a local church, she has the right to manage all of the worship [services] performed in her church and the procedures of the services. On the other hand, the range of women vice-pastors' activities is limited to doing preaching for the Sunday evening service, dawn prayer service, or irregular meetings with the congregation. The social prejudice against women's leadership is still prevailing in Korean churches. Especially, local churches are too conservative to allow women to lead worship. In general, they are expected to give assistance to male leaders. Even the women faculty members in seminaries are given few opportunities to be engaged in campus chapel or other worship services.[17]

Professors Sara and Guidoberto Mahecha — a husband and wife team who have taught in seminaries in Colombia, Brazil, and Costa Rica — report that while many women in Latin America are present in church and worship, "many of them are not prepared to struggle in a movement to take leadership in worship. They have other struggles: to obtain an education, to avoid being beaten, to care for their children because many of them are single mothers, and to be accepted as persons by their pastors, husbands, and family."[18]

Furthermore, the training women receive en route to ordination is not always sympathetic to or inclusive of theology from a woman's perspective. In many Reformed seminaries of Europe and North America, male professors still treat theologies written from a woman's perspective as if they are "peripheral" or "marginal" theologies, not to be considered on the same par with the more "normative" theologies of the Western European predominantly male tradition. Women's theology is often either denigrated or ignored altogether in the training of pastors (male and female), and, as a result, pastors emerge from seminary with little cognizance of what women of their own and other traditions are contributing to theological dialogue. Less than ten Reformed seminaries (globally) currently have women as their presidents,[19] and

---

17. Correspondence to the author from Sang Chang, October 6, 2000.

18. Correspondence to the author from Sara and Guidoberto Machecha, professors in the Universidad Biblica Latinoamericana in San José, Costa Rica, September 21, 2000.

19. In her March 1998 address, "Reflections on Women in the World Church," Jane Dempsey Douglass stated that there were then eight Reformed seminaries with women as presidents: three in North America, three in Latin America, one in Australia, and one in Lebanon.

in some parts of the world, women seminary faculty are either very rare or nonexistent.[20]

Nevertheless, women theologians and worship leaders are giving voice to theology from their perspectives when given the opportunity, and, as a result, are challenging the Reformed churches to continue their ongoing reformation process.

In some contexts, for example, women have been pressing the churches to recognize that the ways in which we name God and speak of God in worship have a profound influence upon the ways in which we think (theologically) about God. If we only refer to God with masculine language (constantly referring to God as "He" or "Him," or exclusively as "Father" or "King"), we also give the impression through our language (a) that God is male and (b) that women, therefore, are not fully created in God's own image. Consequently many women have been urging their churches to use language — in prayers, hymns, sermons, and other liturgical elements — that is more representative of the fullness of who God is.

Admittedly this issue varies in importance from culture to culture and language to language. While in some cultures the language used for God is predominantly masculine (as in the Lingala language of Congo), in other cultures the language for God is either neuter (as in the Cameroon term *Zambe* or the Togo term *Mawu*), or incorporates both masculine and feminine terms for God (as in French, where the different terms and images used for God can be masculine, feminine, or neuter).[21]

The *Directory for Worship* of my own denomination, the Presbyterian Church (U.S.A.), currently states, "The church shall strive in its worship to use language about God which is intentionally as diverse and varied as the Bible and our theological traditions. The church is committed to using language in such a way that all members of the community of faith may recognize themselves to be included, addressed, and equally cherished before God."[22] These two statements are integrally connected, since the ways in which we speak of God also shape the ways in which we think of humanity.

While the God language issue has received a great deal of attention in some Reformed churches, it is only one of the many junctures at which women as worship planners and leaders are "renaming" theology from their own per-

20. Nyambura Njoroge reports, for example, that of the women ordained since 1982 in Kenya, none is a theological educator.

21. For a fuller discussion of this issue within the African context, see "The Togo Report," pp. 15-16.

22. *The Constitution of the Presbyterian Church (U.S.A.) Part II: Book of Order 1999-2000,* W-1.2006b.

spectives. Women are also questioning the ways in which traditional doctrines, such as sin and salvation, and forgiveness and atonement, have been interpreted in worship and liturgy. For example, feminist theologians have questioned whether the church's traditional understanding of sin as "pride" is a helpful or appropriate understanding for women, who, due to their socialization and oppression, may suffer from low self-esteem or a lack of confidence in their own God-given gifts and abilities.[23] Are prayers of confession that repeatedly ask women to confess their "pride" appropriate for those whose sin may more accurately lie in their refusal to claim and live into their own competencies?

In like manner, the traditional Christian language of self-sacrifice and self-denial is being challenged by women, who note that such language has often been used to keep women in abusive relationships or to reinforce women's servitude and passivity. While social location as well as gender plays a significant role in determining what we in the church need to confess (so that women of privilege may well need to confess sins of arrogance and pride toward those of other social classes or races), women clergy are challenging the church to rethink the theological interpretations reflected in our hymns and prayers.

In preaching, too, women are reinterpreting Reformed theology from their own perspectives. As women bring into the pulpit their own images and experiences of grace and forgiveness, conversion and salvation, they offer the church new lenses through which to consider old doctrines. Indeed, by their very selection of biblical texts and themes for preaching, women are opening up theological horizons too long overlooked or ignored in Reformed pulpits. (I think in this instance of the sermons I have heard by women in my preaching classes on oft-ignored biblical texts such as the story of Vashti, Miriam's song and dance after the crossing of the Red Sea, or on biblical "texts of terror" such as the story of the sacrifice of Jephthah's daughter.) Women are also introducing into their preaching and prayers topics too long considered "taboo" in worship, such as domestic violence against women, child abuse, or the sorrow that accompanies miscarriage.

Nyambura Njoroge recounts a story that cuts to the heart of why it is imperative that women's theological perspectives be encouraged in the pub-

23. For a helpful discussion of this issue, see Carol Lakey Hess, *Caretakers of Our Common House: Women's Development in Communities of Faith* (Nashville: Abingdon Press, 1997), pp. 31-54. Hess states: "many women, due to socialized patterns of subordination, are tempted *to give themselves away.* 'Self-possession' is precisely what women need, not the prison from which they should escape" (p. 37).

lic worship arena. Njoroge was worshiping with a congregation in Kenya (this congregation happened to be Baptist) where the preacher was a principal of a theological seminary. The focus of the service was on mission among the members themselves, but the preacher chose to dwell on prayer. She writes:

> He gave about three examples where he prayed for people and the prayers were answered. One of these had to do with "A Big African Problem" as he put it. The family involved a headmaster of a well-known school whose wife only gave birth to girls. So despite the fact that they were Christians the relationship was bad because the wife could not produce a son. And so the preacher man held several prayer sessions. The wife conceived and a baby boy was born!
>
> Well, I looked to see the reaction of those sitting next to me and I was caught by my sister's empty stare of surprise and disappointment. We come from a family of nine daughters with no brother! Are we less important in the eyes of God, we wondered as we dissected the sermon? To make the matters more serious, my sister has been married for twenty years without a child! Does it mean she and her husband who are committed Christians lack the faith of the preacher? Furthermore, I could not help but remember the day (1980s, I think) Kenyans woke to the horror of reading in the headlines of every newspaper in town, how a husband with the help of a friend, gouged out his wife's eyes because she only gave birth to girls and at that point she was pregnant with the sixth child who happened to be a girl. Why not, if these men were listening to such sermons!
>
> Unfortunately, many sermons and bad counseling have led women to their graves while others have been maimed physically or emotionally. I had hoped the preacher would have counseled the family (including the extended family) to appreciate that girls are made in God's image and that children are gifts from God and ours is to raise them responsibly and in joy. Let alone other biological explanations of who determines what sex.[24]

While the example happens to come from an African Baptist congregation and may seem extreme to some readers, the truth is that women and girls from almost any Christian congregation in any part of the globe could recount a similar experience in which their own worth as children of God was denied, undermined, or denigrated by a similar occurrence within worship. If women are to claim their rightful place as equal partners in God's household of freedom, then it is imperative that their theologies be voiced, heard, and respected

24. October 2000 correspondence to author from Nyambura Njoroge.

by the larger church. Worship is a critical juncture at which those voices will increasingly be raised.

Women's Rituals and Worship

In their book *Women at Worship: Interpretations of North American Diversity*, Marjorie Proctor-Smith and Janet R. Walton contend that North American women have spiritual and ritual needs that are not being met by traditional Christian and Jewish congregations. Consequently,

> Women are pushing the decision beyond questions of the use of inclusive language and the ordination of women to questions of identity: What does it mean to be a Christian or a Jewish woman? Who decides: How do we worship the deity? Who is the one whom we worship? What is the best way to offer worship? Such questions go to the very heart of our religious identity, which is precisely where women wish to be.
>
> Moreover, when women ask such questions we are not asking abstract philosophical questions or even aesthetic questions so much as ethical questions. The feminist liturgical movement has pointed out the harm that is done to women by the exclusion of women from ordination or by the use of male-dominated language, as well as by patriarchal liturgical structures. The development of feminist liturgies and rituals is often motivated as much by women's need to recover from deep hurt as by anything. Many of the earliest feminist liturgies were healing rituals.[25]

Often it is when women gather with other women for worship — in safe and sacred spaces where they are free to reshape worship according to their own needs and perspectives — that such healing rituals emerge. At women's conferences, in church women's organizations, in ecumenical gatherings of clergy and lay women, in homes, and in seminary communities, women are crafting and creating their own liturgies that are reflective of feminist principles and that provide avenues for ritual acts not found in other church structures.

Mary Collins (a Roman Catholic) says that feminist liturgies operate according to five principles:

1. They ritualize relationships that emancipate and empower women.
2. They are the production of the community of worshipers, not of special experts or authorities.

25. Marjorie Proctor-Smith and Janet R. Walton, eds., *Women at Worship: Interpretations of North American Diversity* (Louisville: Westminster/John Knox Press, 1993), p. 3.

3. They critique patriarchal liturgies.
4. They have begun to develop a distinctive repertoire of ritual symbols and strategies.
5. They tend to produce liturgical events, not liturgical texts.[26]

Because such rituals are designed in community (and often ecumenically and internationally), it is not always easy to single out or to identify specifically "Reformed" contributions to them. However, Reformed women are certainly participating in the groups that are shaping these rituals, and the rituals' increasing availability to Reformed churches will influence the ongoing practice of our common worship life.

In Korea, for instance, members of ecumenical organizations that are fostering the equal partnership of women and men in the church — such as the Institute for Women's Theological Studies at Ewha Women's University and the Korean Association for Women Theologians — are developing new forms of rituals for use by local churches. Some of the rituals utilize and reclaim traditional Korean music, dance, and drama as a part of their liturgies.[27]

In Germany, Reformed pastor Sabine Dreßler Kromminga reports that she regularly gathered for several years with an ecumenical group of women for "liturgy nights," evenings in which the women (ordained and lay) designed and participated in liturgies reflective of women's theology, concerns, and life experience. A collection of these liturgies has now been compiled and published and is available for broader church use.[28]

In the North American context, there has been a burgeoning interest in recent years in the creation of rituals that support women in various transitions and crises of their lives. Today a local pastor or chaplain can find resources for ministering to rape or incest victims, survivors of domestic violence, women who have endured an abortion or a miscarriage, women who have undergone a hysterectomy or mastectomy, girls who are beginning menstruation, women who are entering menopause, or parents who are adopting a child. Most of these worship resources were created by women.

As women around the globe contribute in greater numbers than ever before to the creation of either entire liturgies[29] or parts of liturgies (prayers, lita-

---

26. Mary Collins, "Principles of Feminist Liturgy," in *Women at Worship*, pp. 9-26.

27. October 2000 correspondence from Dr. Sang Chang, President of Ewha Women's University in Seoul, Korea.

28. See Barbara Hennig, Sabine Dreßler, and Waltraud Likenfelt, *Und Mirjam nam die Pauka: Gottesdienste und liturgische Tänze.*

29. For example, two Presbyterian Church (U.S.A.) clergywomen, who previously served as co-pastors of the Downtown Presbyterian Church in Rochester, New York, have pub-

nies, hymn texts or tunes, and other worship elements), and as the language, imagery, and theological themes in these liturgical elements wend their way into church use, worship becomes more inclusive of women's perspectives and experience.

It is also the case, however, that many of the worship resources and rituals designed by Reformed women are never published. More often women design rituals for use in their own local settings, responding to local issues and needs, and helping to enable, reform, and transform worship practice where they are. This more common practice of crafting and leading local rituals probably contributes to Mary Collins's assertion that women tend to produce liturgical "events," not liturgical "texts."

And the Spirit Who Blows Where She Will

While women's gifts in leadership — including worship leadership — are openly celebrated and affirmed in many Reformed churches, there are still churches where women are denied ordination and full participation in worship leadership, or where women's experimental efforts at worship reform are met with suspicion, mistrust, and even outright hostility.[30] Perhaps nowhere is church "tradition" deemed to be more sacred and inviolable than in the rites and rituals in which we regularly engage in Christian worship.

Yet it is precisely because of the enormous power that worship and liturgical rites have to form and re-form us as people of faith that women's per-

---

lished a book of worship services and rituals that were created when a group of women — many of whom were disenchanted with the patriarchal nature of the church's worship — began meeting and worshiping together at their local Presbyterian church on a regular basis in 1987. Their book, *Birthings and Blessings: Liberating Worship Services for the Inclusive Church* (New York: Crossroad, 1991), not only contains services designed to be used with groups of women during the various seasons of the liturgical year; it also incorporates inclusive services and rituals that can be used by the larger church congregation.

30. For example, I know of no conference in the last decade that has elicited more criticism, controversy, and furor within my own denomination (Presbyterian Church [U.S.A.]) than the "Re-Imagining Conference" held in Minneapolis, Minnesota, in 1993. Sponsored by a number of "mainline" U.S. denominations, the conference incorporated liturgical elements that were crafted by women and that used a great deal of overtly feminine imagery (including Sophia imagery for God). While some of the Presbyterian debate that followed the conference was healthy for the ongoing discernment of what it means theologically for the church to be "Reformed yet reforming," the tone and tenor of the debate was often derisive, dismissive, and acrimonious. Some women were literally forced to resign their church positions because of their participation in or support of the conference.

spectives and efforts at worship reform must be taken seriously. If we genuinely believe, as Reformed Christians, in a God who is bigger than male, in a Jesus whose liberating and salvific work embraces women as well as men, in a Spirit that continues to be poured out on *all* flesh, and in a church that is created to be a partnership of equals, then worship is one of the arenas in which Reformed churches must continue pressing toward the goal of gaining "full respect for women and for women's perspectives in theology."

The increasing opportunities afforded women through their ordination are certainly one avenue through which the Spirit's transforming work will continue. But it is not the only avenue. The truth of the matter is that God's Spirit is blowing where She will — with or without our approbation. And we have yet to fully see what those renewing winds will mean for the future shape of Reformed worship.

Further Reading

Berger, Teresa. *Women's Ways of Worship: Gender Analysis and Liturgical History.* Collegeville, Minn.: Liturgical Press, 1999.

Dempsey Douglass, Jane, and James F. Kay, eds. *Women, Gender, and Christian Community.* Louisville: Westminster/John Knox Press, 1997.

Elkins, Heather Murray. *Worshiping Women: Re-forming God's People for Praise.* Nashville: Abingdon Press, 1994.

Hess, Carol Lakey. *Caretakers of Our Common House: Women's Development in Communities of Faith.* Nashville: Abingdon Press, 1997.

Northup, Lesley A. *Ritualizing Women: Patterns of Spirituality.* Cleveland: Pilgrim Press, 1997.

Proctor-Smith, Marjorie, and Janet R. Walton, eds. *Women at Worship: Interpretations of North American Diversity.* Louisville: Westminster/John Knox Press, 1993.

Reformed World issue on "Partnership in God's Mission." 45:2 (June 1995).

Reformed World issue on "Women and the Ordained Ministry." 49:1 and 2 (Spring-Summer 1999).

Reformed World issue on "Gender Awareness and Leadership Development." 50:1 (March 2000).

Rose, Lucy Atkinson. *Sharing the Word: Preaching in the Roundtable Church.* Louisville: Westminster/John Knox Press, 1997.

Russell, Letty M. *Household of Freedom: Authority in Feminist Theology.* Philadelphia: Westminster/John Knox Press, 1987.

————. *Church in the Round: Feminist Interpretation of the Church.* Louisville: Westminster/John Knox Press, 1993.

Woosley, Louisa M. *Shall Woman Preach? Or the Question Answered.* Memphis: Frontier Press, 1989.

Zikmund, Barbara Brown, Adair T. Lummis, and Patricia Mei Yin Chang. *Clergy Women: An Uphill Calling.* Louisville: Westminster/John Knox Press, 1998.

Calendar and Lectionary in
Reformed Perspective and History

Horace T. Allen Jr.

A particularly Reformed perspective on matters of calendar and lectionary requires at the outset a careful and historical note about the relationship between these two liturgical matters. This is important at the present time because of the differing ways by which many Reformed communities are recovering a more intentional use of each or both. Although Reformed churches abandoned much of the pre-Reformation Western calendrical structure, together with the related Roman lectionary for the Lord's Day, the last century has seen a gradual re-appropriation of certain aspects of the ancient feasts and festivals; such recovery has not, however, always been governed by or associated with a comparable interest in the use of lectionaries, much less their reform. In most instances, therefore, much conventional and post-Reformation practice and piety associated with these observances was thoughtlessly picked up without any reference to biblical and more ancient origins. Examples of this process and its problems will be identified further along in this chapter.

In addition, as lectionary systems have slowly come into use there has been a tendency to select biblical materials for these feasts and festivals according to this practice and piety, much of which is more late-Medieval than ancient or patristic. As the Methodist liturgiologist James F. White puts it, "Many medieval pieties and practices remained intact in Protestantism because they were the only models available when reforming items such as daily public prayer."[1]

At stake here is a principle particularly dear to the Reformed heritage —

---

1. James F. White, *A Brief History of Christian Worship* (Nashville: Abingdon Press, 1993), p. 76.

namely, that all of Christian worship should in some way or other be, and be seen to be, governed by the Scriptures, especially those in use on one or another of these calendrical days or seasons. In short, part of the present problem, and therefore of the need for this chapter's twin concerns, is simply that Scripture should determine calendar, not the other way around. But our recent history of recovering calendrical traditions without recourse to one classic lectionary or another has violated what is a significant Reformed commitment and at the same time a demonstrable matter of ancient church history. And, parenthetically, one should always take quite seriously the full title of Calvin's *"The form of prayer according to the custom of the ancient church."*[2]

At least two historical developments have created this contemporary situation. One is the unquestioned fact that the Roman lectionary and calendar had become, by the time of the sixteenth century, incredibly "cluttered up" by the intrusion onto Lord's Day worship of all manner of hagiographical commemorations ("saints days") both local and universal, as well as by Marian festivals and theological emphases (Trinity, for instance). This was of course one of the issues the reformers addressed through their radical simplification of the calendar to re-emphasize the classic Christological center as embodied in Christmas, Easter, Ascension, and Pentecost. The other development relates to the decision of certain reformers such as Zwingli and Calvin to abandon the Roman lectionary in favor of "in course" or continuous reading week by week. Wise as this undoubtedly was in terms of a preaching and teaching agenda, it had the effect of dissociating "days" from lections such that in later centuries when continuous reading gave way to pastoral selection, week by week, the principle of scriptural governance gave way — which in our present time of calendrical recovery has resulted in extraordinary distortions. As noted, more careful analysis will be given to this problem further on; suffice it to be said here by way of example that one of the most catastrophic instances of this is to be found in the displacement of the historical Advent emphasis on the so-called "Second Coming of the Lord" by a kind of "pre-Christmas preparation," symbolized by the increasingly ubiquitous opening ceremony of the lighting of an Advent wreath (which has to do with the First Coming, Christmas).

Another introductory matter needs expression at this point. The reformers understood, both on biblical and patristic bases, the prior significance for all Christian worship of the weekly cycle with its "first day of the week." This was part of their response to the complex annual cycle of the Roman Rite, but also their reaffirmation of the primacy of a resurrection focus on that day. This

---

2. Bard Thompson, *Liturgies of the Western Church* (Cleveland: World Publishing Co., 1961), p. 197.

nicely played into their revision of the annual calendar and may well have informed Calvin's liturgical hermeneutic of preaching from the Old Testament at daily worship and from the New Testament on the Lord's Day (which day he understood not only in its Paschal character but also in its eucharistic norm). The difficulty our contemporary Reformed communities have run into at this point is the later development of a "Sabbath" definition and piety for the Lord's Day. (The use of the pagan name "Sunday" in English has not helped!) Thus in our own day, without either lectionary or paschal focus, weekly or annually, and without a weekly eucharistic norm, we are adrift in a highly nonbiblical, a-historical, and extra-ecumenical definition of Lord's Day worship as something other than essentially a Christological celebration.

For at least these reasons, therefore, we cannot accept uncritically the increasing interest in the so-called Christian year, as evidenced in U.S. Presbyterian books since 1936, Scottish books since 1940, or the Netherlands *Draft Worship Book* of 1955 and other continental books. Rather, must we inform the continuing interest in, and reform of, the calendar — so greatly encouraged by the reforms instigated in the Roman Catholic Church and, more widely, by the decrees of the Second Vatican Council (1962-1965) and its post-conciliar deliverances — by a parallel discussion and analysis of new lectionary systems, both Roman and ecumenical, as most widely represented by the Roman *Ordo lectionum Missae* (OLM) of 1969 or the widely used *Revised Common Lectionary* (RCL) of 1992.

The Calendar

The Calendar: Its Complex Historical Development

The Christian church's various calendars cannot, of course, be directly derived from the New Testament. That wisdom is indicated in Calvin's reference to "the custom of the ancient church," an implied rebuttal to more "leftwing" appeals to the practice of New Testament churches. These temporal cycles developed in stages in the course of church history, and it should be noted at the outset that these developments were daily as well as weekly and annual. There is, however, no indication in the New Testament of principled opposition to the idea of recurring commemorations of "God's great deeds in Christ." Reformed Christians have sometimes argued that liturgical calendars are in contradiction to the spirit of the Bible, with Galatians 4:10 being the primary text referred to. Not much more needs to be said in this regard, however, than to refer to its immediate context: "Formerly when you did not know God, you were enslaved to beings that by nature are not gods" (v. 8). Thus the injunction concerning "special days, and months, and seasons, and years" (v. 10) must be a reference to pagan customs that had nothing to do with Jewish or early Christian practices. Nor could one simplistically say that such a text establishes an anti-calendar principle for the churches. Paul himself (as well as Luke) refers to Pentecost (1 Cor. 16:8), and all the Gospels take considerable care (though in different ways) to relate the crucifixion of Jesus to the Passover festival — hence the continuation immediately thereafter of Christian Paschal celebrations, which became the cornerstone of both annual and weekly cycles.[3] And that forcefully reminds us that in Christian worship we are starting from an incarnational presupposition, a perspective it inherited from the radically historical consciousness of Judaism, by contrast with the paganism of Paul's time.

The consolidation of the church's calendars took several centuries, a process that is ongoing. In principle, the "architecture" of calendars is always open to further developments. In recent times, for instance, the proposal has been made to give more room in the annual calendar for the celebration of God, Creator. As will be noted later, this was one of the innovations proposed by the Scottish scholar, A. Allan McArthur,[4] and later included in a two-year lectionary published by the British Joint Liturgical Group,[5] now replaced by the *Revised Common Lectionary*.

Weekly Calendar

Fundamental for an appropriate understanding of the church's weekly calendar are two New Testament texts, namely Acts 20:7 and Revelation 1:10, with their references to the "first day of the week" and the "Lord's Day." Also relevant are the early references in Acts to the daily table fellowship and prayer life of the Jerusalem community, which seriously indicate the emergence of an eschatological daily and weekly calendar and perspective, contradictory as that may sound. In other words, the one-day-in-seven of the Jewish calendar, the Sabbath, with its double historical references to Creation and Exodus, and its position in the week as the last, "seventh" day, was replaced with a "first" or anticipatory day. The relationship of this first day to the rest of the

3. Cf. Thomas Talley, *The Origins of the Liturgical Year* (New York: Pueblo Publ. Co., 1986).

4. A. Allan McArthur, *The Christian Year and Lectionary Reform* (London: SCM Press, 1958).

5. The Church of England, *Alternative Service Book* (Colchester, England: Clowes Publishing Co., 1980).

week is initiatory on the basis of resurrection, and opens up the weekly Messianic meal-fellowship of the community as a kind of realized eschatology that still awaits the return of Christ as Messiah and Lord of all creation. Karl Barth put this well in his description of "The Time of the Community" in *Church Dogmatics*: "The time of the community is the time between the first *parousia* of Jesus Christ and the second. The community exists between His coming as the risen One and this final coming."[6] Thus the weekly temporal calendar is actually a matter of two transhistorical "times," the resurrection and the return of the Messiah-Lord. Barth's theological student and friend, Paul Lehmann, puts this juxtaposition of past and future quite clearly in his book *The Tranfiguration of Politics:*

> The word *story*, in this context (messianic), refers to the way in which one generation tells another how the future shapes the present out of the past; how destiny draws heritage into the human reality and meaning of experience, which is always a compound of happenings, hope, and remembrance; how promise and disillusionment, celebration and suffering, joy and pain, forgiveness and guilt, renewal and failure, transfigure the human condition and are transfigured in it.[7]

Or in summary, "The past does not cross over the present into the future. The future draws the present toward itself from the past."[8] The Lord's Day, therefore, unlike the Sabbath, does not complete or commemorate a "perfect" history, but rather inaugurates a future that is even more perfect, the *yom Yahweh.* Interestingly, that singular New Testament text that does refer to the (liturgical?) "meetings of the community" (Heb. 10:19-25) explicitly alludes to "encouraging one another, and all the more as you see the Day [of the Lord] approaching." As we take into account the centrality of the weekly calendar in the Reformation moment as the cornerstone of daily, weekly, and annual calendar structures, we cannot but notice this basically eschatological, rather than historical, theological definition of what a calendar, the marking of time, is all about. "Contradictory" indeed: a futuristic calendar!

Sadly, the loss in our era of this daily-weekly pattern and theology of worship as practiced in Geneva (although uniquely in our time, also in Korea), and the concurrent replacement of "Lord's (resurrection) Day" by a kind of "Christian Sabbath," has fatally obscured this eschatological emphasis. This

6. Karl Barth, *Church Dogmatics (IV/2), The Doctrine of Reconciliation,* tr. G. W. Bromiley (Edinburgh: T&T Clark, 1958), p. 725.

7. Paul Lehmann, *The Transfiguration of Politics* (New York: Harper and Row, 1975), p. 7.

8. Lehmann, *The Transfiguration of Politics,* p. xi.

has also taken its toll on our understanding especially of the Lord's Supper.[9] These reflections provide us with at least two lessons concerning a Reformed understanding of the weekly cycle:

1. The Lord's Day as celebration of death and resurrection must be recovered. This is no sixteenth-century innovation. It was for good reason that the Council of Nicea determined that the annual Christian Paschal festival should fall on a Lord's Day, thus emphasizing as its primary liturgy *baptism,* as the beginning of the Christian's life by virtue of Christ's resurrection (Rom. 6:3-11; 1 Peter 3:21-22). This suggests something about our timing of the celebration of that sacrament. For as long as the first day of the week does not connote resurrection among our churches, then we should beware of the indiscriminate way we have of baptizing (often with little notice) on any Sunday, and perhaps return to the early church's practice of relating that rite to Easter and Pentecost or such other Christological festivals as Epiphany, the Baptism of the Lord, First Lent, or All Saints'. As the well-known aphorism puts it, Time tells all.

2. It is this daily-weekly calendar that provides the occasion for the great Reformed tradition of the continuous reading *(lectio continua)* of the Scriptures in public worship, now so emphatically embodied in the Roman system of 1969 and its progeny — *Common Lectionary* of 1983 and its successor, *Revised Common Lectionary* of 1992. English-speaking Presbyterianism's foundational liturgical document, the *Westminster Directory for Public Worship,* itself suggests such a manner of weekly public proclamation of the Old and New Testaments (chap. 3).

The Annual Calendar

Bearing in mind that the weekly cycle is primary for the history of calendrical celebration, and that its basic function is to provide for the continuous reading of Holy Scripture in the context of worship as well as to provide the occasion for the weekly celebration of the Lord's resurrection and daily presence in the community, we may now turn to the annually celebrated festivals. These festivals focus on the two cycles of Sundays that surround the two principal festivals in the year, Pascha (Easter)/Pentecost and Christmas/Epiphany. This

---

9. The symmetry between the Lord's Supper and the Lord's Day has been magisterially expounded by Willy Rordorf in *Sunday: The History of the Day of Rest and Worship in the Earliest Centuries of the Christian Church* (Philadelphia: Westminster Press, 1968), pp. 274-93.

alerts us that in fact these two cycles do not form an entire "year." Most Sundays of any year (thirty-three or thirty-four, designated in the three-year systems as "Ordinary Time," a somewhat misleading English expression that translates the Latin *Dominica per annum,* "Lord's Days through the Year") form two blocks. These blocks fall between Epiphany and Lent, and between Pentecost and Advent, which respects the fact that the Lord's Day, as we have said, is a festival in its own right, and the time when the Synoptic Gospels are read through, in a continuous or semi-continuous manner, as well as most of the Pauline or pseudo-Pauline Epistles. This accords quite closely with what the Calvinist reformers did.

Thus these two blocks of ordinary time should not be thought of as "seasons" as such, although the Anglican tradition tends to think of the post-Epiphany days as a season of "manifestation." In other words, we do not have a "church year" but a sequence of Lord's Days, which in and around Christmas and Easter employs a *lectio selecta* (as distinct from *lectio continua*) method for choosing scriptural lections, as well as other liturgical actions such as prayers, hymns, and psalmody. For the reformers this also meant the eucharistic celebration, but even that expressive tradition has largely been lost in our time in favor of a strange dependence on monthly (lunar) calculations (first or last Sundays per month, or, worse, quarterly, every three months), which have nothing whatever to do with the gospel or the Christological center of the principle annual feasts, and simply reinforce the unhappy assumption among our people that the Lord's Supper has little or nothing to do with the Lord's Day, and is in fact not essential to the ministry of the word, which does occur each week.[10] Our Roman Catholic brothers and sisters have made the same mistake in their daily eucharistic celebrations! Only the Orthodox have maintained the connection between the Day and the Supper, and gone further yet to insist that there be only one liturgy in one place on each Lord's Day.

We turn now to the two cycles celebrated on an annual basis: Christmas and Easter. (For ease of reading we will use the unfortunate pagan expression "Easter" even though "Pascha" is obviously historically correct and much more suggestive.) It is important to remember that these two cycles occur annually because they are rooted in two historical events, the birth and death of Jesus, which contrasts with the nonhistorical and eschatological significance of the weekly Lord's Day.

---

10. Horace T. Allen Jr., "Lord's Day — Lord's Supper," *Reformed Liturgy and Music* XXI 11/4 (Louisville: Presbyterian Assoc. of Musicians, 1984), and "An Apostolic Warning! Lord's Day and Lord's Supper," *Reformed Liturgy and Music* XXIX/4 (Louisville: Presbyterian Assoc. of Musicians, 1995).

The Easter Cycle: Lent, Holy Week, Easter Day, the Fifty Days, and Pentecost

In terms of historical development, this is the older of the two principal cycles. The New Testament carefully dates the Passion and resurrection of the Lord with reference to the Jewish Pascha and also includes (as noted earlier in this chapter) references to the succeeding fifty days, which on the Jewish calendar formed a post-Passover season culminating in Pentecost. Clearly the sub-apostolic churches continued some sort of celebrations of these dates for their commemoration of the Lord's death and resurrection. By the time of the Council of Nicaea (325 A.D.), however, it was necessary to provide the ecumenical church with a formula for determining the date of Easter on the civil calendar since contact with the Jewish authorities had ceased and, indeed, a vast controversy (*Quartodeciman* for "fourteen" in reference to the Jewish Paschal date of 14/15 Nisan) had erupted. The council included in its decision that the festival should occur on a Lord's Day. Up to that time it could have taken place on any day of the week, Nisan 14-15 being a fixed date (like Christmas).

The Easter celebrations of these first four or five centuries were apparently principally focused on the celebration of baptism, which necessarily would have involved the Supper (especially when, post Nicea, Easter would fall on the Lord's Day). For this reason it was preceded by a one- or two-day fast for those who were to be baptized, the so-called catechumens. And it may have been that their "sponsors" joined them in this. The baptisms would have been effected outside the regular meeting place of the community in order to have "living water" (a river or stream), as required by the late–first-century church order, the *Didache.* This would have taken place during Saturday night (a "vigil" of the Resurrection/Lord's Day according to the Jewish manner of defining "day" as "evening and morning"). The newly baptized were then escorted into church for the exchange of peace, the prayers of the faithful, and their first Communion. The baptismal rite included anointings by the bishop, which in later centuries became separated from the baptismal rite and formed an entirely separate rite known as "Confirmation." Another aspect of this vigil from early times was the parallel reception back into the community of any who had been disciplined by excommunication for a considerable period of time. At the vigil they shed their "sackcloth and ashes" and were also anointed by the bishop. This is the practice that at later date would give us Lent and its Ash Wednesday beginning.

The following fifty days formed a time of sacramental catechesis for the newly baptized and of rejoicing for the whole church, during which Nicea ruled there should be no fasting or kneeling (a penitential gesture) during worship. As for Jews, this time was a kind of annual "Jubilee" (fifty days rather than the fiftieth year), which culminated in the Pentecost celebration of the gift of the Spirit to *all* the nations (just as the Jewish community perhaps celebrated the giving of the Law to Moses on that day). Acts 2 bears many marks of this sort of Christian re-interpretation.

The pre-Easter season of forty days, now known as Lent (another pagan word, which refers to the season of Spring in the northern hemisphere), has its origins in these two disciplinary structures of catechumenal preparation and reconciliation of penitents, and is in fact a much later development. Following the "establishment" of Christianity in the fourth century and the subsequent practice of the universal baptism of infants shortly after birth rather than at the Easter Vigil, the catechumenate effectively disappears from the picture, leaving only reconciliation as the distinctive liturgy. This too declines as the church discliplinary structure weakens. The result of this may be described as the inevitable conservatism of ritual behavior wherein, when the original function of a ritual structure disappears or is forgotten, other reasons rush in to fill the gap. In this case the penitential preoccupation becomes a general practice for the whole community. This becomes quite strong in certain patterns of prayer and penitence among the Irish churches and monastics.

In addition, yet another ritual pattern develops throughout the ecumenical world, derivative of the pilgrimage practices in and around Jerusalem so eloquently witnessed to by the Spanish nun Egeria in the fourth century.[11] These took place during the week before Easter and form the beginnings of what is our present Holy Week, although the symbolism becomes temporal rather than spatial since only Jerusalem had the holy sites. The conjunction of penitence, passion, and death inevitably shifted the focus of the forty days from resurrection to death, thus seriously changing Lent from a pre-Easter preparation to a penitential period, which included fasting. The rites of Holy Week increasingly centered on the cross, with such rites as the Stations of the Cross, Tenebrae, and the Three Hours Devotion taking hold in the medieval period. This week was also necessarily a time for individuals to partake of the sacrament of penance, since all the faithful were required to receive Holy Communion at the Easter Masses.

The Easter Vigil had lost its drama and even timing (during the preceding night), thus separating the Easter celebration of resurrection from the developing Lent–Holy Week penitential anticipation of the Passion. This became elaborated in a two-week period (Holy Week being the second of the two)

11. See John Wilkinson, ed., *Egeria's Travels to the Holy Land,* rev. ed. (Warminster, England: Aris & Phillips, 1981).

whose beginning (the Fifth Sunday in Lent) became known as Passion Sunday. Lent itself was lengthened to include three preparatory Sundays: Septuagesima, Sexagesima, and Quinquagesima. And the Sundays in Lent, marked by largely penitential lections, took on Latin names derived from the first words of the Introits (Psalms) for the day: *Invocabit, Reminiscere, Oculi, Laetare* (more celebrative), *Judica* (Passion Sunday), and *Palmarum*. Finally, it became evident that the "forty days" weren't actually that number, since the Sundays in Lent did not count (a subtle indication that the Sundays of the season were Lord's Days, that is, resurrection days, and originally focused on the annual celebration of baptism/resurrection). To tidy up this situation the count of days was extended back to the Wednesday before the first Sunday in Lent, which became known as Ash Wednesday, with reference to the early penitential practice of the wearing of sackcloth and ashes, except that now the imposition of ashes became a universal requirement. The forty days also acquired a kind of commemorative function in relation to all those forty-day periods in the Old Testament and the forty-day fast of Jesus in his temptations, pericopes of which increasingly appeared in Lent.

This whole development, which spans almost a millennium from the fourth to the fourteenth centuries, powerfully indicates the way in which the church's worship is often shaped by many diverse and sometimes nonliturgical necessities in its ongoing life, such as discipline, its place in culture, its political connections, and waves of particular pieties. This is inevitable over such a lengthy period of time but is also suggestive of the importance of informed liturgical memory and, even more important, of paying careful attention to the liturgical use of Scripture as canonical and theological guidance for worship and piety. This is precisely the agenda that various Reformers — from Cranmer and Luther through Zwingli and Calvin to the Anabaptists — brought to bear on liturgical reform, however widely their solutions may have differed.

In the second part of this chapter we will give some attention to the ways in which in the last several decades both Roman Catholic and Protestant communities have re-shaped their liturgies, largely by reference to ancient practices and lectionary reform. But first, we move on to the Christmas cycle.

The Christmas Cycle: Advent, Christmas, the Twelve Days, Epiphany

The church lived for almost four centuries without this sequence at all, although it may be that Epiphany did precede Christmas in the East, perhaps from the second or third centuries. And according to its scriptural pericopes, there was a water festival of some sort whose gospel was John 1:1–2:11, with the focus being on Jesus' baptism, his calling of the first disciples, and his first "sign" of glory at Cana of Galilee. For churches whose gospel was the Fourth Gospel this made a suitable beginning at what was also the beginning of the civil year (January 6). But more of that date later.

Christmas, the festival of the Nativity (December 25), was a contribution of the Western churches, notably those of Rome and North Africa, sometime in the early fourth century. It is impossible to say when and where it was first celebrated. The "why" question, however, is not quite so difficult. It was during that century that the church was hammering out its Christological and Trinitarian affirmations. One of the important issues of the time was the question of the eternity of the deity of Jesus Christ, the second person of the Holy Trinity. Adoptionism was a significant alternate position, and the Eastern emphasis on the baptism of the Lord at Epiphany seemed to invite just such a misunderstanding. Thus the Western invention of a festival of the Nativity was useful if not deliberate, in effect pushing Christ's deity back to his birth and before. This would also have been quite acceptable to those local churches that used Matthew or Luke as their Gospel; and in the case of the First Gospel, that included the church in Rome.

Traditional liturgical scholarship, well into the twentieth century, noticing the coincidence of the date of December 25 and the Winter Solstice in Rome (December 21), made the assumption that since the church emerged from its minority status with the conversion of Constantine and the declaration of its legitimacy in 325 A.D., the introduction of a Nativity feast at about the same time would indicate an attempt to "baptize" the solstice by way of a parallel between Christ as the "Sun of Righteousness" from the East (Malachi 4:2) and the solstice feast of the sun, *Sol Invictus.* This sociological "history of religions" methodology has recently been seriously and convincingly challenged by the Anglican scholar Thomas Talley.[12] Talley works principally with patristic evidence and lectionary systems of the first centuries. His question is simply, where *did* the date of December 25 come from as the birth of Jesus? (How many children have put this question to parents and pastors, only to receive less than adequate answers!)

Talley identifies an obvious but overlooked consonance between the dates of December (Nativity in the West) or January 6 (Epiphany in the East) and the supposed dates (according to the civil calendar) of Jesus' death (March 25 in the West and April 6 in the East). He reminds us of Jewish mythology that

---

12. See Talley, *Origins of the Liturgical Year.*

all great and holy men are born and die on the same day of the year. For the church's theological purposes, however, birth would have to refer back to conception ("by the holy Spirit and the Virgin Mary"). If the conception date were the same as the death date that would produce a birth date, for the West, of December 25!

This is not Talley's whole argument, however. He has analyzed all available lectionaries from the earliest centuries of the great patriarchal sees of the Middle East, and particularly Egeria's account of the pilgrimage rites in Jerusalem, to suggest that local churches' "course reading" of their Gospels, particularly Mark and John beginning at Epiphany, would quite naturally have brought them to the Passion narratives just at the week before April 6. His argument is quite complex and cannot possibly be summarized here, but its significance is not to be underestimated. Simply put, he argues that the dates of Christmas and Epiphany are a direct and conscious function of the dates various churches held to be those of Christ's death at Passover. Thus, Christmas, at least, not only appears much later on the annual calendar than does Easter, but it is directly dependent on it. So Talley concludes:

> By the early fourth century the projection from April 6th to yield the date of the Epiphany on January 6th was replicated in North Africa and at Rome to give December 25th as the nativity date, based on March 25th as the date of the passion. Later, in the fourth century, that nativity festival on December 25th was adopted at Constantinople, throughout Cappadocia, and at Antioch, while the Epiphany was adopted in the West, albeit with an unfortunate limitation of its meaning to "the manifestation of Christ to the Gentiles," at least in Rome and in Africa.[13]

This leads Talley to identify "the intimate relation that exists between the gospel tradition and its liturgical employment."[14] And for us Reformed Christians this is not only a remarkably suggestive comment about the relationship of canon to calendar but also a serious warning as to what we make of calendars without taking account of their related lectionaries. This leads us "back" to Advent.

Now universally celebrated as a preparatory period for Christmas, Advent is scripturally and historically nothing of the sort. Its history is that of the *last* Sundays of the year (civic and liturgical), wherein the pericopes were eschatological in their thrust, that is, having to do with "last things." The duration of the season was anywhere from four to nine weeks and its lessons

---

13. Talley, *Origins of the Liturgical Year,* p. 235.
14. Talley, *Origins of the Liturgical Year,* p. 235.

tended toward a penitential emphasis, perhaps as parallel to the later development of Lent, but more probably in reference to the Second Coming of the Lord as judge. This is the case with contemporary lectionaries, as we shall shortly see. Nevertheless, much of our Advent worship addresses itself not to the Last Things but to the coming Nativity celebration, including the Advent wreath's "countdown" and the singing of Christmas carols, to say nothing of homiletical allusions to gifts, children, and Christmas "preparations." All of this has nothing whatever to do with the traditional pericopes pointing to the return of the Lord. How strange, in a Reformed congregation, on the first Sunday of Advent, to begin with the lighting of an Advent wreath candle to mark the number of days until the Nativity, and then to hear as the Gospel lesson "watch and pray, for *no one knows* the day or the hour"! Popular piety and cultural conditioning conspire to destroy the gospel's message. (One hears in the background Schleiermacher's panegyric on Christmas Eve.) Once again, history triumphs over eschatology, when, in fact, if Talley is right, the only *history* to which even Christmas refers is in fact the date of the Lord's death, itself a "guess" as to the date of Passover.

Next, what of those twelve days between Christmas and Epiphany (so suggestive of the fifty days between Easter and Pentecost)? Even the popular English folksong, filled with Christian symbolism, "The Twelve Days of Christmas," is worn out by its wearying use throughout Advent well before the "twelve days" have even occurred! Depending on the day of the week of December 25 there can be one or two Sundays during this period, and lectionaries make provision for this by variously scheduling the two birth narratives and the Johannine Prologue (1:1-18). But there are also interesting weekday commemorations, largely hagiographical and, therefore, unhappily foreign to most Reformed churches. Since Christmas may fall on any one of these they are worthy of notice, if only for the unusual theological light they shed on our perhaps too romantic Christmas reflections having to do with snow, children, lights, and possessions. They are as follows: December 26: St. Stephen, Deacon and Martyr; December 27: St. John, Apostle and Evangelist; December 28: The Holy Innocents; December 29: Thomas Becket, Archbishop and Martyr. These persons, suggestively, have come to be known as "the Companions of Jesus." They compose an amazing set of witnesses to the meaning of "this child," to recall Simeon's premonition in Luke (Luke 2.34). They make for distinctive praying and preaching during the twelve days.

Finally, there is Epiphany itself, January 6, affectionately known in some places as "Twelfth night," the time in Great Britain for the "burning of the greens." (In the United States, of course, because the "greens" were probably displayed sometime in late November or early December, they have probably been thrown on the trash heap already shortly after December 26.) As described above, the early history of Epiphany in the East was devoted to the baptism of Jesus and perhaps Christian baptism, including, in Coptic churches, the blessing of wells and village water systems.[15] But as Talley has lamented, in the West this emphasis gave way to the birth narrative's account of the visit of the Magi as a "type" of Christ's "manifestation" to the Gentiles. One would have thought that this theological note was well enough covered at the festival of Pentecost, but for reasons best known to the fourth-century Roman church, the Magi were moved in. (Since Epiphany was a "feast from the East" perhaps the Roman mind decided that these mysterious figures "from the East" were more appropriate.) Perhaps Rome was safeguarding its own Christmas festival by incorporating Epiphany into that narrative. Then, however, the issue that must be raised if Epiphany is used to celebrate the Magi, is what to do with the baptism of the Lord? The solution of the two current three-year systems is to move that to the First Sunday after Epiphany. This needs careful planning, however, because of the shifting day of the week of January 6. In other words, which way should the Epiphany be translated, forward or backward? Preferably, it should go backward onto a Sunday after Christmas so as to guarantee the observance of the baptism of the Lord.

In summary then, concerning the two cycles annually celebrated, a Reformed appropriation needs to be quite clear about early and patristic understandings of these occasions and their biblical underpinnings. The unity of Paschal and eschatological themes in the weekly and annual cycles must be freed from pious and historicist pre- and post-medieval preoccupations, especially at Holy Week, the Great Fifty Days, and Advent. This can only be accomplished in our own time of liturgical change, reform, adaptation, and inculturation by the most serious and detailed consideration of the use and place of Scripture in the context of public worship. For this reason we must turn now to matters of contemporary lectionary reform and creation.

Lectionaries

The strict definition of the word *lectionary* is simply a book in which are collected and printed the readings from canonical literature appointed by a given ecclesiastical authority for a cycle of liturgical occasions, be that the weekly Lord's Day service, a Daily Office pattern, or particular pastoral rites and sacraments other than Mass or Eucharist. Such a book might include all neces-

---

15. George Every, S.S.M., *The Baptismal Sacrifice* (London: SCM Press, 1959).

sary readings, or one or another, such as the Gospel. Such books, called "Comes," began to appear, at the latest, in the fifth century. They have been known as "evangelary," "epistolary," and "full lectionary." Thus, in such traditions the readings were not proclaimed from a full Bible or Testament.

Behind this seemingly simple distinction for the liturgical proclamation of the word of God — from Bible or from lectionary — there lurk significantly different ways of thinking of Scripture in various traditions. At the time of the sixteenth-century Reformation and its technological ally, moveable type, it became practical to publicly use a whole Bible. This crystallized a theological distinction that roughly came to characterize Protestant and Catholic scriptural use and theology; the American lectionary scholar Fritz West has described this as a distinction between "Scripture" (the Protestant use of the whole Bible) and "memory" (the Catholic use of a lectionary book).[16]

This distinction between "Scripture" and "memory" also raises the question of the two classic ways of arranging readings over a given period of time or calendar, which have been mentioned in the previous section of this chapter — i.e., "in course" *(lectio continua)* and "selected" *(lectio selecta)*. Roughly speaking, the divide at the sixteenth century was between the Roman, Anglican, and Lutheran churches, on the one hand, using selected readings, and, on the other hand, the Reformed, including the Zwinglian, Calvinist, and later the Puritan strains, using the "in course" system. Interestingly, the continuous principle seems to be an inheritance of the early church from the synagogue's reading of Torah, whether on a one-year or, as some have supposed, a three-year pattern. Early Christian lectionaries seem also to have used this system for the Gospels, and one would think that such was the only reasonable way to read the epistles as well (Col. 4:16; 1 Thess. 5:27).

One might go so far as to say that the whole history of the liturgical use of Scripture has been a process whereby this "course" reading of the various books of the canon was gradually overtaken by the other "selected" pattern, this having to do with the development, as mentioned earlier, of annual, weekly, or local festivals that came to displace the ordinary course of readings, to say nothing of Marian or hagiographical cycles or particular days devoted to theological, historical, or pious emphases. At the same time, in a development that was certainly never carefully thought out, if only because of local diversity of practice, the use of the Old Testament dropped out of the principal service of the Lord's Day. Although such use is referred to by Justin Martyr (ca. 215), the Apostolic Constitutions, Ambrose of Milan, and Augustine of Hippo

---

16. Fritz West, *Scripture and Memory: The Ecumenical Hermeneutics of the Three-Year Lectionaries* (Collegeville, Minn.: Liturgical Press, 1997).

(with the pericopes mentioned being preponderantly prophetic rather than Torah), this had disappeared altogether by the time of the Reformation, perhaps between the sixth and ninth centuries. Of course, the Daily Office, used only by clerics and monastics, retained extensive course reading of the Old Testament. Thus the Reformation became a critical moment both to reintroduce the Bible, as book, to liturgical worship, and to do so, insofar as possible, in its entirety. This necessitated the drawing up of entirely new tables of readings — which brings us to the more common definition of the word *lectionary* for our own time and for the purpose of this chapter. Even though the strict definition of the term, as stated above, is a book, the word has come to refer also to a table or listing of readings, whether in reference to a Bible in liturgical use or for the purpose of publishing the liturgical books containing the appointed texts. It is in this broader sense that we will now use the term in this chapter.

Recent History

The Daily Office

Lectionary systems, East and West, are primarily devoted to two cycles. The first of these is the daily cycle of prayer, encompassing two to seven or eight brief services of praise and prayer each day, characterized mainly by the use of the Psalter, course reading of the Old and New Testaments, hagiographical readings, and prayers. Although the Anglican Archbishop Thomas Cranmer in the sixteenth century sought to make of this pattern (as a twofold morning and evening structure) a parish-wide experience, as apparently it had been in the case of the early church's so-called "cathedral office," and Calvin and other Reformed leaders at least undertook a daily preaching service, later efforts to move daily prayers and Bible readings into a domestic setting finally failed. Thus the daily office is still a discipline largely of clergy and intentional residential communities. The importance of this cycle is at least twofold: it provides a daily/weekly calendar for Christian worship, and it has always included a full course reading of the Old Testament and repetitive use of the Psalter, in some cycles traversing the entire corpus each week and in others, each month. The new Presbyterian U.S.A. *Book of Common Worship* (1992) does provide such an Office complete with a Psalter to be recited or chanted. In our own time, with the development of a full three-year lectionary for the Lord's Day Service (of which more later), the parity or interplay between daily and weekly cycles has taken on new significance. The North American Consultation on

Common Texts is now working on a plan to integrate these two cycles. And the Roman Catholic Church in the English-speaking world is working on a comprehensive reform of the entire Breviary. The principal issue here is the comprehensive and comprehensible use of the canon of Holy Scripture.

The Weekly Lord's Day Service: Roman Catholic Developments

The Missal of Paul VI (1969), a direct result of Vatican II's document on the liturgy, *Sacrosanctum Concilium,* has radically reformed the Mass of the Roman Catholic liturgy for the first time since the Missal of Paul V (1570). A major part of that reform is to be found in one of the Holy See's publications that same year, *Ordo lectionum Missae.* These two documents define both parts of the Sunday Mass, the Liturgy of the Word and the Liturgy of the Altar, just as the council's deliverance itself stated that "The two parts . . . are so closely connected with each other that they form but one single act of worship" (para. 56). In an earlier paragraph (51) the council ruled that "The treasures of the Bible are to be opened up more lavishly, so that richer fare may be provided for the faithful at the table of God's word. In this way a more representative portion of the Holy Scripture will be read to the people in the course of a prescribed number of years."[17]

The Roman lectionary laid out a three-year cycle in order to read the entirety of the Synoptic Gospels one year at a time — Matthew in year A, Mark in year B, and Luke in year C, with the Fourth Gospel being read on the festival Sundays of Advent/Christmas and Lent/Easter, and John 6 in Mark's year to fill out that shorter Gospel's length. The sequence of Gospel readings is continuous or semi-continuous beginning at Christmas and concluding with the pre-Passion chapters just before Advent, but being interrupted in Lent/Easter for pericopes anticipating Christ's Easter triumph and utilizing pre-baptismal symbolism, and of course for the Passion narrative itself on Passion/Palm Sunday and Good Friday, to be followed during the Great Fifty Days with the resurrection Gospel texts. The Pauline and pseudo-Pauline epistles are read continuously or semi-continuously during the Sundays that comprise "Ordinary Time," namely the thirty-three or thirty-four Sundays following Epiphany and Pentecost. The Johannine Epistles are read "selectively" during the Fifty Days. Thus there is no intended correlation between Gospel and epistle in Ordinary Time, though many preachers and learned commentaries seem never to

17. *The Revised Common Lectionary: Includes Complete List of Lections for Years A, B, and C* (Nashville: Abingdon Press, 1992; for Canada: Winfield, B.C.: Wood Lake Books, Inc., 1992; for England: Norwich: Canterbury Press, 1992).

have noticed that! The Old Testament selections are more or less typologically tied to the Gospel for the day throughout the entire calendar year, and the psalms are always thematically related to the Old Testament passage.

The Weekly Lord's Day Service: North American Ecumenical Developments

With the appearance of the Roman lectionary (which received some minor additions in 1981) an extraordinary ecumenical development opened up in North America. Immediately following Vatican II, Roman Catholic Bishops' Conferences in the English-speaking world had created a Secretariat in Washington, D.C., to coordinate the vast work of translation of the Roman liturgical books into a common English. This is the International Commission on English in the Liturgy (ICEL). Some farsighted and even prophetic individuals in ICEL and certain Protestant churches quickly moved in 1965 to create a parallel ecumenical agency, the Consultation on Common Texts (CCT), representing churches in both the United States and Canada and including ICEL (which became CCT's secretariat in a most generous fashion for over thirty-five years).

Although CCT initially worked principally with liturgical texts such as the creeds and the Lord's Prayer, it provided the venue for subsequent consideration of lectionary matters. This was done in tandem with another ecumenical liturgical body, the Worship Commission of the (United States) Consultation on Church Union (COCU), whose membership significantly overlapped with CCT'S. As early as 1970 certain Presbyterian churches in the United States published a dramatically new service book and hymnal, *The Worshipbook* (1970 and 1972), which included a version of the 1969 Roman lectionary, proposed and prepared by a prescient member of the editorial committee, the Reverend Dr. Lewis Briner, then Dean of the Chapel at McCormick Seminary in Chicago.

In very short order other North American Protestant bodies undertook their own editions and revisions of the Roman *Ordo,* such that by 1974 the COCU Worship Commission had published a consensus version. Then in 1978 CCT assembled a consultation in Washington, D.C., to evaluate the usefulness of the Roman system in Protestant settings. I was the chair of CCT at the time and at its direction assembled a working group that year to prepare an ecumenical version of the Roman document. This work was done and published in 1983 as *Common Lectionary (CL).* It was understood at the time that this was a "proposal" to be used experimentally for a period of nine years (three cycles) and then revised. It adopted virtually unchanged the Gospel and epistle choices of the Roman model. Its major divergence was in the Old Testament set of readings for Ordinary Time. Although the Episcopal and Lutheran constituencies were fairly content with the Roman choices, the more Calvinist groups were unhappy with the "typological" principle of selection, on a Sunday-by-Sunday basis. Reaction had also been registered from Afro-American churches, which missed the lengthy patriarchal and Mosaic narratives and much of the pungent prophetic literature. CCT's decision was to abandon, in Ordinary Time after Pentecost, a close thematic connection between Gospel and Old Testament lections in favor of a more broadly conceived typology and semi-continuous readings from the Hebrew Bible. Thus during the post-Pentecost time in year A (Matthew), the core of the patriarchal and Mosaic narratives was inserted; for the same period in year B (Mark) the Davidic narrative was excerpted, and for year C (Luke) the Elijah-Elisha narrative was included together with one passage from each of the Minor Prophets (with the exception of Obadiah). Toward Advent in each year the Old Testament pericopes were largely drawn from wisdom and eschatological literature, which the Roman table had hardly touched.

British Ecumenical Developments

At about the same time as the Roman lectionary was being created, an ecumenical liturgical body in Great Britain had embarked upon a revision of the various one- or two-year systems then in use there. Based on a proposal of Allan A. McArthur of the Church of Scotland, known as the Peterhead Lectionary,[18] the Joint Liturgical Group (JLG) produced in 1968 a two-year cycle. This system rather radically re-cast the annual calendar along Trinitarian lines, devoting a greatly lengthened Advent season to the Father (rather like the proposal mentioned in the next chapter by Lukas Vischer), the season from Christmas to Pentecost to the Son, and from Pentecost to Advent to the Holy Spirit. The pericopes were selected on the basis of theological themes throughout and included three lessons and a psalm for each Sunday. For the season of the Father the Old Testament pericope was the "controlling" lesson; for the season of the Son the Gospel was the controlling lesson; and for the season of the Holy Spirit the epistle was the controlling lesson.

This lectionary became widely used even by Free churches that had not previously employed any lectionary table. Of course, the Roman Catholic Church in Great Britain was using the Roman 1969 system. Curiously, under the influence of that three-year scheme there even appeared from some members of the JLG a proposal to move to a four-year scheme utilizing the Synop-

18. McArthur, *The Christian Year and Lectionary Reform.*

tic Gospels, as in the Roman and ecumenical patterns, but adding a Johannine year, while at the same time suppressing a weekly dependence on "themes." All of this was overtaken by the events surrounding participation by British representatives in the production of *Revised Common Lectionary* (1992), which both established churches (of Scotland and of England) eventually adopted.

International Developments

As the North American CCT contemplated its further work of revision of *Common Lectionary* at the end of the 1980s, it determined that the rapidly growing convergence in lectionary usage, between its product and the Roman *Ordo lectionum missae (OLM),* needed a more international basis, especially if Roman Catholic authorities were ever to consider allowing the CCT's work to be used in Catholic circles. It also realized that if other linguistic groups were to be drawn in, perhaps through the World Council of Churches, it would be important to set up an international ecumenical body to go beyond CCT's exclusively North American representation; such a group could succeed the international, ecumenical body that ICEL had encouraged in the early seventies (the International Consultation on English Texts, or ICET), which had suspended its meetings in 1974 with the publication of proposed common texts as *Praying Together.*[19] Thus CCT and ICEL invited representatives from the Australian Consultation on Liturgy, JLG from Great Britain, and similar bodies from South Africa, New Zealand, and Ireland in 1985 to form the English Language Liturgical Consultation (ELLC). This group immediately took over stewardship of CL and participated in its revision to produce the Revised Common Lectionary (RCL 1992). This made possible successive if not very successful visits to the Word Council of Churches in Geneva (1993) and the Holy See in Rome (1994).

This narrative thus far has encompassed only English-speaking, Western churches. ELLC has more recently, however, entered into conversations with Catholic German and French liturgical groups and is seeking connections with similar Protestant groupings, having heard that in some French Reformed churches there was an interest in using the Roman OLM. The German Protestant situation is still dominated by the classic Lutheran one-year multilesson lectionary together with its associated "preaching texts" for each Sunday in a six-year cycle. Finally, it can be reported that interest is now being expressed by both Greek and Russian Orthodox communities in North Amer-

---

19. The International Consultation on English Texts, *Prayers We Have in Common, Agreed Liturgical Texts,* rev. ed. (Philadelphia: Fortress Press, 1975).

ica as they are now undertaking the translation of their liturgical books into English. CCT has formally invited the Archbishop of the Greek Orthodox Archdiocese of America, in his capacity as Chair of the Standing Committee of Orthodox Bishops in America, to designate a representative.

Functions and Future of Lectionary Systems

The basic thesis of this chapter has been that the interrelatedness of calendar and lectionary is critical, especially for Reformed churches and their worship. It is also true that the Reformed tradition has always been serious about the ecumenical dimensions of both theology and worship. Therefore, in the present day of extensive liturgical renewal in Protestantism and Catholicism, it is more than essential that the functioning of the canonical pericopes be carefully assessed to provide criteria for the selection of any given lectionary system. And let it not be forgotten that there is always a lectionary system operative, even if it is as casual and spontaneous as the "inspiration" of the local pastor in any given week as the Lord's Day approaches.

To undertake such a "critical" evaluation of extant systems or the creation of new systems it should be noted that the liturgical use of Scripture, in any tradition, time, or place, generally functions in a combination of certain purposes. Since no system is ever going to be "perfect," and since we are in a moment of *semper reformanda*, it might be helpful to delineate the principal ways in which a lectionary does work. They are at least six, which are not necessarily in conflict with one another but which need to be understood in terms of priority and theological importance. These six may be listed as follows, not necessarily in terms of priority but perhaps in terms of historical development:

Full and Catechetical

This is the thrust of the Vatican Council's liturgical document cited above, which speaks of opening up "the treasures of the Bible . . . more lavishly" (para. 51). This is also much of the reason that the three-year systems were developed to cover a longer period than traditional one-year systems did, so as to give full attention to each of the Synoptic Gospels. And of course this is precisely the reason that Scripture was originally read aloud in the assembly, since there was obviously no other way, other than particular catechesis (for catechumens for instance), for the community to become familiar with these texts. This is also the reason that the Reformed tradition returned to "course" reading for both daily and weekly cycles. And in our own modern day, who is to doubt that widespread biblical illiteracy is the fruit both of a thoughtless and unsystematic use of the Scriptures on the Lord's Day and of the collapse of many traditional catechetical structures in the local congregation, such as Sunday church schools? And who is to doubt that recovery of "full" use on the Lord's Day is therefore essential?

Homiletical

The biblical origins of liturgical preaching, as distinct from public, missionary preaching, are notoriously difficult to identify. Certainly, however, the influence of synagogue teaching (Luke 4) was not inconsiderable. And from a very early date in the patristic period sermons begin to appear that are clearly meant for the gathered eucharistic community. This rich tradition was revived and renewed in the sixteenth century. The question for our own time, however, is whether the texts for the day are truly authoritative for the homily or mere pretexts for the preacher to say whatever he or she had planned to do in any event. This is the importance of an ecumenically or ecclesiastically determined lectionary to which, as Scripture and in the liturgical memory of the church, the preacher is responsible and answerable to his or her own local people of God.

Feasts, Festivals, and Seasons

This function of lectionaries usually brings into play the *selecta* principle, which interrupts the *continua* principle, as must have been the practice in the synagogue and in the early church at Paschal-tide and later at Christmas. This is what Fritz West defines as the "memory" aspect of the more catholic lectionaries. RCL, following the 1969 OLM, devotes the Sundays around Christmas and Easter to this pattern. West defines the two principles of "continuous" and "selected" as "two hermeneutical settings interpret[ing] the passages from Scripture which they carry in strikingly different ways."[20] He concludes, with regard to RCL, that it "has arrived at a compelling solution for the balance of the written and communal memories of the Church in the interpretation of Scripture."[21] Clearly, different traditions will have a more or less elaborate pattern at this point, but it is worth noting that the Calvinist position was never as severe as the Puritan (anti–Anglican Prayer Book and pro–Westminster Directory) position.

20. West, *Scripture and Memory*, p. xi.
21. West, *Scripture and Memory*, p. xi.

Cultural, Climatic, Seasonal, and Ethnic

We have already noticed how all of these factors play into the cultic life of all liturgical traditions. This is where the issues of inculturation, adaptation, and "relevance" enter in. This involves difficult decisions, positively and negatively. I am acutely aware, for instance, of the severity with which Korean Reformed churches have rejected much of what the ecumenical tradition would regard as legitimate celebration of All Saints' Day and the communion of the saints, for cultural and evangelistic reasons. Clearly churches from Third World countries and perspectives will want to bring into play their own geographical and temporal contexts. This can impinge very directly on the choice of scriptural material that reflects early Greco-Roman cultural mores (on marriage and family, for instance), or, even more delicately, the use of the terms "Israel" and "Jerusalem" by Christians in a Palestinian context. In North America recent years have seen generous discussion of so-called sexist language throughout the Scriptures. And at the present moment there seems ample evidence of a Roman backlash concerning concessions in this matter, particularly in the forbidding of lectionary use of the New Revised Standard Version of the Bible implied in the document *Liturgiam Authenticam: On the Use of Vernacular Languages in the Publication of the Books of the Roman Liturgy*.[22]

Liturgical and Doxological

A lively debate often breaks out on this issue. Certain traditions, usually on the Catholic side, are wary of the catechetical use intruding upon the strictly doxological. This discussion sometimes simply turns on the question of the length of any given pericope. This is of course particularly problematic in course reading, especially of the Old Testament. Perhaps the most obvious occasion in the church's annual calendar of the kind of accommodation between these two positions is to be found in the extensive set of readings generally associated with the Easter Vigil. It is probably not irrelevant that this rite is itself poised between the catechetical experience of the newly baptized and the climactic eucharistic celebration of the entire year.

---

22. Congregation for Divine Worship and the Discipline of the Sacraments, *Liturgiam Authenticam: On the Use of Vernacular Languages in the Publication of the Books of the Roman Liturgy* (Vatican City, 2001).

Historical and Ecumenical

Particular denominational and theological traditions have their own histories of the use of certain pericopes on certain days or in certain seasons. In the formation of RCL, for instance, we found no way to get around a standoff as to whether the Transfiguration narrative should be read on the last Sunday after Epiphany or on the Second Sunday in Lent. So both were listed as alternatives. And as indicated above, in North America, Afro-American churches require regular attention to the Exodus narrative as virtually equivalent to a Gospel pericope.

No doubt other functions could be discerned by careful analysis but these seem to account for most extant or historical systems. The relative weight given each by any church's lectionary is probably a fairly good indicator of that community's ecclesiology, implicit or explicit. Our Reformed tradition is rightly wary about "days and seasons," but the thesis of this chapter is that by losing, for a protracted period of time, much of the classic liturgy and lectionary of the ecumenical church, it has paid a high price. Our own time, at the turn of the centuries and millennia, and our own churches have, however, been blessed with an extraordinary moment in which the Church of Rome has finally heard the pleas of a Luther or Calvin regarding the use of Scripture in the liturgy. By its thorough liturgical reformation according to Vatican II's *Constitution on the Sacred Liturgy,* it has given us an invaluable guide to our own, necessarily continuing, liturgical reformation. If that should mean an ecumenical appropriation across linguistic, geographical, and denominational boundaries of an already widely used adaptation of a Roman lectionary *(Revised Common Lectionary),* why should this not be the cause for great rejoicing, that at the present moment we may now experience unity at the table of the word of God, even if we must still await such a happy moment at the table of the Supper of the Lord? As my theological mentor, Paul Lehmann, often mused, "the Holy Spirit does have a Semitic sense of humor."

For Further Reading

Allen, Horace T., Jr. Introduction ("Preaching in a Christian Context") to *Handbook for the Revised Common Lectionary,* ed. Peter C. Bower. Louisville: Westminster/John Knox Press, 1996. Pp. 1-24.

———. *Lectionaries: Principles and Problems: A Comparative Analysis.* Studia Liturgica 22, no. 1 (1992): 68-83.

Allen, Horace T., Jr., and Joseph Russell. *On Common Ground.* Norwich, England: Canterbury Press, 1998.

Huitgren, Arland J. *Hermeneutical Tendencies in the Three-Year Lectionary.* Studies in Lutheran Hermeneutics. Ed. John Reumann. Philadelphia: Fortress Press, 1979. Pp. 145-73.

Ordo Lectionum Missae. Vatican City: Polyglot Press, 1969. (English translation: *Lectionary for Mass.* Collegeville, Minn.: Liturgical Press, 1970.)

Ramshaw, Gail. "The First Testament in Christian Lectionaries." *Worship* 64 (1990): 484-510.

Revised Common Lectionary: Includes Complete List of Lections for Year A, B, and C. Nashville: Abingdon Press, 1992; in Canada: Winfield, B.C.: WoodLake Books, Inc. 1992; in England: Norwich: Canterbury Press, 1992.

Sloyan, Gerard Stephen. "Some Suggestions for a Biblical Three-Year Lectionary." *Worship* 63 (1989): 521-35.

West, Fritz. *Scripture and Memory: The Ecumenical Hermeneutic of the Three-Year Lectionaries.* Collegeville, Minn.: Liturgical Press, 1997.

Worship as Christian Witness to Society

Lukas Vischer

Reformed worship has always been public worship. The proclamation of the word has never been confined to spiritual themes but has also included aspects of public life. But the awareness that worship is always taking place *in* the world and has to contribute to the promotion of God's love and will in society has become stronger in recent decades. It is true that worship implies, in a certain sense, a withdrawal from the world. The community gathers in order to concentrate minds and hearts on the essential content of the Christian message — to listen to the word and to praise God's name. It distances itself, for a time, from the world in order to engage afterward in an even more determined service to the world. The life of the community is characterized by the double movement of gathering for worship and being sent into the world, and these two movements cannot be separated. The sending is prepared by the gathering. The witness in the world receives its strength from the relationship with God that has been renewed in worship. From the service in the world the community returns to the praise of God in worship. Appropriately, the witness in the world is often called by Orthodox Christians the "liturgy after the liturgy." This means that the witness to the world is inherent and present in every true act of worship.

The two movements can easily fall apart. Again and again worship is being celebrated as a self-contained event. Again and again worship becomes a refuge from the world and its challenges. Often, the community succumbs to the temptation to leave the world to itself. But the truth stands: God so loved the world — this world — that he gave for it his only begotten Son. The credibility of worship depends on the willingness of the community to share in God's movement of love for the world. Worship will always have an impact; it can either lift up God's love for the world or it can, on the contrary, hide that love behind spiritual walls.

Facing today's ever more rapid social change, the question of the political and social witness through the church's worship must be asked anew. How is the impact of worship on society to be seen? On the one hand, the rapid change calls for an even more determined concentration on the *raison d'être* of the church. On the other hand, there is, in the face of the injustice, violence, and suffering resulting from the change, even greater urgency to appeal to the critical and transforming potential of the gospel. In the course of the last decades, many attempts have been made to relate worship to the world. Many of these attempts were ecumenical, and in many cases Reformed congregations, communities, and churches were directly involved. The debate on the pros and cons of "political worship services" is still far from concluded.

The Public Character of Reformed Worship

The aim of the sixteenth-century Reformation was a comprehensive renewal. Most importantly, the church was to be purified from errors and abuses, but at the same time, society was to be renewed. Without hesitation the reformers — particularly those of the Reformed vein — addressed issues of public life. More than in other Christian traditions, especially more than in the Lutheran tradition, the Reformed churches emphasized the need for the independence of the church from state interference or control. At all times the church was to be free to point to the claims of the gospel on state authorities and on society as a whole. The witness of a church ceasing to enjoy this freedom would inevitably be reduced in its effectiveness. Facing the threat of a totalitarian ideology, the Confessing Church reminded Christians in Germany of the need for this freedom. Thesis 2 of the Barmen Theological Declaration (1934) states that the God who turns to humanity in forgiveness is the master of the entire life of humans and that there is therefore no aspect of human life that would be exempted from God's claim. Thesis 5 both explicitly recognizes and limits the authority of the state. The authority of the state has its legitimacy and its limitation in God's mandate to "be responsible for law and peace." The church is not an organ of the state, but it has the task of reminding people of God's kingdom, commandment, and justice, and of pointing to the responsibilities of both authorities and citizens.[1]

The interaction between church and state also has its place in worship.

1. An English translation of the Barmen Declaration can be found in Presbyterian Church (U.S.A.), *Constitution,* Part I, *Book of Confessions;* cf. also Jack Rogers, *Presbyterian Creeds: A Guide to the Book of Confessions* (Philadelphia: Westminster Press, 1985).

The community gathers in the first place in order to praise God. As it assembles under God's word it also seeks to gain clarity about itself. Who are we who have come together here? Where have we failed? In what direction are we sent by God's forgiving word? The search for clarity also includes the reflection on the place and vocation of the community in society. What has happened around us? What developments are becoming apparent? At what points is the proclamation of the gospel being challenged in a particular way? A common effort at "reading the signs of the time" needs to take place; in other words, an effort needs to be made to understand the events and developments in society in the light of God's liberating message and to judge the degree of their relevance or nonrelevance. The interpretation of developments in society is not automatic. The connection between God's word and the diverse realms of human life needs to be constantly rediscovered. Worship provides the occasion to establish the connection in the first place for the community itself. As the community gains clarity on its vocation in society, God's word begins to be effective also beyond the community's boundaries.

At all times the *sermon* was the privileged instrument in this process of reflection and recognition. Preaching is by nature the attempt to understand God's word and to interpret its significance for today. Throughout history there have been pastors who also included in their preaching the realm of public life; at all times preachers have publicly called injustice by its name. Think of the religious socialists at the beginning of the twentieth century and their efforts to interpret the concerns of the labor movement in the light of the gospel. Think of the significance of preaching in the Confessing Church at the time of the Third Reich. Think of the warnings issued by the churches against economic injustice and the increasing destruction of the environment, and in particular of the role of preaching in the struggle against apartheid. Pastors addressing in their sermons political and social issues are, as a rule, controversial figures. They meet with both applause and criticism. Very often, only their graves will be decorated. But without the dimension of political and social witness, the proclamation of the gospel would lack the salt that the disciples have been promised by their Lord.

Another element of worship in which issues of public life have their place is *intercession,* which is an integral part of every worship service. Through the prayer of intercession the community brings itself, the church, and the entire world before God. It prays that God may make manifest the power of the Spirit, that the church may be strengthened, and especially that all those suffering from illness and despair may experience God's forgiving and healing presence. It gives room to its worry about the future and implores God to set limits to human irresponsibility and prevent further exploitation, violence, and destruction of life. As the psalmists did, it asks God to impose restraint on the "enemies" of the gospel. At all times intercession has included prayers for the government of the country, asking that God would empower the authorities to fulfill their tasks. This intercession is to be understood as an act of loyal solidarity. It becomes an act of political critique when government authorities transgress the function they are mandated to fulfill. Intercession especially acquires a political character when victims of political or economic oppression are mentioned explicitly and by their names.

New Dimensions of Political Worship

Does the political dimension of worship find expression exclusively through preaching and intercession? Or are there other ways of celebrating worship through which the political and social commitment of the community as a whole can even more clearly become visible? Reformed churches around the world have been increasingly preoccupied by this question. Preaching and intercession are fundamental elements of worship. As they are used as instruments of a determined witness in the world, the whole worship is given a new direction. Responsibility for preaching and intercession lies principally with the leaders of worship, since the content of both the sermon and the free prayer of intercession depends largely on their insight and decision. But how can the worship of the community as a whole become a sign to the world? True, preaching and intercession can have the support of the community as a whole; leaders can see themselves as representatives of the community and speak on its behalf, and their witness can be the expression of a position officially adopted by the church. (It may be preceded by a debate in the parish council or even an assembly of the community as a whole.) Nevertheless, preaching and intercession largely rest on the voice of a single person. Are there acts of political worship that involve to a larger extent the community as a whole?

Some attempts that have been made in the course of the last decades may be mentioned here as illustrations:

International Social Justice

In the late fifties and early sixties an awareness grew that the present economic system was the cause of increasing social injustice. The hope for a better world entertained in the first years after World War II vanished. Conscience was faced with the fact of a growing gap between rich and poor nations. At an early date the churches raised their voice to call for a correction of the economic course. Numerous church organizations that sought to alleviate the injustice and develop solutions came into existence. Increasingly, the issue had to be faced how churches in rich countries were to deal with their wealth. Was it not necessary to transcend the barriers of rich and poor, at least within the communion of the church? Was it not necessary to establish a kind of worldwide eucharistic communion and to share the gifts of creation with one another?

One response to these questions was a new interpretation of Lent. In many congregations the period of Ash Wednesday to Easter came to be a time for learning and practicing solidarity with the economically underprivileged. Fasting was practiced not only as the door to a deeper spiritual understanding of Jesus' passion but as an expression of solidarity. More and more development agencies used the period for their campaigns and sought, in diverse ways (often through special worship services), to raise the level of consciousness in the churches with regard to the intolerable disparity between rich and poor nations.

A similar function was fulfilled in many places by the renewal of the *agape,* the ancient tradition of the common meal after the celebration of the Eucharist. Generally, not only in Reformed churches but in the ecumenical movement as a whole, greater emphasis was placed on the meal aspect of the Eucharist. Was not this a way to overcome the concept of worship as mere ritual and to emphasize, through the actual sharing of a meal, the diaconal character of worship? In many places, agape meals were given the meaning of a sign of solidarity with the poor.

Intercession Leading to Intervention on Behalf of the Persecuted and Oppressed

In the 1970s Amnesty International was founded in response to the increased practice in many countries of oppression, torture, and extra-judicial killings. If the vision of a just economic order could not be realized, no effort was to be spared to protect at least the most fundamental human rights. Amnesty International launched a vast campaign against judicial arbitrariness, in particular the use of torture and the death penalty. Numerous congregations participated in this struggle. In worship, at the time of intercession, the names of particular political prisoners were mentioned, and at the end of the service the opportunity was offered to sign petition letters to governments and police of the countries concerned. The intercession in the service was understood as the first step toward concrete action. In certain cases, the intercession resulted in projects with wide ramifications.[2]

Sanctuary

How are we to deal with refugees fleeing from oppression, armed conflicts, and poverty, and seeking security outside their own country? Can churches resign themselves to the restrictive measures adopted by more and more countries, especially the rich industrialized countries, that are meant to reduce the influx of refugees? Can churches remain quiet as refugees are expelled and forced to return to their home countries? Churches have consistently argued in favor of a more generous strategy toward refugees and migrants. Some congregations have gone beyond statements and have offered their churches to refugees as sanctuaries; in other words, they have allowed them to stay in the rooms of the church building and in this way prevented the immediate execution of the expulsion order. An old tradition — biblical and ecclesiastical — thus gained new life.

The intention of such efforts is not to question the authority of the state and establish a separate sphere of law. As congregations accept refugees in their midst they only wish to compel state authorities to interpret the existing laws and administrative rules to the highest possible extent in favor of the refugee. An example: Twenty Kurds who had been expelled from Switzerland sought refuge in a Reformed church of Geneva. The parish council called a parish assembly. It was decided to put at the disposal of the Kurdish group the rooms of the church until their case was examined once more in all its aspects by the competent authority. Several weeks passed without police intervention. Finally, the verdict of the authorities was to maintain the expulsion of two leaders of the group but to grant the rest at least temporary asylum in Switzerland. The sanctuary time was concluded with an interreligious worship service.[3]

---

2. Egon Larsen, *A Flame in Barbed Wire: A History of Amnesty International* (London: F. Muller, 1978). An analogous organization with an explicitly Christian profile — Action des chrétiens pour l'abolition de la torture (ACAT) — was founded in France and spread to other countries.

3. Jill Schaeffer, *Sanctuary and Asylum* (Geneva: WARC, 1990).

Worship Services in Connection
with Political Events or Initiatives

It is one thing to address political and social themes in preaching or intercession, another to devote the whole service to a particular political or social issue. Special worship services can be organized for many reasons, such as to
pray for an end to violence and war, as in the period of increasing tensions in
Yugoslavia; to pray for reconciliation and peace, as for the peaceful reunifica-
tion of Korea; or to pray for the success of a conference, as for the U.N. conferences on economic justice or climate change. Even more than official statements, worship services on a particular political or social theme have become
part of the witness of the churches in public life.

The Community Bearing Witness:
Who Celebrates the Worship and Where?

The political witness of the churches sharply raises the question of the extent
to which the community practices in its own midst the solidarity it is calling
for in society. Is the community a mirror of what it proclaims in public? Again
and again communities lag behind the image of community that corresponds
to the gospel. Is it a community in which the poor have their place? Do the
weak, such as the handicapped, receive the place of honor they deserve? Or is
the Christian community just another association of healthy, strong, and successful people in which the weak and disabled are a foreign body?

More is at stake than the moral integrity of the church's witness. More
and more, in recent decades, an awareness has grown that the inclusiveness of
the community is decisive for the credibility of its witness. Reconciliation cannot be communicated if it is not celebrated by the community as a whole, if the
barriers that separate people from one another are not overcome and transcended within the community itself.

On two issues — the relationship between men and women, and racial
and ethnic barriers within the church — the insistence on the inclusiveness of
the community has led to far-reaching debates and changes.[4] The struggle for
a true community of men and women in the church and a true partnership between them clearly has spiritual dimensions, and inevitably affects ways of

---

4. The debate on the place of the handicapped both in society and in worship is another
illustration of the quest for inclusiveness. Cf. Geiko Müller-Fahrenholz, *Partners in Life,* Faith
and Order Paper 89 (Geneva, 1979).

worship. To what extent do women participate in giving shape to and leading worship? To what extent does the language used in worship reflect the fact that the congregation is a community of men and women? How does worship underline the commitment of the church to inclusiveness in society?[5]

Equally, the inclusiveness of the worshiping community is indispensable in the struggle for reconciliation between races and ethnic groups. In many churches, in the past decades, the common celebration of the Eucharist across racial or ethnic barriers was not only a crucial issue but part of the confession of faith. During the civil rights movement in the United States, sharing or not sharing in the same worship became a test of the commitment of the churches to the rights of the black minority. In the struggle against apartheid in South Africa, the consciousness matured in the Reformed churches that faith in Jesus Christ, the source of reconciliation, inevitably implies communion at the Lord's table. The decisive step was taken by the General Council of the World Alliance of Reformed churches in Ottawa (1982). It decided with an overwhelming majority to declare the *status confessionis* on racial discrimination within the church. In other words, it declared solemnly that racial discrimination was incompatible with the confession of Jesus Christ; the issue was declared to have the status of a fundamental truth. It is important to recall that the impetus for this decision was given at the opening service of the General Council. Through a statement read at the beginning of the service, the delegates of the black churches in South Africa made clear that they felt unable to share in Communion. What was not possible at home could not suddenly be practiced at an international conference. As long as the common celebration of the Eucharist was not permitted in South Africa, they had to refrain from participation at the General Council. More clearly than as the result of any long statement, the delegates were given a choice: would they participate in a Communion service reflecting a distorted fellowship? What was, under these circumstances, Communion at the Lord's table? Can a church that does not admit Christians to the Lord's Supper on racial grounds be considered the church of Christ? The clear language of the General Council on racial discrimination and apartheid thus has its roots in the celebration of the Eucharist.[6]

To make visible God's reconciling work to the world, the inclusiveness of the worshiping community is not the only prerequisite. Very often the question arises as to *where* worship takes place. Again and again congregations have had to decide to celebrate worship not as usual within the walls of their

---

5. See Leonora Tubbs Tisdale's chapter in this volume on the place of women in worship.
6. World Alliance of Reformed Churches, *Ottawa 1982, Proceedings of the 21st General Council*, Geneva 1983, pp. 55 and 176ff.

church building but in places where their witness was more likely to be heard by the public. Instead of waiting for the world to enter the church, they decided to choose places for their witness where the conflict was actually going on. When organized in the world, worship services become to an even higher degree political signs. They acquire symbolic character. Five years after the Tchernobyl accident, various organizations in Switzerland announced a demonstration against the further expansion of nuclear energy in front of the parliament building in the capital Bern. Theology students of the University of Bern decided not only to participate in the demonstration but to organize a worship service in a nearby church and to express in a worship context what they had to say. As police began to use tear gas, many people took refuge in the church. Another example comes from Korea, from the worship service that Pastor Park Hyung-kyu celebrated at Easter 1973 in an open-air theater on the top of Namsan mountain near the center of the capital. The political repression had become harsher and harsher and, in order to show that the opposition could not be muzzled, Pastor Park proclaimed the victory of Christ over all powers of the world at a symbolic place outside the church building. He was arrested before the service had come to an end.

Respect and Responsibility for God's Creation

Among the themes that have preoccupied the churches in the past decades and that also have found an echo in worship, the issue of respect and responsibility toward God's creation holds a special place. Who are we, human beings, in the whole of God's creation? What is our calling in relation to our co-creatures? In the early 1970s, we began to become aware of the ecological crisis, as it became clear that the present technological and economic course would inevitably lead to an intolerable over-exploitation of the resources of the planet. In more and more realms limits began to appear that could not be transgressed without creating dangers for the future. The quality of life began to suffer from the pollution of air, soil, and water. Numerous species of plants and animals disappeared altogether or were in danger of becoming extinct. More and more people recognized that present developments were not sustainable — in other words, they could not be continued without limiting the life chances of future generations.

For many Christians the ecological crisis was at first simply a new and additional political and social theme. Hesitantly, they participated in the public debate. How serious was the threat? What measures needed to be taken? Many warned against exaggerations and against the "greening" of the churches. For others the protection of the environment was a matter of course and needed no special theological legitimation. But soon it became clear that the ecological crisis raised deeper questions for the church. Often in public debate voices could be heard that attributed the responsibility for today's aggressive attitude toward nature to the Jewish-Christian tradition. Though it could easily be shown that the charge rested on a misinterpretation of the biblical sources (both Jewish and Christian), it could not be denied that the theme of creation had been neglected by the churches, receding into the background more and more since the Enlightenment. Confronted with modern natural sciences, theology placed all emphasis on history and human existence in history. Both in theology and in the actual life of the churches, the theme of creation had disappeared from view.

Intensive theological reflection began. The true intention of the biblical texts on creation was recalled and re-stated, and the Christian tradition was re-read and reinterpreted in light of the challenges resulting from the ecological crisis. In many Reformed churches a debate started on the meaning of the first article of the creed. Several churches issued statements on faith in God the Creator and on the responsibilities implied in this faith. Among these texts the statement by the Christian Reformed Church in the United States holds a special place.[7]

Worship also was affected — in the first place, simply by the fact that the theme of creation surfaced more frequently in preaching. In recent decades the hymn tradition has also markedly changed, with new hymns on the Creator and creation finding their way into Reformed worship. In many places, new ways are sought to give more ample room to creation in worship, such as decorating the church with symbols of nature like the sun or water. In some cases, worship services have taken place in which animals were blessed. Attempts have also been made in the opposite direction: instead of bringing nature into the church, services have been celebrated in the open air — on mountains or in the woods, for example. In most cases such services are the occasion for raising concrete political and social issues.

From various sides the proposal has been made that the theme "Creator and creation" should also find its place in the church year. The suggestion is that the period from the Sunday preceding September 1 to the Sunday following October 4 should be observed as a "time of the Creator and creation." It is, indeed, striking that the first article of the creed has no firm place in the church year. The important feast days from the Advent season to Pentecost and

7. Christian Reformed Church, "Our World Belongs to God: A Contemporary Testimony," especially para. 7-10, in *Psalter Hymnal* (Grand Rapids: CRC Publications, 1987).

Trinitatis all recall God's great deeds in Jesus Christ. They lead from the incarnation to the passion and resurrection and then to ascension and the pouring out of the Holy Spirit. True, in all these feasts the theme of creation is indirectly present. But throughout the year the worshiping community is never explicitly guided toward praise of the Creator. The debate on the expansion of the church year through a time of the Creator was launched by a proposal of the Patriarch of Constantinople Dimitrios I (1989) to celebrate September 1 (the beginning of the church year for Orthodox churches) as a day of care for creation. Many Reformed congregations, especially in Switzerland and Italy, have taken up and re-formulated this proposal; they are celebrating a *time* of creation, which extends over several weeks and gives the opportunity for a genuine reflection on the responsibility that flows from faith in God the Creator.[8]

Authentic Worship vs. Succumbing to the World

Reformed churches confess God's reign over the whole world, believing that God's will is valid in all realms of life. Worship, therefore, also needs to be open to all realms of life. It is, however, necessary that the political witness of the church be explicitly rooted in the gospel. Worship must be celebrated in such a way as to make visible — both for the church members and for the world — the center of the Christian message. The political witness must be so formulated that it leads back to the center. The circle must be complete.

The church can lose its freedom and through its worship serve purposes that have little or nothing to do with its true calling. The temptation is real, and the church has often succumbed to it. The world looks for blessing and confirmation, with the result that the church can easily be misused by the powers of the world and subjected to its claims. Its symbols can be used to "humanize" the face of power. Churches are invited to appear at national celebrations at the side of the authorities and to ask for God's blessing on them. After having agreed to bless new bridges, they are eventually also invited to bless armies. To protect the church from this kind of prostitution, clarity needs to be reached on the legitimacy of political options. The church must not degenerate into a lackey of power.

Often, the political witness of the church will therefore consist in rejecting outside claims that threaten to distort the gospel and the *raison d'être* of the Christian community. A good example of this comes from the church of Jesus Christ in Madagascar. In May 1968, the government requested the churches to

8. Lukas Vischer, "A Time of Creation," *Ecumenical Review* 1999/3.

introduce the national flag into all church buildings. The church rejected the demand and declared that the symbol of the state and state power was not an appropriate symbol in a place where Christians worship God. Glory was due to God alone.[9]

When, however, the gospel and its claims are at stake, the politicization of worship is not only admissible, it is required. The decisive criterion will always be solidarity with victims of human power. As much as the church's worship must reject the glorification of human power, it must embrace all those who are being marginalized, oppressed, and exploited.

In practice, political witness in worship services will never be possible without the risk of ambiguity. Even if the arguments in favor of a political, social, or ecological cause seem to be indisputable, errors and misunderstandings remain possible. Political witness often leads to uncomfortable political "neighborhoods." The church can find itself close to parties or groups that, for totally different reasons, happen to be committed to the same cause. The church may be applauded by "friends" whom, for other reasons, it is bound to reject. Such neighborhoods are no reason to avoid witness in society. As long as the church is sure of its cause, it can stand with them with serenity, and also live through the debates and conflicts that may arise within the church.

Despite possible errors and misunderstandings the church has to remain committed to the struggle for true solidarity. It must not withdraw from it; though ambiguity will never be removed, acts of true solidarity have the promise of bearing the fruits of the Spirit.

Further Reading

Abraham, K. C., and Bernadette Mbuy-Beya, eds. *Spirituality of the Third World: A Cry for Life.* Maryknoll, N.Y.: Orbis Books, 1994.

Fowler, Robert Booth. *The Greening of Protestant Thought.* Chapel Hill: University of North Carolina Press, 1995.

Johnston, Carol. *And the Leaves of the Tree Are for the Healing of the Nations.* Louisville: Presbyterian Church (U.S.A.), 1997.

Libânio, J. B. *Spiritual Discernment and Politics: Guidelines for Spiritual Communities.* Trans. Theodore Morrow. Maryknoll, N.Y.: Orbis Books, 1982.

9. Cf. Marc Spindler, "L'usage de la Bible dans le discours politique malgache depuis l'indépendance (1960-1990)," in *Histoire religieuse, Histoire globale, Histoire ouverte,* ed. Jean-Dominique Durand and Régis Ladous (Paris 1991), pp. 204ff.; cf. also *Bulletin d'information de l'Eglise de Jésus-Christ à Madagascar,* no. 1 (January 1969).

Contributors

Horace T. Allen Jr., Professor of Liturgics, Boston University School of Theology; Visiting Professor of Liturgical Studies, Yale Divinity School and Institute for Sacred Music; Member and former Chair of Consultation on Common Text; Founding co-chair of English Language Liturgical Consultation

Marcel Barnard, Professor of Liturgics at the University of Utrecht, Uniting Protestant Churches in the Netherlands, Leiden

Emily R. Brink, Senior Research Fellow, Calvin Institute of Christian Worship, Grand Rapids, Michigan, U.S.A.; Editor of *Reformed Worship*

Livingstone Buama, Moderator of the Evangelical Presbyterian Church, Ghana

Coenraad Burger, Director of BUVTON (an institute for theological training and congregational research), University of Stellenbosch; Moderator of the Cape Synod of the Dutch Reformed Church, South Africa

Bruno Bürki, Pastor of the Church of Neuchâtel; Titular Professor at the University of Fribourg, Switzerland

Gerson Correia de Lacerda, Professor of Church History at the Theological Seminary of São Paulo of the Independent Presbyterian Church of Brazil, São Paulo

Alan D. Falconer, minister in the Church of Scotland; Director of the Faith and Order Commission of the World Council of Churches

Kasonga wa Kasonga, Professor of Practical Theology/Christian Education at Protestant University of Congo, Democratic Republic of the Congo, Kinshasa; Executive Secretary of Christian and Family Life Education at the All Africa Conference of Churches, Nairobi, Kenya

Baranite T. Kirata, Pastor of the Kiribati Congregational Church, Kiribati

Elsie Anne McKee, Archibald Alexander Professor of Reformation Studies and the History of Worship, Princeton Theological Seminary

Seong-Won Park, Pastor of the Presbyterian Church of Korea; Executive Secretary of the Department on Cooperation and Witness of the World Alliance of Reformed Churches, Geneva, Switzerland

Ester Pudjo Widiasih, Professor of Worship Studies and Church Music, Jakarta Theological Seminary, Indonesia

Alan P. F. Sell, Professor of Christian Doctrine and Philosophy of Religion and Director of the Centre of British Christian Thought, United Theological College, Aberystwyth, within the Aberystwyth and Lampeter School of Theology of the University of Wales, United Kingdom

Joseph D. Small, Director of the Department of Theology and Worship of the Presbyterian Church (U.S.A), Louisville, Kentucky, U.S.A.

Bryan D. Spinks, Professor of Liturgical Studies, Yale University Divinity School and Institute of Sacred Music

Leonora Tubbs Tisdale, Elizabeth M. Engle Associate Professor of Preaching and Worship, Princeton Theological Seminary

Lukas Vischer, Professor Emeritus of Ecumenical Theology, University of Bern, Switzerland

Isaiah Wahome Muita, Pastor in the Presbyterian Church of East Africa, Kenya; currently studying in the United States

Geraldine Wheeler, Minister in the Uniting Church in Australia

Marsha M. Wilfong, Assistant Professor of Homiletics and Worship, University of Dubuque Theological Seminary, Dubuque, Iowa; ordained Minister in the Presbyterian Church (U.S.A.)

John D. Witvliet, Director of the Calvin Institute of Christian Worship of Calvin College and Calvin Theological Seminary, Grand Rapids, Michigan, U.S.A.

Index